BOYD LITZINGER AND
K. L. KNICKERBOCKER

THE

BROWNING

CRITICS

UNIVERSITY OF KENTUCKY PRESS

11351292

[ACKNOWLEDGMENTS]

WE ARE GRATEFUL to all those who have permitted us to reprint the following materials:

Richard Altick and the *Yale Review* (copyright Yale University Press) for "The Private Life of Robert Browning," *Yale Review*, XLI (December 1951), 247-62.

William C. DeVane and *Studies in Philology* for "The Harlot and the Thoughtful Young Man," *SP*, XXIX (July 1932), 463-84.

William C. DeVane and the *Yale Review* (copyright Yale University Press) for "The Virgin and the Dragon," *Yale Review*, NS XXXVII (September 1947), 33-46.

Philip Drew and *Victorian Poetry* for "Henry Jones on Browning's Optimism," *Victorian Poetry*, II (Winter 1964), 29-41.

Hoxie N. Fairchild and the *University of Toronto Quarterly* for "Browning the Simple-Hearted Casuist," *UTQ*, XLVIII (April 1949), 234-40.

B. R. Jerman and *PMLA* for "Browning's Witless Duke," *PMLA*, LXXII (June 1957), 488-93.

Roma King and the University of Michigan Press for "Eve and the Virgin" from *The Bow and the Lyre* (1957).

Robert Langbaum and *PMLA* for "*The Ring and the Book*: A Relativist Poem."

Laurence Perrine and *PMLA* for "Browning's Shrewd Duke," *PMLA*, LXXII (June 1957), 488-93.

Robert Preyer and *ELH* (The Johns Hopkins Press) for "Robert Browning: A Reading of the Early Narratives," *ELH*, XXVI (December 1959), 531-48.

F. E. L. Priestley and the *University of Toronto Quarterly*

ACKNOWLEDGMENTS

for "Blougram's Apologetics," UTQ, XV (January 1946), 139-47.

W. O. Raymond and the University of Toronto Press for "The Infinite Moment" from *The Infinite Moment and Other Essays*, 1950.

Donald Smalley and the Harvard University Press for "Special-Pleading in the Laboratory" from *Browning's Essay on Chatterton*, 1948.

Stanford University Press for Frances T. Russell's "His Saving Grace of Pessimism" from *One Word More on Browning*, 1927.

Tennessee Studies in Literature for K. L. Knickerbocker's "A Tentative Apology for Browning," I (1956), 75-82.

During the process of choosing essays for inclusion in this volume, we were given good advice by a number of Browning specialists. We particularly wish to thank Richard Altick and Donald Smalley for their generous help. We, of course, absolve them and others from any responsibility for the contents and the arrangement finally settled upon. We acknowledge finally and with special feeling our great debt to the late William C. DeVane and lament deeply his sudden passing.

Boyd Litzinger   K. L. Knickerbocker
St. Bonaventure University   *University of Tennessee*

[CONTENTS]

CONTENTS

[INTRODUCTION]

MANY POST-VICTORIANS, like the post-Classicists of the Romantic period, were vigorous iconoclasts eager to demolish the household deities of their fathers, and they went about their work with relish. Tennyson and Browning, dominant for the better part of a century and succeeded by no two poets of similar stature, had to be denigrated or what would become of a sophistication forged in the fire of war and tempered by the roaring meaninglessness of the twenties and the despair of the thirties?

I

There is no cosmic scale in sight for weighing the absolute worth of a poet. Once a poet is dead, normally the evidence is in, final and complete. As with Shelley's letters to Harriet, there may be biographical finds which can disturb critical judgment, but the poet's creative work is done. Judgment of this work shifts because new eyes, conditioned to a new world, send new impressions to brains frequently out of tune with the generations of the past. Criticism of a later period, therefore, is normally at odds with the critics of an earlier period and simply expresses, for the most part, a different set of values. The poet then becomes the middle man, caught between what was thought of him and what is thought of him.

Browning has not benefited from the way the world now wags. From being a comfort to his century, a stay against confusion, he has become an irritant to ours. Indeed, in spite of all the corrective, perceptive studies, such as Walter

E. Houghton's *The Victorian Frame of Mind* and Jerome H. Buckley's *The Victorian Temper,* the lingering impression is maintained that somehow the twentieth century grew out of the seventeenth, not the nineteenth. Browning, clearly, is not the only Victorian to suffer from the scrutiny of new eyes, but perhaps he has suffered most.

Now, Browning's fame has passed its nadir. It is perhaps a good moment to gather into one volume examples of some of the best that has been said about this poet. We believe that such a volume will serve four purposes: it will make readily available a group of twenty-two essays now scattered through as many books and journals; it will illustrate the great variety of critical methods applied to Browning; it will provide an opportunity to judge the criticism as well as the poetry it criticizes; it will stimulate, perhaps, many a twenty-third essay setting straight all the wrong thinking about Browning.

We have chosen to present the essays of this volume in chronological order. This arrangement accomplishes the obvious: it displays Browning criticism in historical perspective, with some of its ups and downs. Perhaps if a reader starts at the beginning of this book and proceeds to the end, he will detect progress towards a fuller understanding of the poet, certainly towards an exhaustion of the possible attitudes which may be reasonably set forth. Most of the essayists in this volume have looked not only at Browning but also at the preceding criticism of Browning, both amateur and professional, and have observed with approval or disapproval public response to the poet. Most of the articles, then, are linked to each other in such a way as to make it profitable to consider them in chronological order.

We have not, however, attempted to trace the decline in Browning's popularity, nor to demonstrate that the later the criticism the better it becomes. Some recent criticism has been good indeed, but some of the earlier critics have been reasonably perceptive too. Insofar as possible, we have presented complete essays or entire chapters of books; or, as is the case with the selection from Santayana, such parts of longer essays as seem to form complete units. Conversely, and at the expense of omitting from our table of contents some important names (Henry James, T. S. Eliot, Ezra Pound, among others), we have avoided isolated comments or interesting snippets out of context. We have also reluctantly but of necessity foregone extracting from books on *The Ring and the Book* or from such lengthy studies as that of J. Hillis Miller in *The Disappearance of God.* Our bibliography will give readers the opportunity to see where we may have erred in what we have included and in what we have left out.

Because twenty-two essays can reflect only imperfectly the tremendous mass of printed comment on the poet, we will attempt first to show in broad terms how the early selections differ as a group from the later selections, also regarded as a group. Then in sections II and III we will briefly consider in chronological sequence each essay and offer occasional critical judgments of our own.

Our first seven essays, ranging in date from 1891 to 1916, are strongly impressionistic critiques which demonstrate, above all else, that Browning was still a living force, a power not to be ignored. Disinterestedness is lacking. The critics from Henry Jones to Dixon Scott, excepting Saintsbury, were all eager to find a single explanation for a complex poetic phenomenon, or a single purpose agitating this phenomenon. Such endeavors are of great historical interest, but it takes no great effort to show that Browning's poetry is not of a piece. The poet could say, and possibly did say on occasion:

> But when I sit down to reason,
> think to take my stand nor swerve . . .

In you come with your cold music
till I creep thro' every nerve.

Reason, in short, could provoke a reasonable distrust of itself.
Our first seven critics, whether for or against the poet's life
view and almost in imitation of their subject, took Browning
as a case study. Evidence for or against the poet was easily
marshalled and had only the defect of ignoring the counter-
weights.

The eighth essay, Frances Russell's tour de force "His
Saving Grace of Pessimism," continues the impressionistic
response to the poet. By 1927, however, one notes that it was
not a commercial but a university press which published
Russell's *One Word More on Browning*. Browning as a force,
a power, had lost the large market. The professors, the
scholars now took over from the literary men and philosophers.[1]

Our ninth essay, William C. DeVane's "The Harlot and the
Thoughtful Young Man," shows a radical change in tone
from the preceding selections. Scholarly objectivity is apparent, and the remaining thirteen articles of this book, with
perhaps an exception or two, maintain reasonably well this
sort of cool noninvolvement. Browning's work no longer
compelled either acceptance or rejection. Instead, it invited
careful study and analysis of its form and effectiveness.

II

We begin with Henry Jones, who as professor of Moral
Philosophy at Glasgow and, late in his life, author of *A Faith
That Enquires*, must have felt himself under compulsion to
answer Browning. If Browning was right, he was wrong.
Jones's method is that of the seventeenth-century religious
pamphleteer. He reasons, and if one grants his basic assumption—a belief in testimonies and revelation—he wins. Be-

cause Browning did not accept this sort of knowledge as certain, because he saw no gain from reason *if* this sort of knowledge were certain, Jones exclaims: "What greater depth of agnosticism is possible?" That Browning was, indeed, an agnostic is true, and Jones was the first to make the discovery and to be disturbed by it. Browning represented, to Jones and later to Santayana, the dominant's persistence which must be answered. Answers normally inspire replies, but Jones had mounted an attack so formidable that nearly seventy-five years passed before, as we shall see, his conclusions and method were persuasively challenged.[2]

To move from Jones to Saintsbury is to shift violently from close reasoning to simple, though discriminating, appreciation. Saintsbury took all English literature as his province and swept up Browning in the process. High churchman and militant Tory, he found nothing in Browning to disturb him, nothing to be answered. Fiercely eclectic, he is undismayed by *Sordello* but cool to *The Ring and the Book*, taken by *Fifine* and more than dubious about *Prince Hohenstiel-Schwangau*, sure that "The Last Ride Together" as a love poem is "the best that we have produced for two hundred years" and equally sure that "Count Gismond"—except for four and a half lines—"is no great matter." Browning did not offer "much of a philosophy" but a "poet is always saved by his poetry." One will recall this estimate when one reaches Santayana and his view that Browning's philosophy is epitomized in "The Last Ride Together," which stands not as a great love poem but as a revelation of the poet's barbarism.

John Chapman's method stands somewhere between Jones's tightly controlled, methodical analysis and Saintsbury's swift pronouncements. As with Saintsbury, Chapman in writing about Browning responded more to enlistment than to compulsion. He records his opinions with reasonable objectivity.

Possibly he was the first to conclude that Browning "was not a thinker, for he was never in doubt." Clearly, Chapman did not interpret Browning as Jones had: ever a doubter, said Jones; never, said Chapman. Yet, the disagreement is not as complete as may appear, for Chapman also echoes Jones: "the force of [Browning's] feelings is so much greater than his intellect that his mind serves his soul like a valet." This issue of heart versus head, Chapman predicts, will lose its significance to a posterity which "will want only art." This sort of demand from posterity will be a huge disadvantage to Browning, who is not a singer and is virtually unquotable. Whereas Tennyson will occupy "page after page" in a volume of Familiar Quotations, Browning will be missing. One cannot resist a quick check on this last prophecy: Bartlett's *Familiar Quotations,* tenth edition, contains 227 quotations covering 21⅓ columns from Tennyson, 188 quotations covering 20 columns from Browning. In summary, Chapman was dubious about Browning's lasting qualities because his "verse is bad."

Chesterton was to challenge this negative opinion with vigor, but Santayana comes next and he was very little concerned with Browning's technique. If the poet's philosophic position disturbed Henry Jones, it painfully offended George Santayana, passionate apostle of higher things. In "The Poetry of Barbarism," the sophisticated philosopher unleashed a frontal assault designed to settle the Browning question forever. With annihilation as the goal, the mystic used every weapon at hand, including the highly unmystical technique of *argumentum ad hominem* and selective omissions. The effect was awesome, and many Browning scholars have since tiptoed around the ruins, full of wonder at the devastation. Santayana, of course, has been answered more than once, but the myth persists that he is unanswerable. Every student of Browning must, of necessity, take "The Poetry of Barbarism" into account, for, as a powerful negation, it stands as the most significant and best expressed critique available.

With a mind as keen as Santayana's and a style even more zestful, Gilbert K. Chesterton demonstrated that, for him at least, Browning remained very much alive. Both the philosopher and the literary man recognized Browning's tremendous energy; but to Santayana this very energy produced "a thought and an art inchoate and ill-digested, . . . a volcanic eruption that tosses itself quite blindly and ineffectually into the sky," while to Chesterton the poet's artistic energy made him care "more for form than any other English poet who ever lived."

It was not, however, Santayana who turned Chesterton to a defense of Browning as a literary artist. Chapman, no doubt, with other traditionalists who found Browning's verse bad, stimulated Chesterton to have a look at this charge. Since Chesterton, many critics have found it possible to defend Browning's prosody.

Paul Elmer More, intellectual and humanist, takes exception to Browning's intellectualism ("Browning is nearly the most intellectual poet in the language") and to his humanism, his concentration upon and concern for the individual. Ostensibly More is commenting on the outpouring of scholarly and semischolarly work on Browning, particularly C. H. Herford's *Robert Browning,* but actually, the essay "Why Is Browning Popular?" is a long approving footnote to Santayana's bolder attack.

The most ebullient and bouncy of Browning's early critics, Dixon Scott, offers little evidence of having read Jones, Santayana, or More. His exultation represents a sort of apotheosis of the Browningite who believed he saw the poet steadily and saw him whole. The key to Browning, avers Scott, is that he subordinated poetry to life—his life and the living thereof. This view is not an impossible one, but nearly so. It does help account for the obvious pleasure the poet took during his later years in being a celebrity. It does not, however, "dive by the spirit-sense" into the mystery of Browning, which surely cannot be fully summarized in the word, "homeliness."

If one finds that Scott's key to Browning only jams the lock, one may feel that Frances T. Russell has filed more expertly and that her key does indeed open a door. Taking her cue from Chesterton, actually scolding him mildly for missing the paradox, she demonstrates persuasively "the shrinkage" Browning's "optimism suffers when scrutinized in relation to his total output." Even though this critic rides her thesis too hard and makes it too obvious that saving Browning as a power for good in a wasteland world is the purpose of the evangelical peroration at the end of the essay, nevertheless the correction is successfully made that Browning is not an easy optimist.

III

William C. DeVane completed at Yale in 1926 his prize-winning dissertation, *A Critical Study of Browning's Parleyings with Certain People of Importance in Their Day.* This work, published in 1927 as *Browning's Parleyings: The Autobiography of a Mind,* set a standard for the new Browning scholarship. Although it might be something of an exaggeration to say that all the remaining essayists in our volume belong to the "DeVane school," it is nevertheless hardly possible to imagine any serious student of Browning getting very far without taking DeVane into account. This is not to say that DeVane, himself, does not have debts to many of his predecessors, to W. H. Griffin, W. O. Raymond, T. L. Hood, and to many others including, no doubt, the best of the nonscholars, William Lyon Phelps. What DeVane added to the impressionistic criticism which came before him was a meticulous attention to detail, to fact, to the basic materials.

One may note that this sort of attention does not lead to simplification, to terms such as optimism, pessimism, barbarism, mysticism, homeliness. It does lead to exciting discoveries of single facets in the poet's life and poetry. "The Harlot and the Thoughtful Young Man" reveals convincingly, and with proper use of suspense, the curious relationship between Browning and Rossetti. Perhaps Browning suffers somewhat from this sort of exposure, but fancy portraits are not the concern of the scholar.

Departing just slightly from our chronology, which should bring us next to Priestley's study, we may consider the second of DeVane's essays, "The Virgin and the Dragon," which, though printed in 1947, celebrates appropriately the hundredth wedding anniversary of the Brownings. Again, very careful reading led to a significant discovery: Browning's lifelong preoccupation with the Perseus-Andromeda myth, a preoccupation which not only influenced his poetry but also revealed the sort of image the poet had of himself. One may observe that, contrary to the Dixon Scott thesis, the poet projected his life into his poetry and then this very poetry reinforced, made firmer the image.

We may now move back a step to the Priestley exegesis of "Bishop Blougram's Apology." This sort of analysis of single poems began with the formation of the first Browning Society and has continued at an accelerated rate ever since. The Blougram poem, with its curious mixture of subtlety and blatancy, has puzzled many a reader and, consequently, has produced a spate of explanations. Priestley, by centering attention on the listener, Gigadibs, gives us a coherent, persuasive reading of the poem. One may wish to question, mildly, the statement that "in no other monologue of Browning's is the *muta persona* so important." Lucrezia in

"Andrea del Sarto" is perhaps not the stimulus to Andrea that Gigadibs was to Blougram, but she surely is just as essential to the monologue. One may also observe that Browning provided Blougram with the only antagonist—an atheist—the Bishop could defeat with his hedonistic arguments. However, the foregoing remarks do not detract from the essential correctness of Priestley's interpretation.

Our next essay throws further light on "Bishop Blougram's Apology." Along with several other long monologues "Blougram" reveals a method, a device for entering alien minds. Donald Smalley, who had the astuteness to identify Browning as the author of the *Essay on Chatterton*, has given significance to his discovery by demonstrating convincingly that the *Essay* "exhibited what may be called [Browning's] system of special-pleading—a method of portraying character based upon what a man might 'say for himself' against the world's misinterpretation of his conduct." Although special pleading or case making had long been recognized as Browning's great forte as an artist, Smalley was the first to discover the origin of the method and to show how it was used in some of the poet's most sinewy works.

At first glance Fairchild's essay—"Browning the Simple-Hearted Casuist"—seems an echo of Dixon Scott's "The Homeliness of Browning." The very title is reminiscent of earlier attempts to find *the* phrase which will encompass the Browning phenomenon. Indeed the terms "brain truth" and "heart truth" take us back to Jones's "The Heart and the Head." Fairchild, however, is mainly concerned with what he calls "the giveaway," the intrusion of heart truths (Browning's truth) into what might have otherwise been simply brain truths capable of misinterpretation. Readers will decide whether or not all the alleged giveaways cited by Fairchild are legitimate examples of the poet's intrusiveness. Clearly, the postscript to "Blougram" is interpreted entirely differently by Priestley. And can the final line of

"Porphyria's Lover" be regarded as "editorializing"? If so, what does the editorial mean? Browning certainly does intrude into many of his poems, and Fairchild helps us to recognize the voice of the poet.

W. O. Raymond, who wrote his dissertation on Browning nearly fifty years ago and who has enriched Browning scholarship and criticism ever since, takes a quick look at the adverse critics—Santayana, F. L. Lucas, Irving Babbitt in particular—and then, quietly scolds them for fastening "exclusively on the negative rather than the positive aspect of the poet's elemental attribute." Professor Raymond does not deny that there is a negative—indeed, he may admit to too much—but he shows how the poet's "incomparable gusto" was hardly a quality to be dismissed as barbarian, for it produced, more often than not, splendid poetry.

Browning's "incomparable gusto," his vast energy, his extraordinarily good health have been staple observations of biographers and critics for over a century. Just as Frances T. Russell became weary of the word *optimist* applied so uncritically to Browning and decided a case could be made for an opposite finding, so too it was perhaps inevitable that someone would weary of the harping on Browning's healthiness and, aided by Freudian insights, decide to look more deeply into the truth or falsity of this common observation. Professor Richard D. Altick, one of the keenest and most readable of modern scholars, "unsatisfied with the description of Browning's inner being which the commentators have customarily inferred from his writings" has proposed some opposite conclusions in his "The Private Life of Robert Browning." To Professor Altick's article are appended some comments under the title, "A Tentative Apology for Browning."

At one point in "The Private Life of Robert Browning" the observation is made that "No one who had not himself known the ashen flavor of failure could have written that moving poem": "Andrea del Sarto." Roma King in his "Eve and the Virgin: Andrea del Sarto" shows in great detail the artistry of the poem and emphasizes the central position occupied by Lucrezia. (Is it likely that Browning, if he identified himself with Andrea, also identified Mrs. Browning with Lucrezia? Professor Altick does not go this far, but Betty Miller does in her *Robert Browning: A Portrait*.)[3] Professor King, following the method of the New Critics, does not seek out biographical hints in this finest, and most objective, of Browning's monologues. Instead, he shows how the poet achieved his effects through a disciplined choice of words and rhythms appropriate to the picture of a man threshing about feebly in a welter of rationalizations.

Priestley's close reading of "Blougram" and King's of "Andrea del Sarto" is now followed by Professor Robert Langbaum's perceptive envelopment of *The Ring and the Book*. The poet, Langbaum contends, was steadily concerned in his poem with the "disequilibrium between truth and machinery." All the machinery of the society of 1698 failed to discover the truth which was instinctively present in Pompilia. With the same facts available for all to appraise, judgments were different because the men who pronounced them were different and used the machinery for their own purposes. The poem, then, is adjudged relativist because "the social and religious absolutes are not the means for understanding the right and the wrong" as represented by Pompilia and Guido. Without saying so, Langbaum has shown how Browning, also without saying so, has dramatized Matthew Arnold's contention that modern society depends too much on machinery, the machinery of the church, of the state, of even such shibboleths as "the right of free speech." Certainly Professor Langbaum has helped give twentieth-century relevance to a poem written in the nineteenth century about an event which occurred in the seventeenth.

No volume attempting to represent Browning criticism would be complete without a sampling of the numerous exegeses of "My Last Duchess," the most tantalizing, and, because it is so short, the most frequently analyzed of all Browning's poems. We have chosen B. R. Jerman's "Browning's Witless Duke" and Laurence Perrine's reply, "Browning's Shrewd Duke," not because they exhaust the possible interpretations of "My Last Duchess" (they, of course, do not) but because they illustrate a novel approach (Jerman's) and the more traditional reading (Perrine's).

One may easily follow the arguments over "My Last Duchess," and immediately take a stand. Articles such as innocent-sounding "Robert Browning: A Reading of the Early Narratives" are another matter. Robert Preyer widens the use of the psychological method to find a cultural significance in Browning's changing concept of the poet's vision. If Browning shifts direction, so did Tennyson and others. Therefore, the shift probably is not a matter of personal psychology but is a response to the *Zeitgeist,* for authors of the 1830s in England appeared to be "stunned by the inhumanity of both Tory repression and middle class industrialism." Preyer's is a highly suggestive essay which, along with such speculations as those of Betty Miller and Richard Altick, opens the way for further attempts to crack the Browning conundrum.

With our final essay we come full circle. Philip Drew's "Henry Jones on Browning's Optimism" is a reply to the first essay in this volume. There is, however, more than neatness in this circle. Drew succeeds in reviving a respect for the dilemma Browning faced, a dilemma which Jones thought the poet should have resolved but which, Drew makes clear, has never been rationally resolved by anybody. Browning "characteristically finds himself in a situation where he must choose between hope and despair." How does this situation differ from the modern situation? Do the existentialists, for example, facing this oldest of problems, have a better answer? "It is only after he has proved, or even enacted, the inefficacy of the intellectual processes that Browning decides to perform the crucial act of trust." And *this* is unavoidably an intellectual decision. Another decision would have been possible, of course: the decision of distrust, the modern disaffirmation. But this stance, too, must be based on faith, a depressingly blithe faith which displays a curious sort of rigor mortis energy. The dilemma will not evaporate no matter how hard the prevailing winds of nihilism blow.

One may easily grant that Browning does not provide our time with an appealing answer to an old problem. He did, however, face the problem, and, as this collection of essays demonstrates, he has stood up well both to blame and praise. He can hardly be all the things he has been called, and yet, perhaps he was: agnostic, optimist, pessimist, obscure, simple-hearted, barbarian, homely (or homey), triumphant, defeated. As we said at the outset, the cosmic scales cannot be read from our distance. Meantime, each of us has his own balances and no doubt, for at least a while to come, Browning will invite attempts, in more than three books, at proving absurd all written hitherto.

[1891]

HENRY JONES

THE HEART AND THE HEAD

IT HAS BEEN shown that Browning appeals, in defence of his optimistic faith, from the intellect to the heart. His theory rests on three main assumptions:—namely (1) that knowledge of the true nature of things is impossible to man, and that, therefore, it is necessary to find other and better evidence than the intellect can give for the victory of good over evil; (2) that the failure of knowledge is a necessary condition of the moral life, inasmuch as certain knowledge would render all moral effort either futile or needless; (3) that after the failure of knowledge there still remains possible a faith of the heart; which can furnish a sufficient objective basis to morality and religion. Let us consider these last two assumptions.

Demonstrative, or certain, or absolute knowledge of the actual nature of things would, Browning asserts, destroy the very possibility of a moral life. For such knowledge would show either that evil is evil, or that evil is good; and, in both cases alike, the benevolent activity of love would be futile. In the first case, it would be thwarted and arrested by despair; for, if evil be evil, it must remain evil for aught that man can do. Man cannot effect a change in the nature of things; nor create a good in a world dominated by evil. In the second case, the saving effect of moral love would be unnecessary; for, if evil be only seeming, then all things are perfect and complete, and there is no need of interference. It is necessary, therefore, that man should be in a permanent state of doubt as to the real existence of evil; and, whether evil does exist or not, it must seem, and only seem to exist to man, in order that he may devote himself to the service of good.

Now, if this view of the poet be taken in the strict sense in which he uses it in this argument, it admits of a very easy refutation. It takes us beyond the bounds of all possible human experience, into an imaginary region, as to which all assertions are equally valueless. It is impossible to conceive how the conduct of a being who is moral would be affected by absolute knowledge; or, indeed, to conceive the existence of such a being. For morality, as the poet insists, is a process in which an ideal is gradually realized through conflict with the actual—an actual which it both produces and transmutes at every stage of the progress. But complete knowledge would be above all process. Hence we would have, on Browning's hypothesis, to conceive of a being in whom perfect knowledge was combined with an undeveloped will. A being so constituted would be an agglomerate of utterly disparate elements, the interaction of which in a single character it would be impossible to make intelligible.

But, setting aside this point, there is a curious flaw in Browning's argument, which indicates that he had not distinguished between two forms of optimism which are essentially different from each other,—namely, the pantheistic and the Christian.

To know that evil is only apparent, that pain is only pleasure's mask, that all forms of wickedness and misery are only illusions of an incomplete intelligence, would, he argues, arrest all moral action and stultify love. For love—which necessarily implies need in its object—is the principle of all right action. In this he argues justly, for the moral life is essentially a conflict and progress; and, in a world in which "white ruled unchecked along the line," there would be neither the need of conflict nor the possibility of progress. And, on the other hand, if the good were merely a phantom, and evil the reality, the same destruction of moral activity would follow. "White may not triumph," in this absolute manner, nor may we "clean abolish, once and evermore, white's faintest trace." There must be "the constant shade cast on life's shine."

All this is true; but the admission of it in no way militates against the conception of absolutely valid knowledge; nor is it any proof that we need live in the twilight of perpetual doubt, in order to be moral. For the knowledge, of which Browning speaks, would be knowledge of a state of things in which morality would be really impossible; that is, it would be knowledge of a world in which all was evil or all was good. On the other hand, valid knowledge of a world in which good and evil are in conflict, and in which the former is realized through victory over the latter, would not destroy morality. What is inconsistent with the moral life is the conception of a world where there is no movement from evil to good, no evolution of character, but merely the standstill life of "Rephan." But absolutely certain knowledge that the good is at issue with sin in the world, that there is no way of attaining goodness except through conflict with evil, and that moral life, as the poet so frequently insists, is a process which converts all actual attainment into a dead self, from which we can rise to higher things—a self, therefore, which is relatively evil—would, and does, inspire morality. It is the deification of evil not negated or overcome, of evil as it is in itself and apart from all process, which destroys morality. And the same is equally true of a pantheistic optimism, which asserts that all things *are* good. But it is not true of a Christian optimism, which asserts that all things are *working together for* good. For such optimism implies that the process of negating or overcoming evil is essential to the attainment of goodness; it does not imply that evil, as evil, is ever good. Evil is unreal, only in the sense that it cannot withstand the power which is set against it. It is not *mere* semblance, a mere negation or absence of being; it is opposed to the good, and its opposition can be overcome, only by the moral effort which it calls forth. An optimistic faith of this kind can find room for morality; and, indeed, it furnishes it with the religious basis it needs. Browning, however, has confused these two forms of optimism; and, therefore, he has been driven to condemn knowledge, because he knew no alternative but that of either making evil eternally real, or making it absolutely unreal. A third alternative, however, is supplied by the conception of moral evolution. Knowledge of the conditions on which good can be attained—a knowledge that amounts to conviction—is the spring of all moral effort; whereas an attitude of permanent doubt as to the distinction between good and evil would paralyse it. Such a doubt must be solved before man can act at all, or choose one end rather than another. All action implies belief, and the ardour and vigour of moral action can only come from a belief which is wholehearted.

The further assertion, which the poet makes in *La Saisiaz*, and repeats elsewhere, that sure knowledge of the consequences that follow good and evil actions would necessarily lead to the choice of good and the avoidance of evil, and destroy morality by destroying liberty of choice, raises the whole question of the relation of knowledge and conduct, and cannot be adequately discussed here. It may be said, however, that it rests upon a confusion between two forms of necessity: namely, natural and spiritual necessity. In asserting that knowledge of the consequences of evil would determine human action in a necessary way, the poet virtually treats man as if he were a natural being. But the assumption that man is responsible and liable to punishment, involves that he is capable of withstanding all such determination. And knowledge does not and cannot lead to such necessary determination. Reason brings freedom; for reason constitutes the ends of action.

It is the constant desire of the good to attain to such a convincing knowledge of the worth and dignity of the moral law that they shall be able to make themselves its devoted instruments. Their desire is that "the good" shall supplant in them all motives that conflict against it, and be the inner principle, or necessity, of all their actions. Such complete devotion to the good is expressed, for instance, in the words of the Hebrew Psalmist: "Thy testimonies have I taken as an heritage for ever; for they are the rejoicing of my heart. I have inclined mine heart to perform Thy statutes alway, even unto the end. I hate vain thoughts, but Thy law do I love." "Nevertheless I live," said the Christian apostle, "yet not I, but Christ liveth in me; and the life which I now live in the flesh I live by the faith of the Son of God." In these words there is expressed that highest form of the moral life, in which the individual is so identified in desire with his ideal, that he lives only to actualize it in his character. The natural self is represented as dead, and the victory of the new principle is viewed as complete. This full obedience to the ideal is the service of a necessity; but the necessity is within, and the service is, therefore, perfect freedom. The authority of the law is absolute, but the law is self-imposed.

[5]

The whole man is convinced of its goodness. He has acquired something even fuller than a mere intellectual demonstration of it; for his knowledge has ripened into wisdom, possessed his sympathies, and become a disposition of his heart. And the fulness and certainty of his knowledge, so 'far from rendering morality impossible, is its very perfection. To bring about such a knowledge of the good of goodness and the evil of evil, as will engender love of the former and hatred of the latter, is the aim of all moral education. Thus, the history of human life, in so far as it is progressive, may be concentrated in the saying that it is the ascent from the power of a necessity which is natural, to the power of a necessity which is moral. And this latter necessity can come only through fuller and more convincing knowledge of the law that rules the world, and is also the inner principle of man's nature.

There remains now the third element in Browning's view, —namely, that the faith in the good, implied in morality and religion, can be firmly established, after knowledge has turned out deceptive, upon the individual's consciousness of the power of love within himself. In other words, I must now try to estimate the value of Browning's appeal from the intellect to the heart.

Before doing so, however, it may be well to repeat once more that Browning's condemnation of knowledge, in his philosophical poems, is not partial or hesitating. On the contrary, he confines it definitely to the individual's consciousness of his own inner states.

> Myself I solely recognize.
> They, too, may recognize themselves, not me,
> For aught I know or care.

Nor does Browning endeavour to correct this limited testimony of the intellect as to its own states, by bringing in the miraculous aid of revelation, or by postulating an unerring moral faculty. He does not assume an intuitive power of knowing right from wrong; but he maintains that ignorance enwraps man's moral sense.

And, not only are we unable to know the rule of right and wrong in details, but we cannot know whether there *is* right or wrong. At times the poet seems inclined to say that evil is a phenomenon conjured up by the frail intelligence of man.

> Man's fancy makes the fault!
> Man, with the narrow mind, must cram inside
> His finite God's infinitude,—earth's vault
> He bids comprise the heavenly far and wide,
> Since Man may claim a right to understand
> What passes understanding.

God's ways are past finding out. Nay, God Himself is unknown. At times, indeed, the power to love within man seems to the poet to be a clue to the nature of the Power without, and God is all but revealed in this surpassing emotion of the human heart. But, when philosophizing, he withdraws even this amount of knowledge. He is

> Assured that, whatsoe'er the quality
> Of love's cause, save that love was caused thereby,
> This—nigh upon revealment as it seemed
> A minute since—defies thy longing looks,
> Withdrawn into the unknowable once more.

Thus—to sum up Browning's view of knowledge—we are ignorant of the world; we do not know even whether it is good, or evil, or only their semblance, that is presented to us in human life; and we know nothing of God, except that He is the cause of love in man. What greater depth of agnosticism is possible?

When the doctrine is put in this bald form, the moral and religious consciousness of man, on behalf of which the theory was invented, revolts against it. Nevertheless, the distinction made by Browning between the intellectual and emotional elements of human life is very common in religious thought. It is not often, indeed, that either the worth of love, or the weakness of knowledge receives such emphatic expression as that which is given to them by the poet; but the same general idea of their relation is often expressed, and still more often implied. Browning differs from our ordinary teachers mainly in the boldness of his affirmatives and negatives. They, too, regard the intellect as merely human, and the emotion of love as divine. They, too, shrink from identifying the reason of man with the reason of God; even though they may recognize that morality and religion must postulate some kind of unity between God and man. They, too, conceive that human knowledge differs *in nature* from that of God, while they maintain that human goodness is the same in nature with that of God, though different in degree and fulness. There are two *kinds* of knowledge, but there is only one kind of justice, or mercy, or loving-kindness. Man must be content with a semblance of a knowledge of truth; but a semblance of goodness would be intolerable. God really reveals Himself to man in morality and religion, and He communicates to man nothing less than "the divine love." But there is no such close connection on the side of reason. The religious life of man is a divine principle, the indwelling of God in him; but there is a final and fatal defect in man's knowledge. The divine love's manifestation of itself is ever incomplete, it is true, even in the best of men; but there is no defect in its nature.

As a consequence of this doctrine, few religious opinions are more common at the present day, than that it is necessary to appeal, on all the high concerns of man's moral and religious life, from the intellect to the heart. Where we cannot know, we may still feel; and the religious man may have, in his own feeling of the divine, a more intimate conviction of the reality of that in which he trusts, than could be produced by any intellectual process.

> Enough to say, "I feel
> Love's sure effect, and, being loved, must love
> The love its cause behind,—I can and do."

Reason, in trying to scale the heights of truth, falls back, impotent and broken, into doubt and despair; not by that way can we come to that which is best and highest.

> I found Him not in world or sun,
>   Or eagle's wing, or insect's eye;
>   Nor thro' the questions men may try,
> The petty cobwebs we have spun.

But there is another way to find God and to conquer doubt.

> If e'er when faith had fall'n asleep,
>   I heard a voice "believe no more,"
>   And heard an ever-breaking shore
> That tumbled in the Godless deep;
>
> A warmth within the breast would melt
>   The freezing reason's colder part,
>   And like a man in wrath the heart
> Stood up and answer'd "I have felt."

What, then, I have now to ask, is the meaning and value of this appeal to emotion? Can love, or emotion in any of its forms, reveal truths to man which his intellect cannot discover? If so, how? If not, how shall we account for the general conviction of good men that it can? We have, in a word, either to justify the appeal to the heart, by explaining how the heart may utter truths that are hidden from reason; or else to account for the illusion, by which religious emotion seems to reveal such truths.

The first requirement is shown to be unreasonable by the

very terms in which it is made. The intuitive insight of faith, the immediate conviction of the heart, cannot render, and must not try to render, any account of itself. Proof is a process; but there is no process in this direct conviction of truth. Its assertion is just the denial of process; it is a repudiation of all connections; in such a faith of feeling there are no cob-web lines relating fact to fact, which doubt could break. Feeling is the immediate unity of the subject and object. I am pained, because I cannot rid myself of an element which is already within me; I am lifted into the emotion of pleasure, or happiness, or bliss, by the consciousness that I am already at one with an object that fulfills my longings and satisfies my needs. Hence, there seems to be ground for saying that, in this instance, the witness cannot lie; for it cannot go before the fact, as it is itself the effect of the fact. If the emotion is pleasurable it is the consciousness of the unity within; if it is painful, of the disunity. In feeling, I am absolutely with myself; and there seems, therefore, to be no need of attempting to justify, by means of reason, a faith in God which manifests itself in emotion. The emotion itself is its own sufficient witness, a direct result of the intimate union of man with the object of devotion. Nay, we may go further, and say that the demand is an unjust one, which betrays ignorance of the true nature of moral intuition and religious feeling.

I am not concerned to deny the truth that lies in the view here stated; and no advocate of the dignity of human reason, or of the worth of human knowledge, is called upon to deny it. There is a sense in which the conviction of "faith" or "feeling" is more intimate and strong than any process of proof. But this does not in any wise justify the contention of those who maintain that we can feel what we do not in any sense know, or that the heart can testify to that of which the intellect is absolutely silent.

So let us say—not "Since we know, we love,"
But rather, "Since we love, we know enough."

In these two lines there are combined the truth I would
acknowledge, and the error I would confute. Love is, in one
way, sufficient knowledge; or, rather, it is the direct testimony of that completest knowledge, in which subject and
object interpenetrate. For, where love is, all foreign elements have been eliminated. There is not "one and one
with a shadowy third"; but the object is brought within the
self as constituting part of its very life. This is involved in
all the great forms of human thought—in science and art,
no less than in morality and religion. It is the truth that we
love, and only that, which is altogether ours. By means of
love the poet is

> Made one with Nature. There is heard
> His voice in all her music, from the moan
> Of thunder to the song of night's sweet bird

and it is because he is made one with her that he is able to
reveal her inmost secrets. "Man," said Fichte, "can will
nothing but what he loves; his love is the sole and at the
same time the infallible spring of his volition, and of all his
life's striving and movement." It is only when we have
identified ourselves with an ideal, and made its realization
our own interest, that we strive to attain it. Love is revelation in knowledge, inspiration in art, motive in morality,
and the fulness of religious joy.

But, although in this sense love is greater than knowledge,
it is a grave error to separate it from knowledge. In the life
of man at least, the separation of the emotional and intellectual elements extinguishes both. We cannot know that
in which we have no interest. The very effort to comprehend an object rests on interest, or the feeling of ourselves in

it; so that knowledge, as well as morality, may be said to begin in love. We cannot know except we love; but, on the other hand, we cannot love that which we do not in some degree know. Wherever the frontiers of knowledge may be it is certain that there is nothing beyond them which can either arouse feeling, or be a steadying centre for it. Emotion is like a climbing plant. It clings to the tree of knowledge, adding beauty to its strength. But, without knowledge, it is impossible for man. There is no feeling which is not also incipient knowledge; for feeling is only the subjective side of knowledge—that face of the known fact which is turned inwards.

If, therefore, the poet's agnosticism were taken literally, and, in his philosophical poems he obviously means it to be taken literally, it would lead to a denial of the very principles of religion and morality, which it was meant to support. His appeal to love would then, strictly speaking, be an appeal to the love of nothing known, or knowable; and such love is impossible. For love, if it is to be distinguished from the organic impulse of beast towards beast, must have an object. A mere instinctive activity of benevolence in man, by means of which he lightened the sorrows of his brethren, if not informed with knowledge, would have no more moral worth than the grateful warmth of the sun. Such love as this there may be in the animal creation. If the bird is not rational, we may say that it builds its nest and lines it for its brood, pines for its partner and loves it, at the bidding of the returning spring, in much the same way as the meadows burst into flower. Without knowledge, the whole process is merely a natural one; or, if it be more, it is so only in so far as the life of emotion can be regarded as a foretaste of the life of thought. But such a natural process is not possible to man. Every activity in him is relative to his self-consciousness, and takes a new character from that relation. His love at the best and worst is the love of something that he knows, and in which he seeks to find himself made rich with new sufficiency. Thus love can not "ally" itself with ignorance. It is, indeed, an impulse pressing for the closer communion of the lover with the object of his love.

> Like two meteors of expanding flame,
> Those spheres instinct with it become the same,
> Touch, mingle, are transfigured; ever still
> Burning, yet ever inconsumable;
> In one another's substance finding food.

But, for a being such as Browning describes, who is shut up within the blind walls of his own self, the self-transcending impulse of love would be impossible. If man's inner consciousness is to be conceived as a dark room shutting out the world, upon whose shadowy phenomena the candle of introspection throws a dim and uncertain light, then he can have no interest outside of himself; nor can he ever take that first step in goodness, which carries him beyond his narrow individuality to seek and find a larger self in others. Morality, even in its lowest form, implies knowledge, and knowledge of something better than "those *apparent* other mortals." With the first dawn of the moral life comes the consciousness of an ideal, which is not actual; and such a break with the natural is not possible except to him who has known a better and desired it. The ethical endeavour of man is the attempt to convert ideas into actuality; and all his activity as moral agent takes place within the sphere that is illumined by the light of knowledge. If knowledge breaks down, there is no law of action which he can obey. The moral law that must be apprehended, and whose authority must be recognized by man, either sinks out of being or becomes an illusive phantom, if man is doomed to ignorance or false knowledge. To extinguish truth is to extinguish goodness.

In like manner, religion, which the poet would fain

defend for man by means of agnosticism, becomes impossible, if knowledge be denied. Religion is not blind emotion; nor can mere feeling, however ecstatic, ascend to God. Animals feel, but they are not, and cannot be, religious—unless they can know. The love of God implies knowledge. "I know Him whom I have believed" is the language of religion. For what is religion but a conscious identification of the self with One who is known to fulfil its needs and satisfy its aspirations? Agnosticism is thus directly destructive of it. We cannot, indeed, prove God as the conclusion of a syllogism, for He is the primary hypothesis of all proof. But, nevertheless, we cannot reach Him without knowledge. Emotion reveals no object, but is consequent upon the revelation of it; feeling yields no truth, but is the witness of the worth of a truth for the individual. If man were shut up to mere feeling, even the awe of the devout agnostic would be impossible. For the Unknowable cannot generate any emotion. It appears to do so, only because the Unknowable of the agnostic is not altogether unknown to him; but is a vast, abysmal "Something," that has occupied with its shadowy presence the field of his imagination. It is paganism stricken with the plague, and philosophy afflicted with blindness, that build altars to an unknown God. The highest and the strongest faith, the deepest trust and the most loving, come with the fullest knowledge. Indeed, the distinction between the awe of the agnostic, which is the lowest form of religion, and that highest form in which perfect love casteth out fear, springs from the fuller knowledge of the nature of the object of worship, which the latter implies. Thus, religion and morality grow with the growth of knowledge; and neither has a worse enemy than ignorance. The human spirit cannot grow in a one-sided manner. Devotion to great moral ends is possible, only through the deepening and widening of man's knowledge of the nature of the world. Those who know God best, render unto Him the purest service.

So evident is this, that it seems at first sight to be difficult to account for that antagonism to the intellect and distrust of its deliverances, which are so emphatically expressed in the writings of Browning, and which are marked characteristics of the ordinary religious opinion of our day. On closer examination, however, we shall discover that it is not pure emotion, or mere feeling, whose authority is set above that of reason, but rather the emotion which is the result of knowledge. The appeal of the religious man from the doubts and difficulties, which reason levels against "the faith," is really an appeal to the character that lies behind the emotion. The conviction of the heart, that refuses to yield to the arguments of the understanding, is not *mere* feeling; but, rather, the complex experience of the past life, that manifests itself in feeling. When an individual, clinging to his moral or religious faith, says, "I have felt it," he opposes to the doubt, not his feeling as such, but his personality in all the wealth of its experience. The appeal to the heart is the appeal to the unproved, but not, therefore, unauthorized, testimony of the best men at their best moments, when their vision of truth is clearest. No one pretends that "the loud and empty voice of untrained passion and prejudice" has any authority in matters of moral and religious faith; though, in such cases, "feeling" may lack neither depth nor intensity. If the "feelings" of the good man were dissociated from his character, and stripped bare of all the significance they obtain therefrom, their worthlessness would become apparent. The profound error of condemning knowledge in order to honour feeling is hidden only by the fact that the feeling is already informed and inspired with knowledge. Religious agnosticism, like all other forms of the theory of nescience, derives its plausibility from the adventitious help it purloins from the knowledge which it condemns.

That it is to such feeling that Browning really appeals against knowledge becomes abundantly evident, when we bear in mind that he always calls it "love." For love in man is never ignorant. It knows its object, and is a conscious identification of the self with it. And to Browning, the object of love, when love is at its best—of that love by means of which he refutes intellectual pessimism—is mankind. The revolt of the heart against all evil is a desire for the good of all men. In other words, his refuge against the assailing doubts which spring from the intellect, is in the moral consciousness. But that consciousness is no mere emotion; it is a consciousness which knows the highest good, and moves in sympathy with it. It is our maturest wisdom; for it is the manifestation of the presence and activity of the ideal, the fullest knowledge and the surest. Compared with this, the emotion linked to ignorance, of which the poet speaks in his philosophic theory, is a very poor thing. It is poorer than the lowest human love.

Now, if this higher interpretation of the term "heart" be accepted, it is easily seen why its authority should seem higher than that of reason; and particularly, if it be remembered that, while the heart is thus widened to take in all direct consciousness of the ideal, "the reason" is reduced to the power of reflection, or mental analysis. "The heart," in this sense, is the intensest unity of the complex experiences of a whole life, while "the reason" is taken merely as a faculty which invents arguments, and provides grounds and evidences; it is what is called, in the language of German philosophy, the "understanding." Now, in this sense, the understanding has, at best, only a borrowed authority. It is the faculty of rules rather than of principles. It is ever dogmatic, assertive, repellent, hard; and it always advances its forces in single line. Its logic never convinced any one of truth or error, unless, beneath the arguments which it advanced, there lay some deeper principle of concord. Thus, the opposition between "faith and reason," rightly interpreted, is that between a concrete experience, instinct with life and conviction, and a mechanical arrangement of abstract arguments. The quarrel of the heart is not with reason, but with reasons. "Evidences of Christianity?" said Coleridge; "I am weary of the word." It is this weariness of evidence, of the endless arguments *pro* and *con,* which has caused so many to distrust reason and knowledge, and which has sometimes driven believers to the dangerous expedient of making their faith dogmatic and absolute. Nor have the opponents of "the faith" been slow to seize the opportunity thus offered them. "From the moment that a religion solicits the aid of philosophy, its ruin is inevitable," said Heine. "In the attempt at defence, it prates itself into destruction. Religion, like every absolutism, must not seek to justify itself. Prometheus is bound to the rock by a silent force. Yea, Aeschylus permits not personified power to utter a single word. It must remain mute. The moment that a religion ventures to print a catechism supported by arguments, the moment that a political absolutism publishes an official newspaper, both are near their end. But therein consists our triumph: we have brought our adversaries to speech, and they must reckon with us." But, we may answer, religion is *not* an absolutism; and, therefore, it is *not* near its end when it ventures to justify itself. On the contrary, no spiritual power, be it moral or religious, can maintain its authority, if it assumes a despotic attitude; for the human spirit inevitably moves towards freedom, and that movement is the deepest necessity of its nature, which it cannot escape. "Religion, on the ground of its sanctity, and law, on the ground of its majesty, often resist the sifting of their claims. But in so doing, they inevitably awake a not unjust suspicion that their claims are ill-founded. They can command the unfeigned homage of man, only when they have shown themselves able to stand the test of free inquiry."

And if it is an error to suppose, with Browning, that the primary truths of the moral and religious consciousness belong to a region which is higher than knowledge, and can, from that side, be neither assailed nor defended; it is also an error to suppose that reason is essentially antagonistic to them. The facts of morality and religion are precisely the richest facts of knowledge; and that faith is the most secure which is most completely illumined by reason. Religion at its best is not a dogmatic despotism, nor is reason a merely critical and destructive faculty. If reason is loyal to the truth of religion on which it is exercised, it will reach beneath all the conflict and clamour of disputation, to the principle of unity, on which, as we have seen, both reason and religion rest.

The "faith" to which religious spirits appeal against all the attacks of doubt, "the love" of Browning, is really implicit reason; it is "abbreviated" or concentrated knowledge; it is the manifold experiences of life focussed into an intense unity. And, on the other hand, the "reason" which they condemn is what Carlyle calls the logic-chopping faculty. In taking the side of faith when troubled with difficulties which they cannot lay, they are really defending the cause of reason against that of the understanding. For it is quite true that the understanding, that is, the reason as reflective or critical, can never bring about either a moral or religious life. It cannot create a religion, any more than physiology can produce men. The reflection which brings doubt is always secondary; it can only exercise itself on a given material. As Hegel frequently pointed out, it is not the function of moral philosophy to create or to institute a morality or religion, but to understand them. The facts must first be given; they must be actual experiences of the human spirit. Moral philosophy and theology differ from the moral or religious life, in the same way as geology differs from the earth, or astronomy from the heavenly bodies. The latter are facts; the former are theories about the facts. Religion is an attitude of the human spirit towards the highest; morality is the realization of character; and these are not to be confused with their reflective interpretations. Much of the difficulty in these matters comes from the lack of a clear distinction between *beliefs* and *creeds*.

Further, not only are the utterances of the heart prior to the deliverances of the intellect in this sense, but it may also be admitted that the latter can never do full justice to the contents of the former. So rich is character in content and so complex is spiritual life, that we can never, by means of reflection, lift into clear consciousness all the elements that enter into it. Into the organism of our experience, which is our faith, there is continually absorbed the subtle influences of our complex natural and social environment. We grow by means of them, as the plant grows by feeding on the soil and the sunshine and dew. It is as impossible for us to set forth, one by one, the truths and errors which we have thus worked into our mental and moral life, as it is to keep a reckoning of the physical atoms with which the natural life builds up the body. Hence, every attempt to justify these truths seems inadequate; and the defence which the understanding sets up for the faith, always seems partial and cold. Who ever fully expressed his deepest convictions? The consciousness of the dignity of the moral law affected Kant like the view of the starry firmament, and generated a feeling of the sublime which words could not express; and the religious ecstasy of the saints cannot be confined within the channels of speech, but floods the soul with overmastering power, possessing all its faculties. In this respect, it will always remain true that the greatest facts of human experience reach beyond all knowledge. Nay, we may add further, that in this respect the simplest of these facts passes all understanding. Still, as we have already seen, it is reason that constitutes them; that which is presented to reason for explanation, in knowledge and morality and religion, is itself the product of reason. Reason is the power which, by interaction with our environment, has generated the whole of our experience. And, just as natural science interprets the phenomena given to it by ordinary opinion, i.e., interprets and purifies a lower form of knowledge by converting it into a higher; so the task of reason when it is exercised upon morality and religion, is simply to evolve, and amplify the meaning of its own products. The movement from morality and religion to moral philosophy and the philosophy of religion, is thus a movement from reason to reason, from the implicit to the explicit, from the germ to the developed fulness of life and structure. In this matter, as in all others wherein the human spirit is concerned, that which is first by nature is last in genesis—νικᾶ δ᾽ ὁ πρῶτος καὶ τελευταῖος δραμών. The whole history of the moral and religious experience of mankind is comprised in the statement, that the implicit reason which we call "faith" is ever developing towards full consciousness of itself; and that, at its first beginning, and throughout the whole ascending process of this development, the highest is present in it as a self-manifesting power.

But this process from the almost instinctive intuitions of the heart towards the morality and religion of freedom, being a process of evolution, necessarily involves conflict. There are men, it is true, the unity of whose moral and religious faith is never completely broken by doubt; just as there are men who are not forced by the contradictions in the first interpretation of the world by ordinary experience to attempt to re-interpret it by means of science and philosophy.

Throughout their lives they may say like Pompilia—

I know the right place by foot's feel,
I took it and tread firm there; wherefore change?

Jean Paul Richter said that he knew another way of being happy, beside that of soaring away so far above the clouds of life, that its miseries looked small, and the whole external world shrunk into a little child's garden. It was, "Simply to sink down into this little garden; and there to nestle yourself so snugly, so homewise, in some furrow, that in looking out from your warm lark-nest, you likewise can discern no wolf-dens, charnel-houses, or thunder-rods, but only blades and ears, every one of which, for the nest-bird, is a tree, and a sun-screen, and rain-screen." There is a similar way of being good, with a goodness which, though limited, is pure and perfect in nature. Nay, we may even admit that such lives are frequently the most complete and beautiful, just as the fairest flowers grow, not on the tallest trees, but on the fragile plants at their foot. Nevertheless, even in the case of those persons who have never broken from the traditional faith of the past, or felt it to be inadequate, that faith has been silently reconstructed in a new synthesis of knowledge. Spiritual life cannot come by inheritance; but every individual must acquire a faith for himself, and turn his spiritual environment into personal experience. "A man may be a heretic in the truth," said Milton, "and if he believe things only because his pastor says so, or the assembly so determines, without knowing other reason, though his belief be true, yet the very truth he holds becomes his heresy." It is truth to another but tradition to him; it is a creed and not a conviction.

Browning fully recognizes the need of this conflict—

> Is it not this ignoble confidence,
> Cowardly hardihood, that dulls and damps,
> Makes the old heroism impossible?

asks the Pope. The stream of truth when it ceases to flow onward, becomes a malarious swamp. Movement is the law of life; and knowledge of the principles of morality and religion, as of all other principles, must, in order to grow, be felt from time to time as inadequate and untrue. There are men and ages whose mission is—

> to shake
> This torpor of assurance from our creed,
> Re-introduce the doubt discarded, bring
> That formidable danger back, we drove
> Long ago to the distance and the dark.

Such a spirit of criticism seems to many to exercise a merely destructive power, and those who have not felt the inadequacy of the inherited faith defend themselves against it, as the enemy of their lives. But no logic, or assailing doubt, could have power against the testimony of "the heart," unless it was rooted in deeper and truer principles than those which it attacked. Nothing can overpower truth except a larger truth; and, in such a conflict, the truth in the old view will ultimately take the side of the new, and find its subordinate position within it. It has happened, not infrequently, as in the case of the Encylopædists, that the explicit truths of reason were more abstract, that is, less true, than the implicit "faith" which they assailed. The central truths of religion have often proved themselves to possess some stubborn, though semiarticulate power, which could ultimately overcome or subordinate the more partial and explicit truths of abstract science. It is this that gives plausibility to the idea, that the testimony of the heart is more reliable than that of the intellect. But, in this case also, it was really reason that triumphed. It was the truth which proved itself to be immortal, and not any mere emotion. The insurrection of the intellect against the heart is quelled, only when the untruth, or abstract character, of the principle of the assailants has been made manifest, and when the old faith has yielded up its unjust gains, and proved its vitality and strength by absorbing the truth that gave vigour to the attack. Just as in morality it is the ideal, or the unity of the

whole moral life, that breaks up into differences, so also here
it is the implicit faith which, as it grows, breaks forth into
doubts. In both cases alike, the negative movement which
induces despair, is only a phase of a positive process—the
process of reason towards a fuller, a more articulate and
complex, realization of itself.

Hence it follows that the value and strength of a faith
corresponds accurately to the doubts it has overcome. Those
who never went forth to battle cannot come home heroes.
It is only when the earthquake has tried the towers, and
destroyed the sense of security, that

> Man stands out again, pale, resolute,
> Prepared to die,—that is, alive at last.
> As we broke up that old faith of the world,
> Have we, next age, to break up this the new—
> Faith, in the thing, grown faith in the report—
> Whence need to bravely disbelieve report
> Through increased faith i' the thing reports belie?

"Well knows he who uses to consider, that our faith and
knowledge thrive by exercise, as well as our limbs and
complexion."

It was, thus, I conclude, a deep speculative error into
which Browning fell, when, in order to substantiate his
optimistic faith, he stigmatized human knowledge as merely
apparent. Knowledge does not fail, except in the sense in
which morality also fails; it does not at any time attain to
the ultimate truth, any more than the moral life is in any of
its activities a complete embodiment of the absolute good.
It is not given to man, who is essentially progressive, to
reach the ultimate term of development. For there is no
ultimate term: life never stands still. But, for the same
reason, there is no ultimate failure. The whole history of
man is a history of growth. If, however, knowledge did
fail, then morality too must fail; and the appeal which the

poet makes from the intellect to the heart, would be an appeal to mere emotion. Finally, even if we take a generous view of the poet's meaning, and put out of consideration the theory he expresses when he is deliberately philosophizing, there is still no appeal from the reason to an alien and higher authority. The appeal to "the heart" is, at best, only an appeal from the understanding to the reason, from a conscious logic to the more concrete fact constituted by reason, which reflection has failed to comprehend in its completeness; at its worst, it is an appeal from truth to prejudice, from belief to dogma.

And in both cases alike, the appeal is futile; for, whether "the heart be wiser than the head," or not, whether the faith which is assailed be richer or poorer, truer or more false, than the logic which is directed against it, an appeal to the heart cannot any longer restore the unity of the broken life. Once reflection has set in, there is no way of turning away its destructive might, except by deeper reflection. The implicit faith of the heart must become the explicit faith of reason. "There is no final and satisfactory issue from such an endless internal debate and conflict, until the 'heart' has learnt to speak the language of the head—i.e., until the permanent principles, which underlay and gave strength to faith, have been brought into the light of distinct consciousness."

I conclude, therefore, that the poet was right in saying that, in order to comprehend human character,

> I needs must blend the quality of man
> With quality of God, and so assist
> Mere human sight to understand my Life.

But it was a profound error, which contained in it the destruction of morality and religion, as well as of knowledge, to make "the quality of God" a love that excludes reason, and the quality of man an intellect incapable of knowing truth. Such incongruous elements could never be combined into the unity of a character. A love that was mere emotion could not yield a motive for morality, or a principle of religion. A philosophy of life which is based on agnosticism is an explicit self-contradiction, which can help no one. We must appeal from Browning the philosopher to Browning the poet.

[1895]

GEORGE SAINTSBURY: *BROWNING*

WHENEVER it happens to me to write about Robert Browning, I am always a little apprehensive of the fate of the Trimmer. I have loved and admired his work for full thirty years; but I do not belong to any of the four parties wherein most of mankind are included as regards him. There are those who were Browningites from the first, or almost the first, and have been faithful all through,—a race now naturally diminishing by efflux of time. There are those who began to like him after he himself began to be fashionable, and who, whether they have gone the whole way with the Browning Society or not, regard him as one of the greatest of poets and philosophers. There are those who, from the sturdy English standpoint, have always been unable to tolerate him at all, at whatever time he was presented to them. And there are those who, though chronologically contemporaries of the rage for him, either had other rages which kept them from appreciating him, or are young enough (not necessarily in years) to think him already *vieux jeu*. All these are more or less "prevailing parties," as Lord Foppington says, and can encourage one another by dint of fellowship.

But my case is a little different. It so happened that Browning never fell in my way when I was a boy, except in very small and casual extracts. These I owed, I think, chiefly to that godsend to the youth of the late fifties and early sixties, Dr. Holden's *Foliorum Silvula*, which, if it was the occasion of much deplorable Greek and Latin verse, must have laid the foundation of acquaintance with the very best of English. I cannot remember reading a single volume of Browning as a volume before I became an undergraduate. But the collected edition of his *Poems* appeared almost directly afterwards, and I got it, while no long time passed before the appearance of *Dramatis Personæ*. Then I became very much addicted to Browning, and used to read him night and day. I have never myself quite understood what people meant and still sometimes seem to mean by the "obscurity," the "difficulty" of *Sordello*. It is distinctly breathless and it is unduly affected; but if anybody has got a brain at all, that brain ought not to be very much exercised in following the fortunes of Sordello and Taurello, Alberic and Ezzelin, Adelaide and the rest. It appeared to me that *Paracelsus* didn't prove much, and like *Sordello* was breathless, while I did not and do not care much more for Aprile than for Paul Dombey. But who could miss the splendid, and for its date, wholly novel poetry of it? The plays were mainly a bore—I have scarcely ever read a serious play younger than the seventeenth century that was not more or less of a bore to me—but there too the poet appeared. And as for *Men and Women*, and the *Lyrics*, and so forth, there was no possible mistake about them, when they were at their best. I never loved the most popular pieces much. "Ghent to Aix" is only a *tour de force,* and I can remember that when as a boy I first heard of it I thought that the good man rode to Aix in Provence (which would have been something like a ride), and was desperately disappointed at the actual achievement. In "Count Gismond" there is a passage of four and a half lines which is good enough for anything, but the rest is no great matter. "The Glove" contains other lines which stick in the memory, but the moral is mainly rubbish, and Marot *was* a poet.

And so on and so on. But I had never read, and I have never read, anything like even the least of half a hundred of the others in its best parts. "Christina" (what devil ever tempted Mr. Browning to run the double lines of the earlier version into single ones?); "In a Gondola" and "The Last Ride Together," which I will uphold for two of the best love poems of the century, be the others what they may, the last named being perhaps the very best that we have produced for two hundred years; "Mesmerism" and "Porphyria's Lover," a pair on a plane only a little lower; the first stanza of "Meeting at Night," in which Browning has for once met and matched his great contemporary and rival on his own ground; the delightful rococo of "Women and Roses"; yet another pair, "Life in a Love" and "Love in a Life"; "Love among the Ruins" and "Two in the Campagna," which ought, like so many of Browning's poems, to be taken together; "Prospice," great among the greatest, and such a quiet essence of heroic combativeness that I never could understand how my friend Mr. Henley failed to include it in his Lyra Heroica; "Childe Roland," best of its own class, though "The Flight of the Duchess" runs it hard; and crowning the whole "Rabbi ben Ezra";—these were things (and I have not mentioned a quarter of my own favourites) to set the blood coursing rarely. And yet, though I believe I love and loved them with a sum that twenty thousand members of Browning Societies could not make up, I never could and cannot now call myself exactly a Browningite. Even then, even in his heyday, the man (it is surely permissible to use slang of one who used so much) "jawed" at times; he was not to be depended upon for certainty of taste or touch; he would drop hideous negligences or more hideous outrages of intention in the middle of a masterpiece; it was clear that he wanted to teach; and so forth.

The works which followed *Dramatis Personæ* were not very well suited to convert a half-hearted though at times intense worshipper of this kind into a wholehearted one. I am told that *The Ring and the Book* did actually bring about that change which its author anticipated in the famous address to the British public who "might like him yet." I cannot say that it brought about a contrary change in me. A man does not once appreciate to the full "The Last Ride Together," or "Love among the Ruins," and get tired of them afterwards. But I own that this huge poem itself gave me little pleasure. Of course there are fine things in it, and the traits of "criticism of life" as well as the achievements of poetical expression are often admirable. But it is so tyrannously long without any action; so mercilessly voluble without much justification for the volubility; it has such a false air of wisdom and philosophy which is after all not particularly recondite or novel,—that I remember thinking of "Porphyria's Lover," and wishing that some one had applied that person's drastic procedure to the poet on his own principles.

Nevertheless I persevered, much enduring, and except *Red Cotton Nightcap Country*, which I do not believe I have ever read through yet, and *People of Importance*, which I missed by accident and have never picked up, I do not believe there is a volume or a line of Browning's that I have not read. It was tribulation mostly in those days, but there was comfort sometimes. *Fifine* is really a great book (the Browningites, I am told, do not like it), and there are

gleanings even in the volumes where Mr. Browning thought
to make up for a not wholly perfect knowledge of Greek by
calling a Nymph a "numph." And at the evening time there
was light. Even in the darkest days of the *Conciones ad
Vulgus Browningense* appeared flashes of the old splendour,
never seen on any other land or sea; the final poem of
Pachiarotto was an almost flawless gem, and the latest volumes of all, especially *Asolando,* showed a wonderful recovery. It was a case of *eripitur persona, manet res.* The
mask that the Browning Society had admired, and that had
been constantly touched up and made more mask-like to
please it, fell off, and Browning—not in his first vigour, not
as when he wrote "In a Gondola" or "After," but still Browning—reappeared.

It is of course a very great misfortune to be thus con-
stitutionally unable to be "in the tune." In 1863 one ran
the risk of being thought an affected and presumptuous
youth for saying that, whatever faults *Sordello* might have, it
was not half so obscure as even then one of Mr. Gladstone's
speeches was, and that "The Last Ride Together" was worth
the weight of the lady and her lover and their horses in
gold. In 1883 one ran the risk of being dismissed as a
grizzling fossil because one failed to admire volume after
volume of blank-verse "jaw," where for the most part mannerism took the place of thought and facile ruggedness
that of originality. I am not sure that in 1894 the light,
light wheel is not already on the point of turning again, and
that anybody who admires Browning at all will not be soon
despised as something or other—it really does not much
matter what. Nevertheless, as there are nearly always the
seven thousand or thereabouts who have not bowed the
knee to the Baal of any particular moment, who do not take
their admirations or their dislikes at the stall which happens
to be prescribed by fashion, it may not be impertinent to
examine a little further the reasons which have made one

person of the class a lover of Browning who was never a Browningite,—a critic of Browning, who never would join in the cry about "harshness" and "obscurity," and all the rest of it. If outsiders do indeed see most of the game, such a one should at any rate have been able to see a little of it; and perhaps even his enthusiasm may cease to be suspected when it is taken in conjunction with his objections.

I do not know that there is any English writer to whom the motto *Qualis ab incepto* may be applied with more propriety than to Robert Browning,—any whose works are more intimately connected with his life. I am not one of those who take a very great interest in the biography of poets, and I think that its importance as illustrating their works has been as a rule exaggerated. But certainly, if a tolerably instructed student of books and men were set the problem of Browning's works without any knowledge of Browning's life, it would not give him much trouble to lay down the main lines of the latter. A man who had had to write for a living, or to devote himself to writing in the intervals for any regular occupation, could hardly have produced so much and have produced it with such a complete disregard of the public taste and the consequent chances of profit. A man who had had the advantages of that school and university education which as a rule happens to the upper and upper-middle classes of Englishmen would hardly have produced his work with such an entire disregard of authority as well as of popularity. The first influence was no doubt wholly good, for, copy-books notwithstanding, the instances of men who without private means or practical sinecures have produced large quantities of very fine poetry are very rare, and for the last couple of centuries almost nonexistent. The circumstances of Browning's education, on the other hand, no doubt had a good influence as well as a bad. It is open to any one to contend that his natural genius was too irregular, too recalcitrant to the file, to have admitted the labour of that instrument; and that therefore, if he had had a classical and critical taste implanted in him, the struggle of the two would have condemned him to silence. But it is quite certain that his worst faults are exactly those of a privately educated middle-class Englishman, and it is of the very highest interest to compare his career and performance in this respect with the career and performance of Mr. Ruskin, who was in many respects his analogue in genius and circumstances, but whose sojourn at Oxford gave just the differentiating touch.

Allow however, as we may, less or more influence to these things, I think it will hardly be denied that the effect manifested itself very early, and that even by the appearance of *Bells and Pomegranates* prediction of their author's characteristics and career as a whole was pretty easy. It certainly had become so by the time that I myself, as I have said, was "entered" in Browning. It was obvious on the credit side that here was a man with an almost entirely novel conception of poetical vocabulary and style, with a true and wonderful lyrical gift, with a faculty of argument and narrative in verse which, diametrically as it was opposed in kind to the Drydenian tradition, had been in kind and volume unsurpassed since Dryden, and with an enormous range and versatility of subject. He could, it was clear, not merely manipulate words and verse in a manner almost suggesting prestidigitation, but was also much more than a mere word- and metre-monger. On certain sides of the great problem of life he could think with boldness and originality, if not with depth: the depth of Mr. Browning's thought belongs to the same mistaken tradition as his obscurity, and reminds me of those inky pools in the limestone districts which look and are popularly reputed to be bottomless till somebody tries them and finds them to be about nineteen foot two. He had above all a command of the most universally appealing, if not also the loftiest, style of poetry,—

that which deals with love,—hardly equalled except by the very greatest, and not often excelled even by them.

But these great merits were accompanied by uncommon and sometimes very ugly defects. It was obvious that his occasional cacophonies and vulgarities were not merely an exaggeration of his recognition of the truth that the vernacular can be made to impart vigour, and that discords and degradations of scale and tone heighten and brighten musical effects. They were at any rate sometimes clearly the result of a combination of indolence and bad taste,—indolence that would not take the trouble to remove, bad taste that did not fully perceive, the gravity of the blemishes that wanted removing in his very finest passages. There was also that most fatal defect which the ill-natured fairy so often annexes to the gifts of vigorous and fertile command of language,—an excessive voluminousness and volubility. Lastly there was the celebrated "obscurity," which taken to pieces and judged coolly was simply the combined result of the good and bad gifts just mentioned. Mr. Browning had plenty to say on whatsoever subject he took up; he had a fresh, original, vigorous manner of saying it; he was naturally inclined to and had indulged his inclination for odd and striking locutions; he was very allusive; and he was both impatient of the labour of correction and rather insensitive to the necessity of it. Hence what he himself has rather damagingly called in a probably unintentional satire and caricature of himself the "monstr' inform' ingens-horrendous demoniaco-seraphic penman's latest piece of graphic" which occurs so often in his work, which the admirers take for something very obscure but very precious, requiring the aid of Browning dictionaries and so forth, which the honest public gapes at, from which the primmer kind of academic critic turns away disgusted, and which more catholic and tolerant appreciation regards, if not exactly with disgust, certainly with regret and disapproval.

Now it was practically certain that when, from such a man, the very last restaining or dissuading checks in the shape of public disapproval or (more powerful still) indifference were removed, he would take the bit in his teeth and run away with himself. This was what Browning practically did in the score of volumes in improvised blank verse chiefly, but also in other metres, which he poured forth after 1868. The greater part of this matter I feel tolerably confident that futurity will relegate to the same shelf with Southey's epics and Dryden's plays. Indeed, I myself would much rather read the worst of either group than *Prince Hohenstiel Schwangau*, or the *Balaustion* books. But if the said posterity is well served by its editors, from time to time certain things will be rescued from even this part, and, added to the earlier harvest, will form a poetical *corpus* not by any means contemptible in respect of bulk even when ranked with the sheaves of pretty fertile poets, and full of admirable if rarely perfect poetry. Few philosophical poets have lived long—Lucretius and Dante are the only great exceptions—and I am as certain as it is not rash to be that Mr. Browning in his philosophical pieces will not rank with these. Indeed, it was not much of a philosophy, this which the poet half echoed from and half taught to the second half of the nineteenth century. A sort of undogmatic Theism heightened by a very little undogmatic Christianity; a theory of doing and living more optimist than Carlylism and less fantastic than Ruskinism, but as vague and as unpractical as either; a fancy for what is called analogy and a marvellous gift of rhetorical exposition,—these made it up. It looks vast enough and various enough in form and colour at a distance; it shrinks and crumbles up pretty small when you come to examine it.

But a poet is always saved by his poetry, and of that, thank Heaven, Mr. Browning had plenty to secure his salvation. Those volumes of selections by which in an even narrower compass than that already hinted at he is perhaps destined to live most securely and longest (though the second wants refreshing and rearranging) display a perfect Aurora Borealis of poetical flashes of the intensest luminosity and the most endless variety of colour. The sabre-and-stirrup clang of the *i* rhymes in "Through the Metidja"; the astonishingly various music and imagery of the songs of "In a Gondola"; the steady hopeless swing—too full of passion for rant—of "The Last Ride"; the strange throbbing measure of "Mesmerism"; and a hundred other things which I must not mention lest I be accused of mere catalogue-making;— these are the things which generation after generation of lovers of poetry will read and rejoice in, just as we now read and rejoice in Donne and Marvell, and the rest of the seventeenth century lyrists. Indeed, I sometimes wonder whether on one of their sides Browning did not come nearer to these than Coleridge or Shelley, Keats or Tennyson. For if he had not the finest seventeenth century magic in remoteness of matter and melody of form, he had the odd ups and downs, the queer admixture of ore and dross, the want of criticism, the incompleteness which mark all but one or two of our seventeenth century men.

And if any one must needs, to complete his idea of a great poet, have something more than poetry and passion, than music and moonlight, I shall at least allow that Browning's life philosophy, if exposed to the criticisms made above, did once or twice, notably in the above-mentioned "Rabbi ben Ezra," receive a very noble and lasting enshrinement and expression. A little optimistic perhaps, but certainly not with the optimism which blinks the facts of life; a little pantheistic, as perhaps are all the great religions and all the great philosophies when you come to examine them from certain points of view and mood; a trifle unsubstantial, as divine philosophy must always be. But full of a generous and indomitable spirit, free from the whining and cavilling to which poetic philosophy so often inclines; throbbing with that remembrance of delight which is perhaps better than any delight itself; not covetous but not despairing of more; content to comprehend as far as may be, to labour as much as need be, to hope as much as is rational,—the philosophy in short of a poet who is also a man, which duplicate advantage poets have not always possessed.

[1898]

JOHN J. CHAPMAN

ROBERT BROWNING

THERE is a period in the advance of any great man's influence between the moment when he appears and the moment when he has become historical, during which it is difficult to give any succinct account of him. We are ourselves a part of the thing we would describe. The element which we attempt to isolate for purposes of study is still living within us. Our science becomes tinged with autobiography. Such must be the fate of any essay on Browning written at the present time.

The generation to whom his works were unmeaning has hardly passed away. The generation he spoke for still lives. His influence seems still to be expanding. The literature of Browning dictionaries, phrasebooks, treatises, and philosophical studies grows daily. Mr. Cooke in his guide to Browning gives a condensed catalogue of the best books and essays on Browning, which covers many finely printed pages. This class of book—the textbook—is not the product of impulse. The textbook is a commercial article and follows the demand as closely as the reaper follows the crop. We can tell the acreage under cultivation by looking over the account books of the makers of farm implements. Thousands of people are now studying Browning, following in his footsteps, reading lives of his heroes, and hunting up the subjects he treated.

This Browningism which we are disposed to laugh at is a most interesting secondary outcome of his influence. It has its roots in natural piety, and the educational value of it is very great.

Browning's individuality created for him a personal following, and he was able to respond to the call to leadership. Unlike Carlyle, he had something to give his disciples beside the immediate satisfaction of a spiritual need. He gave them not only meal but seed. In this he was like Emerson; but Emerson's little store of finest grain is of a different soil. Emerson lived in a cottage and saw the stars over his head through his skylight. Browning, on the other hand, loved pictures, places, music, men, and women, and his works are like the house of a rich man,—a treasury of plunder from many provinces and many ages, whose manners and passions are vividly recalled to us. In Emerson's house there was not a peg to hang a note upon,—"this is his bookshelf, this his bed." But Browning's palace craves a catalogue. And a proper catalogue to such a palace becomes a liberal education.

Robert Browning was a strong, glowing, whole-souled human being, who enjoyed life more intensely than any Englishman since Walter Scott. He was born among books; and circumstances enabled him to follow his inclinations and become a writer,—a poet by profession. He was, from early youth to venerable age, a centre of bounding vitality, the very embodiment of spontaneous life; and the forms of poetry in which he so fully and so accurately expressed himself enable us to know him well. Indeed, only great poets are known so intimately as we know Robert Browning.

Religion was at the basis of his character, and it was the function of religious poetry that his work fulfilled. Inasmuch as no man invents his own theology, but takes it from the current world and moulds it to his needs, it was inevitable that Robert Browning should find and seize upon as his own all that was optimistic in Christian theology. Everything that was hopeful his spirit accepted; everything that was sunny and joyful and good for the brave soul he embraced. What was distressing he rejected or explained away. In the world of Robert Browning *everything* was right.

The range of subject covered by his poems is wider than that of any other poet that ever lived; but the range of his ideas is exceedingly small. We need not apologize for treating Browning as a theologian and a doctor of philosophy, for he spent a long life in trying to show that a poet is always really both—and he has almost convinced us. The expositors and writers of textbooks have had no difficulty in formulating his theology, for it is of the simplest kind; and his views on morality and art are logically a part of it. The "message" which poets are conventionally presumed to deliver, was, in Browning's case, a very definite creed, which may be found fully set forth in any one of twenty poems. Every line of his poetry is logically dedicated to it.

He believes that the development of the individual soul is the main end of existence. The strain and stress of life are incidental to growth, and therefore desirable. Development and growth means a closer union with God. In fact, God is of not so much importance in Himself, but as the end towards which man tends. That irreverent person who said that Browning uses "God" as a pigment made an accurate criticism of his theology. In Browning, God is adjective to man. Browning believes that all conventional morality must be reviewed from the standpoint of how conduct affects the actor himself, and what effect it has on his individual growth. The province of art and of all thinking and working is to make these truths clear and to grapple with the problems they give rise to.

The first two fundamental beliefs of Browning—namely: (1) that, ultimately speaking, the most important matter in the world is the soul of a man; and (2) that a sense of effort is coincident with development—are probably true. We instinctively feel them to be true, and they seem to be receiving support from those quarters of research to which we look for light, however dim. In the application of his dogmas to specific cases in the field of ethics, Browning often reaches conclusions which are fair subjects for disagreement. Since most of our conventional morality is framed to repress the individual, he finds himself at war with it—in revolt against it. He is habitually pitted against it, and thus acquires modes of thought which sometimes lead him into paradox—at least, to conclusions at odds with his premises. It is in the course of exposition, and incidentally to his main purpose as a teacher of a few fundamental ideas, that Browning has created his masterpieces of poetry.

Never was there a man who in the course of a long life changed less. What as a boy he dreamed of doing, that he did. The thoughts of his earliest poems are the thoughts of his latest. His tales, his songs, his monologues, his dramas, his jests, his sermons, his rage, his prayer, are all upon the same theme: whatever fed his mind nourished these beliefs. His interest in the world was solely an interest in them. He saw them in history and in music; his travels and studies brought him back nothing else but proofs of them; the universe in each of its manifestations was a commentary upon them. His nature was the simplest, the most positive, the least given to abstract speculation, which England can show in his time. He was not a thinker, for he was never in doubt.

He had recourse to disputation as a means of inculcating truth, but he used it like a lawyer arguing a case. His conclusions are fixed from the start. Standing, from his infancy, upon a faith as absolute as that of a martyr, he has never for one instant undergone the experience of doubt, and only knows that there is such a thing because he has met with it in other people. The force of his feelings is so much greater than his intellect that his mind serves his soul like a valet. Out of the whole cosmos he takes what belongs to him and sustains him, leaving the rest, or not noting it.

There never was a great poet whose scope was so definite. That is the reason why the world is so cleanly divided into people who do and who do not care for Browning. One real glimpse into him gives you the whole of him. The public which loves him is made up of people who have been through certain spiritual experiences to which he is the antidote. The public which loves him not consists of people who have escaped these experiences. To some he is a strong, rare, and precious elixir, which nothing else will replace. To others, who do not need him, he is a boisterous and eccentric person,—a Heracles in the House of mourning.

Let us remember his main belief,—the value of the individual. The needs of society constantly require that the individual be suppressed. They hold him down and punish him at every point. The tyranny of order and organization —of monarch or public opinion—weights him and presses him down. This is the inevitable tendency of all stable social arrangements. Now and again there arises some strong nature that revolts against the influence of conformity which is becoming intolerable,—against the atmosphere of caste or theory; of Egyptian priest or Manchester economist; of absolutism or of democracy.

And this strong nature cries out that the souls of men are being injured, and that they are important; that your soul and my soul are more important than Cæsar—or than the survival of the fittest. Such a voice was the voice of Christ, and the lesser saviors of the world bring always a like message of revolt: they arise to fulfil the same fundamental need of the world.

Carlyle, Emerson, Victor Hugo, Browning, were prophets to a generation oppressed in spirit, whose education had oppressed them with a Jewish law of Adam Smith and Jeremy Bentham and Malthus, of Clarkson and Cobden,—of thought for the millions, and for man in the aggregate. "To what end is all this beneficence, all this conscience, all this theory?" some one at length cries out. "For whom is it in the last analysis that you legislate? You talk of *man*, I see only *men*."

To men suffering from an age of devotion to humanity came Robert Browning as a liberator. Like Carlyle, he was understood first in this country because we had begun earlier with our theoretical and practical philanthropies, and had taken them more seriously. We had suffered more. We needed to be told that it was right to love, hate, and be angry, to sin and repent. It was a revelation to us to think that we had some inheritance in the joys and passions of mankind. We needed to be told these things as a tired child needs to be comforted. Browning gave them to us in the form of a religion. There was no one else sane or deep or wise or strong enough to know what we lacked.

If ever a generation had need of a poet,—of some one to tell them they might cry and not be ashamed, rejoice and not find the reason in John Stuart Mill; some one who should justify the claims of the spirit which was starving on the religion of humanity,—it was the generation for whom Browning wrote.

Carlyle had seized upon the French Revolution, which served his ends because it was filled with striking, with powerful, with grotesque examples of individual force. In his Hero Worship he gives his countrymen a philosophy of history based on nothing but worship of the individual. Browning with the same end in view gave us pictures of the fifteenth and sixteenth centuries in France and Italy. He glorified what we had thought crime and error, and made men of us. He was the apostle to the educated of a most complex period, but such as he was, he was complete. Those people to whom he has been a poet know what it is for the heart to receive full expression from the lips of another.

The second thesis which Browning insists on—the identity of spiritual suffering with spiritual growth—is the one balm of the world. It is said that recent physiological experiment shows that muscles do not develop unless exercised up to what is called the "distress point." If this shall prove to be an instance of a general law,—if the struggles and agony of the spirit are really signs of an increase of that spiritual life which is the only sort of life we can conceive of now or hereafter,—then the truth-to-feeling of much of Browning's poetry has a scientific basis. It cannot be denied that Browning held firmly two of the most moving and far-reaching ideas of the world, and he expanded them in the root, leaf, flower, and fruit of a whole world of poetic disquisition.

It is unnecessary at this day to point out the beauties of Browning or the sagacity with which he chose his effects. He gives us the sallow wife of James Lee, whose soul is known to him, Pippa the silk-spinning girl, three men found in the morgue, persons lost, forgotten, or misunderstood. He searches the world till he finds the man whom everybody will concur in despising, the mediæval grammarian, and he writes to him the most powerful ode in English, the mightiest tribute ever paid to a man. His culture and his learning are all subdued to what he works in; they are all in harness to draw his thought. He mines in antiquity or drags his net over German philosophy or modern drawing-rooms,—all to the same end.

[43]

In that miracle of power and beauty—"The Flight of the Duchess"—he has improvised a whole civilization in order to make the setting of contrast which shall cause the soul of the little duchess to shine clearly. In "Childe Roland" he creates a cycle, an epoch of romance and mysticism, because he requires it as a stage property. In "A Death in the Desert" you have the East in the first century—so vividly given that you wish instantly to travel there, Bible in hand, to feel the atmosphere with which your Bible ought always to have been filled. His reading brings him to Euripides. He sees that Alcestis can be set to his theme; and with a week or two of labor, while staying in a country house, he draws out of the Greek fable the world of his own meaning and shows it shining forth in a living picture of the Greek theatre which has no counterpart for vitality in any modern tongue.

The descriptive and narrative powers of Browning are above, beyond, and outside of all that has been done in English in our time, as the odd moments prove which he gave to the "Pied Piper," "The Ride from Ghent to Aix," "Incident in the French Camp." These chips from his workshop passed instantly into popular favor because they were written in familiar forms.

How powerfully his gifts of utterance were brought to bear upon the souls of men will be recorded, even if never understood, by literary historians. It is idle to look to the present generation for an intelligible account of "One Word More," "Rabbi Ben Ezra," "Prospice," "Saul," A *Blot in the 'Scutcheon.* They must be judged by the future and by men who can speak of them with a steady lip.

It must be conceded that the conventional judgments of society are sometimes right, and Browning's mission led him occasionally into paradox and *jeux d'esprit.* "Bishop Blougram" is an attempt to discover whether a good case cannot be made out for the individual hypocrite. "The Statue and the Bust" is frankly a *reductio ad absurdum,* and ends with a query.

JOHN J. CHAPMAN

There is more serious trouble with others. "The Grammarian's Funeral" is false to fact, and will appear so to posterity. The grammarian was not a hero, and our calmer moments show us that the poem is not a great ode. It gave certain people the glow of a great truth, but it remains a paradox and a piece of exaggeration. The same must be said of a large part of Browning. The New Testament is full of such paradoxes of exaggeration, like the parable of the unjust steward, the rich man's chance for heaven, the wedding garment; but in these, the truth is apparent,—we are not betrayed. In Browning's paradoxes we are often led on and involved in an emotion over some situation which does not honestly call for the emotion.

The most noble quality in Browning is his temper. He does not proceed, as liberators generally do, by railing and pulling down. He builds up; he is positive, not negative. He is less bitter than Christianity itself.

While there is no more doubt as to the permanent value of the content of Browning than of the value of the spiritual truths of the New Testament, there is very little likelihood that his poems will be understood in the remote future. At present, they are following the waves of influence of the education which they correct. They are built like Palladio's Theatre at Vicenza, where the perspective converges toward a single seat. In order to be subject to the illusion, the spectator must occupy the duke's place. The colors are dropping from the poems already. The feeblest of them lose it first. There was a steady falling off in power accompanied by a constant increase in his peculiarities during the last twenty years of his life, and we may make some surmise as to how *Balaustion's Adventure* will strike posterity by reading *Parleyings with Certain People*.

The distinctions between Browning's characters—which to us are so vivid—will to others seem less so. Paracelsus and Rabbi Ben Ezra, Lippo Lippi, Karshish, Caponsacchi, and Ferishtah will all appear to be run in the same mould. They will seem to be the thinnest disguises which a poet ever assumed. The lack of the dramatic element in Browning— a lack which is concealed from us by our intense sympathy for him and by his fondness for the trappings of the drama —will be apparent to the after-comers. They will say that all the characters in A Blot in the 'Scutcheon take essentially the same view of the catastrophe of the play; that Pippa and Pompilia and Phene are the same person in the same state of mind. In fact, the family likeness is great. They will say that the philosophic monologues are repetitions of each other. It cannot be denied that there is much repetition,—much threshing out of old straw. Those who have read Browning for years and are used to the monologues are better pleased to find the old ideas than new ones, which they could not understand so readily. When the later Browning takes us on one of those long afternoon rambles through his mind,—over moor and fen, through jungle, down precipice, past cataract,—we know just where we are coming out in the end. We know the place better than he did himself. Nor will posterity like Browning's manners,—the dig in the ribs, the personal application, and de te fabula of most of his talking. These unpleasant things are part of his success with us to whom he means life, not art. Posterity will want only art. We needed doctrine. If he had not preached, we would not have listened to him. But posterity evades the preachers and accepts only singers. Posterity is so dainty that it lives on nothing but choice morsels. It will cull such out of the body of Browning as the anthologists are beginning to do already, and will leave the great mass of him to be rediscovered from time to time by belated sufferers from the philosophy of the nineteenth century.

There is a class of persons who claim for Browning that his verse is really good verse, and that he was a master of euphony. This cannot be admitted except as to particular instances in which his success is due to his conformity to law, not to his violation of it.

The rules of verse in English are merely a body of custom which has grown up unconsciously, and most of which rests upon some simple requirement of the ear.

In speaking of the power of poetry we are dealing with what is essentially a mystery, the outcome of infinitely subtle, numerous, and complex forces.

The rhythm of versification seems to serve the purpose of a prompter. It lets us know in advance just what syllables are to receive the emphasis which shall make the sense clear. There are many lines in poetry which become obscure the instant they are written in prose, and probably the advantages of poetry over prose, or, to express it modestly, the excuse for poetry at all, is that the form facilitates the comprehension of the matter. Rhyme is itself an indication that a turning-point has been reached. It punctuates and sets off the sense, and relieves our attention from the strain of suspended interest. All of the artifices of poetical form seem designed to a like end. Naturalness of speech is somewhat sacrificed, but we gain by the sacrifice a certain uniformity of speech which rests and exhilarates. We need not, for the present, examine the question of euphony any further, nor ask whether euphony be not a positive element in verse,—an element which belongs to music.

The negative advantages of poetry over prose are probably sufficient to account for most of its power. A few more considerations of the same negative nature, and which affect the vividness of either prose or verse, may be touched upon by way of preface to the inquiry, why Browning is hard to understand and why his verse is bad.

Every one is more at ease in his mind when he reads a language which observes the ordinary rules of grammar, proceeds by means of sentences having subjects and predicates, and of which the adjectives and adverbs fall easily into place. A doubt about the grammar is a doubt about the sense. And this is so true that sometimes when our fears are allayed by faultless grammar we may read absolute nonsense with satisfaction. We sometimes hear it stated as a bitter epigram, that poetry is likely to endure just in proportion as the form of it is superior to the content. As to the "inferiority" of the content, a moment's reflection shows that the ideas and feelings which prevail from age to age, and in which we may expect posterity to delight, are in their nature, and of necessity, commonplace. And if by "superiority of form" it is meant that these ideas shall be conveyed in flowing metres,—in words which are easy to pronounce, put together according to the rules of grammar, and largely drawn from the vulgar tongue,—we need not wonder that posterity should enjoy it. In fact, it is just such verse as this which survives from age to age.

Browning possesses one superlative excellence, and it is upon this that he relies. It is upon this that he has emerged and attacked the heart of man. It is upon this that he may possibly fight his way down to posterity and live like a fire forever in the bosom of mankind.

His language is the language of common speech; his force, the immediate force of life. His language makes no compromises of any sort. It is not subdued to form. The emphasis demanded by the sense is very often not the emphasis demanded by the metre. He cuts off his words and forces them ruthlessly into lines as a giant might force his limbs into the armor of a mortal. The joints and members of the speech fall in the wrong places and have no relation to the joints and members of the metre.

He writes like a lion devouring an antelope. He rends his subject, breaks its bones, and tears out the heart of it. He is not made more, but less, comprehensible by the verse-forms in which he writes. The sign-posts of the metre lead us astray. He would be easier to understand if his poems were printed in the form of prose. That is the reason why Browning becomes easy when read aloud; for in reading aloud we give the emphasis of speech, and throw over all effort to follow the emphasis of the metre. This is also the reason why Browning is so unquotable—why he has made so little effect upon the language—why so few of the phrases and turns of thought and metaphor with which poets enrich a language have been thrown into English by him. Let a man who does not read poetry take up a volume of Familiar Quotations, and he will find page after page of lines and phrases which he knows by heart—from Tennyson, Milton, Wordsworth—things made familiar to him not by the poets, but by the men whom the poets educated, and who adopted their speech. Of Browning he will know not a word. And yet Browning's poetry is full of words that glow and smite, and which have been burnt into and struck into the most influential minds of the last fifty years.

But Browning's phrases are almost impossible to remember, because they are speech not reduced to poetry. They do not sing, they do not carry. They have no artificial buoys to float them in our memories.

It follows from this uncompromising nature of Browning that when, by the grace of inspiration, the accents of his speech do fall into rhythm, his words will have unimaginable sweetness. The music is so much a part of the words—so truly spontaneous—that other verse seems tame and manufactured beside his.

Rhyme is generally so used by Browning as not to subserve the true function of rhyme. It is forced into a sort of superficial conformity, but marks no epoch in the verse. The clusters of rhymes are clusters only to the eye and not to the ear. The necessity of rhyming leads Browning into inversions,—into expansions of sentences beyond the natural close of the form,—into every sort of contortion. The rhymes clog and distress the sentences.

As to grammar, Browning is negligent. Some of his most eloquent and wonderful passages have no grammar whatever. In *Sordello* grammar does not exist; and the want of it, the strain upon the mind caused by an effort to make coherent sentences out of a fleeting, ever-changing, iridescent maze of talk, wearies and exasperates the reader. Of course no one but a schoolmaster desires that poetry shall be capable of being parsed; but every one has a right to expect that he shall be left without a sense of grammatical deficiency.

The Invocation in *The Ring and the Book* is one of the most beautiful openings that can be imagined.

O lyric love, half angel and half bird,
And all a wonder and a wild desire—
Boldest of hearts that ever braved the sun,
Took sanctuary within the holier blue,
And sang a kindred soul out to his face—
Yet human at the red-ripe of the heart—
When the first summons from the darkling earth
Reached thee amid thy chambers, blanched their blue,
And bared them of the glory—to drop down,
To toil for man, to suffer or to die—
This is the same voice: can thy soul know change?
Hail then, and hearken from the realms of help!
Never may I commence my song, my due
To God who best taught song by gift of thee,
Except with bent head and beseeching hand—
That still, despite the distance and the dark
What was, again may be; some interchange
Of grace, some splendor once thy very thought,
Some benediction anciently thy smile;—
Never conclude, but raising hand and head.
Thither where eyes, that cannot reach, yet yearn
For all hope, all sustainment, all reward,
Their utmost up and on—so blessing back
In those thy realms of help, that heaven thy home,
Some whiteness, which, I judge, thy face makes proud,
Some wanness where, I think, thy foot may fall.

These sublime lines are marred by apparent grammatical obscurity. The face of beauty is marred when one of the eyes seems sightless. We re-read the lines to see if we are mistaken. If they were in a foreign language, we should say we did not *fully* understand them.

In the dramatic monologues, as, for instance, in *The Ring and the Book* and in the innumerable other narratives and contemplations where a single speaker holds forth, we are especially called upon to forget grammar. The speaker relates and reflects,—pours out his ideas in the order in which they occur to him,—pursues two or three trains of thought at the same time, claims every license which either poetry or conversation could accord him. The effect of this method is so startling, that when we are vigorous enough to follow the sense, we forgive all faults of metre and grammar, and feel that this natural Niagara of speech is the only way for the turbulent mind of man to get complete utterance. We forget that it is possible for the same thing to be done, and yet to be subdued, and stilled, and charmed into music.

Prospero is as natural and as individual as Bishop Blougram. His grammar is as incomplete, yet we do not note it. He talks to himself, to Miranda, to Ariel, all at once, weaving all together his passions, his philosophy, his narrative, and his commands. His reflections are as profuse and as metaphysical as anything in Browning, and yet all is clear,—all is so managed that it lends magic. The characteristic and unfathomable significance of this particular character Prospero comes out of it.

> *Prospero.* My brother and thy uncle, called Antonio—
> I pray thee mark me,—that a brother should
> Be so perfidious!—he whom next thyself,
> Of all the world I lov'd, and to him put
> The manage of my state; as at that time
> Through all the seignories it was the first,
> And Prospero, the Prime Duke, being so reputed
> In dignity and for the liberal arts,
> Without a parallel: those being all my study,

The government I cast upon my brother,
And to my state grew stranger, being transported
And wrapped in secret studies. Thy false uncle—
Dost thou attend me?

It is unnecessary to give examples from Browning of defective verse, of passages which cannot be understood, which cannot be construed, which cannot be parodied, and which can scarcely be pronounced. They are mentioned only as throwing light on Browning's cast of mind and methods of work. His inability to recast and correct his work cost the world a master. He seems to have been condemned to create at white heat and to stand before the astonishing draft, which his energy had flung out, powerless to complete it.

We have a few examples of things which came forth perfect, but many of even the most beautiful and most original of the shorter poems are marred by some blotches that hurt us and which one feels might have been struck out or corrected in half an hour. How many of the poems are too long! It is not that Browning went on writing after he had completed his thought,—for the burst of beauty is as likely to come at the end as at the beginning,—but that his thought had to unwind itself like web from a spider. He could not command it. He could only unwind and unwind.

"Pan and Luna" is a sketch, as luminous as a Correggio, but not finished. "Caliban upon Setebos," on the other hand, shows creative genius, beyond all modern reach, but flounders and drags on too long. In the poems which he revised, as, for instance, "Hervé Riel," which exists in two or more forms, the corrections are verbal, and were evidently done with the same fierce haste with which the poems were written.

We must not for an instant imagine that Browning was indolent or indifferent; it is known that he was a taskmaster to himself. But he *could* not write other than he did. When the music came and the verse caught the flame, and his words became sweeter, and his thought clearer, then he could sweep down like an archangel bringing new strains of beauty to the earth. But the occasions when he did this are a handful of passages in a body of writing as large as the Bible. Just as Browning could not stop, so he found it hard to begin. His way of beginning is to seize the end of the thread just where he can, and write down the first sentence.

> She should never have looked at me,
> If she meant I should not love her!
>
> Water your damned flowerpots, do—
>
> No! for I'll save it! Seven years since.
>
> But give them me, the mouth, the eyes, the brow!
>
> Fear Death? to feel the fog in my throat.

Sometimes his verse fell into coils as it came, but he himself, as he wrote the first line of a poem, never knew in what form of verse the poem would come forth. Hence the novel figures and strange counterpoint. Having evolved the first group of lines at haphazard, he will sometimes repeat the form (a very complex form, perhaps, which, in order to have any organic effect, would have to be tuned to the ear most nicely), and repeat it clumsily. Individual taste must be judge of his success in these experiments. Sometimes the ear is worried by an attempt to trace the logic of the rhymes which are concealed by the rough jolting of the metre. Sometimes he makes no attempt to repeat the first verse, but continues in irregular improvisation.

Browning never really stoops to literature; he makes perfunctory obeisance to it. The truth is that Browning is expressed by his defects. He would not be Robert Browning without them. In the technical part of his art, as well as in his spirit, Browning represents a reaction of a violent sort. He was too great an artist not to feel that his violations of form helped him. The blemishes in "The Grammarian's Funeral"—*hoti's business, the enclitic de*—were stimulants; they heightened his effects. They helped him make clear his meaning, that life is greater than art. These savageries spoke to the hearts of men tired of smoothness and platitude, and who were relieved by just such a breaking up of the ice. Men loved Browning not only for what he was, but also for what he was not.

These blemishes were, under the circumstances, and for a limited audience, strokes of art. It is not to be pretended that, even from this point of view, they were always successful, only that they are organic. The nineteenth century would have to be lived over again to wipe these passages out of Browning's poetry.

In that century he stands as one of the great men of England. His doctrines are the mere effulgence of his personality. He himself was the truth which he taught. His life was the life of one of his own heroes; and in the close of his life—by a coincidence which is not sad, but full of meaning—may be seen one of those apparent paradoxes in which he himself delighted.

Through youth and manhood Browning rose like a planet calmly following the laws of his own being. From time to time he put forth his volumes which the world did not understand. Neglect caused him to suffer, but not to change. It was not until his work was all but finished, not till after the publication of *The Ring and the Book,* that complete recognition came to him. It was given him by men and women who had been in the nursery when he began writing, who had passed their youth with his minor poems, and who understood him.

In later life Browning's powers declined. The torrent of feeling could no longer float the raft of doctrine, as it had done so lightly and for so long. His poems, always difficult, grew dry as well.

But Browning was true to himself. He had all his life loved converse with men and women, and still enjoyed it. He wrote constantly and to his uttermost. It was not for him to know that his work was done. He wrote on manfully to the end, showing, occasionally, his old power, and always his old spirit. And on his death-bed it was not only his doctrine, but his life that blazed out in the words:—

One who never turned his back, but marched breast forward,
Never doubted clouds would break,
Never dreamed, though right were worsted, wrong would triumph.
Held, we fall to rise—are baffled to fight better—
Sleep to wake.

GEORGE SANTAYANA

THE POETRY OF BARBARISM

IF WE WOULD do justice to Browning's work as a human document, and at the same time perceive its relation to the rational ideals of the imagination and to that poetry which passes into religion, we must keep, as in the case of Whitman, two things in mind. One is the genuineness of the achievement, the sterling quality of the vision and inspiration; these are their own justification when we approach them from below and regard them as manifesting a more direct or impassioned grasp of experience than is given to mildly blatant, convention-ridden minds. The other thing to remember is the short distance to which this comprehension is carried, its failure to approach any finality, or to achieve a recognition even of the traditional ideals of poetry and religion.

In the case of Walt Whitman such a failure will be generally felt; it is obvious that both his music and his philosophy are those of a barbarian, nay, almost of a savage. Accordingly there is need of dwelling rather on the veracity and simple dignity of his thought and art, on their expression of an order of ideas latent in all better experience. But in the case of Browning it is the success that is obvious to most people. Apart from a certain superficial grotesqueness to which we are soon accustomed, he easily arouses and engages the reader by the pithiness of his phrase, the volume of his passion, the vigour of his moral judgment, the liveliness of his historical fancy. It is obvious that we are in the presence of a great writer, of a great imaginative force, of a master in the expression of emotion. What is perhaps not so obvious, but no less true, is that we are in the presence of a barbaric genius, of a truncated imagination, of a thought and an art inchoate and ill-digested, of a volcanic eruption that tosses itself quite blindly and ineffectually into the sky.

The points of comparsion by which this becomes clear are perhaps not in every one's mind, although they are merely the elements of traditional culture, æsthetic and moral. Yet even without reference to ultimate ideals, one may notice in Browning many superficial signs of that deepest of all failures, the failure in rationality and the indifference to perfection. Such a sign is the turgid style, weighty without nobility, pointed without naturalness or precision. Another sign is the "realism" of the personages, who, quite like men and women in actual life, are always displaying traits of character and never attaining character as a whole. Other hints might be found in the structure of the poems, where the dramatic substance does not achieve a dramatic form; in the metaphysical discussion, with its confused prolixity and absence of result; in the moral ideal, where all energies figure without their ultimate purposes; in the religion, which breaks off the expression of this life in the middle, and finds in that suspense an argument for immortality. In all this, and much more that might be recalled, a person coming to Browning with the habits of a cultivated mind might see evidence of some profound incapacity in the poet; but more careful reflection is necessary to understand the nature of this incapacity, its cause, and the peculiar accent which its presence gives to those ideas and impulses which Browning stimulates in us.

There is the more reason for developing this criticism (which might seem needlessly hostile and which time and posterity will doubtless make in their own quiet and decisive fashion) in that Browning did not keep within the sphere of drama and analysis, where he was strong, but allowed his own temperament and opinions to vitiate his representation of life, so that he sometimes turned the expression of a violent passion into the last word of what he thought a religion. He had a didactic vein, a habit of judging the spectacle he evoked and of loading the passions he depicted with his visible sympathy or scorn.

Now a chief support of Browning's popularity is that he is, for many, an initiator into the deeper mysteries of passion, a means of escaping from the moral poverty of their own lives and of feeling the rhythm and compulsion of the general striving. He figures, therefore, distinctly as a prophet, as a bearer of glad tidings, and it is easy for those who hail him as such to imagine that, knowing the labour of life so well, he must know something also of its fruits, and that in giving us the feeling of existence, he is also giving us its meaning. There is serious danger that a mind gathering from his pages the raw materials of truth, the unthreshed harvest of reality, may take him for a philosopher, for a rationalizer of what he describes. Awakening may be mistaken for enlightenment, and the galvanizing of torpid sensations and impulses for wisdom.

Against such fatuity reason should raise her voice. The vital and historic forces that produce illusions of this sort in large groups of men are indeed beyond the control of criticism. The ideas of passion are more vivid than those of memory, until they become memories in turn. They must be allowed to fight out their desperate battle against the laws of Nature and reason. But it is worthwhile in the meantime, for the sake of the truth and of a just philosophy, to meet the varying though perpetual charlatanism of the world with a steady protest. As soon as Browning is proposed to us as a leader, as soon as we are asked to be not the occasional patrons of his art, but the pupils of his philosophy, we have a right to express the radical dissatisfaction which we must feel, if we are rational, with his whole attitude and temper of mind.

The great dramatists have seldom dealt with perfectly virtuous characters. The great poets have seldom represented mythologies that would bear scientific criticism. But by an instinct which constituted their greatness they have cast these mixed materials furnished by life into forms congenial to the specific principles of their art, and by this transformation they have made acceptable in the æsthetic sphere things that in the sphere of reality were evil or imperfect: in a word, their works have been beautiful as works of art. Or, if their genius exceeded that of the technical poet and rose to prophetic intuition, they have known how to create ideal characters, not possessed, perhaps, of every virtue accidentally needed in this world, but possessed of what is ideally better, of internal greatness and perfection. They have also known how to select and reconstruct their mythology so as to make it a true interpretation of moral life. When we read the maxims of Iago, Falstaff, or Hamlet, we are delighted if the thought strikes us as true, but we are not less delighted if it strikes us as false. These characters are not presented to us in order to enlarge our capacities of passion nor in order to justify themselves as processes of redemption; they are there, clothed in poetry and imbedded in plot, to entertain us with their imaginable feelings and their interesting errors. The poet, without being especially a philosopher, stands by virtue of his superlative genius on the plane of universal reason, far above the passionate experience which he overlooks and on which he reflects; and he raises us for the moment to his own level, to send us back again, if not better endowed for practical life, at least not unacquainted with speculation.

With Browning the case is essentially different. When his heroes are blinded by passion and warped by circumstance, as they almost always are, he does not describe the fact from the vantage-ground of the intellect and invite us to look at it from that point of view. On the contrary, his art is all self-expression or satire. For the most part his hero, like Whitman's, is himself; not appearing, as in the case of the American bard, *in puris naturalibus,* but masked in all sorts of historical and romantic finery. Sometimes, however, the personage, like Guido in *The Ring and the Book* or the "frustrate ghosts" of other poems, is merely a Marsyas, shown flayed and quivering to the greater glory of the poet's ideal Apollo. The impulsive utterances and the crudities of most of the speakers are passionately adopted by the poet as his own. He thus perverts what might have been a triumph of imagination into a failure of reason.

This circumstance has much to do with the fact that Browning, in spite of his extraordinary gift for expressing emotion, has hardly produced works purely and unconditionally delightful. They not only portray passion, which is interesting, but they betray it, which is odious. His art was still in the service of the will. He had not attained, in studying the beauty of things, that detachment of the phenomenon, that love of the form for its own sake, which is the secret of contemplative satisfaction. Therefore, the lamentable accidents of his personality and opinions, in themselves no worse than those of other mortals, passed into his art. He did not seek to elude them: he had no free speculative faculty to dominate them by. Or, to put the same thing differently, he was too much in earnest in his fictions, he threw himself too unreservedly into his creations. His imagination, like the imagination we have in dreams, was merely a vent for personal preoccupations. His art was inspired by purposes less simple and universal than the ends of imagination itself. His play of mind consequently could not be free or pure. The creative impulse could not reach its goal or manifest in any notable degree its own organic ideal.

We may illustrate these assertions by considering Browning's treatment of the passion of love, a passion which he gives great prominence and in which he finds the highest significance.

Love is depicted by Browning with truth, with vehemence, and with the constant conviction that it is the supreme thing in life. The great variety of occasions in which it appears in his pages and the different degrees of elaboration it receives, leave it always of the same quality —the quality of passion. It never sinks into sensuality; in spite of its frequent extreme crudeness, it is always, in Browning's hands, a passion of the imagination; it is always love. On the other hand it never rises into contemplation: mingled as it may be with friendship, with religion, or with various forms of natural tenderness, it always remains a passion; it always remains a personal impulse, a hypnotization, with another person for its object or its cause. Kept within these limits it is represented, in a series of powerful sketches, which are for most readers the gems of the Browning gallery, as the last word of experience, the highest phase of human life.

> The woman yonder, there's no use in life
> But just to obtain her! Heap earth's woes in one
> And bear them—make a pile of all earth's joys

And spurn them, as they help or help not this;
Only, obtain her!

When I do come, she will speak not, she will stand,
Either hand
On my shoulder, give her eyes the first embrace
Of my face,
Ere we rush, ere we extinguish sight and speech
Each on each. . . .
O heart, O blood that freezes, blood that burns!
Earth's returns
For whole centuries of folly, noise, and sin—
Shut them in—
With their triumphs and their follies and the rest.
Love is best.

In the piece called "In a Gondola" the lady says to her lover:—

Heart to heart
And lips to lips! Yet once more, ere we part,
Clasp me and make me thine, as mine thou art.

And he, after being surprised and stabbed in her arms, replies:—

It was ordained to be so, sweet!—and best
Comes now, beneath thine eyes, upon thy breast:
Still kiss me! Care not for the cowards; care
Only to put aside thy beauteous hair
My blood will hurt! The Three I do not scorn
To death, because they never lived, but I
Have lived indeed, and so—(yet one more kiss)—can die.

We are not allowed to regard these expressions as the cries of souls blinded by the agony of passion and lust. Browning unmistakably adopts them as expressing his own highest intuitions. He so much admires the strength of this weakness that he does not admit that it is a weakness at all. It is with the strut of self-satisfaction, with the sensation, almost, of

muscular Christianity, that he boasts of it through the mouth
of one of his heroes, who is explaining to his mistress the
motive of his faithful services as a minister of the queen:—

> She thinks there was more cause
> In love of power, high fame, pure loyalty?
> Perhaps she fancies men wear out their lives
> Chasing such shades. . . .
> I worked because I want you with my soul.

Readers need not be reminded of the contrast which this
method of understanding love offers to that adopted by the
real masters of passion and imagination. They began with
that crude emotion with which Browning ends; they lived
it down, they exalted it by thought, they extracted the pure
gold of it in a long purgation of discipline and suffering.
The fierce paroxysm which for him is heaven, was for them
the proof that heaven cannot be found on earth, that the
value of experience is not in experience itself but in the
ideals which it reveals. The intense, voluminous emotion,
the sudden, overwhelming self-surrender in which he rests
was for them the starting-point of a life of rational worship,
of an austere and impersonal religion, by which the fire of
love, kindled for a moment by the sight of some creature,
was put, as it were, into a censer, to burn incense before
every image of the Highest Good. Thus love ceased to be a
passion and became the energy of contemplation: it diffused
over the universe, natural and ideal, that light of tenderness
and that faculty of worship which the passion of love often
is first to quicken in a man's breast.

Of this art, recommended by Plato and practised in the
Christian Church by all adepts of the spiritual life, Browning
knew absolutely nothing. About the object of love he had
no misgivings. What could the object be except somebody
or other? The important thing was to love intensely and to
love often. He remained in the phenomenal sphere: he was

a lover of experience; the ideal did not exist for him. No conception could be farther from his thought than the essential conception of any rational philosophy, namely, that feeling is to be treated as raw material for thought, and that the destiny of emotion is to pass into objects which shall contain all its value while losing all its formlessness. This transformation of sense and emotion into objects agreeable to the intellect, into clear ideas and beautiful things, is the natural work of reason; when it has been accomplished very imperfectly, or not at all, we have a barbarous mind, a mind full of chaotic sensations, objectless passions, and undigested ideas. Such a mind Browning's was, to a degree remarkable in one with so rich a heritage of civilization.

The nineteenth century, as we have already said, has nourished the hope of abolishing the past as a force while it studies it as an object; and Browning, with his fondness for a historical stage setting and for the gossip of history, rebelled equally against the Pagan and the Christian discipline. The "Soul" which he trusted in was the barbarous soul, the "Spontaneous Me" of his half-brother Whitman. It was a restless personal impulse, conscious of obscure depths within itself which it fancied to be infinite, and of a certain vague sympathy with wind and cloud and with the universal mutation. It was the soul that might have animated Attila and Alaric when they came down into Italy, a soul not incurious of the tawdriness and corruption of the strange civilization it beheld, but incapable of understanding its original spirit; a soul maintaining in the presence of that noble, unappreciated ruin all its own lordliness and energy, and all its native vulgarity.

Browning, who had not had the education traditional in his own country, used to say that Italy had been his university. But it was a school for which he was ill-prepared, and he did not sit under its best teachers. For the superficial ferment, the worldly passions, and the crimes of the Italian

Renaissance he had a keen interest and intelligence. But Italy has been always a civilized country, and beneath the trappings and suits of civilization which at that particular time it flaunted so gayly, it preserved a civilized heart to which Browning's insight could never penetrate. There subsisted in the best minds a trained imagination and a cogent ideal of virtue. Italy had a religion, and that religion permeated all its life, and was the background without which even its secular art and secular passions would not be truly intelligible. The most commanding and representative, the deepest and most appealing of Italian natures are permeated with this religious inspiration. A Saint Francis, a Dante, a Michael Angelo, breathe hardly anything else. Yet for Browning these men and what they represented may be said not to have existed. He saw, he studied, and he painted a decapitated Italy. His vision could not mount so high as her head.

One of the elements of that higher tradition which Browning was not prepared to imbibe was the idealization of love. The passion he represents is lava hot from the crater, in no way moulded, smelted, or refined. He had no thought of subjugating impulses into the harmony of reason. He did not master life, but was mastered by it. Accordingly the love he describes has no wings; it issues in nothing. His lovers "extinguish sight and speech, each on each"; sense, as he says elsewhere, drowning soul. The man in the gondola may well boast that he can die; it is the only thing he can properly do. Death is the only solution of a love that is tied to its individual object and inseparable from the alloy of passion and illusion within itself. Browning's hero, because he has loved intensely, says that he has lived; he would be right, if the significance of life were to be measured by the intensity of the feeling it contained, and if intelligence were not the highest form of vitality. But had that hero known how to love better and had he had enough spirit to dominate

his love, he might perhaps have been able to carry away the
better part of it and to say that he could not die; for one half
of himself and of his love would have been dead already
and the other half would have been eternal, having fed—

> On death, that feeds on men;
> And death once dead, there's no more dying then.

The irrationality of the passions which Browning glorifies,
making them the crown of life, is so gross that at times he
cannot help perceiving it.

> How perplexed
> Grows belief! Well, this cold clay clod
> Was man's heart:
> Crumble it, and what comes next? Is it God?

Yes, he will tell us. These passions and follies, however
desperate in themselves and however vain for the individual,
are excellent as parts of the dispensation of Providence:—

> Be hate that fruit or love that fruit,
> It forwards the general deed of man,
> And each of the many helps to recruit
> The life of the race by a general plan,
> Each living his own to boot.

If we doubt, then, the value of our own experience, even
perhaps of our experience of love, we may appeal to the
interdependence of goods and evils in the world to assure
ourselves that, in view of its consequences elsewhere, this
experience was great and important after all. We need not
stop to consider this supposed solution, which bristles with
contradictions; it would not satisfy Browning himself, if he
did not back it up with something more to his purpose,
something nearer to warm and transitive feeling. The compensation for our defeats, the answer to our doubts, is not

to be found merely in a proof of the essential necessity and
perfection of the universe; that would be cold comfort,
especially to so uncontemplative a mind. No: that answer,
and compensation are to come very soon and very vividly to
every private bosom. There is another life, a series of other
lives, for this to happen in. Death will come, and—

> I shall thereupon
> Take rest, ere I be gone
> Once more on my adventure brave and new,
> Fearless and unperplexed,
> When I wage battle next,
> What weapons to select, what armour to endue.
>
> For sudden the worst turns the best to the brave,
> The black minute's at end,
> And the element's rage, the fiend-voices that rave
> Shall dwindle, shall blend,
> Shall change, shall become first a peace out of pain,
> Then a light, then thy breast,
> O thou soul of my soul! I shall clasp thee again
> And with God be the rest!

Into this conception of continued life Browning has put,
as a collection of further passages might easily show, all the
items furnished by fancy or tradition which at the moment
satisfied his imagination—new adventures, reunion with
friends, and even, after a severe strain and for a short while,
a little peace and quiet. The gist of the matter is that we
are to live indefinitely, that all our faults can be turned to
good, all our unfinished business settled, and that therefore
there is time for anything we like in this world and for all
we need in the other. It is in spirit the direct opposite of the
philosophic maxim of regarding the end, of taking care to
leave a finished life and a perfect character behind us. It
is the opposite, also, of the religious *memento mori,* of the
warning that the time is short before we go to our account.
According to Browning, there is no account: we have an

infinite credit. With an unconscious and characteristic mixture of heathen instinct with Christian doctrine, he thinks of the other world as heaven, but of the life to be led there as of the life of Nature.

Aristotle observes that we do not think the business of life worthy of the gods, to whom we can only attribute contemplation; if Browning had had the idea of perfecting and rationalizing this life rather than of continuing it indefinitely, he would have followed Aristotle and the Church in this matter. But he had no idea of anything eternal; and so he gave, as he would probably have said, a filling to the empty Christian immortality by making every man busy in it about many things. And to the irrational man, to the boy, it is no unpleasant idea to have an infinite number of days to live through, an infinite number of dinners to eat, with an infinity of fresh fights and new love-affairs, and no end of last rides together.

But it is a mere euphemism to call this perpetual vagrancy a development of the soul. A development means the unfolding of a definite nature, the gradual manifestation of a known idea. A series of phases, like the successive leaps of a water-fall, is no development. And Browning has no idea of an intelligible good which the phases of life might approach and with reference to which they might constitute a progress. His notion is simply that the game of life, the exhilaration of action, is inexhaustible. You may set up your tenpins again after you have bowled them over, and you may keep up the sport for ever. The point is to bring them down as often as possible with a master-stroke and a big bang. That will tend to invigorate in you that self-confidence which in this system passes for faith. But it is unmeaning to call such an exercise heaven, or to talk of being "with God" in such a life, in any sense in which we are not with God already and under all circumstances. Our destiny would rather be, as Browning himself expresses it in

GEORGE SANTAYANA

a phrase which Attila or Alaric might have composed, "bound dizzily to the wheel of change to slake the thirst of God."

Such an optimism and such a doctrine of immortality can give no justification to experience which it does not already have in its detached parts. Indeed, those dogmas are not the basis of Browning's attitude, not conditions of his satisfaction in living, but rather overflowings of that satisfaction. The present life is presumably a fair average of the whole series of "adventures brave and new" which fall to each man's share; were it not found delightful in itself, there would be no motive for imagining and asserting that it is reproduced *in infinitum*. So too if we did not think that the evil in experience is actually utilized and visibly swallowed up in its good effects, we should hardly venture to think that God could have regarded as a good something which has evil for its condition and which is for that reason profoundly sad and equivocal. But Browning's philosophy of life and habit of imagination do not require the support of any metaphysical theory. His temperament is perfectly self-sufficient and primary; what doctrines he has are suggested by it and are too loose to give it more than a hesitant expression; they are quite powerless to give it any justification which it might lack on its face.

It is the temperament, then, that speaks; we may brush aside as unsubstantial, and even as distorting, the web of arguments and theories which it has spun out of itself. And what does the temperament say? That life is an adventure, not a discipline; that the exercise of energy is the absolute good, irrespective of motives or of consequences. These are the maxims of a frank barbarism; nothing could express better the lust of life, the dogged unwillingness to learn from experience, the contempt for rationality, the carelessness about perfection, the admiration for mere force, in which barbarism always betrays itself. The vague religion which

[69]

seeks to justify this attitude is really only another outburst of the same irrational impulse.

In Browning this religion takes the name of Christianity, and identifies itself with one or two Christian ideas arbitrarily selected; but at heart it has far more affinity to the worship of Thor or of Odin than to the religion of the Cross. The zest of life becomes a cosmic emotion; we lump the whole together and cry, "Hurrah for the Universe!" A faith which is thus a pure matter of lustiness and inebriation rises and falls, attracts or repels, with the ebb and flow of the mood from which it springs. It is invincible because unseizable; it is as safe from refutation as it is rebellious to embodiment. But it cannot enlighten or correct the passions on which it feeds. Like a servile priest, it flatters them in the name of Heaven. It cloaks irrationality in sanctimony; and its admiration for every bluff folly, being thus justified by a theory, becomes a positive fanaticism, eager to defend any wayward impulse.

Such barbarism of temper and thought could hardly, in a man of Browning's independence and spontaneity, be without its counterpart in his art. When a man's personal religion is passive, as Shakespeare's seems to have been, and is adopted without question or particular interest from the society around him, we may not observe any analogy between it and the free creations of that man's mind. Not so when the religion is created afresh by the private imagination; it is then merely one among many personal works of art, and will naturally bear a family likeness to the others. The same individual temperament, with its limitations and its bias, will appear in the art which has appeared in the religion. And such is the case with Browning. His limitations as a poet are the counterpart of his limitations as a moralist and theologian; only in the poet they are not so regrettable. Philosophy and religion are nothing if not ultimate; it is their business to deal with general principles

and final aims. Now it is in the conception of things fundamental and ultimate that Browning is weak; he is strong
in the conception of things immediate. The pulse of the
emotion, the bobbing up of the thought, the streaming of the
reveries—these he can note down with picturesque force or
imagine with admirable fecundity.
Yet the limits of such excellence are narrow, for no man
can safely go far without the guidance of reason. His long
poems have no structure—for that name cannot be given
to the singular mechanical division of *The Ring and the
Book*. Even his short poems have no completeness, no
limpidity. They are little torsos made broken so as to
stimulate the reader to the restoration of their missing legs
and arms. What is admirable in them is pregnancy of
phrase, vividness of passion and sentiment, heaped-up scraps
of observation, occasional flashes of light, occasional beauties
of versification,—all like

> the quick sharp scratch
> And blue spurt of a lighted match.

There is never anything largely composed in the spirit of
pure beauty, nothing devotedly finished, nothing simple and
truly just. The poet's mind cannot reach equilibrium; at
best he oscillates between opposed extravagances; his final
word is still a *boutade*, still an explosion. He has no sustained
nobility of style. He affects with the reader a confidential
and vulgar manner, so as to be more sincere and to feel more
at home. Even in the poems where the effort at imper-
sonality is most successful, the dramatic disguise is usually
thrown off in a preface, epilogue or parenthesis. The author
likes to remind us of himself by some confidential wink or
genial poke in the ribs, by some little interlarded sneer. We
get in these tricks of manner a taste of that essential vulgarity, that indifference to purity and distinction, which is

latent but pervasive in all the products of this mind. The same disdain of perfection which appears in his ethics appears here in his verse, and impairs its beauty by allowing it to remain too often obscure, affected, and grotesque.

Such a correspondence is natural: for the same powers of conception and expression are needed in fiction, which, if turned to reflection, would produce a good philosophy. Reason is necessary to the perception of high beauty. Discipline is indispensable to art. Work from which these qualities are absent must be barbaric; it can have no ideal form and must appeal to us only through the sensuousness and profusion of its materials. We are invited by it to lapse into a miscellaneous appreciativeness, into a subservience to every detached impression. And yet, if we would only reflect even on these disordered beauties, we should see that the principle by which they delight us is a principle by which an ideal, an image of perfection, is inevitably evoked. We can have no pleasure or pain, nor any preference whatsoever, without implicitly setting up a standard of excellence, an ideal of what would satisfy us there. To make these implicit ideals explicit, to catch their hint, to work out their theme, and express clearly to ourselves and to the world what they are demanding in the place of the actual—that is the labour of reason and the task of genius. The two cannot be divided. Clarification of ideas and disentanglement of values are as essential to æsthetic activity as to intelligence. A failure of reason is a failure of art and taste.

The limits of Browning's art, like the limits of Whitman's, can therefore be understood by considering his mental habit. Both poets had powerful imaginations, but the type of their imaginations was low. In Whitman imagination was limited to marshalling sensations in single file; the embroideries he made around that central line were simple and insignificant. His energy was concentrated on that somewhat animal form of contemplation, of which, for the rest, he was a great, perhaps an unequalled master. Browning rose above that level; with him sensation is usually in the background; he is not particularly a poet of the senses or of ocular vision. His favourite subject-matter is rather the stream of thought and feeling in the mind; he is the poet of soliloquy. Nature and life as they really are, rather than as they may appear to the ignorant and passionate participant in them, lie beyond his range. Even in his best dramas, like *A Blot in the 'Scutcheon* or *Colombe's Birthday*, the interest remains in the experience of the several persons as they explain it to us. The same is the case in *The Ring and the Book*, the conception of which, in twelve monstrous soliloquies, is a striking evidence of the poet's predilection for this form.

The method is, to penetrate by sympathy rather than to portray by intelligence. The most authoritative insight is not the poet's or the spectator's, aroused and enlightened by the spectacle, but the various heroes' own, in their moment of intensest passion. We therefore miss the tragic relief and exaltation, and come away instead with the uncomfortable feeling that an obstinate folly is apparently the most glorious and choiceworthy thing in the world. This is evidently the poet's own illusion, and those who do not happen to share it must feel that if life were really as irrational as he thinks it, it would be not only profoundly discouraging, which it often is, but profoundly disgusting, which it surely is not; for at least it reveals the ideal which it fails to attain.

This ideal Browning never disentangles. For him the crude experience is the only end, the endless struggle the only ideal, and the perturbed "Soul" the only organon of truth. The arrest of his intelligence at this point, before it has envisaged any rational object, explains the arrest of his dramatic art at soliloquy. His immersion in the forms of self-consciousness prevents him from dramatizing the real relations of men and their thinkings to one another, to Nature, and to destiny. For in order to do so he would have had to view his characters from above (as Cervantes did, for instance), and to see them not merely as they appeared to themselves, but as they appear to reason. This higher attitude, however, was not only beyond Browning's scope, it was positively contrary to his inspiration. Had he reached it, he would no longer have seen the universe through the "Soul," but through the intellect, and he would not have been able to cry, "How the world is made for each one of us!" On the contrary, the "Soul" would have figured only in its true conditions, in all its ignorance and dependence, and also in its essential teachableness, a point against which Browning's barbaric wilfulness particularly rebelled. Rooted in his persuasion that the soul is essentially omnipotent and that to live hard can never be to live wrong, he remained fascinated by the march and method of self-consciousness, and never allowed himself to be weaned from that romantic fatuity by the energy of rational imagination, which prompts us not to regard our ideas as mere filling of a dream, but rather to build on them the conception of permanent objects and overruling principles, such as Nature, society, and the other ideals of reason. A full-grown imagination deals with these things, which do not obey the laws of psychological progression, and cannot be described by the methods of soliloquy.

We thus see that Browning's sphere, though more subtle and complex than Whitman's, was still elementary. It lay far below the spheres of social and historical reality in which Shakespeare moved; far below the comprehensive and cosmic sphere of every great epic poet. Browning did not even reach the intellectual plane of such contemporary poets as Tennyson and Matthew Arnold, who, whatever may be thought of their powers, did not study consciousness for itself, but for the sake of its meaning and of the objects which it revealed. The best things that come into a man's consciousness are the things that take him out of it—the rational things that are independent of his personal perception and of his personal existence. These he approaches with his reason, and they, in the same measure, endow him with their immortality. But precisely these things—the objects of science and of the constructive imagination—Browning always saw askance, in the outskirts of his field of vision, for his eye was fixed and riveted on the soliloquizing Soul. And this Soul being, to his apprehension, irrational, did not give itself over to those permanent objects which might otherwise have occupied it, but ruminated on its own accidental emotions, on its love-affairs, and on its hopes of going on so ruminating for ever.

The pathology of the human mind—for the normal, too, is pathological when it is not referred to the ideal—the pathology of the human mind is a very interesting subject, demanding great gifts and great ingenuity in its treatment. Browning ministers to this interest, and possesses this ingenuity and these gifts. More than any other poet he keeps a kind of speculation alive in the now large body of sentimental, eager-minded people, who no longer can find in a definite religion a form and language for their imaginative life. That this service is greatly appreciated speaks well for the ineradicable tendency in man to study himself and his destiny. We do not deny the achievement when we point out its nature and limitations. It does not cease to be something because it is taken to be more than it is.

In every imaginative sphere the nineteenth century has been an era of chaos, as it has been an era of order and growing organization in the spheres of science and of industry. An ancient doctrine of the philosophers asserts that to chaos the world must ultimately return. And what is perhaps true of the cycles of cosmic change is certainly true of the revolutions of culture. Nothing lasts for ever: languages, arts, and religions disintegrate with time. Yet the perfecting of such forms is the only criterion of progress; the destruction of them the chief evidence of decay. Perhaps

fate intends that we should have, in our imaginative deca-
dence, the consolation of fancying that we are still pro-
gressing, and that the disintegration of religion and the arts
is bringing us nearer to the protoplasm of sensation and
passion. If energy and actuality are all that we care for,
chaos is as good as order, and barbarism as good as discipline
—better, perhaps, since impulse is not then restrained within
any bounds of reason or beauty. But if the powers of the
human mind are at any time adequate to the task of digesting
experience, clearness and order inevitably supervene. The
moulds of thought are imposed upon Nature, and the conviction of a definite truth arises together with the vision of a
supreme perfection. It is only at such periods that the
human animal vindicates his title of rational. If such an
epoch should return, people will no doubt retrace our
present gropings with interest and see in them gradual
approaches to their own achievement. Whitman and Browning might well figure then as representatives of our time.
For the merit of being representative cannot be denied them.
The mind of our age, like theirs, is choked with materials,
emotional, and inconclusive. They merely aggravate our
characteristics, and their success with us is due partly to
their own absolute strength and partly to our common weakness. If once, however, this imaginative weakness could be
overcome, and a form found for the crude matter of experience, men might look back from the height of a new religion
and a new poetry upon the present troubles of the spirit; and
perhaps even these things might then be pleasant to remember.

GILBERT K. CHESTERTON

BROWNING AS A LITERARY ARTIST

M R. WILLIAM SHARP, in his *Life* of Browning, quotes the remarks of another critic to the following effect: "The poet's processes of thought are scientific in their precision and analysis; the sudden conclusion that he imposes upon them is transcendental and inept."

This is a very fair but a very curious example of the way in which Browning is treated. For what is the state of affairs? A man publishes a series of poems, vigorous, perplexing, and unique. The critics read them, and they decide that he has failed as a poet, but that he is a remarkable philosopher and logician. They then proceed to examine his philosophy, and show with great triumph that it is unphilosophical, and to examine his logic and show with great triumph that it is not logical, but "transcendental and inept." In other words, Browning is first denounced for being a logician and not a poet, and then denounced for insisting on being a poet when they have decided that he is to be a logician. It is just as if a man were to say first that a garden was so neglected that it was only fit for a boys' playground, and then complain of the unsuitability in a boys' playground of rockeries and flowerbeds.

As we find, after this manner, that Browning does not act satisfactorily as that which we have decided that he shall be —a logician—it might possibly be worth while to make another attempt to see whether he may not, after all, be more valid than we thought as to what he himself professed to be —a poet. And if we study this seriously and sympathetically, we shall soon come to a conclusion. It is a gross and complete slander upon Browning to say that his processes of thought are scientific in their precision and analysis. They are nothing of the sort; if they were, Browning could not be a good poet. The critic speaks of the conclusions of a poem as "transcendental and inept"; but the conclusions of a poem, if they are not transcendental, must be inept. Do the people who call one of Browning's poems scientific in its analysis realise the meaning of what they say? One is tempted to think that they know a scientific analysis when they see it as little as they know a good poem. The one supreme difference between the scientific method and the artistic method is, roughly speaking, simply this—that a scientific statement means the same thing wherever and whenever it is uttered, and that an artistic statement means something entirely different, according to the relation in which it stands to its surroundings. The remark, let us say, that the whale is a mammal, or the remark that sixteen ounces go to a pound, is equally true, and means exactly the same thing, whether we state it at the beginning of a conversation or at the end, whether we print it in a dictionary or chalk it up on a wall. But if we take some phrase commonly used in the art of literature—such a sentence, for the sake of example, as "the dawn was breaking"—the matter is quite different.

If the sentence came at the beginning of a short story, it might be a mere descriptive prelude. If it were the last sentence in a short story, it might be poignant with some peculiar irony or triumph. Can any one read Browning's great monologues and not feel that they are built up like a good short story entirely on this principle of the value of language arising from its arrangement? Take such an example as "Caliban upon Setebos," a wonderful poem designed to describe the way in which a primitive nature may at once be afraid of its gods and yet familiar with them. Caliban in describing his deity starts with a more or less natural and obvious parallel between the deity and himself, carries out the comparison with consistency and an almost revolting simplicity, and ends in a kind of blasphemous extravaganza of anthropomorphism, basing his conduct not merely on the greatness and wisdom, but also on the manifest weaknesses and stupidities, of the Creator of all things. Then suddenly a thunderstorm breaks over Caliban's island, and the profane speculator falls flat upon his face—

> Lo! 'Lieth flat and loveth Setebos!
> 'Maketh his teeth meet through his upper lip,
> Will let those quails fly, will not eat this month
> One little mess of whelks, so he may 'scape!

Surely it would be very difficult to persuade oneself that this thunderstorm would have meant exactly the same thing if it had occurred at the beginning of "Caliban upon Setebos." It does not mean the same thing, but something very different; and the deduction from this is the curious fact that Browning is an artist, and that consequently his processes of thought are not "scientific in their precision and analysis."

No criticism of Browning's poems can be vital, none in the face of the poems themselves can be even intelligible, which is not based upon the fact that he was successfully or otherwise a conscious and deliberate artist. He may have failed as an artist, though I do not think so; that is quite a different matter. But it is one thing to say that a man through vanity or ignorance has built an ugly cathedral, and quite another to say that he built it in a fit of absence of mind, and did not know whether he was building a lighthouse or a first-class hotel. Browning knew perfectly well what he was doing; and if the reader does not like his art, at least the author did. The general sentiment expressed in the statement that he did not care about form is simply the most ridiculous criticism that could be conceived. It would be far nearer the truth to say that he cared more for form than any other English poet who ever lived. He was always weaving and modelling and inventing new forms. Among all his two hundred to three hundred poems it would scarcely be an exaggeration to say that there are half as many different metres as there are different poems.

The great English poets who are supposed to have cared more for form than Browning did cared less at least in this sense—that they were content to use old forms so long as they were certain that they had new ideas. Browning, on the other hand, no sooner had a new idea than he tried to make a new form to express it. Wordsworth and Shelley were really original poets; their attitude of thought and feeling marked without doubt certain great changes in literature and philosophy. Nevertheless, the "Ode on the Intimations of Immortality" is a perfectly normal and traditional ode, and *Prometheus Unbound* is a perfectly genuine and traditional Greek lyrical drama. But if we study Browning honestly, nothing will strike us more than that he really created a large number of quite novel and quite admirable artistic forms. It is too often forgotten what and how excellent these were. *The Ring and the Book*, for example, is an illuminating departure in literary method—the method of telling the same story several times and trusting to the variety of human character to turn it into several different and equally interesting stories. *Pippa Passes,* to take another example, is a new and most fruitful form, a series of detached dramas connected only by the presence of one fugitive and isolated figure. The invention of these things is not merely like the writing of a good poem—it is something like the invention of the sonnet or the Gothic arch. The poet who makes them does not merely create himself—he creates other poets. It is so in a degree long past enumeration with regard to Browning's smaller poems. Such a pious and horrible lyric as "The Heretic's Tragedy," for instance, is absolutely original, with its weird and almost blood-curdling echo verses, mocking echoes indeed—

> And clipt of his wings in Paris square,
> They bring him now to be burned alive.
>
> [*And wanteth there grace of lute or clavicithern,*
>   *ye shall say to confirm him who singeth—*
>
> We bring John now to be burned alive.

A hundred instances might, of course, be given. Milton's "Sonnet on his Blindness," or Keats's "Ode on a Grecian Urn," are both thoroughly original, but still we can point to other such sonnets and other such odes. But can any one mention any poem of exactly the same structural and literary type as "Fears and Scruples," as "The Householder," as "House" or "Shop," as "Nationality in Drinks," as "Sibrandus Schafnaburgensis," as "My Star," as "A Portrait," as any of "Ferishtah's Fancies," as any of the "Bad Dreams"?

The thing which ought to be said about Browning by those who do not enjoy him is simply that they do not like his form; that they have studied the form, and think it a bad form. If more people said things of this sort, the world of criticism would gain almost unspeakably in clarity and common honesty. Browning put himself before the world as a good poet. Let those who think he failed call him a bad poet, and there will be an end of the matter. There are many styles in art which perfectly competent æsthetic judges cannot endure. For instance, it would be perfectly legitimate for a strict lover of Gothic to say that one of the monstrous rococo altar-pieces in the Belgian churches with bulbous clouds and oaken sun-rays seven feet long, was, in his opinion, ugly. But surely it would be perfectly ridiculous for any one to say that it had no form. A man's actual feelings about it might be better expressed by saying that it had too much. To say that Browning was merely a thinker because you think "Caliban upon Setebos" ugly, is precisely as absurd as it would be to call the author of the old Belgian altar-piece a man devoted only to the abstractions of religion. The truth about Browning is not that he was indifferent to technical beauty, but that he invented a particular kind of technical beauty to which any one else is free to be as indifferent as he chooses.

There is in this matter an extraordinary tendency to vague and unmeaning criticism. The usual way of criticising an author, particularly an author who has added something to the literary forms of the world, is to complain that his work does not contain something which is obviously the speciality of somebody else. The correct thing to say about Maeterlinck is that some play of his in which, let us say, a princess dies in a deserted tower by the sea, has a certain beauty, but that we look in vain in it for that robust geniality, that really boisterous will to live which may be found in *Martin Chuzzlewit*. The right thing to say about *Cyrano de Bergerac* is that it may have a certain kind of wit and spirit, but that it really throws no light on the duty of middle-aged married couples in Norway. It cannot be too much insisted upon that at least three-quarters of the blame and criticism commonly directed against artists and authors falls under this general objection, and is essentially valueless. Authors both great and small are, like everything else in existence, upon the whole greatly underrated. They are blamed for not doing, not only what they have failed to do to reach their own ideal, but what they have never tried to do to reach every other writer's ideal. If we can show that Browning had a definite ideal of beauty and loyally pursued it, it is not necessary to prove that he could have written *In Memoriam* if he had tried.

Browning has suffered far more injustice from his admirers than from his opponents, for his admirers have for the most part got hold of the matter, so to speak, by the wrong end. They believe that what is ordinarily called the grotesque style of Browning was a kind of necessity boldly adopted by a great genius in order to express novel and profound ideas. But this is an entire mistake. What is called ugliness was to Browning not in the least a necessary evil, but a quite unnecessary luxury, which he enjoyed for its own sake. For reasons that we shall see presently in discussing the philosophical use of the grotesque, it did so happen that Browning's grotesque style was very suitable for the expression of his peculiar moral and metaphysical view. But the whole mass of poems will be misunderstood if we do not realise first of all that he had a love of the grotesque of the nature of art for art's sake. Here, for example, is a short distinct poem merely descriptive of one of those elfish German jugs in which it is to be presumed Tokay had been served to him. This is the whole poem, and a very good poem too—

Up jumped Tokay on our table,
Like a pigmy castle-warder,
Dwarfish to see, but stout and able,
Arms and accoutrements all in order;
And fierce he looked North, then, wheeling South
Blew with his bugle a challenge to Drouth,
Cocked his flap-hat with the tosspot-feather,
Twisted his thumb in his red moustache,
Jingled his huge brass spurs together,

Tightened his waist with its Buda sash,
And then, with an impudence nought could abash,
Shrugged his hump-shoulder, to tell the beholder,
For twenty such knaves he would laugh but the bolder:
And so, with his sword-hilt gallantly jutting,
And dexter-hand on his haunch abutting,
Went the little man, Sir Ausbruch, strutting!

I suppose there are Browning students in existence who would think that this poem contained something pregnant about the Temperance question, or was a marvellously subtle analysis of the romantic movement in Germany. But surely to most of us it is sufficiently apparent that Browning was simply fashioning a ridiculous knick-knack, exactly as if he were actually moulding one of these preposterous German jugs. Now before studying the real character of this Browningesque style, there is one general truth to be recognised about Browning's work. It is this—that it is absolutely necessary to remember that Browning had, like every other poet, his simple and indisputable failures, and that it is one thing to speak of the badness of his artistic failures, and quite another thing to speak of the badness of his artistic aim. Browning's style may be a good style, and yet exhibit many examples of a thoroughly bad use of it. On this point there is indeed a singularly unfair system of judgment used by the public towards the poets. It is very little realised that the vast majority of great poets have written an enormous amount of very bad poetry. The unfortunate Wordsworth is generally supposed to be almost alone in this; but any one who thinks so can scarcely have read a certain number of the minor poems of Byron and Shelley and Tennyson.

Now it is only just to Browning that his more uncouth effusions should not be treated as masterpieces by which he must stand or fall, but treated simply as his failures. It is really true that such a line as

Irks care the crop-full bird, frets doubt the maw-crammed beast?

is a very ugly and a very bad line. But it is quite equally true that Tennyson's

And that good man, the clergyman, has told me words of peace,

is a very ugly and a very bad line. But people do not say that this proves that Tennyson was a mere crabbed controversialist and metaphysician. They say that it is a bad example of Tennyson's form; they do not say that it is a good example of Tennyson's indifference to form. Upon the whole, Browning exhibits far fewer instances of this failure in his own style than any other of the great poets, with the exception of one or two like Spenser and Keats, who seem to have a mysterious incapacity for writing bad poetry. But almost all original poets, particularly poets who have invented an artistic style, are subject to one most disastrous habit—the habit of writing imitations of themselves. Every now and then in the works of the noblest classical poets you will come upon passages which read like extracts from an American book of parodies. Swinburne, for example, when he wrote the couplet—

From the lilies and languors of virtue
To the raptures and roses of vice,

wrote what is nothing but a bad imitation of himself, an imitation which seems indeed to have the wholly unjust and uncritical object of proving that the Swinburnian melody is a mechanical scheme of initial letters. Or again, Mr. Rudyard Kipling when he wrote the line—

Or ride with the reckless seraphim on the rim of a redmaned star,

was caricaturing himself in the harshest and least sympathetic spirit of American humour. This tendency is, of course, the result of the self-consciousness and theatricality of modern life in which each of us is forced to conceive ourselves as part of a *dramatis personæ* and act perpetually in character. Browning sometimes yielded to this temptation to be a great deal too like himself.

> Will I widen thee out till thou turnest
> From Margaret Minnikin mou' by God's grace,
> To Muckle-mouth Meg in good earnest.

This sort of thing is not to be defended in Browning any more than in Swinburne. But, on the other hand, it is not to be attributed in Swinburne to a momentary exaggeration, and in Browning to a vital æsthetic deficiency. In the case of Swinburne, we all feel that the question is not whether that particular preposterous couplet about lilies and roses redounds to the credit of the Swinburnian style, but whether it would be possible in any other style than the Swinburnian to have written the "Hymn to Proserpine." In the same way, the essential issue about Browning as an artist is not whether he, in common with Byron, Wordsworth, Shelley, Tennyson, and Swinburne, sometimes wrote bad poetry, but whether in any other style except Browning's you could have achieved the precise artistic effect which is achieved by such incomparable lyrics as "The Patriot" or "The Laboratory." The answer must be in the negative, and in that answer lies the whole justification of Browning as an artist.

The question now arises, therefore, what was his conception of his functions as an artist? We have already agreed that his artistic originality concerned itself chiefly with the serious use of the grotesque. It becomes necessary, therefore, to ask what is the serious use of the grotesque, and what relation does the grotesque bear to the eternal and fundamental elements in life?

One of the most curious things to notice about popular æsthetic criticism is the number of phrases it will be found to use which are intended to express an æsthetic failure, and which express merely an æsthetic variety. Thus, for instance, the traveller will often hear the advice from local lovers of the picturesque, "The scenery round such and such a place has no interest; it is quite flat." To disparage scenery as quite flat is, of course, like disparaging a swan as quite white, or an Italian sky as quite blue. Flatness is a sublime quality in certain landscapes, just as rockiness is a sublime quality in others. In the same way there are a great number of phrases commonly used in order to disparage such writers as Browning which do not in fact disparage, but merely describe them. One of the most distinguished of Browning's biographers and critics says of him, for example, "He has never meant to be rugged, but has become so in striving after strength." To say that Browning never tried to be rugged is to say that Edgar Allan Poe never tried to be gloomy, or that Mr. W. S. Gilbert never tried to be extravagant. The whole issue depends upon whether we realise the simple and essential fact that ruggedness is a mode of art like gloominess or extravagance. Some poems ought to be rugged, just as some poems ought to be smooth. When we see a drift of stormy and fantastic clouds at sunset, we do not say that the cloud is beautiful although it is ragged at the edges. When we see a gnarled and sprawling oak, we do not say that it is fine although it is twisted. When we see a mountain, we do not say that it is impressive although it is rugged, nor do we say apologetically that it never meant to be rugged, but became so in its striving after strength. Now, to say that Browning's poems, artistically considered, are fine although they are rugged, is quite as absurd as to say that a rock, artistically considered, is fine although it is rugged. Ruggedness being an essential quality in the universe, there is that in man which responds to it as to the striking of any other chord of the eternal harmonies. As the children of nature, we are akin not only to the stars and flowers, but also to the toadstools and the monstrous tropical birds. And it is to be repeated as the essential of the question that on this side of our nature we do emphatically love the form of the toadstools, and not merely some complicated botanical and moral lessons which the philosopher may draw from them. For example, just as there is such a thing as a poetical metre being beautifully light or beautifully grave and haunting, so there is such a thing as a poetical metre being beautifully rugged. In the old ballads, for instance, every person of literary taste will be struck by a certain attractiveness in the bold, varying, irregular verse—

> He is either himsell a devil frae hell,
> Or else his mother a witch maun be;
> I wadna have ridden that wan water
> For a' the gowd in Christentie,

is quite as pleasing to the ear in its own way as

> There's a bower of roses by Bendemeer stream,
> And the nightingale sings in it all the night long,

is in another way. Browning had an unrivalled ear for this particular kind of staccato music. The absurd notion that he had no sense of melody in verse is only possible to people who think that there is no melody in verse which is not an imitation of Swinburne. To give a satisfactory idea of Browning's rhythmic originality would be impossible without quotations more copious than entertaining. But the essential point has been suggested.

> They were purple of raiment and golden,
> Filled full of thee, fiery with wine,
> Thy lovers in haunts unbeholden,
> In marvellous chambers of thine,

is beautiful language, but not the only sort of beautiful language. This, for instance, has also a tune in it—

GILBERT K. CHESTERTON

I—"Next Poet?" No, my hearties,
I nor am, nor fain would be!
Choose your chiefs and pick your parties,
Not one soul revolt to me!

.   .   .   .   .

Which of you did I enable
Once to slip inside my breast,
There to catalogue and label
What I like least, what love best,
Hope and fear, believe and doubt of,
Seek and shun, respect, deride,
Who has right to make a rout of
Rarities he found inside?

This quick, gallantly stepping measure also has its own kind of music, and the man who cannot feel it can never have enjoyed the sound of soldiers marching by. This, then, roughly is the main fact to remember about Browning's poetical method, or about any one's poetical method—that the question is not whether that method is the best in the world, but the question whether there are not certain things which can only be conveyed by that method. It is perfectly true, for instance, that a really lofty and lucid line of Tennyson, such as—

Thou art the highest, and most human too

and

We needs must love the highest when we see it

would really be made the worse for being translated into Browning. It would probably become

High's human; man loves best, best visible,

and would lose its peculiar clarity and dignity and courtly plainness. But it is quite equally true that any really char-

[89]

acteristic fragment of Browning, if it were only the tempestuous scolding of the organist in "Master Hugues of Saxe-Gotha"—

> Hallo, you sacristan, show us a light there!
> Down it dips, gone like a rocket.
> What, you want, do you, to come unawares,
> Sweeping the church up for first morning-prayers,
> And find a poor devil has ended his cares
> At the foot of your rotten-runged rat-riddled stairs?
> Do I carry the moon in my pocket?

—it is quite equally true that this outrageous gallop of rhymes ending with a frantic astronomical image would lose in energy and spirit if it were written in a conventional and classical style, and ran—

> What must I deem then that thou dreamest to find
> Disjected bones adrift upon the stair
> Thou sweepest clean, or that thou deemest that I
> Pouch in my wallet the vice-regal sun?

Is it not obvious that this statelier version might be excellent poetry of its kind, and yet would be bad exactly in so far as it was good; that it would lose all the swing, the rush, the energy of the preposterous and grotesque original? In fact, we may see how unmanageable is this classical treatment of the essentially absurd in Tennyson himself. The humorous passages in *The Princess,* though often really humorous in themselves, always appear forced and feeble because they have to be restrained by a certain metrical dignity, and the mere idea of such restraint is incompatible with humour. If Browning had written the passage which opens *The Princess,* descriptive of the "larking" of the villagers in the magnate's park, he would have spared us nothing; he would not have spared us the shrill uneducated voices and the unburied bottles of ginger beer. He would have crammed the poem with uncouth similes; he would have changed the metre a hundred times; he would have broken into doggerel and into rhapsody; but he would have left, when all is said and done, as he leaves in the paltry fragment of the grumbling organist, the impression of a certain eternal human energy. Energy and joy, the father and the mother of the grotesque, would have ruled the poem. We should have felt of that rowdy gathering little but the sensation of which Mr. Henley writes—

> Praise the generous gods for giving,
> In this world of sin and strife,
> With some little time for living,
> Unto each the joy of life,

the thought that every wise man has when looking at a Bank Holiday crowd at Margate.

To ask why Browning enjoyed this perverse and fantastic style most would be to go very deep into his spirit indeed, probably a great deal deeper than it is possible to go. But it is worth while to suggest tentatively the general function of the grotesque in art generally and in his art in particular. There is one very curious idea into which we have been hypnotized by the more eloquent poets, and that is that nature in the sense of what is ordinarily called the country is a thing entirely stately and beautiful as those terms are commonly understood. The whole world of the fantastic, all things top-heavy, lop-sided, and nonsensical are conceived as the work of man, gargoyles, German jugs, Chinese pots, political caricatures, burlesque epics, the pictures of Mr. Aubrey Beardsley and the puns of Robert Browning. But in truth a part, and a very large part, of the sanity and power of nature lies in the fact that out of her comes all this instinct of caricature. Nature may present itself to the poet too often as consisting of stars and lilies; but these are not poets who live in the country; they are men who go to the country for inspiration and could no more live in the country than they could go to bed in Westminster Abbey. Men who live in the heart of nature, farmers and peasants, know that nature means cows and pigs, and creatures more humorous than can be found in a whole sketch-book of Callot. And the element of the grotesque in art, like the element of the grotesque in nature, means, in the main, energy, the energy which takes it own forms and goes its own way. Browning's verse, in so far as it is grotesque, is not complex or artificial; it is natural and in the legitimate tradition of nature. The verse sprawls like the trees, dances like the dust; it is ragged like the thunder-cloud, it is top-heavy like the toadstool. Energy which disregards the standard of classical art is in nature as it is in Browning. The same sense of the uproarious force in things which makes Browning dwell on the oddity of a fungus or a jellyfish makes him dwell on the oddity of a philosophical idea. Here, for example, we have a random instance from "The Englishman in Italy" of the way in which Browning, when he was most Browning, regarded physical nature.

> And pitch down his basket before us,
>   All trembling alive
> With pink and grey jellies, your sea-fruit;
>   You touch the strange lumps,
> And mouths gape there, eyes open, all manner
>   Of horns and of humps,
> Which only the fisher looks grave at.

Nature might mean flowers to Wordsworth and grass to Walt Whitman, but to Browning it really meant such things as these, the monstrosities and living mysteries of the sea. And just as these strange things meant to Browning energy in the physical world, so strange thoughts and strange images meant to him energy in the mental world. When, in one of his later poems, the professional mystic is seeking in a supreme moment of sincerity to explain that small things may be filled with God as well as great, he uses the very same kind of image, the image of a shapeless sea-beast, to embody that noble conception.

The Name comes close behind a stomach-cyst,
The simplest of creations, just a sac
That's mouth, heart, legs, and belly at once, yet lives
And feels, and could do neither, we conclude,
If simplified still further one degree.

These bulbous, indescribable sea-goblins are the first thing on which the eye of the poet lights in looking on a landscape, and the last in the significance of which he trusts in demonstrating the mercy of the Everlasting.

There is another and but slightly different use of the grotesque, but which is definitely valuable in Browning's poetry, and indeed in all poetry. To present a matter in a grotesque manner does certainly tend to touch the nerve of surprise and thus to draw attention to the intrinsically miraculous character of the object itself. It is difficult to give examples of the proper use of grotesqueness without becoming too grotesque. But we should all agree that if St. Paul's Cathedral were suddenly presented to us upside down we should, for the moment, be more surprised at it, and look at it more than we have done all the centuries during which it has rested on its foundations. Now it is the supreme function of the philosopher of the grotesque to make the world stand on its head that people may look at it. If we say "a man is a man", we awaken no sense of the fantastic, however much we ought to, but if we say, in the language of the old satirist, "that man is a two-legged bird, without feathers," the phrase does, for a moment, make us look at man from the outside and gives us a thrill in his presence. When the author of the Book of Job insists upon the huge, half-witted, apparently unmeaning magnificence and might of Behemoth, the hippopotamus, he is appealing precisely to this sense of wonder provoked by the grotesque. "Canst thou play with him as with a bird, canst thou bind him for thy maidens?" he says in an admirable passage. The notion of the hippopotamus as a household pet is curiously in the spirit of the humour of Browning.

But when it is clearly understood that Browning's love of the fantastic in style was a perfectly serious artistic love, when we understand that he enjoyed working in that style, as a Chinese potter might enjoy making dragons, or a mediæval mason making devils, there yet remains something definite which must be laid to his account as a fault. He certainly had a capacity for becoming perfectly childish in his indulgence in ingenuities that have nothing to do with poetry at all, such as puns, and rhymes, and grammatical structures that only just fit into each other like a Chinese puzzle. Probably it was only one of the marks of his singular vitality, curiosity, and interest in details. He was certainly one of those somewhat rare men who are fierily ambitious both in large things and in small. He prided himself on having written *The Ring and the Book,* and he also prided himself on knowing good wine when he tasted it. He prided himself on re-establishing optimism on a new foundation, and it is to be presumed, though it is somewhat difficult to imagine, that he prided himself on such rhymes as the following in *Pacchiarotto*:—

> The wolf, fox, bear, and monkey,
> By piping advice in one key—
> That his pipe should play a prelude
> To something heaven-tinged not hell-hued,
> Something not harsh but docile,
> Man-liquid, not man-fossil.

This writing, considered as writing, can only be regarded as a kind of joke, and most probably Browning considered it so himself. It has nothing at all to do with that powerful and symbolic use of the grotesque which may be found in such admirable passages as this from "Holy Cross Day":—

> Give your first groan—compunction's at work;
> And soft! from a Jew you mount to a Turk.
> Lo, Micah—the self-same beard on chin
> He was four times already converted in!

This is the serious use of the grotesque. Through it passion and philosophy are as well expressed as through any other medium. But the rhyming frenzy of Browning has no particular relation even to the poems in which it occurs. It is not a dance to any measure; it can only be called the horseplay of literature. It may be noted, for example, as a rather curious fact, that the ingenious rhymes are generally only mathematical triumphs, not triumphs of any kind of assonance. "The Pied Piper of Hamelin," a poem written for children, and bound in general to be lucid and readable, ends with a rhyme which it is physically impossible for any one to say:—

> And, whether they pipe us free, fróm rats or from mice,
> If we've promised them aught, let us keep our promise!

This queer trait in Browning, his inability to keep a kind of demented ingenuity even out of poems in which it was quite inappropriate, is a thing which must be recognized, and recognized all the more because as a whole he was a very perfect artist, and a particularly perfect artist in the use of the grotesque. But everywhere when we go a little below the surface in Browning we find that there was something in him perverse and unusual despite all his working normality and simplicity. His mind was perfectly wholesome, but it was not made exactly like the ordinary mind. It was like a piece of strong wood with a knot in it.

The quality of what can only be called buffoonery which is under discussion is indeed one of the many things in which Browning was more of an Elizabethan than a Victorian. He was like the Elizabethans in their belief in the normal man, in their gorgeous and overloaded language, above all in their feeling for learning as an enjoyment and almost a frivolity. But there was nothing in which he was so thoroughly Elizabethan, and even Shakespearian, as in this fact, that when he felt inclined to write a page of quite uninteresting nonsense, he immediately did so. Many great writers have contrived to be tedious, and apparently aimless, while expounding some thought which they believed to be grave and profitable; but this frivolous stupidity had not been found in any great writer since the time of Rabelais and the time of the Elizabethans. In many of the comic scenes of Shakespeare we have precisely this elephantine ingenuity, this hunting of a pun to death through three pages. In the Elizabethan dramatists and in Browning it is no doubt to a certain extent the mark of a real hilarity. People must be very happy to be so easily amused.

In the case of what is called Browning's obscurity, the question is somewhat more difficult to handle. Many people have supposed Browning to be profound because he was obscure, and many other people, hardly less mistaken, have supposed him to be obscure because he was profound. He was frequently profound, he was occasionally obscure, but as a matter of fact the two have little or nothing to do with each other. Browning's dark and elliptical mode of speech, like his love of the grotesque, was simply a characteristic of his, a trick of his temperament, and had little or nothing to do with whether what he was expressing was profound or superficial. Suppose, for example, that a person well read in English poetry but unacquainted with Browning's style were earnestly invited to consider the following verse:—

Hobbs hints blue—straight he turtle eats.
Nobbs prints blue—claret crowns his cup.
Nokes outdares Stokes in azure feats—
  Both gorge. Who fished the murex up?
What porridge had John Keats?

The individual so confronted would say without hesitation
that it must indeed be an abstruse and indescribable thought
which could only be conveyed by remarks so completely
disconnected. But the point of the matter is that the thought
contained in this amazing verse is not abstruse or philosophical at all, but is a perfectly ordinary and straightforward comment, which any one might have made upon an
obvious fact of life. The whole verse of course begins to
explain itself, if we know the meaning of the word "murex,"
which is the name of a sea-shell, out of which was made the
celebrated blue dye of Tyre. The poet takes this blue dye
as a simile for a new fashion in literature, and points out that
Hobbs, Nobbs, etc., obtain fame and comfort by merely
using the dye from the shell; and adds the perfectly natural
comment:—

        . . . Who fished the murex up?
    What porridge had John Keats?

So that the verse is not subtle, and was not meant to be
subtle, but is a perfectly casual piece of sentiment at the end
of a light poem. Browning is not obscure because he has
such deep things to say, any more than he is grotesque
because he has such new things to say. He is both of these
things primarily, because he likes to express himself in a
particular manner. The manner is as natural to him as a
man's physical voice, and it is abrupt, sketchy, allusive, and
full of gaps. Here comes in the fundamental difference
between Browning and such a writer as George Meredith,
with whom the Philistine satirist would so often in the

matter of complexity class him. The works of George Meredith are, as it were, obscure even when we know what they mean. They deal with nameless emotions, fugitive sensations, subconscious certainties and uncertainties, and it really requires a somewhat curious and unfamiliar mode of speech to indicate the presence of these. But the great part of Browning's actual sentiments, and almost all the finest and most literary of them, are perfectly plain and popular and eternal sentiments. Meredith is really a singer producing strange notes and cadences difficult to follow because of the delicate rhythm of the song he sings. Browning is simply a great demagogue, with an impediment in his speech. Or rather, to speak more strictly, Browning is a man whose excitement for the glory of the obvious is so great that his speech becomes disjointed and precipitate: he becomes eccentric through his advocacy of the ordinary, and goes mad for the love of sanity.

If Browning and George Meredith were each describing the same act, they might both be obscure, but their obscurities would be entirely different. Suppose, for instance, they were describing even so prosaic and material an act as a man being knocked downstairs by another man to whom he had given the lie, Meredith's description would refer to something which an ordinary observer would not see, or at least could not describe. It might be a sudden sense of anarchy in the brain of the assaulter, or a stupefaction and stunned serenity in that of the object of the assault. He might write, "Wainwood's 'Men vary in veracity,' brought the baronet's arm up. He felt the doors of his brain burst, and Wainwood a swift rushing of himself through air accompanied with a clarity as of the annihilated." Meredith, in other words, would speak queerly because he was describing queer mental experiences. But Browning might simply be describing the material incident of the man being knocked downstairs, and his description would run:—

What then? "You lie" and doormat below stairs
Takes bump from back.

This is not subtlety, but merely a kind of insane swiftness.
Browning is not like Meredith, anxious to pause and examine
the sensations of the combatants, nor does he become obscure through this anxiety. He is only so anxious to get his
man to the bottom of the stairs quickly that he leaves out
about half the story.

Many who could understand that ruggedness might be an
artistic quality, would decisively, and in most cases rightly,
deny that obscurity could under any conceivable circumstances be an artistic quality. But here again Browning's
work requires a somewhat more cautious and sympathetic
analysis. There is a certain kind of fascination, a strictly
artistic fascination, which arises from a matter being hinted
at in such a way as to leave a certain tormenting uncertainty
even at the end. It is well sometimes to half understand a
poem in the same manner that we half understand the world.
One of the deepest and strangest of all human moods is the
mood which will suddenly strike us perhaps in a garden at
night, or deep in sloping meadows, the feeling that every
flower and leaf has just uttered something stupendously
direct and important, and that we have by a prodigy of
imbecility not heard or understood it. There is a certain
poetic value, and that a genuine one, in this sense of having
missed the full meaning of things. There is beauty, not only
in wisdom, but in this dazed and dramatic ignorance.

But in truth it is very difficult to keep pace with all the
strange and unclassified artistic merits of Browning. He was
always trying experiments; sometimes he failed, producing
clumsy and irritating metres, top-heavy and over-concen-
trated thought. Far more often he triumphed, producing a
crowd of boldly designed poems, every one of which taken
separately might have founded an artistic school. But

whether successful or unsuccessful, he never ceased from his fierce hunt after poetic novelty. He never became a conservative. The last book he published in his lifetime, *Parleyings with Certain People of Importance in their Day*, was a new poem, and more revolutionary than *Paracelsus*. This is the true light in which to regard Browning as an artist. He had determined to leave no spot of the cosmos unadorned by his poetry which he could find it possible to adorn. An admirable example can be found in that splendid poem "Childe Roland to the Dark Tower Came." It is the hint of an entirely new and curious type of poetry, the poetry of the shabby and hungry aspect of the earth itself. Daring poets who wished to escape from conventional gardens and orchards had long been in the habit of celebrating the poetry of rugged and gloomy landscapes, but Browning is not content with this. He insists upon celebrating the poetry of mean landscapes. That sense of scrubbiness in nature, as of a man unshaved, had never been conveyed with this enthusiasm and primeval gusto before.

> If there pushed any ragged thistle-stalk
>   Above its mates, the head was chopped; the bents
>   Were jealous else. What made those holes and rents
> In the dock's harsh swarth leaves, bruised as to baulk
> All hope of greenness? 'tis a brute must walk
>   Pashing their life out, with a brute's intents.

This is a perfect realization of that eerie sentiment which comes upon us, not so often among mountains and waterfalls, as it does on some half-starved common at twilight, or in walking down some grey mean street. It is the song of the beauty of refuse; and Browning was the first to sing it. Oddly enough it has been one of the poems about which most of those pedantic and trivial questions have been asked, which are asked invariably by those who treat Browning as a science instead of a poet, "What does the poem of

'Childe Roland' mean?" The only genuine answer to this is, "What does anything mean?" Does the earth mean nothing? Do grey skies and wastes covered with thistles mean nothing? Does an old horse turned out to graze mean nothing? If it does, there is but one further truth to be added—that everything means nothing.

[1905]

PAUL ELMER MORE

WHY IS BROWNING POPULAR?

It has come to be a matter of course that some new book on Browning shall appear with every season. Already the number of these manuals has grown so large that any one interested in critical literature finds he must devote a whole corner of his library to them—where, the cynical may add, they are better lodged than in his brain. To name only a few of the more recent publications: there was Stopford Brooke's volume, which partitioned the poet's philosophy into convenient compartments, labelled nature, human life, art, love, etc. Then came Mr. Chesterton, with his biting paradoxes and his bold justification of Browning's work, not as it ought to be, but as it is. Professor Dowden followed with what is, on the whole, the best *vade mecum* for those who wish to preserve their enthusiasm with a little salt of common sense; and, latest of all, we have now a critical study by Prof. C. H. Herford, of the University of Manchester, which once more

unrolls in all its gleaming aspects the poet's "joy in soul."
Two things would seem to be clear from this succession of
commentaries: Browning must need a deal of exegesis, and
he must be a subject of wide curiosity. Now obscurity and
popularity do not commonly go together, and I fail to remember that any of the critics named has paused long
enough in his own admiration to explain just why Browning
has caught the breath of favour; in a word, to answer the
question: Why is Browning popular?

There is, indeed, one response to such a question, so
obvious and so simple that it might well be taken for
granted. It would hardly seem worth while to say that
despite his difficulty Browning is esteemed because he has
written great poetry; and in the most primitive and un-
equivocal manner this is to a certain extent true. At intervals
the staccato of his lines, like the drilling of a woodpecker,
is interrupted by a burst of pure and liquid music, as if that
vigorous and exploring bird were suddenly gifted with the
melodious throat of the lark. It is not necessary to hunt
curiously for examples of this power; they are fairly frequent
and the best known are the most striking. Consider the first
lines that sing themselves in the memory:

> O lyric Love, half-angel and half-bird,
> And all a wonder and a wild desire—

there needs no cunning exegete to point out the beauty of
these. Their rhythm is of the singing, traditional kind that
is familiar to us in all the true poets of the language; the
harmony of the vowel sounds and of the consonants, the very
trick of alliteration, are obvious to the least critical; yet
withal there is that miraculous suggestion in their charm
which may be felt but cannot be converted into a prosaic
equivalent. They stand out from the lines that precede and
follow them in *The Ring and the Book,* as differing not so

much in degree as in kind; they are lyrical, poetical, in the midst of a passage which is neither lyrical nor, precisely speaking, poetical. Elsewhere the surprise may be on the lower plane of mere description. So, throughout the peroration of *Paracelsus,* despite the glory and eloquence of the dying scholar's vision, one feels continually an alien element which just prevents a complete acquiescence in their magic, some residue of clogging analysis which has not quite been subdued to poetry—and then suddenly, as if some discordant instrument were silenced in an orchestra and unvexed music floated to the ear, the manner changes, thus:

> The herded pines commune and have deep thoughts,
> A secret they assemble to discuss
> When the sun drops behind their trunks which glare
> Like grates of hell.

And, take his works throughout, there is a good deal of this writing which has the ordinary, direct appeal to the emotions. Yet it is scattered, accidental so to speak; nor is it any pabulum of the soul as simple as this which converts the lover of poetry into the Browningite. Even his common-sense admirers are probably held by something more recondite than this occasional charm.

> You see one lad o'erstride a chimney-stack;
> Him you must watch—he's sure to fall, yet stands!
> Our interest's on the dangerous edge of things—

says Bishop Blougram, and the attraction of Browning to many is just in watching what may be called his acrobatic psychology. Consider this same "Bishop Blougram's Apology," in some respects the most characteristic, as it is certainly not the least prodigious, of his poems. "Over his wine so smiled and talked his hour Sylvester Blougram"— talked and smiled to a silent listener concerning the strange

PAUL ELMER MORE

mixture of doubt and faith which lie snugly side by side in
the mind of an ecclesiastic who is at once a hypocrite and a
sincere believer in the Church. The mental attitude of the
speaker is subtle enough in itself to be fascinating, but the
real suspense does not lie there. The very balancing of the
priest's argument may at first work a kind of deception, but
read more attentively and it begins to grow clear that no
man in the wily bishop's predicament ever talked in this way
over his wine or anywhere else. And here lies the real
piquancy of the situation. His words are something more
than a confession; they are this and at the same time the
poet's, or if you will the bishop's own, comment to himself
on that confession. He who talks is never quite in the
privacy of solitude, nor is he ever quite conscious of his
listener, who as a matter of fact is not so much a person as
some half-personified opinion of the world or abstract notion
set against the character of the speaker. And this is Browning's regular procedure not only in those wonderful dramatic
monologues, *Men and Women,* that form the heart of his
work, but in *Paracelsus,* in *The Ring and the Book,* even in
the songs and the formal dramas.

Perhaps the most remarkable and most obvious example
of this suspended psychology is to be found in *The Ring and
the Book.* Take the canto in which Giuseppe Caponsacchi
relates to the judges his share in the tangled story. It is clear
that the interest here is not primarily in the event itself, nor
does it lie in that phase of the speaker's character which
would be revealed by his confession before such a court as
he is supposed to confront. The fact is, that Caponsacchi's
language is not such as under the circumstances he could
possibly be conceived to use. As the situation forms itself
in my mind, he might be in his cell awaiting the summons
to appear. In that solitude and uncertainty he goes over in
memory the days in Arezzo, when the temptation first came
to him, and once more takes the perilous ride with Pompilia

to Rome. He lives again through the great crisis, dissecting all his motives, balancing the pros and cons of each step; yet all the time he has in mind the opinion of the world as personified in the judges he is to face. The psychology is suspended dexterously between self-examination and open confession, and the reader who accepts the actual dramatic situation as suggested by Browning loses the finest and subtlest savour of the speech. In many places it would be simply preposterous to suppose we are listening to words really uttered by the priest.

> We did go on all night; but at its close
> She was troubled, restless, moaned low, talked at whiles
> To herself, her brow on quiver with the dream:
> Once, wide awake, she menaced, at arms' length
> Waved away something—"Never again with you!
> My soul is mine, my body is my soul's:
> You and I are divided ever more
> In soul and body: get you gone!" Then I—
> "Why, in my whole life I have never prayed!
> Oh, if the God, that only can, would help!
> Am I his priest with power to cast out fiends?
> Let God arise and all his enemies
> Be scattered!" By morn, there was peace, no sigh
> Out of the deep sleep—

no, those words were never spoken in the ears of a sceptical, worldly tribunal; they belong to the most sacred recesses of memory; yet at the same time that memory is coloured by a consciousness of the world's clumsy judgment.

It would be exaggeration to say that all Browning's greater poems proceed in this involved manner, yet the method is so constant as to be the most significant feature of his work. And it bestows on him the honour of having created a new genre which follows neither the fashion of lyric on the one hand nor that of drama or narrative on the other, but is a curious and illusive hybrid of the two. The passions are not uttered directly as having validity and meaning in the heart of the speaker alone, nor are they revealed through action and reaction upon the emotions of another. His dramas, if read attentively, will be found really to fall into the same mixed genre as his monologues. And a comparison of his *Sordello* with such a poem as Goethe's *Tasso* (which is more the dialogue of a narrative poem than a true drama) will show how far he fails to make a character move visibly amid opposing circumstances. In both poems we have a contrast of the poetical temperament with the practical world. In Browning it is difficult to distinguish the poet's own thought from the words of the hero; the narrative is in reality a long confession of Sordello to himself who is conscious of a hostile power without. In Goethe this hostile power stands out as distinctly as Tasso himself, and they act side by side each to his own end.

There is even a certain significance in what is perhaps the most immediately personal poem Browning ever wrote, that "One Word More" which he appended to his *Men and Women*. Did he himself quite understand this lament for Raphael's lost sonnets and Dante's interrupted angel, this desire to find his love a language,

> Fit and fair and simple and sufficient—
> Using nature that's an art to others,
> Not, this one time, art that's turned his nature?

It would seem rather the uneasiness of his own mind when brought face to face with strong feeling where no escape remains into his oblique mode of expression. And the man Browning of real life, with his training in a dissenting Camberwell home and later his somewhat dapper acceptance of the London social season, accords with such a view of the writer. It is, too, worthy of note that almost invariably he impressed those who first met him as being a successful

[107]

merchant, a banker, a diplomat—anything but a poet. There was passion enough below the surface, as his outburst of rage against FitzGerald and other incidents of the kind declare; but the direct exhibition of it was painful if not grotesque.

Yet in this matter, as in everything that touches Browning's psychology, it is well to proceed cautiously. Because he approached the emotions thus obliquely, as it were in a style hybrid between the lyric and the drama, it does not follow that his work is void of emotion or that he questioned the validity of human passion. The very contrary is true. I remember, indeed, once hearing a lady, whose taste was as frank as it was modern, say that she liked Browning better than Shakespeare because he was more emotional and less intellectual than the older dramatist. Her distinction was somewhat confused, but it leads to an important consideration; I do not know but it points to the very heart of the question of Browning's popularity. He is not in reality more emotional than Shakespeare, but his emotion is of a kind more readily felt by the reader of today; nor does he require less use of the intellect, but he does demand less of that peculiar translation of the intellect from the particular to the general point of view which is necessary to raise the reader into what may be called the poetical mood. In one sense Browning is nearly the most intellectual poet in the language. The action of his brain was so nimble, his seizure of every associated idea was so quick and subtle, his elliptical style is so supercilious of the reader's needs, that often to understand him is like following a long mathematical demonstration in which many of the intermediate equations are omitted. And then his very trick of approaching the emotions indirectly, his suspended psychology as I have called it, requires a peculiar flexibility of the reader's mind. But in a way these roughnesses of the shell possess an attraction for the educated public which has been sated with what lies too accessibly on the surface. They hold out the flattering promise of an initiation into mysteries not open to all the world. Our wits have become pretty well sharpened by the complexities of modern life, and we are ready enough to prove our analytical powers on any riddle of poetry or economics. And once we have penetrated to the heart of these enigmas we are quite at our ease. His emotional content is of a sort that requires no further adjustment; it demands none of that poetical displacement of the person which is so uncomfortable to the keen but prosaic intelligence. And here that tenth Muse, who has been added to the Pantheon for the guidance of the critical writer, trembles and starts back. She beholds to the right and the left a quaking bog of abstractions and metaphysical definitions, whereon if a critic so much as set his foot he is sucked down into the bottomless mire. She plucks me by the ear and bids me keep to the strait and beaten path, whispering the self-admonition of one who was the darling of her sisters:

I *won't* philosophise, and *will* be read.

Indeed, the question that arises is no less than the ultimate distinction between poetry and prose, and "ultimates" may well have an ugly sound to one who is content if he can comprehend what is concrete and very near at hand. And, as for that, those who would care to hear the matter debated in terms of *Idee* and *Begriff, Objektivität* and *Subjektivität*, must already be familiar with those extraordinary chapters in Schopenhauer wherein philosophy and literature are married as they have seldom been elsewhere since the days of Plato. And yet without any such formidable apparatus as that, it is not difficult to see that the peculiar procedure of Browning's mind offers to the reader a pleasure different more in kind than in degree from what is commonly associated with the word poetry. His very manner of approaching the passions obliquely, his habit of holding his portrayal of character in suspense between direct exposition and dramatic reaction, tends to keep the attention riveted on the individual speaker or problem, and prevents that escape into the larger and more general vision which marks just the transition from prose to poetry. It is not always so. Into that cry "O lyric Love" there breaks the note which from the beginning has made lovers forget themselves in their song—the note that passes so easily from the lips of Persian Omar to the mouth of British FitzGerald:

> Ah Love! could you and I with Him conspire
> To grasp this sorry Scheme of Things entire,
> Would not we shatter it to bits—and then
> Re-mould it nearer to the Heart's Desire!

Is it not clear how, in these direct and lyrical expressions, the passion of the individual is carried up into some region where it is blended with currents of emotion broader than any one man's loss or gain? and how, reading these words, we, too, feel that sudden enlargement of the heart which it is the special office of the poet to bestow? But it is equally true that Browning's treatment of love, as in "James Lee's Wife" and "In a Balcony," to name the poems nearest at hand, is for the most part so involved in his peculiar psychological method that we cannot for a moment forget ourselves in this freer emotion.

And in his attitude towards nature it is the same thing. I have not read Schopenhauer for many years, but I remember as if it were yesterday my sensation of joy as in the course of his argument I came upon these two lines quoted from Horace:

> Nox erat et cælo fulgebat luna sereno
> Inter minora sidera.

How perfectly simple the words, and yet it was as if the splendour of the heavens had broken upon me—rather, in some strange way, within me. And that, I suppose, is the real function of descriptive poetry—not to present a detailed scene to the eye, but in its mysterious manner to sink our sense of individual life in this larger sympathy with the world. Now and then, no doubt, Browning, too, strikes this universal note, as, for instance, in those lines from *Paracelsus* already quoted. But for the most part, his description, like his lyrical passion, is adapted with remarkable skill towards individualising still further the problem or character that he is analysing. Take that famous passage in "Easter-Day":

> And as I said
> This nonsense, throwing back my head
> With light complacent laugh, I found
> Suddenly all the midnight round
> One fire. The dome of heaven had stood
> As made up of a multitude
> Of handbreadth cloudlets, one vast rack
> Of ripples infinite and black,
> From sky to sky. Sudden there went,
> Like horror and astonishment,
> A fierce vindictive scribble of red
> Quick flame across, as if one said
> (The angry scribe of Judgment), "There—
> Burn it!" And straight I was aware
> That the whole ribwork round, minute
> Cloud touching cloud beyond compute,
> Was tinted, each with its own spot
> Of burning at the core, till clot
> Jammed against clot, and spilt its fire
> Over all heaven. . . .

We are far enough from the "Nox erat" of Horace or even the "trunks that glare like grates of hell"; we are seeing the world with the eye of a man whose mind is perplexed and whose imagination is narrowed down by terror to a single question: "How hard it is to be A Christian!"

[111]

And nothing, perhaps, confirms this impression of a body of writing which is neither quite prose nor quite poetry more than the rhythm of Browning's verse. Lady Burne-Jones in the Memorials of her husband tells of meeting the poet at Denmark Hill, when some talk went on about the rate at which the pulse of different people beat. Browning suddenly leaned toward her, saying, "Do me the honour to feel my pulse"—but to her surprise there was none to feel. His pulse was, in fact, never perceptible to touch. The notion may seem fantastic, but, in view of certain recent investigations of psychology into the relation between our pulse and our sense of rhythm, I have wondered whether the lack of any regular systole and diastole in Browning's verse may not rest on a physical basis. There is undoubtedly a kind of proper motion in his language, but it is neither the regular rise and fall of verse nor the more loosely balanced cadences of prose; or, rather, it vacillates from one movement to the other, in a way which keeps the rhythmically trained ear in a state of acute tension. But it has at least the interest of corresponding curiously to the writer's trick of steering between the elevation of poetry and the analysis of prose. It rounds out completely our impression of watching the most expert funambulist in English letters. Nor is there anything strange in this intimate relation between the content of his writing and the mechanism of his metre. "The purpose of rhythm," says Mr. Yeats in a striking passage of one of his essays, "it has always seemed to me, is to prolong the moment of contemplation, the moment when we are both asleep and awake, which is the one moment of creation, by hushing us with an alluring monotony, while it holds us waking by variety." That is the neo-Celt's mystical way of putting a truth that all have felt—the fact that the regular sing-song of verse exerts a species of enchantment on the senses, lulling to sleep the individual within us and translating our thoughts and emotions into something significant of the larger experience of mankind.

But I would not leave this aspect of Browning's work without making a reservation which may seem to some (though wrongly, I think) to invalidate all that has been said. For it does happen now and again that he somehow produces the unmistakable exaltation of poetry through the very exaggeration of his unpoetical method. Nothing could be more indirect, more oblique, than his way of approaching the climax in "Cleon." The ancient Greek poet, writing from the sprinkled isles, Lily on lily, that o'erlace the sea," answers certain queries of Protus the Tyrant. He contrasts the insufficiency of the artistic life with that of his master, and laments bitterly the vanity of pursuing ideal beauty when the goal at the end is only death:

> It is so horrible,
> I dare at times imagine to my need
> Some future state revealed to us by Zeus,
> Unlimited in capability
> For joy, as this is in desire for joy.
> .   .   .   .   .   . But no!
> Zeus has not yet revealed it; and alas,
> He must have done so, were it possible!

The poem, one begins to suspect, is a specimen of Browning's peculiar manner of indirection; in reality, through this monologue, suspended delicately between self-examination and dramatic confession, he is focussing in one individual heart the doom of the great civilisation that is passing away and the splendid triumph of the new. And then follows the climax, as it were an accidental afterthought:

> And for the rest,
> I cannot tell thy messenger aright
> Where to deliver what he bears of thine
> To one called Paulus; we have heard his fame
> Indeed, if Christus be not one with him—
> *I know not, nor am troubled much to know.*
> Thou canst not think a mere barbarian Jew,

[113]

As Paulus proves to be, one circumcised,
Hath access to a secret shut from us?
Thou wrongest our philosophy, O King,
In stooping to inquire of such an one,
As if his answer could impose at all!
He writeth, doth he? well, and he may write.
Oh, the Jew findeth scholars! certain slaves
Who touched on this same isle, preached him and Christ;
And (as I gathered from a bystander)
Their doctrine could be held by no sane man.

It is not revoking what has been said to admit that the superb audacity of the indirection in these underscored lines touches on the sublime; the individual is involuntarily rapt into communion with the great currents that sweep through human affairs, and the interest of psychology is lost in the elevation of poetry. At the same time it ought to be added that this effect would scarcely have been possible were not the rhythm and the mechanism of the verse unusually free of Browning's prosaic mannerism.

It might seem that enough had been said to explain why Browning is popular. The attitude of the ordinary intelligent reader toward him is, I presume, easily stated. A good many of Browning's mystifications, *Sordello,* for one, he simply refuses to bother himself with. *Le jeu,* he says candidly, *ne vaut pas les chandelles.* Other works he goes through with some impatience, but with an amount of exhilarating surprise sufficient to compensate for the annoyances. If he is trained in literary distinctions, he will be likely to lay down the book with the exclamation: *C'est magnifique, mais ce n'est pas la poésie!* And probably such a distinction will not lessen his admiration; for it cannot be asserted too often that the reading public today is ready to accede to any legitimate demand on its analytical understanding, but that it responds sluggishly, or only spasmodically, to that readjustment of the emotions necessary for the sustained enjoyment of such a poem as *Paradise Lost.*

But I suspect that we have not yet touched the real heart of the problem. All this does not explain that other phase of Browning's popularity, which depends upon anything but the common sense of the average reader; and, least of all, does it account for the library of books, of which Professor Herford's is the latest example. There is another public which craves a different food from the mere display of human nature; it is recruited largely by the women's clubs and by men who are unwilling or afraid to hold their minds in a state of self-centred expectancy toward the meaning of a civilisation shot through by threads of many ages and confused colours; it is kept in a state of excitation by critics who write lengthily and systematically of "joy in soul." Now there is a certain philosophy which is in a particular way adapted to such readers and writers. Its beginnings, no doubt, are rooted in the naturalism of Rousseau and the eighteenth century, but the flower of it belongs wholly to our own age. It is the philosophy whose purest essence may be found distilled in Browning's magical alembic, and a single drop of it will affect the brain of some people with a strange giddiness.

And here again I am tempted to abscond behind those blessed words *Platonische Ideen* and *Begriffe, universalia ante rem* and *universalia post rem,* which offer so convenient an escape from the difficulty of meaning what one says. It would be so easy with those counters of German metaphysicians and the schoolmen to explain how it is that Browning has a philosophy of generalised notions, and yet so often misses the form of generalisation special to the poet. The fact is his philosophy is not so much inherent in his writing as imposed on it from the outside. His theory of love does not expand like Dante's into a great vision of life wherein symbol and reality are fused together, but is added as a commentary on the action or situation. And on the other hand he does not accept the simple and pathetic

incompleteness of life as a humbler poet might, but must
try with his reason to reconcile it with an ideal system:

> Over the ball of it,
> Peering and prying,
> How I see all of it,
> Life there, outlying!
> Roughness and smoothness,
> Shine and defilement,
> Grace and uncouthness:
> One reconcilement.

Yet "ideal" and "reconcilement" are scarcely the words; for
Browning's philosophy, when detached, as it may be, from
its context, teaches just the acceptance of life in itself as
needing no conversion into something beyond its own impulsive desires:

> Let us not always say,
> "Spite of this flesh to-day
> I strove, made head, gained ground upon the whole!"
> As the bird wings and sings,
> Let us cry, "All good things
> Are ours, nor soul helps flesh more, now, than flesh helps soul!"

Passion to Shakespeare was the source of tragedy; there is
no tragedy, properly speaking, in Browning, for the reason
that passion is to him essentially good. By sheer bravado
of human emotion we justify our existence, nay—

> We have to live alone to set forth well
> God's praise.

His notion of "moral strength," as Professor Santayana so
forcibly says, "is a blind and miscellaneous vehemence."
But if all the passions have their own validity, one of them
in particular is the power that moves through all and renders
them all good:

In my own heart love had not been made wise
To trace love's faint beginnings in mankind,
To know even hate is but a mask of love's.

It is the power that reaches up from earth to heaven, and
the divine nature is no more than a higher, more vehement
manifestation of its energy:

For the loving worm within its clod
Were diviner than a loveless god.

And in the closing vision of *Saul* this thought of the identity
of man's love and God's love is uttered by David in a kind
of delirious ecstasy:

'Tis the weakness in strength, that I cry for! my flesh, that I seek
In the Godhead! I seek and I find it. O Saul, it shall be
A Face like my face that receives thee; a Man like to me,
Thou shalt love and be loved by, forever: a Hand like this hand
Shall throw open the gates of new life to thee! See the Christ stand!

But there is no need to multiply quotations. The point is
that in all Browning's rhapsody there is nowhere a hint of
any break between the lower and the higher nature of man,
or between the human and the celestial character. Not that
his philosophy is pantheistic, for it is Hebraic in its vivid
sense of God's distinct personality; but that man's love is
itself divine, only lesser in degree. There is nothing that
corresponds to the tremendous words of Beatrice to Dante
when he meets her face to face in the Terrestrial Paradise:

Guardami ben: ben son, ben son Beatrice.
Come degnasti d' accedere al monte?
Non sapei tu che qui è l'uom felice?

(Behold me well: lo, Beatrice am I.
And thou, how daredst thou to this mount draw nigh?
Knew'st thou not here was man's felicity?) —

nothing that corresponds to the "scot of penitence," the tears, and the plunge into the river of Lethe before the new, transcendent love begins. Indeed, the point of the matter is not that Browning magnifies human love in its own sphere of beauty, but that he speaks of it with the voice of a prophet of spiritual things and proclaims it as a complete doctrine of salvation. Often, as I read the books on Browning's gospel of human passion, my mind recurs to that scene in the Gospel of St. John, wherein it is told how a certain Nicodemus of the Pharisees came to Jesus by night and was puzzled by the hard saying: "Except a man be born again, he cannot see the kingdom of God." There is no lack of confessions from that day to this of men to whom it has seemed that they were born again, and always, I believe, the new birth, like the birth of the body, was consummated with wailing and anguish, and afterwards the great peace. This is a mystery into which it is no business of mine to enter, but with the singularly uniform record of these confessions in my memory, I cannot but wonder at the light message of the new prophet: "If you desire faith—then you've faith enough," and "For God is glorified in man." I am even sceptical enough to believe that the vaunted conclusion of *Fifine at the Fair,* "I end with—Love is all and Death is naught," sounds like the wisdom of a schoolgirl. There is an element in Browning's popularity which springs from those readers who are content to look upon the world as it is; they feel the power of his lyric song when at rare intervals it flows in pure and untroubled grace, and they enjoy the intellectual legerdemain of his suspended psychology. But there is another element in that popularity (and this, unhappily, is the inspiration of the clubs and of the formulating critics) which is concerned too much with this flattering substitute for spirituality. Undoubtedly, a good deal of restiveness exists under what is called the materialism of modern life, and many are looking in this way and that for an escape into the purer joy which they hear has passed from the world. It used to be believed that Calderon was a bearer of the message, Calderon who expressed the doctrine of the saints and the poets:

> Pues el delito mayor
> Del hombre es haber nacido—

(since the greatest transgression of man is to have been born). It was believed that the spiritual life was bought with a price, and that the desires of this world must first suffer a permutation into something not themselves. I am not holding a brief for that austere doctrine; I am not even sure that I quite understand it, although it is written at large in many books. But I do know that those who think they have found its equivalent in the poetry of Browning are misled by wandering and futile lights. The secret of his more esoteric fame is just this, that he dresses a worldly and easy philosophy in the forms of spiritual faith and so deceives the troubled seekers after the higher life.

It is not pleasant to be convicted of throwing stones at the prophets, as I shall appear to many to have done. My only consolation is that, if the prophet is a true teacher, these stones of the casual passer-by merely raise a more conspicuous monument to his honour; but if he turns out in the end to be a false prophet (as I believe Browning to have been)—why, then, let his disciples look to it.

[1912]

DIXON SCOTT

THE HOMELINESS OF BROWNING:

A CENTENARY ARTICLE

CRITICISM being what she is, and the stir of Tennyson's
hundredth birthday party having but newly subsided,
today's proceedings will scarcely be expected to go through
without at least one complacent side glance at the rival
celebration. It has by now almost become the official
opening indeed; all through the sweltering days of the
eighties and nineties, when both suns were blazing together,
it was a refuge used without stint: instead of attempting to
reconcile matters, explain the phenomenon, or of honestly
tackling each in turn, our cunning writers used to make a
labour saving device of the difficulty—pit one giant against
the other, and saunter off coolly dusting their hands as
though things had been neatly cancelled out. And such
comparisons can be commodious. Indulged in for a moment,
they would bring us sharply face to face at once with
the most interesting problem now left—the sole remaining
Browning conundrum. For one of the chief characteristics

of the Tennysonian affair was a certain tameness and per-functoriness: the toasts seemed tepid and formal, the old enthusiasm to have waned. But with our man—how richly the reverse! Never has he had so many, or such hearty and lusty, admirers as today. The haughty Browning Society, that used to hug itself in a grim isolation, is now only a black speck in the middle of a genial mob. The books that baffled a Ruskin and were too tough for a Jowett are every-body's reading today—the only feature about them that bewilders us being the report that they ever bewildered any one. We need cribs for *Sordello* no longer; Polonius's occupation is gone. Miss Lilian Whiting has taken his place. The correct thing now is to run through *Pacchiarotto* with a smile, lay it down with a laugh, and then ask for something really craggy to break our minds on.

Now, there is more in this than the natural desire of us young folk to smile indulgently down upon our parents. It is not just posterity's pertness. Nor is it even due—altogether —to our unavoidable superiority. Nor yet to the way our musical ears have been genuinely quickened and toughened of late by the last crashing multiplex choruses, crisscrossed so variously, of the great late-Victorian choir. The main reason is something so simple—and yet, at the same time, so terribly like gawky paradox—that it is possible to feel shy about naming it. Named, however, it must be, for, being true, it involves a high tribute, and probably the tribute which Browning himself would most have liked to see us bringing. It was just his sweet sanity, then, that made him seem a madcap eccentric; it was his friendly normality and family likeness to themselves that filled our grandfathers with expostulating terror. No escaping this conclusion: look where you will, fresh evidence leaps up and locks you in. Take, first, the larger literary aspect. Seen suddenly against the elaborate curtain of nineteenth-century song, Browning does seem to stand out with an abrupt incongruity, like a work-man in front of a tapestry. But when we step fifty years or so back from it, the figure not only falls into focus, but becomes a kind of centrepiece and summary, a concentration of all the colours behind: he almost looks the artist who wove them—if he differs from each of the dim decorative figures that brood there, it is because he resembles them all. In *Paracelsus* alone it is possible to find a match for almost every tint—for Keats's famous blue and the lunar rainbow lights of Shelley, for the romantic tartan of Sir Walter and Wordsworth's missionary black, and—yes!—even the cool, delicious dyes of Lotusland itself:—

> Heap cassia, sandal-buds and stripes
> Of labdanum and aloe-balls,
> Smeared with dull nard an Indian wipes
> From out her hair: such balsam falls
> Down seaside mountain pedestals. . . .

He can stalk Byronically—soar like his Suntreader, come to earth again as true and right as Tennyson. And the biography explains. "You might as well apply to a gin-shop for a leg of mutton as ask for any thing human and earthly from me," said Shelley. But "Browning is good at everything," wrote one of his friends. Poetry was but one of his passions: he boxed and he rode, he danced, fenced, fished, and travelled, painted, played, was a pattern man of affairs, had all the sound suburban virtues, lay awake at night if he owed a bill, and as a bank clerk would have been as great a success as his assiduous grandfather. One of his eyes, we are told, was exceptionally long-sighted, the other exceptionally short, and the blend gave him a vision of splendid balance and completeness. It is finely characteristic of the man who differed from other men not because he had one function hyperdeveloped but because he had all their faculties in noble measure, so that the result was a radiant normality. In no other two volumes of verse on our shelves, accordingly, do we find so much of life, in such right proportions and so prismatically mixed. Both halves of Rome are here. And, roughly, it may be said that it differed from the work of the figures behind in being—not the sudden exceptional song of a man touched to ecstasy, but just the voice of a giant speaking. At once, as a consequence, came an almost purely mechanical difficulty. When men saw poetry passing up to her lectern they had grown accustomed to assume a certain portly mental attitude; the mere sight of verse was enough (is still perhaps in some places) to set the mind involuntarily swaying with a certain grave formality, and the eager quest and recovery and directness of thought stepping with a conversational swing knocked this for a moment out of time. But it was scarcely more than a physiological difficulty, a matter of optical deportment; it was never a misalliance of matter and form, nor yet the diviner difficulty of thought supernaturally swift. It was simply that the voice was more frank and convivial than the mood which its environment summoned up. The reader's eye wanted time to readjust itself—nothing more. The interval has been granted it, and now it falls into step automatically. And there you have one of the simpler ways in which Browning's friendly humanity made him seem bizarre.

And helping it, scarcely less superficial, there was another difficulty, half dead too by now, which ought to be mentioned and dismissed. *Sibrandus Schafnaburgensis; Johannes Ceutonicus; Mic. Toxetis, Onomastica; Her. Tom. Agrippa, De Occult Philosoph.* Consternation may well have seized plain minds when they saw poetry sprinkled with names like these. But we know now (it is the mocking conclusion which heavy research now finds itself facing askance) that these titles really testify, not to anything monstrous or fantastic in the way of learning, but to a kind of fireside simplicity and homeliness. They are only the names young Browning picked out of the books that were his nursery toys. Paracelsus, for instance, was his father's pet hobby. To make rhymes about the Piper of Hamelin was almost an

established family game. The more we learn of his life the
plainer do we see that his air of dangerous abstruseness is
largely due to a kind of domestic economy, to the sensible
practice, which he maintained to the end of his life, of using
the material that lay nearest to his hand.

But these are minor matters after all. Like his later
levities—his willingness to guy his critics, to scribble ribaldry
on the tabernacle walls of his verse, to out-Browning Browning and to live up to—and beyond—his reputation; they are
just offshoots and illustrations of a yet more profoundly
wholesome and philistine quality—his inability, that is, to
see poetry as anything but a tool, a useful subordinate to
life, to be treated like a servant. He could never be one of
those who crush their lives to produce the wine of their art.
He would never sell himself for a new song. And this
sterling refusal to allow life to approach art with salaams
flustered his fellow philistines in all sorts of curious ways.
One of the most interesting relates to the notorious difficulty
of *Sordello*—the "mountain of unintelligibilities." When he
wrote it, in his twenties, he was indeed determined to succeed as a poet, but only as part of his programme for making
a thorough success of the larger business of life; and when
he took up his pen it was less to learn how to write than to
learn how to act and eat and comport himself. In it, and in
Paracelsus and *Pauline*, those companion studies of "aspiring
souls," you see him using poetry—not only to educate his
faculties gymnastically, as Sordello did—

> Fondling, in turn of fancy, verse; the Art
> Developing his soul a thousand ways—

but actually to work out his position, map out his life, make
a rough trial draft of his career, a private rehearsal, and cast
a sort of horoscope. It is usual to praise *Paracelsus* and
Sordello for "the completeness with which they portray
remote historical personages." The hero of each certainly is

an historical personage. But he was not born before May 7, 1812. These sketches are not retrospects, they are prospects —are, in fact, prospectuses—preliminary announcements of the proposed extensive development of the going concern called Robert Browning. It is just here that we young bloods of today are perhaps a little unfair to our elders. We forget that in their time, when the clear-cut aiguilles and gullies of the *Dramatic Lyrics* were still in the clouds, there was only one route up Browning, and that was over the vast slithering slopes of *Sordello*. Nowadays, if we read it at all, it is on our descent, confidently skipping and glissading— slurring the difficulties lightheartedly, sustained by our knowledge of the peak. But to tackle it as Tennyson and Ruskin did, working heavily up into the unknown, is still to find *Sordello* pretty stiff. "Hard, very hard, it undoubtedly is," even that keen climber Mr. Symons has openly admitted. Yet not, as he suggested, for its "cragginess." It is scree— that is the difficulty; the debris of his wanderyear, made out of his changing moods and impressions, the stuff he quarried as he went seeking the Philosopher's Stone. And if the litter is thus due to a kind of canny levelheadedness, to a dedication of poetry to the service of his life instead of his life to the service of poetry, there was something even more magnificently practical to follow. Like some emperor of old at the mouth of a dubious labyrinth, he had sent in these creatures of his, Paracelsus and Sordello, in advance, in order to test the way. Both expired, painfully. But each, before the end, gasped out a certain piece of advice. "Regard me," says the dying Paracelsus—

> Regard me and the poet dead long ago,
> Who loved too rashly—and shape forth a third
> And better-tempered spirit, warned by both.

The life of the intellect, urged both, must be balanced by some exterior devotion; egoism unlinked with love means horrid dooms. So said these Browning *manqués*. We know how he took the warning. The second half of *Paracelsus*, as inspection makes clear, is just an empty shell, a dummy, stuck on for the sake of symmetry. The true conclusion was not effected until that brave September morning of 1846 when the poet swept down upon 50, Wimpole Street— snatched Miss Barrett out of her darkened room, heavy with opiates—and away to Florence and the sun-sluiced Apennines:

> I have gained her!
> Her soul's mine, and now, grown perfect,
> I shall pass my life's remainder.

Perfection! Was it really that? We can only guess at the alternatives: who shall say? Yet one or two points, apt to our main argument, cannot be concealed. It is plain, to begin with, that it was this practical attitude towards poetry, continued in his later work, that both gained him his intimidating title of philosopher and robbed him of any real right to it. He was no true speculator, in spite of his followers: all he sought was a safe investment for his time. Long before Harvard had invented the word he was only a pragmatist. His Rabbi Ben Ezras and Blougrams and Karshish are all agents acting on his behalf, sent out to find him the Elixir if they can. Far more a physician than a metaphysician, he delights in discussing the problems of the body, and sees the soul as a superior drug or stimulus, a medicine for the man who encloses it—not greatly different in character from the large restoratives of arts or gems or seas. If renunciation is recommended, it is only that the world may be more perfectly won. It is the conqueror's code, not the prophet's—the voice of the visible world. His judgments are those of the fireside and the club (though a good club, of course, and a bright fireside). You can give some of these earthly songs a heavenly meaning if you will:—

Then welcome each rebuff
That turns earth's smoothness rough,
Each sting that bids nor sit nor stand but go!
Be our joys three parts pain!
Strive and hold cheap the strain;
Learn, nor account the pang; dare, never grudge the throe.

But though you fill it with mystical wine the cup is still of clay—good, red clay. An icier and exacter philosophy, for instance, would perhaps have judged less cruelly those lovers in "The Statue and the Bust," still seeing in their frustration a fine achievement, fitly symbolized by the more enduring beauty of the marble and the bronze. The earthly love Sordello urged remains the supreme ideal, rarely even made a symbol of the finer devotions to which it has sometimes—has it not?—to be sacrificed, a devotion that knows nothing of sex. Even from Luria, his supreme renunciant, he never dares demand that sacrifice. It was perhaps the abnegation Browning dreaded his calculations to commend. Perhaps he instinctively falsified the crystal. For it has to be remembered—though it rarely is—that his fifteen superb married years were, poetically, the most barren of his life, that it was in his years of desirous youth and aching widowerhood that his best work was done.

But this is not the occasion to put such questions, to ask whether there may not have been a misappropriation of poetic capital. And our dividend—even if we do not count the compensation to be got from the sight of his love affair, rounded and radiant as a myth—is already high. These limitations made him an incomplete philosopher and an imperfect dramatist, but they made him a model man. They are the lines that frame the picture. Restrained on the one hand from sitting beside Shelley, on the other from a seat by Shakspere, he is left ruler of a midway kingdom, made our chief poet of familiar life. He is the Laureate of life in undress, of life emulous and muscular and mirthful. All the physical satisfactions—of touch, sight, taste, and sound—are rendered here irresistibly. The best drinking songs in the language are here, and the best riding songs, and some of our best rhymed tales. All the treasures, fruits, and gems of the world are fingered for us with a satisfying voluptuousness; the lines are littered with loot, heaped like a pirate's hold; we prowl in an Aladdin's Cave. And the rich sounds of life echo here too. From bee's kiss to thunderclap he can race up the full scale, missing never a note, and then come rippling back again through the semitones of art, from Abt Vogler's to Galuppi's. Who has painted us better landscapes and seascapes or such curtains of sunset and dawn? With Swinburne he can rejoice simultaneously in the boom and lash of the living wave and the kiss and lilt of the line that records it. And, unlike the poets of nature, he sees the country as but a pedestal to the town, as part of that wide apparatus of life which it is man's business to learn how to use. It was from this safe, normal centre that he drew his arch, the full rainbow of earthly reassurances, and it was thus that he became, at his zenith, the supreme celebrant in our time of the ultimate solace of love.

Higher than that he does not go; it is the keystone of his arch. The transcendentalism of which we used to hear so much is merely the vapour on which the prism was cast; its very weakness, as we have seen, was woven up with the strength of his life—it was just because it was of the earth, watery, that it reflected the divine colours so well. There are still solemn persons, it is true, stout sons of their fathers, who will insist on going out, with little clattering pails, and returning to us proudly with indubitable rain water—which they assure us is the very blood and essence of the bow. Dear, queer, estimable people! "Does Browning urge this?" they ask; and "Did he mean us to regard the other?"; and go gathering maxims in his poems—gleaning fossils in a field of corn and poppies. How much they would have us miss!

One instance, a central one, to end with. "Entirely honest merchant" that he was, Browning shows in nothing the hearty simplicity of his nature so well as in his uneasy anxiety to convince himself that he is doing something more than merely sing. *Pippa* itself, as is too rarely recognized, is just an attempt to prove the practical value of song, the material importance of the poet; so, of course, is *Saul*. He felt fidgety without a tangible purpose—and so would often self-deceptively assuage his sterling conscience by budding his roses on solid intellectual trunks. If he painted a landscape he must have a stout peg to hang it on—and then a wall to justify the nail—and then a house for the wall—and there, in a winking, you have a humming community of hastily banded and organized theories. His skill at this kind of swift buttressing was superb—and to fail to perceive that it is improvisation is not only to overestimate their solidity rather dangerously but to miss, as well, more lamentably, the high sport of watching rapid cunning and resource in full cry. He could twist anything into a stanza; somewhere in his exact and abounding memory he could always pounce upon some alloy of epithet or incident which made the perfect amalgam. Examples are everywhere: *Dramatis Personæ* is full of them; for one of the daintier instances turn to "Love in a Gondola," where a casual potpourri of petals is so safely compressed and so craftily tinted that it looks like a dense group in bronze. Much of the "cragginess" of his later work is only the result of his desire for plenty of rifts to load with ore. Sometimes, of course, he did tackle stubborn trees of thought out of a sheer lad's love of climbing. But most often he is only using them as Christmas trees to hang with little lamps and gems and precious toys.

Not to realize that is to sell your Christmas tree for firewood, to spend your time painfully struggling up a maypole instead of catching its ribands and joining the dance. It is the last word to be said today—a warning and a salute.

[129]

Approach Browning solemnly, with a frown of perplexity, and he will frown back at you fiercely. But come to him heartily, as convivially as he came to verse, and you find him speaking in your own vernacular, dealing more directly with your humble troubles, hopes, and appetites—good leg-of-mutton poet that he is—than any other singer of our age. He has been held captive too long by those dark banditti, the Browningites. Let us hail him now as the poet for plain people, for honest, friendly souls like you and me. The wise Landor saw that long ago, when he linked him with an earlier democrat:—

> Since Chaucer was alive and hale,
> No man hath walk'd along our roads with step
> So active, so inquiring eye, or tongue
> So varied in discourse.

But even Landor's tribute has been outdone, in fundamental completeness, by the proud testimony of Lockhart. It is the perfect exposition of his secret. Let it stand for peroration here. "I like Browning," said he. "He's not the least bit like one of your damned literary men." *Ave!*

FRANCES T. RUSSELL

HIS SAVING GRACE OF PESSIMISM

IT OCCURRED to Chesterton that he could perpetrate an-other paradox through his perception that Bret Harte was a humorist, an American, yet not an American humorist. But he failed to recognize still another opportunity in spite of its staring him in the face as he composed his brisk biography of Browning. Perhaps he considered it enough to discover the optimism of Byron, and so left at large the equally important pessimism of Browning. For although Browning was certainly robust and ostensibly optimistic, he was not the robust optimist that popular report declared him to be.

Optimism, it seems, is always robust, just as materialism is always crass. And it was, to be sure, on the swelling tide of this robust optimism that the poet finally sailed into the south of public opinion.

The tide itself was augmented by the double service of that willing epithet, Robust. It naturally propelled the quality, Optimism; it chanced to be attached to this man Browning. Presto, the robust Browning becomes a robust optimist. The manipulated adjective is indeed not wholly superfluous. There is a flabby optimism and a robust pessimism and, for that matter, a flabby pessimism. But the point of interest here is the strange case of his own "Time's Revenges" that beset the poet on this issue.

For it happened that the very merit for which he was crowned by his contemporaries became thereafter less a badge of honor than an inglorious brand. But in the meantime he is found to be less deserving of it, whether badge or brand, than had been supposed.—Wherefore he is by way of saving his reputation through what would formerly have lost it.

It was one exception to his otherwise fortunate fate that placed a poet all compact of hard sense and soft sentiment in a generation that encouraged the latter more than the former. For this generation mistook a glittering surface for a vasty deep, stimulated by approval the expansion of that surface, and wisely refrained from probing beneath it. It was so much easier, and quite sufficient, to cull a few comforting and inspiring sentiments, and give them a multiple effect by constant use. By these facile repetitions Browning's "message" grew to sound like a fugue with the theme, "There shall never be one lost good." This was fine music at the time, but recently it has begun to take on the character of a hurdy-gurdy grinding out its little round of tunes—"The evil is null, is naught"; "The best is yet to be"; "I know there shall dawn a day." That is the reason the much-quoted poet is nowadays having his "God's in his heaven—All's right with the world!" continually thrown in his teeth by people whose knowledge of him is confined to that one fragment— and they evidently are unaware that in its context, as Pippa's morning song, it struck just the right note.

But what practically all of Browning's readers, those who

ridicule and patronize his optimism as well as those who applaud it, are unaware of is the shrinkage that optimism suffers when scrutinized in relation to his total output. In actual amount it is far outweighed by his pessimistic pronouncements. In quality, the pessimism is the more sincere and spontaneous, the optimism labored and rationalized.

From the youthful melancholy of *Pauline* to the aged sadness of the "Epilogue" to *Ferishtah's Fancies*, the poet pours forth a fairly steady stream of testimony to the unlivableness of life. His indictments are both specific and general, and are filed against both camps in the cosmic battle—the visible pygmy, Humanity, and the hidden giant, Fate.

The historical character Paracelsus is but a transparent mask for the youth of Camberwell, himself just awakening to the masked nature of his beautiful universe. We may be God's creatures, he exclaims, but it is certain that He takes no pride in us. Life is a poor cheat, a stupid bungle, a wretched failure, and he for one protests against it and hurls it back in scorn. With equal scorn he hurls back also the sustaining solace of immortality. Why should this world be only a makeshift, a mere foil to some fine life to come? Man must be fed with angels' food, forsooth, the unsubstantial diet of belief in his own divinity. But in that he flatters himself, for his own strongest driving emotion is not love but hate; his mind is nothing but disease and his natural health ignorance. Blind and endless is the struggle with evil, futile the frenzy to instruct those who lack the capacity to understand. Most eloquent of all is Paracelsus over the fallacy of a beneficent Providence. Let us smile at the idea that we have vast, God-given longings, satiable by lust or gold, or that we see the divine will charactered on heaven's vault that he who lifts his eyes may read. For himself, he knows as much of any such will as knows the dumb and tortured beast the will of his stern master from the perplexing blows that plague him every way. (So later said Ixion and Ferishtah's Camel Driver.) He waxes ironic over God's intimations that fail rather in clearness than in energy, as did Caliban in due time with his sneer at Setebos:

> Not He!
> There is the sport; discover how or die!

Not more bitter is Thomas Hardy over the treatment of his Tess by the President of the Immortals than is this medieval rebel over a world of Durbeyfields:

> You are to understand that we who make
> Sport for the gods, are hunted to the end.

Nay, more:

> Jove strikes the Titans down,
> Not when they set about their mountain-piling
> But when another rock would crown the work.

What could be left but the desire he expresses that the farce be quickly shuffled through to its dispiriting end? And does he then recant when on the approach of the end he has a consoling vision of the evolutionary nature of existence, in the grand perspective of which these partial evils are seen merging into a final good? Call it rather an anticipation of Francis Furini, of whom Browning suggested—

> That, on his death-bed, weakness played the thief
> With wisdom, folly ousted reason quite.

Or perchance this whole poem, together with *Pauline*, *Strafford*, and *Sordello*, the quartette forming a symphony on the theme of failure, is to be taken as a lad's sowing of his pessimistic wild oats. Did not their author recover from these growing pains and emerge into a cheerful and whole-

some manhood? Was not his fifth production, the gladsome
Pippa Passes, at once a confession of error and a peace
offering?

One might suppose so, for the passage of Pippa is so
brilliant that it dazzles into obscurity the significance of what
she passes. What is the dire actuality among "Asolo's Four
Happiest Ones"? What is discovered about those four types
of love from whose hierarchy of radiance the lonely child
was to extract a reflected light to illumine her ungraced path
withal? The first exhibits adultery, murder, ingratitude; the
second, vulgarity blasting by a vile practical joke an artist's
lustrous dream; the third, another young idealist made the
cat's paw of scheming politicians; the fourth, a high ecclesiastic hearkening to a scoundrel's malignant plots. These
choice samples of human behavior, amalgamated by a rubble
of spies, police, and women of the street, form a cross section
of life as it is lived. These incidents are credible realism.
The violent wrenching of the situations whereby all the
sinners are saved on the brink of their respective perditions
by the accidental appropriateness of the passing Pippa's
songs is sheer fantastic romanticism. You can chant "All's
right with the world," so long as you skirt the outside edges
of it like an angel unaware; and you can make the world
right by performing a row of miracles.

Yet was Browning at this time only in his early maturity.
What from the ripened, clarified writer of his epic masterpiece? It is indeed in *The Ring and the Book* that the poet
reaches the peak of his own mountain, and it is from this
height that the panorama appears like the Dark Tower
district in "Childe Roland." Fools and knaves in high places
and low, greedy, cynicism, wanton torture, and selfish refusal
of aid to the helpless, result in a vortex of overwhelming
catastrophe submerging guilty and innocent alike. This is
redeemed only by the intrepid initiative of a terrified,
hounded girl, the chivalry of a priest suddenly sobered out

of his convivial gayety, and the insight of a wise and saintly pope. Even this partial redemption is ignored in the conclusion to the whole matter, which is a strange reversal or nullification of what little compensation has survived. We are not to draw from the vindication of Pompilia's purity the inference that all truth triumphs in the end. "Learn one lesson hence," warns Browning emphatically, and recites that lesson as the utter nothingness of human testimony and estimation. With which whistling down the wind of mortal veracity and judgment, the curtain falls on a scene of truly Stygian gloom and ruin irremediable.

This great poem, however, momentous as it is, is only Browning's penultimate. Is not that final "Epilogue" the last word? Years before the poet had said: "I shall know, being old." Now that he is old, what does he know? Quite literally, he does not know what he is talking about. His subject is himself and his career in the next life. As to the first, the portrait drawn is so subtly specious, mistaking as it does disposition for character and accomplishment, that it is invalidated as a trustworthy report. The second is a concluding instance of his habit of accepting hope as certainty.

In the meantime there are many other pictures of another color. There is the tale of the mischievous Apollo, who wickedly converts the Three Fates from bitterness to mirth by the judicious gift of Bacchus' flowing bowl. Even the dread divinities, as well as our human Tam o'Shanters, become glorious only when their minds are drowned in drink. And as Burns found retrospect drear and prospect fearful, so Browning (in his "Bean-Stripe") sees "humanity reeling beneath its burden," for—

> Life, from birth to death,
> Means—either looking back on harm escaped,
> Or looking forward to that harm's return
> With tenfold power of harming.

Not more pensive is Koheleth over the vanity of human wishes, not more caustic is Omar over the futility of human hopes, than the author of "Earth's Immortalities," "Misconceptions," "The Last Ride Together," "In a Year," and other memorials to the frustration that comes more from a man's stars than from himself.

As for the humanity that tries to shape its own ends, or does not even try—"Some with lives that came to nothing, some with deeds as well undone"—the record of its "centuries of folly, noise and sin" is summarized in "Love Among the Ruins":

> Lust of glory pricked their hearts up, dread of shame
> Struck them tame;
> And that glory and that shame alike, the gold
> Bought and sold.

In the aggregate these beings arouse in Browning only contempt, a sentiment he has illustrated many times by sarcastic descriptions of mobs and crowds; this low opinion being offset by no brief whatever for earth's inhabitants in the lump and by very few instances of high personal distinction. Out of his battalion of men and women the poet produces a scant corporal's guard of the spirtual aristocracy, and of these none is nobly triumphant: all meet with defeat or a discounted victory. Out of man's weakness springs his selfishness, and from this under pressure are derived his deceitfulness, injustice, and cruelty.

What, then, says this present generation when asked to give a candidate for fame a propelling push along the twentieth century? It is a dubious business for any individual to play the prophet; but perhaps the consensus of thoughtful and candid opinion would voice itself somewhat as follows:

Robert Browning, as we define our terms, you look to us like a good normal mixture of the optimistic and the pessimistic, not, however, distinguished by robustness in either attitude. And since to us pessimism is no longer identified with the morbid and pathological, nor is optimism granted a monopoly of sanity and truth, you gain on the whole more than you lose by a reevaluation.

For the tremendous popular approval that the optimistic theory has always enjoyed we account on psychological rather than ethical grounds. The universal prejudice in its favor comes from our natural impulse to elevate a biological asset to a moral plane. Man has become an expert at making a virtue out of his necessity. Reconciliation with the life he has to live is as primal a necessity as food, shelter, and companionship. The gratification of that instinct is as wise, under similar restrictions, as is the satisfaction of the others. It is precisely as virtuous as any other act of self-preservation, and not a whit more to be imputed to us for righteousness.

Accordingly, Robert Browning, the things about you for which we care the least are the very ones for which you were blue-ribboned by your own generation. They have been allowed by default ever since, but you will now have to begin living them down. And conversely, what we prize are the darker streaks in your "veined humanity," not for their darkness, but for their richness, depth, and truth. We cannot be terribly impressed by your vaunted discovery that when you stoop you pluck a posy and when you stand and stare all's blue, since obviously if you had chanced to be stooping over the desert sands or staring at a thunderstorm, your botanizing would have been less bonny and your sky gazing less blithe. We take little stock in the mighty to-do you make to establish your wishes as facts, your zeal in nursing your hope to keep it warm.

"Take away love," sings Fra Lippo Lippi, "and our earth is a tomb." Take away also material comfort, scope for healthful activity, recompense for effort, and religious faith,

and what is our earth but a charnel house? Yet hordes of
your fellow beings are doomed to live and die on a minimum
physical and spiritual ration, and few indeed are endowed
with your *aes triplex* of happy environment, buoyant disposition, and naïve theology. Since life for you never was
reduced to its lowest terms, you naturally are not qualified to
grapple with ultimates. Yet even you voiced this admission:

I must say—or choke in silence—"Howsoever came my fate,
Sorrow did, and joy did nowise—life well weighed—preponderate."

Here you touch the responsive chord, Robert Browning,
and for this shall you be saved. Not for your love of the
garish day, of shawms and trumpets, of C major and the
Mode Palestrina, do we welcome and speed you on, but for
the wistful minor of your "Toccata," the ineffable unfulfill-
ment of your "Campagna," your confession that our joy may
be three parts pain and dearly bought at that with strain
and throe, your recognition that this curse will come upon
us—to see our idols perish. In your redoubtable harrying of
evil through Bishop Blougram, Bernard de Mandeville,
Mihrab Shah, and lesser lights, we see more of an oratorical
gesture than a pugilistic blow; but in the embarrassed
wondering of Karshish and in the scornful groping of Cleon
—who "sees the wider but to sigh the more"—we find the
simple, sincere handclasp of human fellowship. It is not your
David of inspired prophecy, but the young shepherd who
consoled and encouraged his friend that we love. And more
than Ben Ezra, prating of "plastic circumstance," do we trust
del Sarto's "So free we seem, so fettered fast we are!"

This aspect of you we appreciate not because we love
felicity and blessed assurance less, but honesty more. It is
not that we revel in misery and enjoy our poor health. We
too "desire joy and thank God for it," although we do not
expect Him to furnish it on demand. Our hearts also beat

that it is good to live and learn; only we are beginning to be more concerned that we learn aright.

It is when you celebrate the heroisms and loyalties of the ambiguous creatures, discouragingly weak and incredibly strong, summoned into this life, it is when you sing of the beauty and the wonder and the power of this world, that you enter into our common human heritage of grief and bliss and mystery, and render it more luminous and endurable. And thus from your manifold pages we shall select and hold parley with Certain Poems of Importance, enshrining them along with the "Grecian Urn," "Dover Beach," "Gloucester Moors," and "Pulvis et Umbra."

[1932]

WILLIAM C. DeVANE

THE HARLOT AND THE

THOUGHTFUL YOUNG MAN

Early in June 1872, Dante Gabriel Rossetti, already in a desperate mental condition, read the presentation copy of Robert Browning's *Fifine at the Fair,* flung it from him under the strong conviction that the poem was an attack upon his character, and thus ended a friendship of twenty-five years' standing. His suspicions have never been explained, except upon grounds of irrationality. His brother, William Michael Rossetti, who was present and in possession of most of the facts of the situation, was compelled at last to conclude that Dante Rossetti was "not entirely sane." Upon inspection *Fifine* does not immediately yield the secret of Rossetti's belief that his old friend and master, Browning, had joined the conspiracy with Robert Buchanan "to hound him from the society of honest men." The clue to the mystery, I think, lies in the inordinate value which Rossetti put upon his own poem, "Jenny." This poem, because of its long and eventful career and the personal implications of its contents, had become identified by Rossetti with his own moral character. In *Fifine,* he read a running commentary upon "Jenny." If there was an element of madness in Rossetti's belief that Browning had attacked him, I think I can show that it was a madness not altogether without reason in it. The history of the personal and intellectual relationship between Robert Browning and Dante Gabriel Rossetti has hardly been more than suggested.[1] In the present paper I shall do little more than sketch a few of the events of their friendship from Rossetti's early idolatry of the elder poet to his complete repudiation of Browning in 1872. The tale of Rossetti's discovery of the anonymous *Pauline* in the British Museum in 1847,[2] and Rossetti's consequent taxing of Browning with the authorship, is not quite the beginning of the connection between the two. Earlier in the same year Browning had become, after Dante, the chief poet of the world to Rossetti, then an apprentice painter of nineteen years of age. "At last . . . ," says William Michael Rossetti in his account of this time,

everything took a secondary place in comparison with Robert Browning. *Paracelsus, Sordello, Pippa Passes, A Blot in the 'Scutcheon,* and the short poems in the *Bells and Pomegranates* series, were endless delights; endless were the readings, and endless the recitations. Allowing for a labyrinthine passage here and there, Rossetti never seemed to find this poet difficult to understand; he discerned in him plenty of sonorous rhythmical effect, and revelled in what, to some other readers, was mere crabbedness. Confronted with Browning, all else seemed pale and in neutral tint. Here was passion, observation, aspiration, medievalism, the dramatic perception of character, act, and incident. In short, if at this date Rossetti had been accomplished in the art of painting, he would have carried out in that art very much the same range of subject and treatment which he found in Browning's poetry.[3]

Indeed, we know that Browning's poem, "The Laboratory," was the subject of Rossetti's first watercolor. But the young Rossetti was a poet as well as a painter, and in this year he began at least two poems in Browning's manner, "A Last Confession" and "Jenny." Such was the quality of Rossetti's admiration for Browning that he had the distinction for many years of being almost the only admirer, save the author, of *Sordello*. He was in the habit of reading that poem to the Pre-Raphaelite Brothers at the rate of fifty pages at a sitting with all the will of an Ancient Mariner. This fact probably accounts in part for the early dissolution of the society. Rossetti's admiration survived the publication of *Christmas-Eve and Easter-Day*, *Men and Women*, *Dramatis Personae*, *The Ring and the Book*, and even *Hohenstiel-Schwangau*. In 1871 he was a little apprehensive over Browning's undertaking a Greek subject in *Balaustion's Adventure*, but he was sure that Browning could do it if anyone could. "Browning seems," he wrote, "likely to remain, with all his sins, the most original and varied mind, by long odds, which betakes itself to poetry in our time."[4]

The admiration was nourished and the affection reciprocated on personal acquaintance. The famous meeting at Browning's residence in Dorset Street on September 27, 1855, when Tennyson read "Maud" and Browning read "Fra Lippo Lippi," remained long in Rossetti's memory. The death of Mrs. Rossetti in February 1862 brought a quick and ready sympathy from Browning, for he had been bereaved of his wife the year before. Browning wrote a friend:

While I write my heart is sore for a great calamity just befallen poor Rossetti, which I only heard of last night: his wife, who had been, as an invalid, in the habit of taking laudanum, swallowed an overdose, was found by the poor fellow on his return from the working-men's class in the evening under the effects of it. Help was called in, the stomach pump used, but she died in the night, about a week ago: & there has hardly been a day when I have not thought "if I can, tomorrow, I will go & see him, & thank him for his book [Rossetti's translations], & return his sister's poems." Poor, dear fellow.[5]

There were many pleasant exchanges of friendliness during the Sixties. In 1863 Browning sent Rossetti a copy of *Selections from the Poetical Works of Robert Browning* which had been compiled by John Forster and Barry Cornwall (B. W. Proctor). Rossetti wrote in answer:

Concerning this book, all your lieges of oldest standing will feel some pangs of selfishness. "Had I," each will say, "but had the doing of it." For not even the poking of one's own fire, perhaps, is so peculiarly unapproachable a privilege as the insight into one's own poet.[6]

But as the decade progressed on toward 1870, Browning and Rossetti moved more and more in different social worlds. When Rossetti's poems appeared in 1870, Browning was indeed among the many who wrote to him in laudatory strain. This must have been the mere form of courtesy, for, as we shall see, it was not his true opinion.

Actually the publication of Rossetti's *Poems* on April 25, 1870, began a chain of events which was to end in the complete rupture of this long and cordial, if not intimate, friendship. The *Poems* went into several editions and caused much talk in literary circles. They finally brought forth Robert Buchanan's article in the *Contemporary Review* for October 1871, called "The Fleshly School of Poetry—Mr. D. G. Rossetti," which assailed Rossetti for his sensuality. This caused Rossetti's vindication of himself in the *Athenaeum* for December 1871, in an article called "The Stealthy School of Criticism," so named because Buchanan had not signed the attack with his own name, but had permitted the pseudonym "Thomas Maitland" to be used. Rossetti came off clearly the victor, but in May 1872 Buchanan issued his article in pamphlet form, enlarged and envenomed, but retaining the same title. The article in the *Contemporary Review*, as W. M. Rossetti testifies, had no ill effects upon Rossetti, but the pamphlet of 1872 drove him to the verge of madness.

Certain it is that, when the pamphlet-edition appeared (which was towards the middle of May 1872), with its greatly enhanced virus of imputation and suggestion, he received it in a spirit very different from that with which he had encountered the review-article, and had confuted it in *The Stealthy School of Criticism*. His fancies now ran away with him, and he thought that the pamphlet was a first symptom in a widespread conspiracy for crushing his fair fame as an artist and a man, and for hounding him out of honest society.[7]

Buchanan's pamphlet changed the course of Rossetti's life. The crisis was immediate. To cure his insomnia and anguish Rossetti took enormous doses of chloral and whisky. On one occasion, probably shortly after the appearance of the pamphlet, he startled a group of friends at a dinner party at William Bell Scott's house:

One day [says Scott] I had some friends to dinner: ten used to be my number, two or three times in the season before leaving town. On this particular day one of the friends was D.G.R.; we were loitering about the drawing-room waiting for the latest man, who was Gabriel himself. At last we heard a tremendous peal at the bell, and knocking, a great noise ascended the stair, and he burst in upon us, shouting out the name Robert Buchanan. . . . He was too excited to observe or to care who were present, and all the evening he continued unable to contain himself, or to avoid shouting out the name of his enemy.[8]

On June 2, 1872, William Michael Rossetti was with his

brother all day at No. 16 Cheyne Walk. "It was one of the most miserable days of my life," he says in the *Memoir*, "not to speak of his. From his wild ways of talking—about conspiracies and what not—I was astounded to perceive that he was, past question, not entirely sane."[9]

A day or two later Rossetti received from Browning a presentation copy of that poet's new volume, *Fifine at the Fair*, which had just been published. "Rossetti," says his brother,

looked into the book; and to the astonishment of by-standers, he at once fastened upon some lines at its close as being intended as an attack upon him, or as a spiteful reference to something which occurred, or might be alleged to have occurred at his house. In a moment he relented, with an effusion of tenderness to this old, attached, and illustrious friend; but in another moment the scarcely credible delusion returned. Browning was regarded as a leading member of the "conspiracy"; and, from first to last, I was never able to discern that this miserable bugbear had ever been expelled from the purlieus of my brother's mind. He saw no more of Browning, and communicated with him no more; and on one or two occasions when the great poet, the object of Rossetti's early and unbounded homage, kindly enquired of me concerning him, and expressed a wish to look him up, I was compelled to fence with the suggestion, lest worse should ensue—no doubt putting myself in a very absurd and unaccountable position. Whether Browning ever knew that Dante Rossetti had conceived a real dislike of him, or supposed himself to have motive of definite complaint, I am unable to say. He was certainly far too keen to miss seeing that there was something amiss, and something which was kept studiously unexplained.[10]

W. B. Scott also records that Rossetti believed that Browning's *Fifine at the Fair* "was entirely written about him, and against him, all the innuendoes and insinuations being aimed at him."[11] Writing his reminiscences, years later, William

Michael Rossetti confessed his complete inability to understand his brother's action, and finally set it down as "unreasonable prejudice." "My firm conviction is," he added, "that Browning never wrote or did anything hostile to my brother. . . ."[12]

In this manner ended a friendship of twenty-five years' standing. Rossetti and Browning never met again, and save that the elder poet continued to send copies of his works as they appeared, they never communicated. Rossetti, in wretched health, and in gradually worsening mental condition, lived the ten years of life which were now left to him as a recluse, shunning company, suffering hallucinations of persecution, and going abroad for the most part only after night had fallen. Browning continued in the highroad of his literary and social success. But was there nothing in Rossetti's suspicion that Browning had joined the conspiracy under Robert Buchanan's leadership against him? Does Browning's *Fifine* yield nothing that the fevered mind of Rossetti might reasonably think was intended as an attack against him? In the text of *Fifine* there is no allusion, no suggestion, to indicate that Browning is doing more than making his usual subtle analysis of one of his slippery characters. Commentators have therefore given the matter up, and have been content to call Rossetti mad. But in my opinion the critics have not seen what Rossetti saw in *Fifine*, because most of them have not read *Fifine* with the facts of Rossetti's recent history in mind. I think there was considerable ground for Rossetti's suspicions, and I think the clue to his actions lies in the history of the quarrel he had with Buchanan. In short, I think that Browning gave comfort and friendship to Rossetti's assailant, and that his poem, *Fifine*, is a commentary upon Rossetti's poem, "Jenny," a poem very near to Rossetti's heart, and the piece which had borne the brunt of Buchanan's attack.

The history of "Jenny" is a strange one, and as eventful as

the lives of most ladies of the heroine's class. Rossetti kept the poem by him for twenty-three years, writing and re-writing it from time to time in his earnest desire to perfect his treatment of a theme in which he was deeply interested. "*Jenny* (in a first form)," he says, "was written almost as early as *The Blessed Damozel,* which I wrote . . . when I was eighteen. . . . Of the first *Jenny,* perhaps fifty lines survive here and there, but I felt it was quite beyond me then (a world I was then happy enough to be a stranger to), and later I re-wrote it completely."[13] The year of the first draft of "Jenny" was 1847, a notable one, for in that year Rossetti became a painter, a poet, and discovered the poetry of Blake and of Browning. The poem of 1870 differs enormously, no doubt, from the first draft: new lines and new incidents have been added. But the original situation of the poem, which is its chief point, and its manner are constant from 1847 to 1870, and in the latter year a number of critics, friendly and unfriendly, were still able to detect the influence of Browning in the dramatic monologue in spite of the years and changes. One may observe also the hand of Blake in the choice of subject and the sympathy of treatment. Blake was a close second to Browning in Rossetti's affections in 1847, and had already contributed to "The Blessed Damozel." The seed from which "Jenny" sprang may be the quatrain from Blake's poem called "London":

> But most, through midnight streets I hear
> How the youthful harlot's curse
> Blasts the new-born infant's tear,
> And blights with plagues the marriage-hearse.

Further, William Bell Scott's conviction that his own poem, "Rosabell," afterwards called "Mary Anne," in which the poet philosophized upon a harlot's life in Edinburgh, was the true genesis of Rossetti's "Jenny" and the picture *Found,*[14] the two most notable instances of Rossetti's handling of a contemporary subject, may well have some foundation in fact. The mediocre artist often sees the excellent themes which he has handled ineptly taken from him by a master craftsman. Such was Greene's complaint against Shakespeare. Whatever its starting point, "Jenny" was Rossetti's own, and moreover it was a daring poem for its day. Jenny is a harlot of London, and the speaker of the poem, or rather the thinker of it, is a "young and thoughtful man of the world," who has come home with Jenny to her lodgings at the evening's end. The thoughtful young man soliloquizes upon the lot of the Jennys of the world while she sleeps, sitting upon the floor, her head upon his knees. So intimate (in the Browningesque manner) was the treatment, and so daring was the subject at the middle of the century, that Rossetti did not publish the poem. As we shall see, he feared the opinions of his own family.

The poem continued to grow in Rossetti's mind. The painting *Found*, which is a slightly different aspect of the same subject, done in pigment instead of rhyme, occupied Rossetti steadily during October 1854 and for some months thereafter.[15] The painting supplied fresh and vivid illustration to the poem. "*Jenny*," says W. M. Rossetti, "appears to have reached substantial completion about 1858. . . ."[16] In the next year Rossetti sent "Jenny" with a few other pieces to Ruskin, eager to know what that great moralist thought of the poem. The reply was not long in coming. Ruskin wrote,

I have read *Jenny*, and nearly all the other poems, with great care and with great admiration. In many of the highest qualities they are entirely great. But I should be sorry if you laid them before the public entirely in their present state.

I do not think *Jenny* would be understood but by few; and even of those few the majority would be offended by the mode of the treatment. *The character of the speaker himself is too doubt-*

ful. He seems, even to me, anomalous. He reasons and feels entirely like a wise and just man—yet is occasionally drunk and brutal: no affection for the girl shows itself—his throwing the money into her hair is disorderly—he is altogether a disorderly person. The right feeling is unnatural in him, and does not therefore truly touch us.

I don't mean that an entirely right-minded person never keeps a mistress: but, if he does, he either loves her—or, not loving her, would blame himself, and be horror-struck for himself no less than for her, in such a moralizing fit.

My chief reason for not sending it to Thackeray [i. e. for the *Cornhill Magazine*] is this discordance and *too great boldness for common readers.* But also in many verses it is unmelodious and incomplete. "Fail" does not rhyme to "belle," nor "Jenny" to "guinea." You can write perfect verses if you choose, and you should never write imperfect ones. . . .[17]

If one is inclined to think that there are more possible psychological states than are dreamed of in John Ruskin's morality, one must admit, nevertheless, that he put his finger upon the cleft in the armor of the poem. Ruskin's criticism gave Rossetti pause, and "Jenny" was not to be published for twelve years. But the evidence favors the opinion that the poet did not think sufficiently of Ruskin's strictures to change his poem materially. The criticism troubled him. The difficulties that so often beset inept users of the dramatic monologue were his. He had been so intent upon his subject and the figure of Jenny that he had not paid proper attention to the character of the speaker. And since the speaker's character suggested Rossetti himself, Ruskin's criticism had something of the force of a comment upon Rossetti's moral rightness, rather than of a condemnation of the bad art of the piece.

But in 1859 Ruskin's comments seemed rather blind. Even William Michael Rossetti, who was a moralist of parts himself, thought Ruskin had missed the point of the poem. Ruskin's remarks are interesting, he admits, "but it appears

to me that he had misapprehended the relation—the merely
casual and extempore relation—which the poem intends to
represent between the male speaker and Jenny."[18]

When Ruskin failed him, Rossetti sent his poems in October of 1860 to William Allingham, and at the end of November received them from him. The criticisms accompanying
the poems had not touched upon the problem which most
interested the author, and on the twenty-ninth of November
he addressed a special inquiry to Allingham:

> Would you tell me as regards *Jenny* (which I reckon the most
> serious thing I have written), whether there is any objection you
> see in the treatment, or in any side of the subject left untouched
> which ought to be included? I really believe I shall print the
> things now, and see whether the magic presence of proof-
> sheets revives my muse sufficiently for a new poem or two to
> add to them. . . .[19]

But Rossetti's plans for the publication of his poems were set
aside, partly by his marriage to Miss Siddal and the desperate
condition of her health, and partly by the formation of
William Morris's great company of craftsmen, of which
Rossetti was a member. Instead of poems, Rossetti published his translations, *The Early Italian Poets,* in the spring
of 1861. In this book he advertised that he would soon
publish a volume to be called *Dante at Verona and Other
Poems.* But these plans came to naught. On the 11th of
February 1862, Mrs. Rossetti died from an overdose of
laudanum. She had dined on the preceding evening with her
husband and Swinburne, and after dinner Rossetti saw her
home, and hurried away, as he said, to the Working Man's
class in which he was interested. When he returned late at
night he discovered her desperate condition and called
doctors, but she died in the morning without regaining
consciousness. Mrs. Rossetti was an invalid, and habitually

used drugs under the doctor's orders. But she was ill and desperately unhappy in a growing conviction that her husband had married her, after their engagement of ten years, through a mistaken sense of loyalty, when in the meantime he had fallen deeply in love with another woman. At any rate, there was a certainty in the minds of some[20] that Mrs. Rossetti's death was not an accident. Rossetti suffered agonies of remorse, accusing himself of having neglected her; and some strange impulse of renunciation impelled him to put his manuscript book of poems under her hair beside her face as she lay in her coffin. It was probably as much his absorption in work, as an interest in another woman, for which he reproached himself, and the complete sacrifice of his poems, written in a manuscript book she had given him, was all the retribution he could now make. When Mrs. Rossetti was buried on the 17th of February, "Jenny" was laid in the grave with her.

"Jenny," a daring poem in 1847, was still daring in 1860. But by 1870 it had lost quite a little of its boldness. Baudelaire had come to be known in England during the Sixties, and Swinburne, his vicar there, had given notoriety to harlots far more shameless than Jenny. One wonders what Rossetti's emotions were as he saw Swinburne's *Poems and Ballads* run their course. Swinburne was Rossetti's pupil and he had reaped a harvest of notoriety and censure, not a little mingled with admiration. The friends of Rossetti urged him to take his place among the poets of the day, and this meant that he would have "to recover the MS. buried in his wife's coffin, and thus to obtain possession, not only of copies of several poems completer than the copies (made up from scraps and reminiscence) which were already in his hands, but also of some compositions of which he retained no example whatever. The chief among these was the important production named *Jenny*."[21] Upon October 10th, 1869, the manuscripts were disinterred, and on the 14th Rossetti wrote,

WILLIAM C. DeVANE

I went to-day to see those MSS. at the Doctor's, and I shall be able to have them in a few days. They are in a disappointing state. The things I have already seem mostly perfect, and there is a great hole right through all the leaves of *Jenny*, which was the thing I most wanted. A good deal is lost; but I have no doubt the things as they are will enable me, with a little more rewriting and a good memory and the rough copies I have, to reestablish the whole in a perfect state. . . .[22]

Twelve days later Rossetti called at his brother's house and read the reconstructed "Jenny" to him. It is certain that some changes and additions were made in the poem at this time.[23]

The care with which Rossetti at last ushered his poems into the world argues that he ventured with a good deal of apprehension. While the volume was still in the press he wrote to F. S. Ellis, his publisher,

Would you send me the proofs of the fly-leaf & binding as soon as you get them. Also please let me know if Forman seems frightened at *Jenny* or anything else.[24]

On the 11th of April, 1870, still before the publication of the poems, Rossetti wrote to Professor C. E. Norton concerning his forthcoming volume in language which he was to use later in answering Buchanan's attack:

I hope that when you get my book you will agree with me as to the justness of including all it contains. I say this because there are a few things—and notably a poem called *Jenny*—which will raise objections in some other quarters. I only know that they have been written neither recklessly nor aggressively (moods which I think are sure to result in the ruin of Art), but from a true impulse to deal with subjects which seem to me capable of being brought rightly within Art's province. Of my own position I feel sure, and so wait the final result without apprehension.[25]

On April 25, 1870, the *Poems* were published and the chorus of laudation began in the reviews. Rossetti had judiciously selected his reviewers—"working the oracle" it was called—and this fact more than any other precipitated the attack upon him in the next year. But in spite of the praise, it was not until May 24 that Rossetti could muster up courage enough to send his poems to his elderly aunt, and he did it then only because she was about to get them without his help.

I just hear from Mama [he wrote], with a pang of remorse, that you have ordered a copy of my *Poems*. You may be sure I did not fail to think of you when I inscribed copies to friends and relatives; but, to speak frankly, I was deterred from sending it to you by the fact of the book including one poem (*Jenny*) of which I felt uncertain whether you would be pleased with it. I am not ashamed of having written it (indeed I assure you that I would never have written it if I thought it unfit to be read with good results); but I feared it might startle you somewhat, and so put off sending you the book. I now do so by this post, and hope that some if not all of the pieces may be quite to your taste. Indeed, I hope that even *Jenny* may be so, for my mother likes it on the whole the best in the volume, after some consideration.[26]

With the approbation of his friends and his family, not to mention the fact that the *Poems* sold well for poetry, Rossetti passed more than a year free from apprehension. October 1871 found him at Kelmscott painting and writing poetry and in a cheerful mood. In that month the first blow fell, for eighteen months after the publication of his poems the *Contemporary Review* printed the article signed by Thomas Maitland and called "The Fleshly School of Poetry—Mr. D. G. Rossetti." As we have seen, the attack did not at first cause him great anguish. He presently found out that Maitland was a pseudonym for his old enemy Buchanan, from

whom he had expected attack.[27] But what Rossetti had long
feared would happen had happened, and Buchanan's unmitigated rancor gradually ate into his mind. Rossetti had
anticipated precisely the points of his enemy's charge, for
"Jenny" was, with three other poems, the salient selected.
The *Review* ran in part:

Whether he [Rossetti] is writing of the holy Damozel, or of
the Virgin herself, or of Lilith, or Helen, or of Dante, or of Jenny
the street-walker, he is fleshly all over, from the roots of his
hair to the tip of his toes; never a true lover merging his identity
into that of the beloved one; never spiritual, never tender; always
self-conscious and aesthetic. "Nothing," says a modern writer,
"in human life is so utterly remorseless—not love, not hate, not
ambition, not vanity—as the artistic or aesthetic instinct morbidly
developed to the suppression of conscience and feeling"; and
at no time do we feel more fully impressed with this truth than
after the perusal of "Jenny," in some respects the finest poem in
the volume, and in all respects the poem best indicative of the
true quality of the writer's humanity. It is a production which
bears signs of having been suggested by Mr. Buchanan's quasi-
lyrical poems, which it copies in the style of title, and particularly by "Artist and Model"; but certainly Mr. Rossetti cannot be accused, as the Scottish writer has been accused, of
maudlin sentiment and affected tenderness. The two first lines
are perfect:—

Lazy laughing languid Jenny,
Fond of a kiss and fond of a guinea;

And the poem is a soliloquy of the poet—who has been spend-
ing the evening in dancing at a casino—over his partner, whom
he has accompanied home to the usual style of lodgings occupied by such ladies, and who has fallen asleep with her head
upon his knee, while he wonders, in a wretched pun—

Whose person or whose purse may be
The lodestar of your reverie?

The soliloquy is long, and in some parts beautiful, despite a very constant suspicion that we are listening to an emasculated Mr. Browning, whose whole tone and gesture, so to speak, is occasionally introduced with startling fidelity; and there are here and there glimpses of actual thought and insight, over and above the picturesque touches which belong to the writer's true profession, such as that where, at daybreak—

> lights creep in
> Past the gauze curtains half drawn-to,
> And *the lamp's doubled shade grows blue.*

What we object to in this poem is not the subject, which any writer may be fairly left to choose for himself; nor any bad blood bursting through in special passages. But the whole tone, without being more than usually coarse, seems heartless. There is not a drop of piteousness in Mr. Rossetti. He is just to the outcast, even generous; severe to the seducer; sad even at the spectacle of lust in dimity and fine ribbons. Notwithstanding all this, and a certain delicacy and refinement of treatment unusual with this poet, the poem repels and revolts us, and we like Mr. Rossetti least after its perusal. We are angry with the fleshly person at last. The "Blessed Damozel" puzzled us, the "Song of the Bower" amused us, the love-sonnet depressed and sickened us, but "Jenny," though distinguished by less special viciousness of thought and style than any of these, fairly makes us lose patience. We detect its fleshliness at a glance; we perceive that the scene was fascinating less through its human tenderness than because it, like all the others, possessed an inherent quality of animalism. "The whole work" ("Jenny"), writes Mr. Swinburne, "is worthy to fill its place for ever as one of the most perfect poems of an age or generation. There is just the same life-blood and breadth of poetic interest in this episode of a London street and lodging as in the song of 'Troy Town' and the song of 'Eden Bower'; just as much, and no jot more,"—to which last statement we cordially assent; for there is bad blood in all, and breadth of poetic interest in none. "Vengeance of Jenny's case," indeed!—when such a poet as this comes fawning over her, with tender compassion in one eye and aesthetic enjoyment in the other.[28]

Compared to Rossetti, Buchanan concluded, Swinburne "was only a little mad boy letting off squibs."

Now there were many things in this grossly unfair assault upon "Jenny" which would strike madness to Rossetti's soul, but perhaps only three need concern us here. In the first place, Buchanan confused Rossetti, the poet, with the speaker in "Jenny," the young and thoughtful man of the world who went home with her. Next, Buchanan suggested that he himself had provided Rossetti with the subject of "Jenny." Finally, and this was an accusation which always cut Rossetti deeply, Buchanan charged Rossetti with a degree of plagiarism; in "Jenny," he said, "we are listening to an emasculated Mr. Browning, whose whole tone and gesture, so to speak, is occasionally introduced with startling fidelity. . . ." Perhaps the crowning blow was that Rossetti began to find that a very considerable and surprising number of people whose judgment he valued were shocked into agreement with Buchanan.

As we know, Rossetti's answer appeared in the *Athenaeum* during December 1871; it was admirably named "The Stealthy School of Criticism," and was a dignified and successful rebuttal of Buchanan. He answers specifically the charges that he is himself the speaker in "Jenny" and that Buchanan suggested his poem. He cannot, as yet, answer the third charge because Browning is still his friend and admired master, and it would be ungrateful, and to some extent untrue, to deny that the elder poet to a considerable degree had given him eyes, ears, and method. But the center of Rossetti's defense of "Jenny" in "The Stealthy School of Criticism" is a vindication of the psychology of the young man of the world who soliloquizes upon the harlot and her fate:

The last of the four quotations grouped by the critic as con-
clusive examples [i.e. of Rossetti's sensuality] consists of two
lines from *Jenny*. Neither some thirteen years ago, when I wrote
this poem, nor last year when I published it, did I fail to foresee
impending charges of recklessness and aggressiveness, or to
perceive that even some among those could really *read* the poem,
and acquit me on these grounds, might still hold that the thought
in it had better have dispensed with the situation which serves
it for framework. Nor did I omit to consider how far a treatment from without might here be possible. But the motive
powers of art reverse the requirement of science, and demand
first of all an *inner* standing-point. The heart of such a mystery
as this must be plucked from the very world in which it beats
or bleeds; and the beauty and pity, the self-questioning and all
questionings which it brings with it, can come with full force
only from the mouth of one alive to its whole appeal, such as
the speaker put forward in the poem,—that is, of a young and
thoughtful man of the world. To such a speaker, many half-
cynical revulsions of feeling and reverie, and a recurrent presence
of the impressions of beauty (however artificial) which first
brought him within such a circle of influence, would be inevitable
features of the dramatic relations portrayed. Here again I can
give the lie, in hearing of honest readers, to the base of trivial
ideas which my critic labours to connect with the poem. There
is another little charge, however, which this minstrel in mufti
brings against *Jenny*, namely, one of plagiarism from that very
poetic self of his which the tutelary prose does but enshroud for
the moment. This question can, fortunately, be settled with ease
by others who have read my critic's poems; and thus I need the
less regret that, not happening myself to be in that position, I
must be content to rank with those who cannot pretend to an
opinion on the subject.[29]

Of course Rossetti was right, but men have continued from
his day to our own to state that "the 'young and thoughtful
man of the world,' postulated by Rossetti as the only speaker
from whose mouth the beauty and pity and questioning of

the poem can come, is again himself,"[30] and to impute therefore a moral unrightness to Rossetti.

Buchanan was not silenced: he answered briefly in the
Athenaeum for December 30, 1871. In the hue and cry
which followed during the first months of 1872 Rossetti had
good cause to think that most conservative readers were
against him. In May, Buchanan returned savagely to the
attack with a pamphlet called *The Fleshly School of Poetry
and other Phenomena of the Day.* The nucleus of this
pamphlet was the article of the year before, but now it was
enlarged and envenomed. Espousing the cause of a middle-
class prudery and firmly convinced of the sinfulness of the
flesh, Buchanan now found Rossetti to be symptomatic of
the evil days upon which English society had fallen. He
prepared elaborately for his attack upon Rossetti: first he
attempted to estimate the influence of "leg," as a token of
sensuality, upon modern society, and concluded desperately
that

It is only in fashionable rooms and in the stalls of the theatre
that Leg is at a discount; but that is not because life there is
more innocent and modest, but because Leg is in the higher
circles altogether eclipsed by its two most formidable rivals—
Bosom and Back.[31]

The way thus cleared, Buchanan approached Rossetti, the
last word in vice, by paying his respects at length to Baudelaire and Swinburne. And then he arrived at Rossetti. In
this new assault the comments upon "Jenny" are considerably augmented, and now Buchanan speaks boldly of "Mr.
Rossetti soliloquizing over Jenny in her London lodging
. . . ," denying Rossetti any impersonal or dramatic powers
whatever. Further, he adds this stinging touch:

Having so far complied with Mr. Rossetti's request, and re-
examined "The House of Life," I retain unchanged my impres-

sion that the sort of house meant should be nameless, but is probably the identical one where the writer found "Jenny."[32]

A moment later these words occur:

The first [poem] is "A Last Confession," which describes, in Mr. Browning's favourite manner, how an Italian, maddened by jealousy, murdered his mistress. This Italian, it may be remarked, is very like our author, for besides being disagreeably affected, he had a morbid habit of *brooding* over unclean ideas and suspicions. . . .[33]

This should have been sufficient, but Buchanan was not content until he had pointed out a model of excellence for Rossetti:

To my thinking, there is no grander passage in literature than that tremendous scene between Ottilia [Buchanan means Ottima] and her paramour, in "Pippa Passes"; no one accuses the author of that, and of the "Ring and the Book," of neglecting love or overlooking the body; and yet I do daily homage to the genius of Robert Browning.[34]

Finally, in the first and longest of three appendices, devoted to further criticism of "Jenny," Rossetti's name is linked once more to Browning's:

The metre at the opening reminds us of one which Mr. Browning uses with characteristic force, but which in Mr. Rossetti's hands soon degenerates into feeble octosyllabic verse.

Is it any wonder, then, that Rossetti, a man most sensitive to criticism in the best of his time and now already shaken in health, should conclude that there was a "widespread conspiracy for crushing his fair fame as an artist and a man," and should become "not entirely sane"? "Jenny," which through many years had come to be to Rossetti the symbol of his poetical and moral nature, was now described as morbid lust. The speaker in "Jenny," who had become even to Rossetti identified with himself, was nothing but an unmitigated sensualist. *The House of Life,* sonnets written to his wife describing with religious fervor the ritual of love, were the songs of the brothel!

The crisis of Rossetti's illness came on June 2, 1872. A day or two later he read Browning's *Fifine at the Fair,* and the friendship of twenty-five years came to an end.

The question, then, which rises from a consideration of the circumstances is this: What is there in Browning's *Fifine* which, though it escaped the comprehension of reasonable friends, could have been conjured by the harassed mind of Rossetti into an attack upon himself? In the first place, it is worthy of note that Browning wrote *Fifine,* according to the manuscript in the library of Balliol College, between December 1871 and April 1872, the very time when the clamor aroused by the Buchanan-Rossetti controversy was at its height in London. In April Browning told his friend Domett that he had "just finished a poem, the most metaphysical and boldest he had written since *Sordello,* and was very doubtful as to its reception by the public."[35] Indeed, Browning seems to have been almost as apprehensive about *Fifine* as Rossetti had been about "Jenny," and for somewhat the same reasons. The woman who gives title to Browning's poem is of the same ancient profession as Jenny, and the hero or speaker is, as in "Jenny," a rather too thoughtful young man of the world who ponders upon the situation of the gypsy girl, Fifine, and upon his own emotions concerning her.

It was in Pornic, a small seacoast town of Brittany, at the fair of St. Gillies that Browning saw the handsome gypsy rope-dancer who suggested Fifine to him, and the scene of the poem is Pornic in fair-time, though the idea of the poem did not crystallize until several years later in London. The speaker in *Fifine* is a man of the world of subtle intelligence, who passes through the fair with his wife, Elvire, a shadowy figure who is little more than the speaker's conscience, his better self. The body of the poem is the speaker's justification, through some of Browning's most cherished principles, of his sensual yearnings for the handsome gypsy girl. He thinks it possible to love Elvire, a "spiritual lady," and at the same time to love Fifine, admittedly a loose woman, in the flesh. The poem is one of Browning's cleverest pieces of "case-making" for a slippery character. He made so good a case, indeed, that he threw not a few of his followers into consternation. The casuist justifying sensuality by quoting Browning was Satan quoting scripture.

There was no need, however, to misapprehend Browning, for the end of the poem clears all. The young man who walks through the fair philosophizing to his wife puts gold into Fifine's tambourine, and as a consequence "finds" a note from her in his glove at the end of his journey. He dashes away from his wife with the purpose, as he says, of clearing up the "misunderstanding" with Fifine, knowing that he will remain away longer than the five minutes he gives himself, and knowing too that if he does not return promptly he runs the danger of losing his wife forever.

The body of the poem is the speaker's casuistical argument; all the action—the finding of the letter from Fifine, the confession that he has put gold into her tambourine, his dashing away to the assignation—all these are crowded into the last twenty lines of the poem. The casuistry of the speaker, by a most sudden turn, is revealed as casuistry by his deeds.

How similar, then, and yet how different, is the situation in *Fifine* from that in "Jenny." While the young and thoughtful man of the world muses upon the harlot in each case, Rossetti's young man leaves Jenny's lodgings at daybreak, innocent in act, compassionate in heart, after flinging gold into Jenny's hair; Browning's young man, in the midst of his musing, slips gold into Fifine's tambourine, and presently, in a most adulterous mood, goes off to encounter her. The moral philosophizings of these two thoughtful young men lead to totally dissimilar actions. Is it not as if Browning had answered Rossetti's "Jenny" through his own *Fifine*, saying, "your young man would not have left Jenny with that innocent, compassionate, wondering heart. If I know anything of human nature, the affair would have ended very differently indeed! They that touch pitch will be defiled." When one remembers also that Rossetti in his own mind had identified himself with the hero of "Jenny," one begins to see how, as William Michael Rossetti said, some lines at the close of *Fifine* convinced the fevered mind of Rossetti that Browning had joined the "conspiracy" against him.

Assuredly Browning meant no attack upon Rossetti's moral character. Yet I believe with equal certainty that Browning wrote *Fifine* with "Jenny" in mind. To him, I think, it was a mere literary disagreement concerning a point of human nature, and he as master in those regions, "subtlest psychologist of the soul in song," was recording his own opinion. Browning had a tendency, which grew upon him as the years went on, to challenge in his verse his contemporaries' readings of life as well as their actions. For example, "The Glove" (1845) is a commentary upon Leigh Hunt's poem, "The Glove and the Lions"; "The Lost Leader" (1845) is a commentary upon Wordsworth's acceptance of a pension from the Civil List in 1842 and the Laureateship in 1843. There, indeed, are both the "handful of silver" and the "riband to stick in his coat." *Christmas-Eve and Easter-Day*, besides being a survey of religious ideas in 1850, is a commentary upon Strauss's *Leben Jesu*. Several poems in *Men and Women* show Browning to be a controversialist, willing to speak for the ideas he holds, and convinced that the function of the poet is to express himself upon contemporary topics. "Bishop Blougram" used Cardinal Wiseman, first Roman Catholic Archbishop in England, as a model. "Cleon" has recently been shown to be Browning's answer to Matthew Arnold's "Empedocles."[36] Almost the whole of *Dramatis Personae* (1864) is controversial in character.[37] Thereafter for ten years half of the poems Browning wrote are upon contemporaneous subjects and filled with topical remarks. The *Pacchiarotto* volume of 1876 is a running commentary, in part, upon contemporary poets and critics. It is possible that the poem, "House," with its significant first line, "Shall I sonnet-sing you about myself?" and the succeeding corroborative detail, may refer to Rossetti and his sonnet-sequence, *The House of Life*.[38] The whole tendency culminates in the *Parleyings* of 1887. In the midst of this period, flanked on one side by *Hohenstiel-Schwangau*, a portrait of Napoleon III, and on the other by *Red Cotton Night-Cap Country*, the account of a celebrated case of suicide in France, came *Fifine* in 1872. This is the time, moreover, when Browning, exhausted by *The Ring and the Book*, was looking about him eagerly for subjects.

Fifine was written, as we have seen, when the Buchanan-Rossetti controversy was at its height. That Browning followed the quarrel with interest there is no room to doubt. His friend Domett recorded that

He did not much admire Rossetti's poetry, 'hated all affectation.' He laughed at the cant about 'délicate harmony' of his rhymes about Haymarket [i.e., "Jenny"]. He quoted Buchanan's parody of them, adding a line or two of his own, similarly rhymed:

> But grog would be sweeter
> And stronger and warmer, etc.[39]

Moreover, Browning's opinion of Rossetti's poetry was essentially in agreement with Buchanan's. At about the same time that he wrote Rossetti the conventional laudatory letter of thanks for the presentation copy of *Poems,* he was writing in another strain to Isa Blagden:

> Yes, I have read Rossetti's Poems, and poetical they are— *scented* with poetry, as it were, like trifles of various sorts you take out of a cedar or sandal-wood box. You know I hate the *effeminacy* of his school; the men that dress up like women; that use obsolete forms, too, and archaic accentuations—fancy a man calling it a lily'—lilies' and so on. Swinburne started this,' with other like Belialisms; witness his 'harp-player,' etc. It is quite different when the object is to *imitate* old ballad-writing, when the thing might be. Then, how I hate 'Love,' as a lubberly naked young man putting his arms here and his wings there, about a pair of lovers; a fellow they would like to kick away in the reality.[40]

These criticisms Browning communicated to Buchanan, possibly forming but certainly strengthening Buchanan's opinion. "Shortly after the publication of my review," wrote Buchanan, "Tennyson avowed to me *vivâ voce* that he considered Rossetti's sonnet on 'Nuptial Sleep' the 'filthiest thing he had ever read.' Browning in private talks had been equally emphatic."[41] It is certain, then, that Browning agreed with Buchanan and gave him comfort. He continued his intimacy with the critic, while George Henry Lewes, for example, hardly more of a friend to Rossetti than was Browning, instantly upon reading the attack upon Rossetti, cut Buchanan's acquaintance.

It is certain that Browning had no realization of the part he had played in Rossetti's catastrophe. He tried several times after 1872 to renew his former friendship. To him the disagreement was not at all personal; it was merely a difference between literary men in the reading of human nature. But Rossetti, reading the ending of *Fifine,* saw clearly the reference to "Jenny." Always identifying himself with the thoughtful young man of the world, he saw himself accused once more of fleshliness. Browning, his admired master, his friend as well as Buchanan's, had joined with that enemy in attacking him. What more Rossetti read than Browning intended, who can say? Did his overwrought mind see in those closing lines, in which the young man bids his wife, if he does not return quickly, to "slip from flesh and blood, and play the ghost again," a reference to those old rumors about his wife's suicide? Whatever he saw, he could scarcely believe such an attack possible from his old, attached, and illustrious friend; but the incredible delusion persisted. His peace was poisoned. For ten years he was a recluse, seldom seen by day, a hypochondriac, a victim of chloral and whisky. He never found health and peace again. To him it seemed that Browning had joined Buchanan in the conspiracy to ruin his fair fame among honest men. And even after ten years Rossetti could say to Hall Caine, who reported to him certain unfavorable comments upon "Jenny," that "it was the old story, which began ten years earlier, and would go on until he had been hunted and hounded into his grave."[42]

[1946]

F. E. L. PRIESTLEY

BLOUGRAM'S APOLOGETICS

,

MOST INTERPRETATIONS of "Bishop Blougram's Apology"
have started with the assumption that the poem represents one of Browning's attempts to present the best that a
generally contemptible character can say for himself, "an
attempt to make a case for a sophistical and indulgent priest
at his possible worst."[1] Such interpretations give to the word
apology its popular meaning of a confession of error with a
plea for lenience in judgment. As Miss Naish pointed out
long ago, Browning's reported comments to Duffy are hard
to reconcile with this view of the poem; if Browning drew a
portrait of Wiseman as "a vulgar, fashionable priest, justifying his own cowardice,"[2] yet declared that the portrait was
not a satire, and had "nothing hostile about it,"[3] then Browning was either a hypocrite more brazen than Gigadibs
thought Blougram, or incredibly naive.

As a matter of fact, the critics in general, even Miss Naish, have paid too little attention to the significance of the title, and far too little attention to Gigadibs. The whole monologue is an *apology* in the sense of a piece of apologetics; its whole course is dictated by Gigadibs. In no other monologue of Browning's is the *muta persona* so important; in no other monologue is Browning so careful to keep us aware of the presence of the auditor. Every word of the Bishop's is uttered with a full understanding of the character of his guest, and of what his guest is thinking.

Consider for a moment who Gigadibs is, and why he is in the Bishop's presence. Gigadibs is a thirty year old journalist, ambitious for "success" (if his name means anything, success in terms of a gig and "dibs"). His contributions to *Blackwood's* have so far attracted no attention; his scholarly work, as yet unprinted, consists of "two points in Hamlet's soul Unseized by the Germans yet"; his one success is an imitation of Dickens, a piece of sensational journalism with a secondhand literary flavour. His mind is that of the ordinary third-rate journalist; the Bishop calls him "You . . . the rough and ready man who write apace, Read somewhat seldomer, think perhaps even less"; he is on the alert for the sensational, the dramatic antithesis, "the honest thief, the tender murderer, The superstitious atheist"; he needs simple labels, neat summary phrases, "man of sense and learning too, The able to think yet act, the this, the that," to embody these dramatic journalistic contrasts. Phrases, indeed, serve him instead of thought; he has never pursued thoughts far enough to reach solid ground; his opinions are "loose cards, Flung daily down, and not the same way twice."

In his own estimation, however, Gigadibs is no ordinary figure. He is an artist-soul, with the artist's nobility of aim and stern integrity; "clever to a fault"; proud of his scepticism, since to him unbelief is a sign of honest thinking; proud of his vague aspirations, of his insistence on being himself, "imperial, plain and true," proud of his rigid certainty that "truth is truth."

He has come to interview the Bishop with a purpose perfectly evident to Blougram from the start. To Gigadibs, it is a self-evident proposition that intelligence and religious faith are incompatible. Consequently, Blougram must be either an imbecile or a hypocrite, a fool or a knave. And he is obviously no fool. Gigadibs is confident that, if granted an interview, he, the shrewd journalist, the trained ferret, can surely penetrate the pretence, and expose the impostor; through his skilful questioning, Blougram can be led to make "The Eccentric Confidence," to admit, at least by implication, that "he's quite above their humbug in his heart."

His very presence is an insult to the Bishop. The problem facing Blougram is quite clear; Gigadibs is a recognizable type, and represents a familiar point of view. To insist that a man may be intelligent and yet accept the articles of Christian faith would merely confirm Gigadibs in his belief that the Bishop is a hypocrite. Moreover, Blougram, nettled by the reporter's smug self-conceit, his secure conviction of the rightness of his own point of view, his patronizing assumption of superior integrity, is in no mood for defence. Gigadibs has arrived, has spoken his home truths, has challenged Blougram to say what he can for his own way of life, assuming always that his own way of life is the only one compatible with truth, honesty, and a lofty morality. Blougram is far from ready to admit that his own is the vulnerable position. He is not defending, but attacking. He has no great hope of changing Gigadibs' prejudices; he can perhaps make him realize that even the Gigadibsian philosophy, beautiful as it is in its simplicity, is not uniquely coherent and reasonable. Being a skilled apologist, he recognizes the necessity for attacking on his opponent's ground; since Gigadibs would scornfully reject all the Bishop's premises, the arguments must proceed from premises acceptable to the sceptic. Throughout, Blougram uses the apologetic method, stating Gigadibs' objections fairly and strongly, then replying to them. The stages in the argument are quite clear in the Bishop's mind as he drives Gigadibs systematically from one position to another, at every point anticipating the movements of his hearer's thoughts.

The Bishop is so much master of the situation, so much superior to his opponent, that he permits himself flourishes or scores a point with insulting ease. The whole performance is shot through with irony, and Blougram enjoys it. He enjoys particularly giving Gigadibs the impression that he is about to hear what he has come to hear. ("These hot long ceremonies of our church Cost us a little—oh, they pay the price, You take me—amply pay it!" Is this a bit of the "truth that peeps Over the glasses' edge?" Or does "price" hold two possible meanings?) Gigadibs' naive conviction that a few glasses of wine will lead an intelligent prelate into indiscreet utterance, and the sight of the eager face across the table, waiting for the wine to work and the eccentric confidence to flow, offer Blougram tempting opportunities. He opens and closes the interview on the same theme: he begins by explaining, to Gigadibs' embarrassment, the sort of confidence Gigadibs expects, and ends by a challenge to Gigadibs to publish what he has learned. The full irony of the challenge is apparent only to those who stop to consider exactly what Gigadibs has learned in the course of the conversation. That will appear if we follow the conversation step by step.

As it opens, Blougram is examining Gigadibs' charges against him, his grounds for despising him. These are: first, that the Bishop's official position implies the possession of a religious faith which in Gigadibs' opinion is impossible to an intelligent man; and secondly, that the Bishop is less ascetic and otherworldly than a bishop, in Gigadibs' opinion, ought to be. If these charges were being made by a pious ascetic, they would be coherent; but they are proceeding from a sceptic and secularist, from one who denies the validity of the religious ideal and the utility of the ascetic ideal. Blougram at once proceeds to the attack. When Gigadibs condemns Blougram's way of life, what is his criterion? What is the ideal way of life by which he is measuring Blougram's? Gigadibs has not thought the matter out; he is sure only that he would like to be something distinguished (Blougram offers an anticlimactic trio of possibilities) and that the chief quality to be sought is integrity, which of course the Bishop lacks. Even as Pope, Blougram could not, thinks Gigadibs, realize the majestic ideal of being himself, "imperial, plain and true."

At this point, a less skilful apologist would have at once challenged Gigadibs' assumption of the unworthiness of the Bishop's way of life. But Blougram is patient and shrewd. The only approach to Gigadibs is through premises he will accept. By way of preliminary groundwork, then, the Bishop establishes the basic premise that a plan of life must relate to life as it is, not to an "abstract intellectual plan of life," but to the life "a man, who is man and nothing more, may lead." This is a premise which Gigadibs must accept. As a sceptic, he cannot admit otherworldly criteria; any admission that man is more than man, the natural being, makes his whole case against Blougram collapse. Measured by his own this-worldly criterion, then, is Gigadibs' plan of life superior to the Bishop's? If mundane values are the only ones we can accept, whose life is the better fitted to realize those values? This question, framed playfully in the "cabin" analogy, confronts Gigadibs at the outset with the basic problem of values, and tends to force him into a recognition of the inconsistency of his own axiology. If no other values than the simply material must guide our plan of life, then why is not the life of a bishop a choice one, since it brings the good things of this world (apart from any other good things)? Why will not Gigadibs be a bishop too?

Gigadibs' answer comes rapidly; he can't believe in any revelation called divine; that is, believe "fixedly And absolutely and exclusively." As Blougram indicates at this point, a great deal depends on what "believe" means, but discussion of that can come later. He is ready to admit ("To you, and over the wine") that there are doctrinal difficulties he cannot solve, dogmas he cannot "believe" in Gigadibs' sense of the word. But before considering the nature of faith, the Bishop proposes to start from Gigadibs' premise of the necessity of total unbelief ("I mean to meet you on your own premise") and examine its consequences.

Since they are both agreed that the primary concern of man is to find the fittest, most coherent way of life, Blougram raises the question, how can we make unbelief bear fruit to us? Gigadibs has challenged the utility of belief; now he must show the utility of unbelief. But first, again by way of applying Gigadibs' own logic to his argument, since he will not accept anything but complete and perfect belief, can he accept anything but complete and perfect unbelief? and how can he be certain of complete unbelief? This argument, combined perhaps with the warmth and evident sincerity of Blougram's assertion of the possibility of a divine purpose, leads Gigadibs to abandon his position of positive unbelief for the agnostic "chessboard."

Blougram is now ready for the next stage in the argument. "We'll proceed a step." The problem of belief or unbelief is not a simple matter of choice between equally tenable propositions of a theoretic nature. "Belief or unbelief Bears upon life, determines its whole course." Every act implies a faith; every effort a man makes implies faith in the value of what he strives for. The only consistent course for the thorough unbeliever is to keep his bed, to "abstain from healthy acts that prove you man." Even on the basis of material values, if Gigadibs wishes to exclude all others, the Bishop can show success in gaining the world's estimation, and its good things. If the sensitive artistic idealism of Gigadibs is repelled by the blunt way in which Blougram proclaims the goodness of worldly power and comforts, he must remember that consistent materialism admits only material values, naturalism only natural values, and draw his own conclusions. At this point he is ready to concede that "it's best believing if we may." He is next asked to concede, still on his own premises of unbelief, that "if once we choose belief, . . . We can't be too decisive in our faith . . . To suit the world which gives us the good things." Success in life (that is, in material terms of riches, honour, pleasure, work, repose) does not come to the indifferent; whatever a man chooses to pursue, we do not call him a fool "so long as he's consistent with his choice." The choice once made is irrevocable. Blougram's own choice, viewed (in accordance with the agreed premise of unbelief) from the merely material point of view, has given his life a singleness and continuity of purpose, and has brought the material returns. Gigadibs would object here that the Bishop's taste is gross; that were he made of "better elements" he would not call this sort of life successful. Again Blougram draws his attention to the logical inconsistency. Gigadibs is denying the validity of the ascetic ideal, and condemning the Bishop for not following it; he is proclaiming that the Bishop cannot be genuinely religious, yet blaming him for not being so. "Grant I'm a beast," says Blougram, "Why, beasts must lead beasts' lives." Gigadibs is trying to have it both ways. Again the "cabin" is brought out to remind him that the discussion is concerned with living life as it is, not as it might be.

But the Bishop is by no means willing to grant that he is a beast; the patronizing assumption of moral superiority by Gigadibs is not patently justified. Gigadibs feels himself nobler simply because he is thoroughly convinced that Blougram is fool or hypocrite, and that he "pines among his million imbeciles" uneasily conscious of the piercing eyes of the Gigadibsian experts. As Verdi looked towards the true judge of music, Rossini, so must Blougram look towards the true judge of values, Gigadibs. But is a journalist the most expert judge of values, of ideals, of men? Is the journalistic habit of mind a critical habit? or does it rather seek the sensational, "see more in a truth than the truth's simple self," find interest only "on the dangerous edge of things," and strive to distinguish only by "gross weights, coarse scales and labels broad?" Why may not the simple truth be that Blougram actually believes what he professes to believe?

But even granted that Blougram's life is not one of which Gigadibs can approve, what is his ideal? The direct question disconcerts Gigadibs; it is one thing to be complacently aware of lofty, if vague, aspirations; to define them is another matter involving more rigorous thinking. The Bishop waits in vain, then offers suggestions. Suppose that Gigadibs aspires to be a Napoleon, a man of action, and granted that he has the requisite qualities ("A large concession, clever as you are," says Blougram), then, remembering that we are still accepting the Gigadibsian premise of unbelief ("We can't believe, you know—We're still at that admission, recollect!"), what guiding principle will justify the life? What possible admirable worldly end can explain such a career? "What's the vague good o' the world, for which you dare With comfort to yourself blow millions up?" If this life is all, Napoleon wins a "dozen noisy years" and "ugly thoughts," while if "doubt may be wrong—there's judgment, life to come!" On either basis, Napoleon's life offers no admirable pattern. If not the man of action, then perhaps the great artist offers an ideal. Should we try to be Shakespeares? What aims in life did Shakespeare pursue? On the material level, he sought the kind of comfort which has come much more abundantly to Blougram: "We want the same things, Shakespeare and myself, And what I want, I have." *If this life's all,* then Blougram beats Shakespeare. With this *re-duction ad absurdum* the attack on Gigadibs' first premise, the assumption of unbelief, is closed. Gigadibs is forced to recognize something beyond this life and its purely temporal and material values.

The discussion can now be moved on to an important new stage. "Believe—and our whole argument breaks up." Gigadibs has been forced by argument from his own premises to abandon them and accept the one basic premise of Blougram's position. He has been brought to acknowledge the use of faith, and as Blougram says, "We're back on Christian ground." What remains now is to proceed from that premise to Blougram's conclusion. The procedure is clearly to examine the nature of faith. Both are now agreed that "enthusiasm's the best thing," that "fire and life Are all, dead matter's nothing," and that faith has power to "penetrate our life with such a glow As fire lends wood and iron"; but fire in itself may be good or ill, enthusiasm may be well or ill directed. Moreover, how can we command it? "Paint a fire, it will not therefore burn." Gigadibs, having granted the value of enthusiasm, is inclined to restrict his approval to enthusiasm like Luther's, enthusiasm "on the denying side." But "ice makes no conflagration." Moreover, there is a limit to denying; after Luther comes Strauss, and once the denying has taught the world that it owes not a farthing (or a duty) to the Church or to St. Paul, what has been gained except the comfort (perhaps temporary) of him who denies? He may feel a Gigadibsian satisfaction at being himself, "imperial, plain and true," but the consequences of following the inner light of doubt may not be all good.

"But," objects Gigadibs, still convinced of the Bishop's secret scepticism, "imperfect faith is no more available to do faith's work than unbelief like mine. Whole faith, or none!" This is the objection Blougram has been waiting for, and, indeed, leading up to. It is time to attack Gigadibs' definition of faith, as he had promised to do earlier. ("Well, I do not believe—If you'll accept no faith that is not fixed, Absolute and exclusive, as you say. You're wrong—I mean to prove it in due time.") Faith is to be distinguished from empirical knowledge; "it is the idea, the feeling and the love, God means mankind should strive for and show forth Whatever be the process to that end." Faith is not solely an act of the intellect; it is a free act of will: "If you desire faith—then you've faith enough: What else seeks God—nay, what else seek ourselves?" "What matter though I doubt at every pore, Head-doubts, heart-doubts . . . If finally I have a life to show?" Gigadibs is demanding, not faith, but factual knowledge verifiable by the senses; like Thomas, he cannot believe until he has seen with his eyes and felt with his hands. Belief, he thinks, must have been easy centuries ago; he might believe in Genesis if he could meet the traveller who has seen the ark. But, Blougram points out, intellectual assent does not constitute a living belief. The important question is not "what could you accept?" but "how should you feel, in such an age, How act?" Faith is something to live by; when it means an inner struggle with doubt, then "A man's worth something." At worst, a struggle to maintain the most difficult beliefs is at all events better than "acquitting God with grace."

If Gigadibs thinks that there have been times, or that there are places, in which belief as he defines it has ever prevailed, he is wrong. No intellectual acceptance of religious doctrines has ever been qualitatively the same as the acceptance of empirically observed experience. No "ragamuffin-saint Believes God watches him continually, As he believes in fire that it will burn, Or rain that it will drench him." The two sorts of knowledge, even as knowledge, are not alike, and can never be equally immediate. It is not part of the divine scheme that they should be so. "Some think, Creation's meant to show him forth: I say it's meant to hide him all it can. . . . Under a vertical sun, the exposed brain . . . less certainly would wither up at once Than mind, confronted with the truth of him."

It follows that the criteria to be applied to empirical knowledge are not applicable to the substance of faith. The demand to "decrassify" faith, to "experimentalize on sacred things," since it eventually means the rejection of all that cannot be empirically verified, must end in "Fichte's clever cut at God himself."

Gigadibs is still inclined to object to "leaving growths of lies unpruned," so Blougram again introduces the "cabin" analogy, to remind his hearer again that the Gigadibsian logic cannot be free to argue from diverse premises: the Bishop cannot be condemned for rejecting an empirical view of faith and in the same breath be condemned for accepting an empirical view of life. The "cabin" and the following "traveller" analogy, besides offering a logical objection, also put forward the characteristic Browning argument of the goodness and significance of this life. Whether this denial of asceticism is an important part of the Bishop's own belief does not, at this point, matter; it serves here to drive Gigadibs into asserting once and for all whether he recognizes absolute values. Presented with this clear-cut issue, Gigadibs meets it by maintaining the value of truth, and the necessity of acting up to it.

Now the attack can be pressed home: Gigadibs, who has accused the Bishop of failure to fit his life to his professed ideals, has now announced the transcendental rule by which *his* life is governed. Does he consistently live by the dictates of reason (as he would define reason) in search of truth (as he would define truth)? If he applies to natural religion the test he has used to demolish the revealed, what is left that checks his will? His behaviour is obviously not unrestrainedly amoral; upon what empirically rational grounds does he base his system of morality? Why is he chaste, for example? After all, he rejects the religious ideal of chastity, and as for a natural law, what authority can it preserve against the analysis of the anthropologist? Natural morality can show no more validity than supernatural. Is Gigadibs chaste, then, from an instinctive feeling that self-restraint is good, and indulgence evil? If so, then his whole pretence of following "reason" breaks down with the introduction of an element which belongs not to his scheme of things, but to the Bishop's. Does he restrain himself from mere timid conformity to convention, because "your fellow-flock Open great eyes at you and even butt?" Conformity to convention can be justified on a utilitarian basis of weighing pleasures against pains, but what then becomes of the lofty pursuit of truth?

With this final challenge, Blougram has finished his argument. It is time to dismiss Gigadibs, and again the Bishop recalls why he has come. He is again aware of the ironic fact that the very worldly position which Gigadibs affects to despise him for valuing is all that makes him important in the journalist's eyes. The real lover of power, rank, luxury, and high worldly place is this same ambitious Gigadibs who is feeling so patronizingly superior. Once more the Bishop is moved to retaliate. Since it is power and social position that Gigadibs admires, it is only fitting to return his condescension with interest by reminding him of his own insignificance. The final insult is to offer the episcopal influence in the publishing world; the implications are that Gigadibs needs (or wants) the money, and that his writing is not good enough to be accepted on its own merits. The irony of the invitation to publish "The Outward-Bound" is effective and complicated. It carries a reminder of the journalist's insignificance, and it also draws attention to Gigadibs' original purpose of "exposing" the Bishop. He is now free to publish to the eager world the startling revelations that the Bishop, though not necessarily granting the good things of this world preeminence, does not despise them and actually enjoys good food, works of art, and a position of eminence; and that he, like most theologians, distinguishes between faith and knowledge, recognizing the activity of the will in belief. It would take more than the Dickens touch to give these revelations the sensational quality Gigadibs had anticipated. And so Gigadibs departs, still detesting Blougram perhaps, still eager to defame him, but at least not despising him as an opponent. There is a deliberate ambiguity, of course, in the Bishop's use of the word "despising."

Blougram, we are told, "believed, say, half he spoke." The rest was shaped "for argumentatory purposes." It should by now be evident enough which half Blougram believed. Quite clearly, the arguments from Gigadibsian premises are not, and are not intended to be, his own beliefs. The "arbitrary accidental thoughts That crossed his mind, amusing because new," are obviously the analogies of the "cabin" and the "traveller"; these are ingenious, are brought in more than once, and represent stages in the argument necessary for the attack on Gigadibs' assumptions. Blougram's own beliefs are indicated by the deeper tone, the heightened poetry of the expression in certain passages; they all deal with the affirmation of faith and the power of faith (ll. 182-97; 560-3; 621-5; 647-61; 693-7; 845-51). His deeper religious thoughts and feelings he did not utter, partly because they are not readily expressed, partly because their expression would have meant nothing to Gigadibs. His purpose was not to make a fruitless exposition of his own point of view for the scoffer's benefit, but to show the scoffer upon what crumbling ground his scoffing rested. After Gigadibs has seen the shallowness of his own thinking, then he can start the process of trying to reach firmer ground ("So, let him sit with me this many a year!").

But Blougram has been more successful than he had expected. Gigadibs, seized with a "sudden healthy vehemence," renounces his ambitions of power and place, of literary eminence, and sails for Australia. He has presumably found an ideal, and is proposing to follow it. Moreover, he is, apparently, intent on the study of the Gospels. He has in fact turned away from precisely those things in Blougram's career which he formerly valued, and is seeking that which he formerly despised; he who doubted above all the possibility of the life of faith is now pursuing it. The victory, unexpected to be sure in its scope, is Blougram's.

[1947]

WILLIAM C. DeVANE

THE VIRGIN AND THE DRAGON

IN BROWNING circles, the year 1946 was one of jubilation. There were ceremonies in London and Florence, abroad, and at home the autumnal but vigorous Browning Societies of such cultural centres as Boston, New York, and Los Angeles were in high celebration, for on September 12, one hundred years ago, Robert Browning, the poet, snatched Elizabeth Barrett, considerably more renowned than himself in her day, from her parental home in Wimpole Street, married her before a handful of witnesses in Marylebone Church, and carried her off to the sun-drenched shores of Italy. On Browning's part as well as Miss Barrett's their flight was an act of decision and courage, and also of entirely legal and moral romance. Legend has endowed their act with qualities and colors which truth compels us to modify and subdue. Romance is swift and dangerous; Miss Barrett took a year and a half to come to her decision, and the only real danger lay in the condition of her health. Mr. Barrett, her father, was surely not the unique prehistoric monster he has been painted.

The episode, however, catches neatly in its totality the character of the hero of the affair, "that infinitely respectable rebel," Robert Browning. It was an event that could have happened in quite the way it did only in the benign and domestic reign of Queen Victoria. A half century earlier, a Shelley or a Byron would have dispensed with the services of the church and the clergy, and a century later the romance would probably have been the fifth or sixth on each side. But here was a marriage made in heaven, or as we say colloquially, "for keeps." The success of the marriage has become proverbial, a legend to posterity. That Browning was at all times conscious of the full implications of his deed, and had in prophetic fashion anticipated and shaped the event itself will be seen from what follows. My present comments fall into three parts, which might be called anticipations of romance, the reality of marriage, and the afterglow of romance.

It ought to be clearly understood that Browning was ready for his moment when it came to him in his thirty-fifth year. He had long dreamed how the event should happen, and had constructed or found a private myth by which the event was to be controlled and shaped. Browning's private myth is a singularly revealing one, reflecting perfectly his romantic, dramatic, and strong-minded character. This myth was the legend of Andromeda. In Greek legend Andromeda was the daughter of Cepheus and Cassiopeia; she lived on the shores of Asia Minor, not far from Joppa. To satisfy Poseidon, the god of the sea, who had been offended by Andromeda's father, she was chained to a rock to be sacrificed to a sea monster. Perseus, the great Athenian hero, was returning from Ethiopia, where he had slain the Gorgon, when he found her in this predicament. He slew the dragon, set the maiden free, and married her in spite of the fact that she had been promised to another prince. She became the ancestress of a great and famous family by Perseus, and Sophocles and Euripides, among others, made the legend of Andromeda the subject of their tragedies. Incidents in the story were represented in numerous works of ancient art.

So great was the fame of Andromeda in the ancient world of the Near East that at her death, as Ovid tells it, she was translated to a constellation in the sky. But as so often happened, the legend was too humanly useful to die or leave the earth, and was merely transferred to a Christian hero and heroine. We know, as a matter of fact, very little about the life of St. George, patron saint of England, Aragon, and Portugal. He seems to have flourished mightily in the third century A.D., and then to have suffered martyrdom at Lydda in Palestine about the year 300. The connection of St. George with the dragon, familiar since the "Golden Legend" of Jacobus de Voraigne, can be traced to the close of the sixth century. At Arsuf or Joppa, neither of them far from Lydda, Perseus had slain the sea monster that threatened the virgin Andromeda, and George, like many another Christian saint, entered into the inheritance of veneration previously enjoyed by a pagan hero. There is no more curious accident in the annuals of hagiography than that St. George should have become the patron saint of England. He was, as we have noted, not English or even European by birth. The veneration of St. George in Europe was one of the results of the Crusades, for the Crusaders it was who brought back his effigy from Asia Minor. When Eleanor of Castile married Henry II of England in 1152, and went with him to England, she carried with her on her shield the effigy of the saint, who in due course of time became England's patron saint. From about the beginning of the fifteenth century, St. George's Day, April 23, has been one of the greatest feasts of the English church. The Red Cross of St.

George has been for five hundred years the great English national emblem, and still shines resplendent at the centre of the Union Jack. Almost every painter of Europe has given us a representation of St. George's struggle with the dragon. The Red Cross Knight of the first book of Spenser's *Faerie Queene* is the most famous literary treatment of the subject. It is clear that the Perseus-Andromeda legend and the St. George legend are cognate, and, as we shall see, Browning will move from one to the other with that assurance. It is only necessary to say here that there were extant many debased forms of the legend, and Browning felt free to make use of them as well.

Readers of Browning's letters and biography will remember that the young poet always wrote at a desk over which there hung a copy of Caravaggio's picture of Andromeda, "the perfect picture," as he called it. As he wrote his first poem, *Pauline,* in the winter of 1832-33, he glanced up at the picture, and recorded what he saw in verse:

> Andromeda!
> And she is with me: years roll, I shall change,
> But change can touch her not—so beautiful
> With her fixed eyes, earnest and still, and hair
> Lifted and spread by the salt-sweeping breeze,
> And one red beam, all the storm leaves in heaven,
> Resting upon her eyes and hair, such hair,
> As she awaits the snake on the wet beach
> By the dark rock and the white wave just breaking
> At her feet; quite naked and alone; a thing
> I doubt not, nor fear for, secure some god
> To save will come in thunder from the stars.

The years rolled, but Browning did not change as much as he imagined he would. Two years before the end of his career, that is, in 1887, in the "Parleying with Francis Furini," he employed for the last time the myth of Andromeda. Furini, the obscure Italian painter, becomes the stalking horse for Browning's defense of nude paintings, and specifically a defense of his son, Pen Browning, whose colossal figures in the nude had been subjected to prudish contemporary criticism. The emphasis in the "Parleying" is upon the nakedness of Andromeda and the goodness of the flesh, but the setting is the same: the blackness, with the single beam of light, the sea and the wind. A little further in the poem the myth of Andromeda is applied differently; this time Andromeda represents Browning's own faith, standing precariously upon the rock of consciousness amidst the growing darkness of the sky and the waters waste and wild, and awaiting destruction from the monsters of new scientific thought, or rescue from heaven.

Early and late, then, Browning uses the Andromeda myth to express his faith. But these brackets must by no means be thought to be empty. In one form or another, the Andromeda pattern may be traced all through the poet's life and works. In the Forties, Count Gismond was the Perseus to rescue the maligned lady of the romance; the ancient Gipsy rescued the Duchess in "The Flight of the Duchess"; in "My Last Duchess" no god came to the rescue of outraged innocence. That was an exception, and the lady of "The Glove" fared better in spite of the established story to the contrary. But Browning had good reason to make the Perseus of this latter story attractive and young, for the poem was written in 1845 under the eye of Miss Barrett. It was a short step from writing these things and thinking habitually in these terms, to performing them in actual life, so we are not surprised when in 1846 Browning plays the part of Perseus to Miss Barrett's Andromeda, with only the part of the dragon left over for the unfortunate and misunderstood Mr. Barrett. Such a stroke as that might well confirm a man's belief in his role for life. In Browning's Italian days, the Perseus-Andromeda pattern finds a more subtle expression—all the obvious rescues have been accomplished—but after Mrs. Browning's death, the pattern becomes prominent again in retrospect. This is especially true in *The Ring and the Book*, where Browning is striving to build his masterpiece on a huge scale, and to make it a masterpiece peculiarly his own. Here we see Pompilia-Mrs. Browning-Andromeda rescued from the dragon Guido by Caponsacchi-Browning-Perseus, first; and later when truth or justice is endangered, Pope Innocent, the Vicegerent of God, is the rescuer.

But this is to anticipate those middle years of Browning's life, mainly spent in Italy, when his romance turned into the reality of marriage. The fine poetic flowering of these years is given to us in *Men and Women*, published in 1855, nine years after his marriage and his flight to Italy, and it is the thinking and feeling of those two superb volumes that I wish to examine at this point. For it is in *Men and Women* that Browning ceases to be the romantic young man, and turns his heart and intelligence to the scrutiny of the relationship in marriage of man to woman and woman to man. Here the poet is not the romantic dreamer, but the observer and the recorder, and assuredly the moralist. To paraphrase King Lear, "he takes upon him the mystery of things, as if he were God's spy"—a passage from Shakespeare's play which Browning used and was particularly fond of. And in these golden volumes of 1855 we get those amazing insights into the human heart upon which Browning's immortality as a poet must in large part ultimately rest.

The first effect of Elizabeth Barrett upon the poetry of her husband was not a happy one. In some of the earliest letters which Elizabeth Barrett wrote to Browning in 1845 she begins to manage and reform him. It seems a malady incident to being a good woman. Miss Barrett is a little unhappy about her suitor's interest in the theatre, and his lack in recent years of evangelical fervor in chapel attendance; she is profoundly uneasy over Browning's habitual poetical technique—she constantly urges him to drop his dramatic mask and speak out in the first person singular, to find, as she might put it, his own voice. She is also eager to have him speak directly upon religious and moral topics especially and become a prophet to his age. Being an obedient husband, he tried his best to be the kind of poet his wife wanted him to be. And so, in 1850, he published the first volume since his marriage, *Christmas Eve and Easter Day,* in which he spoke in the first person upon the problems of religious faith and doubt in contemporary terms. In spite of many splendid passages the result was not significant for its day, and is even less so for ours. *Christmas Eve and Easter Day* must be reckoned a failure also on commercial grounds, for it sold only two hundred copies.

But happily, Mrs. Browning got preoccupied with other things, and in those seemingly idle, sunlit years as the poet strolled about the streets and environs of Florence with Flush at his heels, Browning worked out his poetic salvation. The cares and joys of motherhood absorbed Mrs. Browning, and before long she was also writing about Italian liberty and constructing "Aurora Leigh." It was a release for Browning which he never acknowledged, and perhaps never recognized. But then as he walked about Florence he thought of many things—of the kind of poetry he could write, and only he; of the great artists of earlier times, the musicians and painters, and their relations to their women, of the true function of the poet, and, above all, of the intimate relation between man and woman in the blessed state of matrimony. There was no rebellion towards his wife in him, but rather a profound gratitude and wonder at his own good fortune. In the poem "By the Fireside," he watched her as she sat

> Reading by fire-light, that great brow
> And the spirit-small hand propping it. . . .

And to himself he said:

> . . . If I tread
> This path back, is it not in pride
> To think how little I dreamed it led
> To an age so blest that, by its side,
> Youth seems the waste instead?

For art's sake, the poet transfers the perfect meeting of lovers' spirits in this poem to a forest scene, high in the Apennines. It really just took place in London's dreary Wimpole Street. For that high rare communion of hearts he is everlastingly grateful—

> You might have turned and tried a man,
> Set him a space to weary and wear,
> And prove which suited more your plan,
> His best of hope or his worst despair,
> Yet end as he began.
>
> But you spared me this, like the heart you are,
> And filled my empty heart at a word.
> If two lines join, there is oft a scar,
> They are one and one, with a shadowy third;
> One near one is too far.
>
> A moment after, and hands unseen
> Were hanging the night around as fast;
> But we knew that a bar was broken between
> Life and life: we were mixed at last
> In spite of the mortal screen.
>
> The forests had done it; there they stood;
> We caught for a moment the powers at play:
> They had mingled us so, for once and good,
> Their work was done—we might go or stay,
> They relapsed to their ancient mood.

But such a communion of spirit most men never know, or if they know it, they know it fleetingly and rarely. It is the lot of most of us to live alone, and between us there flows the unplumbed, salt estranging sea. In "Two in the Cam-

pagna" the lovers never meet, in spite of the speaker's strong
desire:

> No. I yearn upward, touch you close,
> Then stand away. I kiss your cheek,
> Catch your soul's warmth,—I pluck the rose
> And love it more than tongue can speak—
> Then the good minute goes.

These are but two poems in *Men and Women*, volumes
which give us the anatomy of married love. Look for a
moment at the titles of the poems: "Love among the Ruins,"
"A Lovers' Quarrel," "A Woman's Last Word," "Any Wife
to Any Husband," "A Serenade at the Villa," "A Pretty
Woman," "Respectability," "A Light Woman," "The Statue
and the Bust," "Love in a Life," "Life in a Love," "The Last
Ride Together," "Andrea del Sarto," "In Three Days," "In a
Year," "Women and Roses," "The Guardian Angel," "One
Way of Love," "Another Way of Love," "Misconceptions,"
"One Word More." Not all the experiences recorded in these
poems happened in their fulness to Browning, of course;
from his own relations with his wife he picked up a hint here
and a suggestion there, and his friends and acquaintances
did not escape his scrutinizing eye. Not since John Donne
had any such intimate revelation of married love been given
us. In the full scope we see love triumphant, and love
rejected; love eager and young, and love satiated; love a
strong support, and love betrayed; love making heroes of
men, and love enslaving and corrupting them. The poet's
theme is love in all its guises. If at one end of the human
scale, love is a foretaste of heaven, at the other end it can
be a foretaste of hell. From the whole we gradually ascertain
the unforgivable sin against love—the sin that is committed
by the lovers of "The Statue and the Bust." For those lovers,
profoundly committed in their hearts to their love for each
other, never dare to take the illicit step which would unite

them. Indecision, respect for convention, and cowardice are the qualities of their failure—

> The counter our lovers staked was lost
> As surely as if it were lawful coin:
> And the sin I impute to each frustrate ghost
>
> Is—the unlit lamp and the ungirt loin. . . .

A colder and more exact judgment would have been kinder to these lovers; but to the generous and impulsive poet, their failure was anathema. These lovers are really lost souls:

> So! While these wait the trump of doom,
> How do their spirits pass, I wonder
> Nights and days in the narrow room?
>
> Still, I suppose, they sit and ponder
> What a gift life was, ages ago,
> Six steps out of the chapel yonder.
>
> Only they see not God, I know,
> Nor all that chivalry of his,
> The soldier-saints who, row on row,
>
> Burn upward each to his point of bliss—

This theme of "love not taken when it is at hand" is the subject of many poems in the poet's next volume, *Dramatis Personae,* of 1864.

But the golden time of Browning's life and genius comes to an end in 1861, for in that year Mrs. Browning died. From that time to the end of his life, his comments upon love are the remembrance of things past. We now enter his third phase in these matters, and it is a phase in which he reverts to his first or Andromeda phase, with experience and memory added. Earlier in this essay I mentioned the large pattern of *The Ring and the Book,* of 1868, where Browning attempted to build his masterpiece on an epic scale, and to make it a work in technique and substance peculiarly his own. In *The Ring and the Book,* we see Pompilia rescued from the dragon Guido by Caponsacchi in the first instance; and later when truth or ultimate justice is endangered, Pope Innocent comes to save it.

But to point to these large patterns in *The Ring and the Book* is to give the barest indication of the manner in which the myth of Andromeda (with which Mrs. Browning is now completely identified) had penetrated and shaped the conscious thinking and the deeper unconscious feeling in the poet's greatest single achievement. I wish now to look at the prevalence, or rather the all-pervasiveness, of the Andromeda legend through certain books of *The Ring and the Book*— including with the Andromeda myth its Christian cognate, the legend of St. George and the dragon. In those books of *The Ring and the Book* where the speakers give favorable judgments upon Pompilia and Caponsacchi, I have counted at least thirty references to the Andromeda and its cognate myth, not counting such facts as this—that Browning, for all his accuracy and care in consulting the Astronomer Royal upon the condition of the moon on the night of Pompilia's flight, April 29-30, 1697, at the last moment changed the date, but not the moon, so that the flight would fall on April 23, St. George's Day. By the light or cynical speakers in *The Ring and the Book,* the flight of Pompilia and Caponsacchi is usually referred to in the terms of the story of Helen and Paris, "De Raptu Helenae"; and Guido's pursuit is likened humorously to Vulcan pursuing Mars to get back his Venus. But it is not too much to say that whenever Browning is representing, favorably to Pompilia and Caponsacchi—and that is a great deal of the time—the great scene at the inn at Castelnuovo where the real conflict between the opposing forces takes place, he habitually and consistently thinks of it in the terms of the Andromeda situation, with Caponsacchi as Perseus, Pompilia as the manacled victim, and Guido as the dragon. Moreover, the scene is generally set as nearly as possible with the colors he imagined in the Andromeda scene. Caponsacchi thus pictures Pompilia in that moment at the inn:

> She started up, stood erect, face to face
> With the husband: back he fell, was buttressed there
> By the window all aflame with morning-red,
> He the black figure, the opprobrious blur
> Against all peace and joy and light and life.

And Pompilia speaking of the same scene describes Guido as "the serpent towering and triumphant." When the Pope thinks of Pompilia in the clutches of Guido, he uses a figure appropriate to Andromeda's plight:

> Such denizens o' the cave now cluster round
> And heat the furnace sevenfold: time indeed
> A bolt from heaven should cleave roof and clear place,
> Transfix and show the world, suspiring flame,
> The main offender, scar and brand the rest
> Hurrying, each miscreant to his hole: then flood
> And purify the scene with outside day—
> Which yet, in the absolutest drench of dark,
> Ne'er wants a witness, some stray beauty-beam
> To the despair of hell.

When Browning himself describes the same situation—Pompilia in the power of Guido and his family—he says:

>   . . . These I saw,
> In recrudescency of baffled hate,
> Prepare to wring the uttermost revenge
> From body and soul thus left them: all was sure,
> Fire laid and cauldron set, the obscene ring traced,
> The victim stripped and prostrate: what of God?
> The cleaving of a cloud, a cry, a crash,
> Quenched lay their cauldron, cowered i' the dust the crew,
> As, in a glory of armour like Saint George,

Out again sprang the young good beauteous priest
Bearing away the lady in his arms. . . .

Indeed, so steadily is the Perseus-St. George legend used in
The Ring and the Book that we may know what to think of
each speaker by the treatment he accords the myth, and by
what version of the myth he employs. The speaker in "The
Other Half-Rome," favorable to Pompilia, gives the legend
a Christian character, but he only faintly realizes his figure.
When he has sketched the miraculous rescue of Pompilia by
Caponsacchi, he turns upon his auditor:

How do you say? It were improbable;
So is the legend of my patron-saint.

In Caponsacchi's monologue the scene of Andromeda's distress before the rescuer comes is set again and again—in the
box at the theatre with Guido lurking in the background,
and in the window of her house, for example—and always
in the same terms of darkness and light. Of course, Caponsacchi was only a partially effective Perseus or St. George,
and being modest, cannot refer to himself in such terms,
except ironically, as he does here when he is addressing the
judges:

I rise in your esteem, sagacious Sirs,
Stand up a renderer of reasons, not
The officious priest would personate Saint George
For a mock Princess in undragoned days.

But there is nothing, or very little, to keep Pompilia in her
monologue from speaking of Caponsacchi as Perseus or St.
George, and she constantly refers to him as such. One of the
legends in the tapestries in her house, she recalls, had as its
subject "the slim young man with wings at head, and wings
at feet, and sword threatening a monster." And, of course,
though she cannot call herself Andromeda, she constantly

recognizes herself in the role of the helpless and innocent victim, and Caponsacchi as the heaven-sent rescuer.

The characters of evil import in *The Ring and the Book* use the same essential myth, but use it in a debased form or for a base purpose. Thus Guido uses it when in his defense he gives an account of one of his ancestors who met death in the region where Perseus and St. George had performed their exploits:

> One of us Franceschini fell long since
> I' the Holy Land, betrayed, tradition runs,
> To Paynims by the feigning of a girl
> He rushed to free from ravisher, and found
> Lay safe enough with friends in ambuscade
> Who flayed him while she clapped her hands and laughed:
> Let me end, falling by a like device.

The keen intelligence of Guido sees the matter clearly, whatever he may make of it, but the dim mind of Bottinius, the lawyer for Pompilia's cause, can only arrive at this approximation of the Andromeda myth in his defense of Pompilia's conduct in arranging for her flight:

> Methinks I view some ancient bas-relief.
> There stands Hesione thrust out by Troy,
> Her father's hand has chained her to a crag,
> Her mother's from the virgin plucked the vest,
> At a safe distance both distressful watch,
> While near and nearer comes the snorting orc.
> I look that, white and perfect to the end,
> She wait till Jove despatch some demigod;
> Not that,—impatient of celestial club
> Alcmena's son should brandish at the beast,—
> She daub, disguise her dainty limbs with pitch,
> And so elude the purblind monster! Ay,
> The trick succeeds, but 'tis an ugly trick,
> Where needs have been no trick! . . .
> Trick, I maintain, had no alternative.
> The heavens were bound with brass,—Jove far at feast . . .

With the unblamed Aethiop,—Hercules spun wool
I' the lap of Omphale, while Virtue shrieked—
The brute came paddling all the faster.   You
Of Troy, who stood at distance, where's the aid
You offered in the extremity? . . .
                                        He,
He only, Caponsacchi 'mid a crowd,
Caught Virtue up, carried Pompilia off. . . .
              . . . what you take for pitch
Is nothing worse, belike, than black and blue,
Mere evanescent proof that hardy hands
Did yeoman's service, cared not where the gripe
Was more than duly energetic . . .

All this is sufficiently far from that other admirer of
Euripides who thought in his youth that "if Virtue feeble
were, Heaven itself would stoop to her," but it is characteristic of Browning and will serve. It must not be
imagined that Browning dropped the Perseus-Andromeda
conception of life after *The Ring and the Book*. Perhaps the
most direct and poignant use of the theme of rescue in all
the poet's writings occurs in *Balaustion's Adventure,* two
years later, where Browning gives us a transcript of Euripides' *Alcestis*. There, it will be remembered, Heracles
rescues the lady from death itself. Both overtly and covertly
the poem is bound to the memory of the poet's dead wife.
But this is only one instance among a dozen. In the "Parleying with Francis Furini" at the end of his life, as we have
seen, Browning made another frank avowal of his myth, and
utilized it this time as an explanation of his religious faith.
How closely Mrs. Browning had become a part of that total
faith one may easily see.

By the time that Browning was writing his "Parleying
with Francis Furini," in 1887, the bright world of his youth
had taken on a sombre hue. In the death of Mrs. Browning
he had suffered an irreparable loss, and after 1861, for all his
dining out and being lionized, he was often a lonely man.

In the realm of his faith, too, the shocks had come. The fierce assaults of the Higher Criticism upon the literal authority of the Bible had undermined and doomed the evangelical position in which Browning had been bred. Science, moreover, had shaken his faith in his dearly loved doctrine of progress, or at least had changed that conception from the triumphal march of an earlier notion to the long, slow evolution of man with many setbacks and retrogressions. Economically and industrially, too, the lines of the graph no longer strained to the upper righthand corner. There was distress in imperial England, and there were wars and rumors of wars in the air. There was not much to comfort the serious observer in 1887. The bright morning of the Forties had turned into an ominous twilight.

The murky atmosphere of this later time is faithfully reflected in Browning's last use of the Andromeda myth. In the "Parleying with Francis Furini" the maiden is once more chained to the rock amidst the dark waters. Here in the dusk she symbolizes the poet's faith in the destiny of man and the providence of God. There is an air of desperation in the scene, for as yet no God has come in thunder from the stars to effect a rescue, and the sea beast comes apace.

And Elizabeth Barrett Browning, dead now for twenty-six years, has become

> Perhaps but a memory, after all!
> —Of what came once when a woman leant
> To feel for my brow where her kiss might fall.

DONALD SMALLEY

SPECIAL PLEADING IN

THE LABORATORY

A FORTNIGHT after the publication of *Prince Hohenstiel-Schwangau, Saviour of Society* (1871) Browning wrote his friend Isa Blagden:

> By this time you have got my little book and seen for yourself whether I make the best or worst of the case. I think in the main, he [Napoleon III] meant to do what I say, and, but for the weakness, grown more apparent in these last years than formerly, would have done what I say he did not.

In his next letter to Miss Blagden, Browning added concerning this monologue: ". . . it is just what I imagine the man might, if he pleased, say for himself."[1] Nearly thirty years earlier, in the *Essay on Chatterton*, Browning had tried his first experiment in making the best of a case and revealing what a character who had been condemned by the world might "say for himself" against the world's interpretation of him.

Browning was happy in his choice of a first client; he believed that Chatterton had a valid defense against the allegations of cynical biographers. Browning argued with earnestness and conviction; he was confident of winning his case. Later he tackled more difficult subjects. In such notable exercises in special pleading as "Bishop Blougram's Apology" (1855), "Mr. Sludge, 'The Medium'" (1864), the monologues of Guido in *The Ring and the Book* (1868-69), *Prince Hohenstiel-Schwangau* (1871), *Fifine at the Fair* (1872), and *Red Cotton Night-Cap Country* (1873), he pleaded the cases of less admirable characters and argued their briefs without the intention of securing a full acquittal. In all but the last named poem he employed the dramatic monologue, allowing his characters to defend their courses of action in their own words. Nevertheless Browning's procedure in these later works remained in most respects the procedure which he had used to defend Chatterton in 1842.

Even before the *Essay*, Browning had been tentatively feeling his way toward a special type of character study. In *The Return of the Druses* he had two years earlier carried his inclination for portraying tortuous mental processes as far as the drama could take him. Farther, indeed, in the opinion of William Charles Macready, who concluded upon reading the play that Browning's intellect was "not quite clear" and that the author of this drama would "*never write again*—to any purpose."[2] The fact was that Browning had fastened upon the general subject matter of his later studies before he had seen the need for a special manner of presenting it. By 1842 he had solved his problem. In the *Essay* he exhibited what may be called his system of special pleading —a method of portraying character based upon what a man might "say for himself" against the world's misinterpretation of his conduct.

The *Essay*, this chapter will attempt to show, was Browning's laboratory experiment in the process of special pleading. Writing anonymously and writing in prose, he was able to put his ideas into practice with unusual freedom. There is a good deal of evidence that he was fully conscious of trying innovations in presenting his defense of Chatterton. To view the matter clearly, however, it is necessary to lay a ghost of Browning's own making. For Browning, in pleading Chatterton's case, professed merely to apply the lessons that he had learned from Richard Henry Wilde.

I

It seems certain that Browning first undertook the task of preparing an article for *The Foreign Quarterly Review* with the purpose of writing a review of Wilde's study of Tasso.[3] The title of Wilde's work alone heads the *Essay*. It is not until the seventh paragraph that Browning mentions the recently published volumes on Chatterton which serve him as a starting point for his discussion of the English poet. His words at this juncture are revealing:

Thinking thus, and grieving over what must be admitted to be the scantiness of the piece of sunshine here, and the narrow and not very novel track it would alone serve to lead us into,— a book was sent to us on a subject not very different from Mr. Wilde's, but on which the service he has sought to render to the memory of Tasso has not hitherto been attempted for a memory more foully outraged. (113-19)[4]

One wonders whether the book "was sent" to Browning by John Forster. If so, Forster was at the outset of his editorship deviating from the previous policy of his periodical and from his own later practice, for the scope of the *Foreign Quarterly* did not include reviews of English books upon English authors. Probably the alteration in subject matter was Browning's own idea. Grieved at the scantiness of new material in Wilde's work, and seeing no particularly interesting track for further discussion of Tasso, he had found in Willcox's edition of Chatterton, prefaced by a new biography of the poet, a convenient means of turning into more fertile fields.

But though Browning speaks lightly of Wilde's subject matter,[5] he professes the highest regard for Wilde's method of handling his material. He praises the American writer especially for confining his study to a single aspect of Tasso's life:

Such as it is, however, in what Mr. Wilde has done, he has gone the right way to work and done it well. He has steadily restricted himself to the single point in question [whether Tasso loved and was beloved by the Princess of Este]. . . . Still it is but a point; and Mr. Wilde has not perhaps done less gracefully and wisely in leaving the rest untouched, than in accomplishing so thoroughly the task he took in hand. He relies upon his subject; is sure of the service he can render by an efficacious treatment of thus much of it; nor entertains any fear lest the bringing in a Before and After, with which he has no immediate concern, should be thought necessary to give interest to the At Present on which he feels he can labour to advantage. We suspect that if we would make any material progress in knowledge of this description, such works must be so undertaken. (82-101)

And Browning proposes to follow Wilde's method in his own attempt to throw a new light upon Chatterton's career:

As the whole of Mr. Wilde's argument may be said to include itself in his commentary upon the opening couplet of the first Sonnet of the collection of *Rime,*

True were the loves and transports which I sung,

so let us say of the Englishman, that his were far from that untruth, that absence of reality, so constantly charged against them. In a word, poor Chatterton's life was not the Lie it is so universally supposed to have been; nor did he "perish in the pride" of refusing to surrender Falsehood and enter on the ways of Truth. We can show, we think, and by some such process as Mr. Wilde adopts in regard to Tasso, that he had already entered on those ways when he was left, without a helping hand, to sink and starve as he might. And to this single point we shall as far as possible restrict ourselves. (136-49)

In the final paragraph of the *Essay* Browning again acknowledges Wilde as his preceptor:

Thus much has been suggested by Mr. Wilde's method with Tasso. As by balancing conflicting statements, interpreting doubtful passages, and reconciling discrepant utterances, he has examined whether Tasso was true or false, loved or did not love the Princess of Este, was or was not beloved by her,—so have we sought, from similar evidences, if Chatterton was towards the end of his life hardening himself in deception or striving to cast it off. (899-906)

Browning is so much impressed with the possibilities of this method for revealing the true natures of men whom the world has misunderstood that he ends the *Essay* with an exhortation:

Let others apply in like manner our inquiry to other great spirits partially obscured, and they will but use us—we hope more effectually—as we have used these able and interesting volumes. (906-909)

Two questions arise from the statements just reviewed and demand to be answered. First, why did Browning give such enthusiastic praise to Wilde's method of working? Second, did Browning actually follow Wilde's method in his own study of Chatterton? The answer to the first question is not far to seek. Even in *Pauline* (1833), his first published poem,

Browning had been concerned primarily with analysis of character. In the preface to *Paracelsus* (1835) he had stated his intention of discarding "the operation of persons and events" and "an external machinery of incidents" in order to "display somewhat minutely the mood itself in its rise and progress" within the mind of Paracelsus. In the preface to *Strafford* (1837) Browning proposed to reveal "Action in Character, rather than Character in Action" in his drama. *Sordello* (1840), *The Return of the Druses* (completed by the midsummer of 1840), and *Pippa Passes* (1841) show a continued desire to subordinate external incident in order to lay all possible stress upon the intense study of character. In Wilde's principle of limiting himself to "the single point in question," a single important issue in Tasso's career, and in Wilde's method of analyzing Tasso's nature by "balancing conflicting statements, interpreting doubtful passages, and reconciling discrepant utterances"—by laying all possible stress upon Tasso's inner history as evidenced in his writings rather than upon the external machinery of incident stressed by biographers—Browning could hardly help recognizing the work of a kindred spirit. Like Sir Willoughby Patterne, he saw his image reflected and found that it was good.

The truth, indeed, is that Browning read a good deal into Wilde's study of Tasso that a disinterested reader cannot find there. To the uninstructed eye, Wilde's method in his two volumes does not seem especially adventurous. Richard Henry Wilde (1789-1847), born in Dublin but arrived in America in 1797, had been an attorney general of Georgia and had served five terms in Congress before he undertook Italian scholarship during an extended visit abroad from 1835 to 1840 or early in 1841. In addition to his discussion of Tasso, Wilde attempted a treatise upon "The Life and Times of Dante" and another upon "The Italian Lyric Poets." The unfinished manuscripts of the last two works are now in the Library of Congress.[6] The aim and the content of

DONALD SMALLEY

Wilde's *Conjectures and Researches* seem fairly described in *The North American Review* for April 1842: "Mr. Wilde has endeavoured to make the poet tell his own story, and, from the vast collection of his letters and minor poems, to cull out and piece together those personal allusions and statements, which may throw light on the principal incidents in his life."[7] Wilde's work is as much a collation of materials as it is an original study. He compiled laboriously from Tasso's critics and biographers, and he translated gracefully and at length from Tasso's verse. He was more interested in presenting the materials upon which a judgment could be formed than he was in impressing his own conclusions upon the reader. Something of his attitude and method can be gathered from his introductory comments:

> Various conjectures respecting [the love, madness, and imprisonment of Tasso] have been offered; none, perhaps, entirely satisfactory. The value of those which follow will depend on their probability, and that, again, on the number of incidents collected and compared, and the candor and sagacity employed in their collation.[8]

His voice continues modest throughout the two volumes. He views himself as a collator, and his most characteristic remark is, "Either the thing proves itself, or we should fail to prove it."[9]

In Browning's account, as we have already seen, Wilde takes on another character. For Browning's curious summary given below, the materials are, to be sure, contained in Wilde; but Wilde was concerned only with suggesting that Tasso's love for the Princess of Este was a reality and that Tasso merely feigned madness when his passion was discovered. Wilde did not in any way attempt to interpret Tasso's actions in terms of a "false step" and a deviation from "the right way." The moral tone and stress here are entirely Browning's:

For Tasso, a few words will say how his first false step was an indiscretion; how, having published love-poetry under a false name, and suffered himself to be suspected its author, he, to avoid the ill-consequences, feigned at the Duke's suggestion, Madness; and how his protracted agony at Saint Anna was but an unremitting attempt to free himself from the effect of this false step without being compelled to reveal the truth, and disavow his whole proceedings since the time of that sad starting-aside from the right way. (167-75)

Through Browning's remarkable habit of creative reading, Wilde's somewhat discursive and elaborately cautious account of Tasso's life has acquired a central moral theme and a unified plot. It has become a tragedy dealing with a fatal error—a "sad starting-aside" from truth—and Tasso's career from his "first false step" onward has assumed new meaning as a dramatic struggle against the meshes of falsehood.

In quoting as his "text" Wilde's statement that Tasso was not "habitually insincere,"[10] Browning turned an incidental remark into a central theme. He might as logically have preached a very different sermon by taking as his text Wilde's comment upon other documents, that a description "false in one point, is probably false in all, and . . . the same deceit once practised, may be suspected wherever there is the same temptation."[11]

It becomes clear that Browning used Wilde, however unconsciously, less as a model than as a stalking-horse. He could follow the example of Wilde's "clever volumes" in shaping his interpretation of Chatterton's life only because he had first remade Wilde's method to his own specifications.

II

In praising Wilde, Browning was actually offering a prospectus of his personal system as a special pleader. Viewed in this light, his zeal as a disciple and a missionary is understandable. It was not until 1871, with the publication of *Prince Hohenstiel-Schwangau,* that Browning once more expressed himself at any length concerning his theories as a special pleader. In that poem through the lips of Hohenstiel-Schwangau, and in *Red Cotton Night-Cap Country* two years later in his own person, he again grew confidential. By comparing his statements of theory in the *Essay* with the statements which he made three decades later in these two poems, and by comparing his practice in the *Essay* with his practice in his mature works,[12] we can see with some clarity to what extent he made his prose work of 1842 a laboratory trial of his method.

In arguing his brief for Chatterton, Browning makes it clear that he is consciously trying out what may be considered the three essentials of his procedure in special pleading. These will be considered separately in the pages that follow.

a. *The very basis of the* Essay *is an attempt to reveal the hero's intimate point of view concerning his career, to defend his actions as he must have defended them to himself in the inner recesses of his mind.*

This is also the basis of every study in special pleading that Browning wrote from the *Essay* onward. The assumption which guides Browning in his work as a pleader of cases is that the hero is powerless to make his own defense to the world at large. He must either have his inner thoughts interpreted for him by the author, acting as narrator, or he must be allowed to speak in the nearest approach to absolute privacy that the conventions of the dramatic monologue can allow.[13] Browning's self-apologist of the dramatic monologues reveals his intimate view of his career to a single individual, and reveals it under peculiarly favorable circumstances. Bishop Blougram is minded to push chairs back after the wine and speak frankly in the intimacy of his own palace. He reveals his course to a single obscure auditor, who cannot hope to be believed if he repeats one word of what the Bishop tells him. Mr. Sludge proposes to reveal all to a host who has already caught him cheating. He makes his revelation in the privacy of his host's drawing room, with the comforting knowledge that he can later contradict or twist to his own ends whatever Horsefall may choose to divulge of his confession. Hohenstiel-Schwangau finds a pretty and attentive listener who, like him, has seen better days. He can talk to her in private without fear that she can later use his confidences against him.

Even under the most favorable of conditions, however, the self-apologist finds a statement of his inner view of his life a difficult matter. Hohenstiel-Schwangau exclaims:

> Alack, one lies oneself
> Even in the stating that one's end was truth,
> Truth only, if one states as much in words!
> Give me the inner chamber of the soul
> For obvious easy argument! 't is there
> One pits the silent truth against a lie—
> . . . But, do your best,
> Words have to come: and somehow words deflect
> As the best cannon ever rifled will.   (2123-34)

In his first exercise in special pleading, and three decades later in *Red Cotton Night-Cap Country*, Browning dispensed with the restrictions of the dramatic monologue. His essential purpose was the same—the enabling his hero to "speak for himself," to counter his own point of view against the world's judgment of him—but in these words Browning, in the capacity of narrator, could proceed more directly to give his hero's thoughts. He could, moreover, explain what he was trying to do. "It is needless for us here to interpose," Browning tells us in the *Essay* (720-24), "that our whole argument goes, not upon what Chatterton said, but what he did: it is part of our proof to show that all his distress arose out of the impossibility of his saying any thing to the real purpose." And in explaining Chatterton's concealed motives for going to London: "It will, of course, be objected, that Chatterton gave the very reasons for his desire to obtain a release from Bristol that we have rejected. But he was forced to say something, and what came more plausibly?" (737-40) The basic principle of Browning's procedure as a special pleader is contained in these two sentences. In *Red Cotton Night-Cap Country*, after many years of practice, Browning stated it even more succinctly:

> How substitute thing meant for thing expressed?
>
> (2959)

Earlier in the poem, Browning had suggested his manner of answering the question:

> "I like these amateurs"—our friend had laughed,
> Could he turn what he felt to what he thought,
> And, that again, to what he put in words . . .
>
> (2833-35)

And later in the poem, Browning elaborates the principle behind his method:

> He thought . . .
>   (Suppose I should prefer "He said?"
> Along with every act—and speech is act—
> There go, a multitude impalpable
> To ordinary human faculty,
> The thoughts which give the act significance.
> Who is a poet needs must apprehend
> Alike both speech and thoughts which prompt to speak.
> Part these, and thought withdraws to poetry:
> Speech is reported in the newspaper.)
> He said, then, probably no word at all,

But thought as follows—in a minute's space—
One particle of ore beats out such leaf! (3276-87)

In basing his defense upon the impossibility of Chatterton's "saying any thing to the real purpose" in justification
of his actions, in attempting to plead Chatterton's case in
terms of what Chatterton intimately thought and felt but
could not say for himself, Browning was entering his special
province as an artist. With "the point of view," as George
Herbert Palmer observed, Browning's "special type of poetry
is inherently connected."[14]

b. The second essential of Browning's procedure is closely
linked with the first: *Browning explains the whole of his
hero's later, superficially complex and ambiguous conduct in
terms of a single tendency of his nature that is with him at
the beginning of his career.*

To understand Chatterton's "true position," Browning tells
us in the *Essay,* "we must remove much of the colouring
which subsequent occurrences imparted to the dim beginnings of his course of deception." (224-26) The typical self-
apologist of the dramatic monologues proceeds in like
manner, first defining the tendency of his career in its "dim
beginnings" and then tracing his later conduct in terms of it.
Bishop Blougram prefers to talk in metaphor:

> Now come, let's backward to the starting-place.
> See my way: we're two college friends, suppose.
> Prepare together for our voyage, then;
> Each note and check the other in his work,—
> Here's mine, a bishop's outfit; criticize!
> What's wrong? why won't you be a bishop too?
>   (144-49)

The Bishop's aim has been to outfit his cabin for the voyage
of life with a view to solid comfort above all else. He traces
the whole of his career in terms of his desire from the
beginning to be "merely much" and to enjoy the pleasures

of an "ideal realized" in mundane luxuries and adulation, in preference to an uncomfortable pursuit of abstract truth.[15] Sludge goes back to his boyhood to show how his tendency to brighten the truth with fable-making became by degrees an ordered system of trickery under the encouragement of his patrons. But it is Hohenstiel-Schwangau who is most expansive among the self-apologists on this, as on the other points of Browning's procedure:

> Good! It shall be! Revealment of myself!
> But listen, for we must co-operate;
> I don't drink tea: permit me the cigar!
>
> First, how to make the matter plain, of course—
> What was the law by which I lived. Let's see:
> Ay, we must take one instant of my life
> Spent sitting by your side in this neat room:
> Watch well the way I use it, and don't laugh!
> Here's paper on the table, pen and ink:
> Give me the soiled bit—not the pretty rose!
> See! having sat an hour, I'm rested now,
> Therefore want work: and spy no better work
> For eye and hand and mind that guides them both,
> During this instant, than to draw my pen
> From blot One—thus—up, up to blot Two—thus—
> Which I at last reach, thus, and here's my line
> Five inches long and tolerably straight:
> Better to draw than leave undrawn, I think,
> Fitter to do than let alone, I hold,
> Though better, fitter, by but one degree.   (22-41)

In this simple action, so the Prince says, he has illustrated his central tendency from the beginning of his career to his downfall; for his aim has been always to patch, to compromise, to keep things safe:

> Make what is absolutely new—I can't,
> Mar what is made already well enough—
> I won't: but turn to best account the thing

[209]

That's half-made—that I can. Two blots, you saw
I knew how to extend into a line
Symmetric on the sheet they blurred before—
Such little act sufficed, this time, such thought.

(85-91)

By following this inclination for patching and preserving through the actions that made up his career, the pretty auditress can understand "what meant certain things he did of old" which had greatly puzzled far wiser heads:

—why, you'll find them plain,
This way, not otherwise: I guarantee,
Understand one, you comprehend the rest.

(62-64)

Monsieur Léonce Miranda of *Red Cotton Night-Cap Country or Turf and Towers* (as the full title goes) also possessed a nature that ran to compromise, and it was by compromise that he perished. In Miranda's nature two forces waged irreconcilable conflict—the earthy and illicit love of his mistress, which Browning symbolizes as "turf," and his religious aspirations, which Browning designates as "towers." It is in terms of this conflict that Miranda's conduct is interpreted from his youth to his apparent suicide. Browning as narrator wanted to make sure that the reader would not miss this fact:

Keep this same
Notion of outside mound and inside mash,
Towers yet intact round turfy rottenness,
Symbolic partial-ravage,—keep in mind!
Here fortune placed his feet who first of all
Found no incumbrance, till head found . . . But hear!

(1144-49)

Returning to the *Essay* after this view of Browning's mature practice, it is possible to see more clearly how the prose piece of 1842 looked forward to Browning's later work in regard to the second essential of his method. Even in turning from Tasso to Chatterton, Browning makes it plain that he intends to trace the labyrinthine ways of Chatterton's career by a single thread:

But before we speak of the corresponding passage in Chatterton's story, something should be premised respecting the characteristic shape his first error took, as induced by the liabilities of that peculiar development of genius of which he was the subject. (175-79)

Chatterton's first error, we learn, was the comparatively harmless imitating of the work of an earlier period. But Chatterton's peculiar powers of simulating the ancient manner involved him almost at once in more serious deceptions. He was urged on by his patrons, and "at every advance in such a career," Browning tells us, "the impossibility of continuing in the spirit of the outset grows more and more apparent" (212-214). Poor Chatterton, unable to give all up, could only determine to produce more Ellas and Godwyns. Yet his genius was essentially moral. Though day after day found him more deeply involved, he fought valiantly to regain the ways of Truth.

It is in terms of Chatterton's struggle to reform under the most adverse circumstances and in spite of his peculiar ability to profit by deception that Browning explains the boy poet's conduct in his ambiguous and puzzling career. His dealings with Walpole became "the predetermined last acts of a course of dissimulation he would fain discard for ever—on their success" (507-508). His departure from Bristol is attributed to "this and no other motive—to break through his slavery—at any sacrifice to get back to truth" (734-35). His suicide is explained in terms of this struggle and as its culmination in spiritual triumph. Even in *Hohenstiel-Schwangau*

Browning did not proceed more directly to his purpose than in his attempt at "showing that [Chatterton] really made the most gallant and manly effort of which his circumstances allowed to break through the sorry meshes that entangled him" (475-78).

c. The third essential of Browning's procedure as a special pleader is again but a dimension of the first and basic fact, his espousal of a special point of view: *Browning concentrates each of his studies upon a single important question in the life of his hero.*

The question may be, to use the language of *Sordello*, "One of God's large ones" that is difficult to condense into a period; nevertheless it is a single question that gives point and coherence to the whole monologue or narrative. Inevitably it bears upon the central tendency of the hero's nature, and it is in terms of this central tendency that the answer is elaborated. The question of Bishop Blougram's life is whether he believes or disbelieves, a difficult question that requires a thousand lines of finely balanced exposition in reply. The Bishop defines it thus:

Fool or knave?
Why needs a bishop be a fool or knave
When there's a thousand diamond weights between?
So, I enlist them. Your picked twelve, you'll find
Profess themselves indignant, scandalized
At thus being held unable to explain
How a superior man who disbelieves
May not believe as well: that's Schelling's way!
It's through my coming in the tail of time,
Nicking the minute with a happy tact.
Had I been born three hundred years ago
They'd say, "What's strange? Blougram of course believes";
And, seventy years since, "disbelieves of course."
But now, "He may believe; and yet, and yet
"How can he?" All eyes turn with interest.

(404-18)

Sludge seems equally direct in posing the question of his life:

> What? If I told you all about the tricks?
> Upon my soul!—the whole truth, and nought else,
> And how there's been some falsehood . . . ?   (55-57)

But the implied question is how Sludge came to indulge in tricks and cheating, how self-desecration came to be his way of life. Hohenstiel-Schwangau, as we have already seen, at first proposes to attempt an almost all inclusive subject:

> Good! It shall be! Revealment of myself!   (22)

He limits his aim as he proceeds:

> —I don't say, to that plaguy quadrature
> "What the whole man meant, whom you wish you knew,
> But, what meant certain things he did of old,
> Which puzzled Europe,— . . . .   (59-62)

Nevertheless the solution to the two questions might have been the same, for small and large are meaningless terms when character is the subject. The answer to both questions is to be found in the central tendency of Hohenstiel-Schwangau's actions. This may in turn be found by the proper analysis of any single action—such coherency is revealed in the nature of a man provided one has the truly analytic eye:

>   I guarantee,
> Understand one [action], you comprehend the rest.
> Rays from all round converge to any point:
> Study the point then ere you track the rays!

The size o' the circle's nothing; subdivide
Earth, and earth's smallest grain of mustard-seed,
You count as many parts, small matching large,
If you can use the mind's eye: otherwise,
Material optics, being gross at best,
Prefer the large and leave our mind the small—
And pray how many folk have minds can see?
                                              (63-73)

Here what may at first seem mere casuistry on the part of the
Prince is actually in its implications an effective description
of Browning's method of working; for in his handling, a
focal point is indeed made but a center for all aspects of his
hero's character. Like Tennyson's little flower, Browning's
single question, his point of focus, is made to mean far
beyond the facts in radial hints and suggestions. In studying
the point, he studied all. It is thus that Blougram, Sludge,
and Hohenstiel-Schwangau reveal themselves.

It is in like manner that Miranda of *Red Cotton Night-Cap
Country* is revealed. The central question with which
Browning concerns himself is what led Miranda to leap from
his belvedere to dash his brains upon the ground below.
Insanity, the villagers believed; but Browning held otherwise. Miranda made his leap, Browning maintained, in the
hope that angels might bear him up and thus vouchsafe
through a miracle his right to keep both his mistress and
his faith. His error was not in his conclusions, but in the
premises that others had taught him:

                    No! sane I say.
        Such being the conditions of his life,
        Such end of life was not irrational.   (3605-607)

Nearly twenty-five hundred lines earlier, after a lengthy and
discursive introduction, Browning had given the point and
theme of his tale:

DONALD SMALLEY

And all at once the climbing landed him
—Where, is my story:
Take its moral first.
Do you advise a climber? Have respect
To the poor head, with more or less of brains
To spill, should breakage follow your advice!
(1123-27)

In the interim, he had gone through the whole of Miranda's
life. Yet all is told in terms of the one question.

As we have already seen, Browning in 1842 praised
Richard Henry Wilde for having "steadily restricted himself
to the single point in question" and proposed to follow
Wilde in tracing Chatterton's career. In the light of his own
later practice, Browning's comments on Wilde's method may
be worth reviewing even at the expense of some repetition:

Still it is but a point; and Mr. Wilde has not perhaps done
less gracefully and wisely in leaving the rest untouched, than
in accomplishing so thoroughly the task he took in hand. He
relies upon his subject; is sure of the service he can render by
an efficacious treatment of thus much of it; nor entertains any
fear lest the bringing in a Before and After, with which he
has no immediate concern, should be thought necessary to give
interest to the At Present on which he feels he can labour to
advantage. We suspect that if we would make any material
progress in knowledge of this description, such works must be
so undertaken. (91-101)

Here the bias seems more important than the literal statement. Browning as a special pleader did not in the *Essay*
or in his later work concentrate so completely on the "At
Present" that he failed to bring in "a Before and After" to
illuminate his immediate subject; but he did direct all his
attention to the "single point in question," and that is
apparently what he considered new and significant in Wilde's
method:

[215]

If, for example, the materials for a complete biography of Tasso are far from exhausted, let some other traveller from the west be now busied in the land of Columbus and Vespucci with the investigation,—say, of the circumstances of the wondrous youth of Tasso; the orations at Naples and the Theses at Padua,—and in the end we should more than probably have two spots of sunshine to find our way by, instead of one such breadth of dubious twilight, as, in a hazy book written on the old principle of doing a little for every part of a subject, and more than a little for none, rarely fails to perplex the more. (102-12)

It was by applying this lesson from Wilde that he hoped to add his own spot of sunshine to Chatterton biography:

We can show, we think, and by some such process as Mr. Wilde adopts in regard to Tasso, that [Chatterton] had already entered on those ways when he was left, without a helping hand, to sink and starve as he might. And to this single point we shall as far as possible restrict ourselves. (145-149)

And it was this aspect of his own practice that Browning at the close of the *Essay* urged others to follow, using his study of Chatterton as he had used Wilde's volumes.

It is clear that Browning considered his concentration upon a single question of Chatterton's career the most notable fact of his method in the *Essay*, the fact which made his method capable of substituting solar radiance for the dubious twilight of earlier writers, which made it worth the study and emulation of other authors.

III

The *Essay*, then, is a tentative exercise, a laboratory model, in the process of special pleading. It possesses the attributes common to laboratory models. There is a patent self-consciousness on the part of its maker regarding his purposes and his means of effecting them; there is little attempt to round surfaces and conceal the angular machinery that does the work.

This is not to say that the *Essay* is without literary merit; Browning's Chatterton can claim a place in Browning's memorable gallery of men and women. But the *Essay* is at least as interesting for what it prophesies as for what it realizes. In this unacknowledged prose work we see clearly for the first time how the essential artist of the 1840's was feeling his way toward *The Ring and the Book* and the great dramatic monologues of his maturity.

[1949]

HOXIE N. FAIRCHILD

BROWNING THE SIMPLE-HEARTED CASUIST

Has any English poet of comparable historical interest and intrinsic merit received so small an amount of respectable critical attention as Robert Browning? Now that the nineteenth-century spate of "inspirational" eulogy and exegesis has dwindled to the merest trickle, there is need and opportunity for disinterested reexamination of his work. One result of such a study will be our awareness of a paradox. Though by no means a profound philosopher, Browning was a man of much intellectual subtlety. He was fascinated by the difficulties and ambiguities of thought, its sinuous twistings and turnings and casuistical rationalizations. But his deeply convoluted brain could never dismiss the obligation to satisfy the demands of his healthy and almost boyishly simple heart. On the one hand, the truth was many-sided, relative, shadowy; on the other hand, it was single, absolute, and plain as a pikestaff. Brain truth was of man; heart truth was of God. The poet, who must faithfully render all the tangled phenomena of mental life, must also apprehend God's truth and impart it to others. Several of Browning's most characteristic poems attempt to reconcile the complex brain and the simple heart. For all his dramatic subtlety, he seldom fails to make the speaker expose the "real" truth which underlies the surface play of intellectual sophistication. Although the assumption that the real is always more simple than the apparent is probably fallacious, one usually admires the skill with which Browning achieves his purpose. Sometimes, however, the speaker unmasks himself with excessively naïve alacrity. And still more regrettably Browning, in his reluctance to bewilder or demoralize the reader and in his eagerness to satisfy the demands of his own wholesome nature, rather often adds a passage which tells the reader precisely what to think. Sometimes he does so within the framework of the poem, and sometimes he frankly speaks in his own person; but in either case the passage is essentially extra-dramatic. Especially when religious issue is at stake, this device is common enough to deserve a label: let us call it "the giveaway."

The earliest clear example of the giveaway occurs in *Sordello*—not of course a dramatic monologue, but an attempt to tell a story in terms of the infinitely tortuous thoughts and feelings of the characters, with a minimum didactic intrusion. In Book VI, just before the poet-patriot's death, Browning mercifully steps in with

> Ah my Sordello, I this once befriend
> And speak for you.

Both hero and reader stand in dire need of such intervention, for the preceding five hundred lines or so have described, in language of almost impenetrable difficulty, the groping of Sordello's mind toward some kind of suprapersonal value.

Since the hero himself does not know what this value is, it is incumbent on Browning to inform us, quite unambiguously, that what Sordello really needs is God incarnate in Jesus Christ.

Naturally, however, it is in the dramatic monologues that the problem of how to be interestingly subtle without placing a stumbling-block in the reader's path becomes acute. Let us examine a few of these giveaways, arranging the examples in a descending order of blatancy. The more specious the case of the speaker, the greater the need of an explicit indication of his falsehood. Mr. Sludge, the medium, is caught barehanded in an outrageous piece of trickery. But Mrs. Browning's spiritualistic hankerings have given her husband as sharp a distaste for the patrons of men like Daniel Home as for the tricksters themselves. Hence the rascally little Yankee is given a good deal to say for himself. His nature has been warped by social and economic factors beyond his control. The normal fancifulness of his childhood has been perverted by the world's craving for marvels and by the vanity of superstitious gentry who develop a vested interest in the validity of his mediumship. "You see, sir, it's your own fault more than mine. . . . It's too bad, I say, Ruining a soul so!" His tricks, moreover, have served the cause of religion in this unbelieving age. He firmly believes in the supernatural, and "can't be sure But there was something in it, tricks and all!" Perhaps he has not actually cheated, but "made believe I led myself" rather than confront the awesome reality of his contact with the spiritual realm. Although this apologia is sprinkled with clues which broadly hint at the speaker's fundamental falsity, Browning will not permit such casuistry to pass without more obvious exposure. Sludge himself is made to show us the "real" truth when he curses his patron, that "brute-beast and blackguard" whom he has just left with a "Good-night!

Bl-l-less you, sir!" He will turn defeat into victory by spreading scandalous reports about this fine gentleman, and then

> An end of him! Begin elsewhere anew!
> Boston's a hole, the herring-pond is wide,
> V-notes are something, liberty still more.
> Besides, is he the only fool in the world?

Having had his fun, Browning does his duty. We are left in no doubt as to what to think of Sludge. Most readers will probably feel that Bishop Blougram's casuistry is that of a cold-hearted, worldly sceptic. At least one scholar, however, has interpreted his apologetics in a different sense [F. E. L. Priestley, "Blougram's Apologetics." See above, pp. 167-80]. Closely examined, the main body of the monologue is a puzzling mixture of a slyness repugnant to Browning and a common sense pragmatism by no means uncongenial with his own philosophy. Hence at the end of the poem Browning makes a rather awkward effort to extract the simple, wholesome truth from subtleties which might otherwise be too darkly ambiguous both for his audience and for himself. Browning the psychologist had made the bishop talk too cleverly to satisfy Browning the moralist. Blougram's insistence on living according to what is, rather than according to what should be, is a favourite doctrine of the poet himself, though it is voiced more frequently in later poems. A snare lurks in the idea that no one can be either a completely sure believer or a completely sure unbeliever: "We call the chessboard white —we call it black." And the argument for exercising something very like the Jamesian will-to-believe in the absence of demonstrative proof is not to be accepted without safeguards which the Bishop himself cannot be expected to provide. Therefore Browning in his own person furnishes the giveaway. The Bishop, we are told, "believed, say,

[221]

half he spoke," and made up the rest for the pleasure of the argument, offering as settled convictions whatever amusing notions chanced to cross his mind, but not revealing "certain hell-deep instincts" which were more fundamental in his nature than the ideas he had expressed. "He said true things, but called them by wrong names." He by no means convinced Gigadibs, his interviewer. Before a week had elapsed the young journalist, with "sudden healthy vehemence," took ship for the less sophistical shores of Australia—

> . . . there, I hope,
> By this time he has tested his first plough,
> And studied his last chapter of St. John.

Thus any possible ambiguity in the monologue proper is clarified by a much simpler wisdom than Blougram's.

Mention of St. John brings to mind "A Death in the Desert." The dying Evangelist's faith is of course untainted by casuistry; and although the historical and physical background of the poem is admirably dramatic, John himself speaks so exactly like Robert Browning that any giveaway would seem to be superfluous. But Browning permits John to foresee the doubts of future generations who will regard the Saviour as "mere projection from man's inmost mind," and who will wish to devise new expressions of the same human love. These doubts are set forth rather more clearly and tellingly than the saint's passionate but vague rebuttal. Hence to the account of John's death in the ancient manuscript "One [Browning in antique costume] added this": a familiar argument for the divinity of Christ, which the poet thought too modern to be expressed through the lips of John. If Jesus was mere man, then he was a wretched failure, or a deceiver, or both. Here again is the attempt to provide external simplification of the complex intellectual drama of the poem.

"An Epistle," in which Karshish mingles notes on medical botany with the story of the raising of Lazarus, might well have been allowed to speak for itself. The way in which the hard-headed Arab physician *almost* doubts his own disbelief is deeply suggestive. The poet, however, makes Karshish conclude with:

> The very God! think, Abib; dost thou think?
> So, the All-Great were the All-Loving too—
> So, through the thunder comes a human voice
> Saying, "O heart I made, a heart beats here!
> Face, my hands fashioned, see it in myself!
> Thou hast no power nor mayst conceive of mine,
> But love I gave thee, with myself to love,
> And thou must love me who have died for thee!"
> The madman [Lazarus] saith He said so: it is strange.

The last line cannot conceal the fact that the rest of this passage is pure Browning. These are not the words of the half-fascinated sceptic who has written the hauntingly ambiguous letter.

In "Cleon" the giveaway is managed so delicately that one feels no rupture of the dramatic framework. The weary old pagan confesses that the thought of death is dreadful to one who has devoted himself to the goods of this world, and especially so to the artist because he savours this fleeting life so intensely. No hope of immortality has ever crossed his mind; and the best he can offer Protus, who has sought his advice, is:

> Live long and happy, and in that thought die,
> Glad for what was!

But rather than seem to recommend such Epicureanism, Browning makes Cleon intimate the existence of a higher hope without realizing that he has done so. Cleon is somewhat offended that Protus should also have written to one Paulus, "a mere barbarian Jew," who may or may not be the same as Christus. At all events—an ironic giveaway—"Their doctrine could be held by no sane man."

If ever a character in a dramatic monologue explicitly betrayed his own benightedness through his own words, surely Caliban does so in his brutish dissertation upon Setebos. That Browning feels the need of suggesting a loftier religious ideal is indicated by Caliban's dim sense that even Setebos is subject to something called "the Quiet." This device does not, however, fully perform the function of a giveaway, for Caliban supposes that "the Quiet" is wholly indifferent to human concerns. This deity finds in the act of creation nothing but a sort of aesthetic pleasure: " 'Tis solace making baubles, ay, and sport." Instead of developing the idea of "the Quiet," Browning concludes the poem by terrifying Caliban with one of Setebos' thunderstorms:

> Fool to gibe at Him!
> Lo! 'Lieth flat and loveth Setebos!
> 'Maketh his teeth meet through his upper lip,
> Will let those quails fly, will not eat this month
> One little mess of whelks, so he may 'scape!

Perhaps this speech is too typical of Caliban to be called a giveaway, but it lays heavy didactic emphasis on the fact that the God whom Caliban has created in his own image becomes for him a source of real terror and an object of superstitious propitiation.

When "Johannes Agricola in Meditation" and "Porphyria's Lover" first appeared in 1842, Browning provided a preliminary giveaway by placing them under the heading "Madhouse Cells." When he later abandoned this crude device, the poems were allowed to stand on their own feet except for the light touch of "editorializing" in the last line of "Porphyria's Lover": "And yet God has not said a word."

This poem, however, is perfectly consistent with Browning's doctrine of the "good minute." Agricola's antinomianism is self-condemnatory, but it is rather surprising that Browning should have withheld his rebuke.

In other dramatic monologues the absence of any give-away is easily explained. Fra Lippo Lippi and Andrea del Sarto preach Browning's own gospel too fervently to require or deserve correction. In "The Bishop Orders His Tomb," the dying sensualist gives *himself* away so obviously that the author has nothing to add. Any reader could be trusted to interpret the poem in relation to the ecclesiastical corruption of the Renaissance. Browning uses a much finer brush for "My Last Duchess," but he is so sympathetic with the poor girl's lack of aristocratic discrimination that he regards the Duke's mere recital of the story as sufficiently explicit condemnation of him. This little masterpiece is, I believe, the only dramatic monologue in which an enemy of Browning's gospel is allowed to speak for himself without heavily underscoring his own error or being exposed by a giveaway.

It is in *The Ring and the Book* that the struggle between subtle brain and simple heart grows most acute. The "old yellow book" richly satisfied Browning's almost perverse love of intellectual complication and ambiguity, his sense of the many-sidedness of truth and the entanglement of good and evil. And yet beneath the conflicting documents lay the real, simple, black and white truth—the truth not of man but of God. The poet must find and reveal this truth by adding the alloy of imagination to the crude ore of fact, thus shaping the formless old "book" into a "ring"—a work of art beautifully instructive and instructively beautiful. In the opening book of the poem he discusses this creative problem and sketches the muddled ferment of Roman opinion on the case. He does not fail, however, to run through the story from a point of view which the reader plainly sees will prove to be the true one.

"Half-Rome," "The Other Half-Rome," and "Tertium Quid" represent Browning's desire to exploit the complexities and ambiguities of his material in psychological studies almost completely uncoloured by any suggestion of a judgment external to that of the speaker. "Tertium Quid" is especially remarkable for the objectivity with which its sophisticated casuistry is rendered. Unfortunately our response to these sections is conditioned by the giveaway which the prefatory book has already provided.

After "Tertium Quid," except in the sections devoted to the grotesque lawyers, the warm-hearted moralizer completely supplants the analyst of mental behaviour. Count Guido makes some effective appeals to the sympathies and prejudices of the court, and he has a legitimate grievance against Pietro and Violante; but even the first of his two speeches leaves no doubt that he is a monster. With the appearance of the hero and heroine, the psychological thriller becomes something very like a religious allegory; the amount of imaginative alloy imposed upon the original documentary ore is now greatly increased. The characters of Caponsacchi and Pompilia exhibit no human mixture of black and white, but a blaze of heavenly radiance. They reveal themselves as God's champions, saints provided for each other's prayers, latter-day incarnations of divine love.

But their own words are not enough. Unwilling to trust the dramatic method as a means of distinguishing absolute good from absolute evil, Browning winds up his *magnum opus* by piling giveaway upon giveaway. Diaphanously disguised as the Pope he reviews the whole case, reaches the already foregone conclusion, dispenses praise and blame, renders judgment. Then he brings Guido before us a second time and makes him talk in such a way as to prove that the good old Pope was perfectly right. Finally he steps forward in his own person and provides the "British Public" with the moral:

This lesson, that our human speech is naught,
Our human testimony false, our fame
And human estimation words and wind.

This is a fair deduction from the utterance of the Romans, of Guido, and of the lawyers. But the human testimony of Caponsacchi and Pompilia has not been false at all, and the human estimation supplied by Browning, though most copiously expressed in words, has been thoroughly sound. Perhaps, however, the hero, the heroine, and the poet are to be regarded as "human" only in a rather special sense. At all events Browning adds the final point that art, which suggests thoughts through things, is a precious means of telling truth "obliquely." Thus the poet may

write a book shall mean beyond the facts,
Suffice the eye and save the soul beside.

That last line points to the core of the whole matter. Broadly interpreted, "suffice the eye" implies the whole scope of Browning's omnivorous curiosity, his lust to render the bewildering but fascinating welter of mental no less than physical phenomena, to

paint these
Just as they are, careless what comes of it.

In the dramatic monologue he found the most congenial medium for the satisfaction of this impulse. But it was necessary to "save the soul beside," and his simple heart could not extract sufficiently clear didactic principles from the complexities in which his subtle brain delighted. Hence his too frequent reliance, in ostensibly dramatic writing, on the essentially undramatic giveaway. Hence also the strange fact that Browning, whose main distinguishing characteristic is his preference for speaking through the lips of others, is one of the least impersonal of English poets.

Some may prefer to say the "real" Browning is genuinely dramatic, and that his soul-saving giveways are reluctant concessions to the Victorian appetite for wholesome messages. But he was a very honest man, and when the writings of an honest man reek with purpose the logical conclusion is that he is honestly purposeful. His naive didacticism represents the "real" Browning no less faithfully than his psychological sophistication. He was inwardly divided against himself, though to some extent the conflict was his personal share of a prevalent nineteenth-century confusion.

[1950]

WILLIAM O. RAYMOND

THE INFINITE MOMENT

THOUGH it is now sixty years since the death of Robert Browning, the time is yet unripe for a definitive estimate of his place amongst English men of letters. During his lifetime he experienced, perhaps to a greater extent than any of his contemporaries, the vicissitudes of a poet's lot. A long period of depreciation, in which his poetry was a by-word for difficulty and obscurity, was followed by a sudden access of fame. From the time of the publication of *The Ring and the Book* in 1868-69 until his death in 1889, his niche beside Tennyson as one of the two master poets of the Victorian era was secure. Criticism was succeeded by panegyric, reaching its acme in the adulation of the Browning Society and its mushroom offshoots in England and America.

In the sixty years that have passed since Browning's death, his poetic reputation has varied as widely as in his lifetime.

The pendulum of critical opinion has again swung violently from one extreme to the other. In particular, Browning has suffered, along with Tennyson, from the general reaction inimical to Victorianism and all its works which has characterized the opening decades of the twentieth century. There are signs that the nadir has been reached, and that a juster and truer appreciation of the Victorian epoch is at hand. But we are still in the wake of that inevitable shift of literary evaluation which marks the transition from one generation to the next. The baiting of Victorianism continues to be a favourite sport of modern writers; and prevailing currents of present-day historical and aesthetic criticism run counter to some of the cherished ideals and standards in life and art of our Victorian forerunners. Part of this censure is wholesome, part is regrettable, but the winnowing of our Victorian inheritance by the fan of time is as yet incomplete.

A tentative estimate, within brief compass, of Browning's place in English letters must strive for centrality of view. In reckoning with a poet of such far-ranging interests, it is important to insist that he be appraised first of all as an artist. However beguiling the bypaths of his work in literature may be, it is essential to keep steadily in sight the beaten highway, lit by the flash of his genius, where his powers are exhibited at full stretch.

Yet such an emphasis should not be inconsistent with a recognition of the composite nature of Browning's contribution to English poetry. In certain ways he is both an intellectual and a moralist, and the philosophical, ethical, and theological aspects of his writings are fruitful subjects of inquiry. Much has been said concerning the confinement of these elements of his work within a set Victorian mould. But in dealing with a mind of a rare order and a poet of genius, stress should be laid upon those gleams of intuition which break through the conventional Victorian framework with keen insight into the heart of life and the problems of man's destiny. Such a reverie as that of Pope Innocent XII, in *The Ring and the Book*, is no mere collection of theological platitudes. It is a definitive summing up of Browning's philosophy of life, and a high watermark of metaphysical thought in nineteenth-century poetry, enriched by acute religious perception.

Nevertheless, it is inevitable that a study of the didactic interests of Browning often leads to the periphery rather than to the centre of his poetry. Within this sphere, prodigious mental energy or moral fervour tends to obscure the poet. There is in him a conflict between imagination and intellect, only resolved in the poems of happiest vein, written between 1840 and 1870, beginning with *Pippa Passes* and ending with *The Ring and the Book*. For the understanding of his view of life, the deep-seated opposition between faith and reason pivotal to his thought, his ethical outlook, his conception of the relation between God and man and of man's place in the universe, a consideration of the earlier and later poems lying outside his golden period of imaginative vision is indispensable. Nor can the depths of Browning's analysis of character be plumbed without a knowledge of those stages of his work which abound in subtle probing of impulse and motive, the incidents in the development of the soul underlying outward action.

In order to comprehend these varying interests, a student must toil through the labyrinth of *Sordello*, "a bewildering potpourri of poetry, psychology, love, romance, humanitarianism, philosophy, fiction, and history."[1] He must wrestle with poems which in the aggregate, at any rate, tax his patience and mental faculties even more than that "Giant Despair" of English letters. Some of the later writings of Browning, while they contain lines and passages of sheer poetic beauty, are jungles of involved argument. The mind reels amid the elusive, ever shifting sophistries of *Fifine at the Fair* and *Aristophanes' Apology*, or is repelled by the sordidness of *Red Cotton Night-Cap Country*. Though the poet tells us that a delectable ortolan is sandwiched between the plain bread of *Ferishtah's Fancies*, the appetite of the average reader is hardly reconciled to the crust he must crunch before reaching the toothsome bird.

Even the wit and dexterity of Browning's numerous studies in casuistry scarcely atone for their redundancy. We are dizzied by their juggling and wearied by their tortuousness. "Mr. Sludge, 'the Medium,'" "Bishop Blougram's Apology," and *Prince Hohenstiel-Schwangau* are overweighted with ratiocination. The hair-splitting arguments of the lawyers in *The Ring and the Book* make gnarly and tiresome reading, and their crabbed forensic quibbles are only slightly enlivened by quaint Latin puns illustrating the humour of pedants. Whatever tribute is due to Browning's ingenuity in constructing these cumbersome leviathans of verse, the most ardent devotee of the poet, when caught in their toils, must compare his state of mind to that of Milton's spirits in torment, who "found no end in wandering mazes lost."

Happily for Browning's enduring fame as an artist, he has written a large body of fine poetry in which he was able to exorcise his intellectual devil. He cast it from him, even as the hero of one of his poems, in rollicking mockery of arid scholasticism, tossed the bulky tome of Sibrandus Schafnaburgensis into the crevice of a garden tree. "Plague take all your pedants, say I!" It is a pleasure to turn from the "grey argument" of tracts of his verse to the magic of such poetry as is garnered in *Dramatic Romances* and *Men and Women*. Here imagination has not been supplanted by dialectic; and passion and intuition are enlisted in the depicting of character and situation with swift and brilliant portraiture. The sweep and vivacity of Browning's humanism are a perpetual source of delight. As a humanist he is of the lineage of Chaucer and Shakespeare, a poet of whose work it may be said, "here is God's plenty." Above all other Victorian writers, he has that spaciousness of mind we are wont to link with the Elizabethans. Spiritually a disciple of the Renaissance, he is akin to that great age in his zest of life, *élan* of temperament, overflowing curiosity regarding the ways and works of man. His creative genius has many facets and in richness and versatility is unsurpassed in nineteenth-century English literature. How far flung is his poetic net and what treasure trove he brings to land! Strange fish sometimes, but all

> Live whelks, each lip's beard dripping fresh,
> As if they still the water's lisp heard
> Through foam the rock-weeds thresh.

I intend to centre my estimate of Browning on his artistic quality. This, in itself, has various aspects, and many of them must be left untouched. His dramatic gift, its capacity and limitation, is a fascinating theme, but it has been exhaustively written on from various points of view. The style and diction of his verse have been the subject of a number of technical treatises. I have in mind, rather, to dwell on what may be called the elemental spirit of Browning's art. This choice is in part due to a wish to take issue with what I conceive to be the general drift of Browning criticism at present. If I interpret this rightly, its quarrel is with the whole tone and temper of the poet's work, not with this or that specific weakness.

An initial definition is, therefore, necessary. What is the basic element which inhabits and glints through the body of Browning's verse as its pervasive and animating soul? Can we in reading his numerous poems, so diverse in theme and setting, "loose their subtle spirit" in a cruce, like the Arab sage of "In a Gondola"?

Writing to Elizabeth Barrett in 1845, Browning spoke of his poetry as momentary escapes of a bright and alive inner power and (in a figure of speech) compared it to flashes of

[233]

light he had seen at sea leaping out at intervals from a narrow chink in a Mediterranean pharos.[2] The vehemence and impulsiveness of Browning's verse have been universally recognized. Both the form and the content of his poetry are vividly impressionistic. His favourite medium is the dramatic monologue, which in his best work is the distillation of a crucial moment of human experience. Light is focused at one point in a white heat of concentration and intensity. In the revelation of the significance of the precipitous moment, vivacity and turbulence are outstanding attributes of his poetic diction and spirit.

Yet the general recognition of the flair or impetuosity of Browning's poetry has by no means been accompanied by unanimity of opinion concerning its merit. Differing judgments of this essential quality have led to a battle of controversy, dividing the poet's admirers and detractors into hostile camps. Before singling it out for praise, it is, therefore, well to glance at some of the criticism it has provoked. "Cockney Sublime, Cockney Energy," was FitzGerald's jaundiced comment.[3] In our own day, Mr. Santayana, in an essay "The Poetry of Barbarism," has scored the work of Browning as that of "a thought and an art inchoate and ill-digested, of a volcanic eruption that tosses itself quite blindly and ineffectually into the sky."[4] Santayana likens Browning to Whitman, and in this comparison has been followed by T. S. Eliot.

The germ of that approach to Browning's writings which emphasizes their so-called barbaric, Gothic, ultra-romantic elements, may be found back in 1864, in Bagehot's "Wordsworth, Tennyson, and Browning, or, Pure, Ornate, and Grotesque Art in English Poetry." It is a conception that was taken up and enlarged upon by Chesterton in his arresting but untrustworthy biography of the poet. Of late it has been made a formidable weapon of attack in the hands of a school of aesthetic thought which extols classical standards and is deeply distrustful of romanticism. F. L. Lucas has given recent expression to this neo-classicist credo in *The Decline and Fall of the Romantic Ideal.* Our appraisal of it will depend on whether we regard romanticism as abnormal and pathological, or as rooted in an experience of life as normative and intrinsic as that on which the classic tradition is based. It is important to recognize that criticism of Browning as voiced by Irving Babbitt, Santayana, F. L. Lucas, and T. S. Eliot is an offshoot of a general neo-classicist position. Viewed as a whole, the modern indictment of the energy of Browning's poetry seems a weighty one. At present, the moral, intellectual, and aesthetic aspects of his outlook on life are all suspect. To Santayana, the poet's vagrancy of impulse is indicative of the barbarity of his genius, the essence of which lies in the fact that to him "life is an adventure, not a discipline; that the exercise of energy is the absolute good, irrespective of motives or of consequences."[5] To Babbitt, Browning's unrestrained emotion is an example of those centrifugal and neurotic tendencies that, from the standpoint of neo-classicism, are regarded as evidence of a decadent romanticism. Passion and sensation, we are told, run riot in his poetry, and there is an utter lack of classical decorum, balance, and repose. To Mr. Lucas, there is a trace of a bouncing vulgarity in Browning's energetic verse, which smacks too much of the hearty hail-fellow-well-met manner of a Philistine. Metaphorically speaking, the unfastidious poet slaps his readers on the back. His "stamping and shouting," the jarring dissonances of his verse, "his hastily scribbled poems as fuzzy and prickly and tangled as a furzebush"[6] are at once excesses of his temperament and an undisciplined romanticism. Such comments are reminiscent of an earlier criticism that all of Browning's poetry is summed up in the line, "*Bang-whang-whang* goes the drum, *tootle-te-tootle* the fife."[7]

Although, in justice to Mr. Lucas, it should be noted that he does recognize the vitality of Browning's dramatic portrayal of human life, the general tenor of his criticism seems to me indicative of a mental twist which inhibits him from depicting the great men of letters of the Victorian age with disinterested objectivity. It is the fate of every generation to have its idols shattered by the hammer blows of the succeeding generation. Since the publication of Lytton Strachey's life of Queen Victoria, there have been many acute and witty *exposés* of the foibles, conventions, and conservatisms of the Victorian era. Yet what so many twentieth-century critics lack is a perception of the dignity, poise, and stability of that era, an ethos contributing to the endowment of its principal personages with nobility of character. To ignore these basic elements in Victorianism in delineating its great men is to view the age through a subtly distorted mirror in which every figure is out of focus.

Every man, it has been said, has the defect of his quality, and it might be added, every poet in his art has the defect of his quality. Browning's energy and vitality at times din the ear and become strident and overpowering. Though "barbarism" is not supposed to be a mid-Victorian vice, there is something unbridled in his rush of passion and the militant romanticism of his verse. He can write metallic poems and rhyming exercises. When he is lost in the Cretan labyrinth of his longer poems, his style is as crabbed and involved as his subject matter.

But the error and insufficiency of the criticism I have been reviewing seems to be that it fastens exclusively on the negative rather than on the positive aspect of the poet's elemental attribute. For it is precisely the dash or verve of his poetry which constitutes its perennial originality and attractiveness. It is a strain running like an *elixir vitae* through his verse in its golden era, giving it headiness and flavour. We are reminded of the violent rush of a mountain torrent frothing and seething amongst rocks and fretting its channel, but compensating for its lack of smooth rhythmical flow by the spin and dance, the spray and sparkle of its waters. "Passion's too fierce to be in fetters bound." From the critical censure of Browning's energy and impulsiveness we turn away, as our eye falls, perchance, with renewed delight on the opening lines of *Pippa Passes:*

> Day!
> Faster and more fast,
> O'er night's brim, day boils at last:
> Boils, pure gold, o'er the cloud-cup's brim
> Where spurting and suppressed it lay. . . .

The relation between the form and the content of the poetry of Browning is often a tension rather than a harmony. All poetry, he once wrote to Ruskin, is the problem of "putting the infinite within the finite."[8] It would carry us too far afield to show how the antithesis of infinite and finite is perpetually in his thought. But it is clear that the crux of the struggle in his life as an artist was the difficulty of bodying forth the content of his imagination and intellect in adequate poetic forms. In *Sordello,* which in many ways is a confessional document, there is a vivid account of the hero's attempt to forge a new language, in an Italian dialect, capable of expressing the novelty of his thoughts and perceptions. The analogy between this and Browning's wrestling with language is unmistakable. Like Sordello, he was striving to make his diction a suitable vehicle for the new type of analytic poetry he was writing. The arduousness of the process is realistically described:

> He left imagining, to try the stuff
> That held the imaged thing, and, let it writhe
> Never so fiercely, scarce allowed a tithe
> To reach the light—his Language. (II. 570-73)

Sordello, from the point of view of style, is a gigantic experiment in artistic technique. It is apprentice work of a faulty kind, yet through its convolutions the poet was feeling his way towards his true manner.

And when, after the murkiness of *Sordello,* the art of Browning begins to clear nobly in *Pippa Passes,* discovers its true bent in *Dramatic Lyrics* and *Dramatic Romances,* and reaches its meridian in *Men and Women,* the triumph of his style is all the more impressive because it has been hardly won. In the dramatic monologue of medium length, he found the poetic instrument he had vainly sought in *Sordello.* His metres and diction instinctively adapt themselves to impressionistic vignettes of picturesque situations and crucial moments in the lives of men and women, often enriched by pregnant historical or artistic backgrounds. Tension of style remains, but it is a close-packed, sensitive tension that is responsive to the subtle and varied play of highly charged thought and emotion. The tempo of Browning's diction in his great dramatic monologues is rapid to the point of abruptness. The metres have the beat of a driving energy. The music of his verse is uneven rather than smooth flowing, involving frequent suspensions and resolutions.

Le style c'est l'homme; and the racy, colloquial style of Browning in the best of his dramatic monologues is a revelation of his intrinsic quality. He has used a greater variety of metres than any other modern poet, but his verse is never rigidly set in a conventional mould. In reading Tennyson's lines,

> All in the blue unclouded weather
> Thick-jewell'd shone the saddle-leather,

we realize that the imagery is enclosed in a sedate metrical framework. But when Browning writes,

> To mine, it serves for the old June weather
> Blue above lane and wall,

there is a natural felicity in the utterance which shakes itself free from formal trappings.

Within its own province, there is a finality in the organic structure, the Sophia and Techné of Greek art; where communication is so wedded to inspiration, form to content, that, as Browning has pointed out in "Old Pictures in Florence," it achieves perfection in the sphere of the finite. But romantic art, as an emanation of the spirit of man in one of the two basic moments of his experience, has a genius of its own. It may lack the radiance of classic art, that clarity and harmony representative of "the depth and not the tumult of the soul." Yet there is a place on the altars of literature for the Dionysiac fire of romantic art: Dionysiac fire at times, but, when it burns as a purer flame, the light of the Holy Grail. Poetry must in certain moods reveal the tension of the spirit straining at the leash of form, and infinite passion shattering the web of finite expression:

> Thoughts hardly to be packed
> Into a narrow act,
> Fancies that broke through language and escaped.

Therefore, despite the frown of the classicist, a lover of Browning's poetry may take pleasure in its romantic beauty and in the free rein given to passion and sensation. He may enjoy its impressionistic glooms and glances, its live and nervous diction responsive to the "moment one and infinite" of electrically charged emotion. He may feel the justification of a content that overweighs the form, and a tension that is like the pent-up energy of a storm cloud:

> There are flashes struck from midnights,
> There are fire-flames noondays kindle. . . .

A few examples of the flair and verve of Browning's verse may be cited at random from the poems composed between 1840 and 1870.

The sensuousness of Browning's imagery is vivid and often

opulent, but never cloying or languorous. He has too much energy ever to indulge in the sleepy sensuousness of Spenser. Frequently his imagery is associated with a wealth and exotic splendour of colour. In "Popularity," his eye revels in the Tyrian blue or purple dye extracted from a secretion in the shell of the murex, and he combines this colour with the lustre of gold in two dazzling pictures. The dye, he tells us, is

> Enough to furnish Solomon
> Such hangings for his cedar-house,
> That, when gold-robed he took the throne
> In that abyss of blue, the Spouse
> Might swear his presence shone
>
> Most like the centre-spike of gold
> Which burns deep in the blue-bell's womb,
> What time, with ardours manifold,
> The bee goes singing to her groom,
> Drunken and overbold.

Images of light, sound, and motion are conjoined in the triumphant close of "Rabbi Ben Ezra," where the philosophic argument of the Jewish sage takes imaginative wings:

> Look not thou down but up!
> To uses of a cup,
> The festal board, lamp's flash and trumpet's peal,
> The new wine's foaming flow,
> The Master's lips a-glow!
> Thou, heaven's consummate cup, what need'st thou
>   with earth's wheel? (ll. 175-80)

"Abt Vogler" is a fine example of a sustained piece of imagery, representing a crescendo of feeling evoked by music. In other poems, imagery flares forth at the peak of an emotional mood like a beacon of passion. How the lines kindle in "The Statue and the Bust" when the cowardly and procrastinating lovers are contrasted with the militant saints of God!

> Only they see not God, I know,
> Nor all that chivalry of his,
> The soldier-saints who, row on row,
> Burn upward each to his point of bliss. . . . (ll.220-23)

Browning's descriptions of nature are as impressionistic as his vistas of human life, and reveal to an equal degree his elemental property. There is occasional tranquillity in his landscapes, but as a rule this is the brief hush that follows or precedes a moment of highly wrought emotional tension. As the lovers in "By the Fire-side" wait for the flash of revelation that is to fuse their lives in one, the brooding quietness of evening o'erhangs woodland and mountain.

> Oh moment, one and infinite!
> The water slips o'er stock and stone;
> The West is tender, hardly bright:
> How grey at once is the evening grown—
> One star, its chrysolite! (ll. 181-85)

But Browning's typical delineation of nature is in keeping with the high tide of dramatic passion that surges through his poetry. In *Pippa Passes,* the lightning seems to search for the guilty lovers, Sebald and Ottima, like the bared sword of divine justice.

> Buried in woods we lay, you recollect;
> Swift ran the searching tempest overhead;
> And ever and anon some bright white shaft
> Burned thro' the pine-tree roof, here burned and there.
> As if God's messenger thro' the close wood screen
> Plunged and replunged his weapon at a venture,
> Feeling for guilty thee and me: then broke
> The thunder like a whole sea overhead. . . .
>
> (I. 190-97)

In *The Ring and the Book,* the Pope's one hope for the salvation of Guido is visualized through a similar piece of fiery landscape painting.

> I stood at Naples once, a night so dark
> I could have scarce conjectured there was earth
> Anywhere, sky or sea or world at all:
> But the night's black was burst through by a blaze—
> Thunder struck blow on blow, earth groaned and bore,
> Through her whole length of mountain visible:
> There lay the city thick and plain with spires,
> And, like a ghost disshrouded, white the sea.
> So may the truth be flashed out by one blow,
> And Guido see, one instant, and be saved. (X. 219-28)

Browning's delight in brilliant and intense colour blends with his love of Italian scenery. In "De Gustibus," he prefers a Mediterranean vista, "the great opaque blue breadth of sea without a break," to the pastoral lanes and coppices of England. He takes particular pleasure in the semitropical bounty of nature in June in these lines of *Pippa Passes:*

> Well for those who live through June!
> Great noontides, thunder-storms, all glaring pomps
> That triumph at the heels of June the god
> Leading his revel through our leafy world. (III. 153-56)

The freshness and animation of the poet's landscapes are as typical as their emotional thrust. He pictures Florence as seen in spring "through the live translucent bath of air," when "river and bridge and street and square" are as clear "as the sights in a magic crystal ball." The common phenomenon of the breaking of ice in a pond gives birth, in "The Flight of the Duchess," to the following exquisite description:

> Well, early in autumn, at first winter-warning,
> When the stag had to break with his foot, of a morning,

A drinking-hole out of the fresh tender ice
That covered the pond till the sun, in a trice,
Loosening it, let out a ripple of gold,
And another and another, and faster and faster,
Till, dimpling to blindness, the wide water
    rolled. . . . (ll. 216-22)

Il fait vivre ses phrases. It is, as I have striven to show, the incomparable gusto of Browning's poetry that is its essential quality. And this gusto is not the outpouring in art of the hearty exuberance of a Philistine, or the pietistic enthusiasm of an irresponsible optimist. It is rather—if one may apply to it words used by Arthur Symons in connection with the humour of "The Pied Piper of Hamelin," and "Confessions"—"the jolly laughter of an unaffected nature, the effervescence of a sparkling and overflowing brain."[9] It has its roots in a sound physical constitution, a fine fibre of intellect, and a glow of life which, to cite Elizabeth Barrett's tribute, "shows a heart within blood-tinctured, of a veined humanity."[10]

Undoubtedly, Browning's superb physical health is an element of this gusto. In "Saul," David sings of "our manhood's prime vigour," the play of muscle and sinew, "the leaping from rock up to rock," and "the plunge in a pool's living water." Idealist though the poet is, there is a genial and aromatic flavour of mother earth in his writings, and he draws sustenance from her which races through his veins like the sap of trees in spring. "Oh, good gigantic smile o' the brown old earth!" he exclaims in "James Lee's Wife." This touch with earth is reflected in his unique chronicling of insect life, that form of animal existence which is in most intimate conjunction with the soil. The prodigal and spawning energy of nature, riotous with life, is whimsically portrayed in "Sibrandus Schafnaburgensis." The worm, slug, eft, water-beetle, and newt, invading the covers of a ponderous volume, are symbolic of sheer animal frolic, mocking dry-as-dust pedantry and the dead bones of a musty scholasticism:

> All that life and fun and romping,
> All that frisking and twisting and coupling,
> While slowly our poor friend's leaves were swamping
> And clasps were cracking and covers suppling!

Allied with this love of energy in the physical world is Browning's keen perception of the grotesque. For the grotesque is a bold and peremptory shattering of conventional moulds. As Chesterton has said: "The element of the grotesque in art, like the element of the grotesque in nature, means, in the main, energy, the energy which takes its own forms and goes its own way."[11]

But the *élan* of the poet's art has more subtle and spiritual springs in his intellectual and emotional gifts. These gifts have their extravagances. The suppleness of Browning's mind and his temperamental impetuosity often lead him to strain at the curb of form. Yet the turns and twists of his verse, his metrical liberties, his unexpected and at times somersaulting rhymes, are usually the bubbling up of irrepressible high spirits, chafing at the yoke of aught that is tame or conventional. It should be noted that he only gives rein to an "outrageous gallop of rhymes" in poems having a certain raciness or bohemianism of content, such as "The Flight of the Duchess," "Old Pictures in Florence," or *Pacchiarotto*. When set in their proper perspective and viewed in relation to the whole body of his poetry, these outward flourishes of style, even when pushed to the verge of idiosyncrasy, are not to be condemned sweepingly as barbaric wilfulness. They are often the frothings of a superabundant vitality, a tang of life like that of Fra Lippo Lippi, shattering the moulds of artistic decorum in a spirit of Puckish impishness.

A laugh, a cry, the business of the world. . . .
And my whole soul revolves, the cup runs over,
The world and life's too big to pass for a dream,
And I do these wild things in sheer despite,
And play the fooleries you catch me at,
In pure rage! (II. 247-54)

Though we must look to the future for an impartial
evaluation of Victorian literature, it is evident that Browning, with the possible exception of Carlyle, had a more
robust and sinewy mind than any of his contemporaries.
He is a great humanist; and however deeply and broadly he
quarries in the mine of the thoughts and emotions of men
and women, the vein never runs thin, though it may lead at
times through tortuous tunnels. The horizons of an intellect
of such power and fertility are vast; and linked with this
amplitude is the gift of communicating the joy and tingle
of his contact with life. In this respect he allies himself with
Chaucer, Fielding, and Scott. Like theirs his interest in
humanity is unflagging, and while he does not maintain
their objectivity of representation, he probes deeper than
any of his forerunners into the inner springs of character.

As we travel imaginatively with Browning in many climes
and ages, a panorama full of light and colour is unrolled. On
a spacious canvas, through an astonishing variety of circumstance, he mirrors the subtle and ceaseless play of impulse
and motive flaming up in moments of highly wrought passion
into the crux of action,

> When a soul declares itself—to wit,
> By its fruit, the thing it does![12]

In speaking of the poems of Browning that culminate with
The Ring and the Book, Mr. Osbert Burdett has said: "If it
be still urged that the poetry of Browning loses for want of
repose, the reply is that, in these poems, we do not miss it

but are carried by the poet while we read into his own world of vigorous healthy imagination, a world so rich, vivid, and finely fashioned that it is one of the most original and dramatic possessions of our literature."[13]

While individual judgments are always relative, it is a test of quality when we can return in later years with unabated pleasure to the work of a poet loved in youth, and "obey the voice at eve, obeyed at prime." Browning measures up to this test, because the volume of his poetry is "the precious life-blood of a master spirit." Into its pages, through the alchemy of genius, the elixir of a generous personality has been distilled. In a large human sense, the best of Browning's work does not date—always a touchstone of worth.

In the most famous passage of *The Advancement of Learning,* Bacon says of poetry: "And, therefore it was ever thought to have some participation of divineness, because it doth raise and erect the mind, by submitting the shows of things to the desires of the mind." The classicist may complain that Browning bullies "the shows of things" into submission. Despite his recognition of "the value and significance of flesh," he does at times wrest the body of art, its sensuous elements, in order to

> Make new hopes shine through the flesh they fray,
> New fears aggrandize the rags and tatters:
> To bring the invisible full into play!
> Let the visible go to the dogs—what matters?[14]

Yet it is the informing presence of a discursive, fully charged mind that is an unfailing source of enjoyment to the sympathetic reader of his poetry. Like Donne, whom in many ways Browning strikingly resembles, he might have spoken of "the sinewy thread my brain lets fall." In this fibre of thought, interwoven with ardour of temperament, lies the genesis of his verve and originality—that flash of life which I have singled out as the essential quality of his poetry.

[1951]

RICHARD D. ALTICK

THE PRIVATE LIFE OF

ROBERT BROWNING

ONLY A FEW of those who knew Robert Browning in the 1870's and 1880's as an immensely healthy, masculine, vigorous, white-maned gentleman, always on hand at fashionable London soirées, teas, concerts, and exhibitions, seem to have sensed any incongruity in the fact that this voluble, affable man was also a great poet. And of the few who did sense an incongruity, only Henry James felt impelled to invent a legend to explain it.

It was not easy to meet him and know him without some resort to the supposition that he had literally mastered the secret of dividing the personal consciousness into a pair of independent compartments. The man of the world—the man who was good enough for the world, such as it was—walked abroad, showed himself, talked, right reasonably, abounded, multiplied his contacts and did his duty; the man of [the poems] . . ., this inscrutable personage sat at home and knew as well as he might in what quarters of *that* sphere to look for suitable company. The poet and the "member of society" were, in a word, dissociated in him as they can rarely elsewhere have been.

Such a *donnée* could not be wasted, and in time James "dramatized" it in his story, "The Private Life," in which Browning was the model for the novelist Clare Vawdrey, a "loud, sound, normal, hearty presence, all so assertive and so whole, all bristling with prompt responses and expected opinions and usual views," who led one to wonder "what lodgement, on such premises, the rich proud genius one adored could . . . ever have contrived." The explanation, as James put it in a later preface, was that "our delightful inconceivable celebrity was *double*, constructed in two quite distinct and 'water-tight' compartments—one of these figured by the gentleman who sat at a table all alone, silent and unseen, and wrote admirably deep and brave and intricate things; while the gentleman who regularly came forth to sit at a quite different table and substantially and promiscuously and multitudinously dine stood for its companion. . . . It was amusing to think of the real great man as a presence known, in the late London days, all and only to himself—unseen of other human eye and converted into his perfectly positive, but quite secondary, *alter ego* by any approach to a social contact."

James, then, recognized that the public Robert Browning was not the whole Browning and, indeed, quite possibly, not the true Browning at all. But he seems never to have wondered *why* Browning was a double being, or what that other self was like who never emerged from the study where he meditated and wrote poetry. So the mystery of Robert Browning persists, to disturb those readers who cannot reconcile the outward man with the poetry signed with his name, and who are unsatisfied with the description of Browning's inner being which the commentators have customarily inferred from his writings.

contributed to it. We are rarely told what he was brooding about at the time, what train of thought, what emotional mood formed the inspiration and background for a particular poem. As Griffin very carefully phrased it, "He seemed, in general society, anxious not to be reminded, or to remind others, that he was a poet." He was delighted, on the contrary, to be mistaken for a successful financier. And when, with the advent of the Browning cult in the 1880's, the poet was plagued with inquiries from earnest explicators of his text, although his innate courtesy forbade turning the inquirers away, he confined himself to clarifying the meaning of an allusion or of a hazy line or two. When it came to discussing the meaning of a whole poem, he preferred to approve an interpretation that was brought to him rather than to offer one of his own. He seemed grateful to have words put into his mouth. When someone asked if the meaning of "Childe Roland" might be summarized by the phrase, "He that endureth to the end shall be saved," he answered (with relief?), "Yes, just about that." No matter if there were obvious difficulties in the way of reading the poem in such a fashion; the question had been answered, and the subject could be dropped. Time after time, most conspicuously in the case of Mrs. Orr, he gave his blessing to the publication of facts about his life and poems, and interpretations of the text, which simply are wrong. He never cared to set the record straight. His only concern was to dispose as quickly as possible of matters which, for some reason, it was extremely distasteful for him to discuss.

Here, it seems to me, we have the key to Browning's inner life. Paradoxical though it may seem, in the light of his enormous productivity, he had come in time to regard his role of poet as a burden. He had found that, for various reasons, he could not possibly do what, in his youth, he had dedicated his life to trying to achieve. Before he was twenty his reading of Shelley had determined his ambition: to be a seer-poet. He had a vocation as passionate, as ineradicable, as that of Milton or Tennyson. And so firmly set was this ambition that success in any other way of poetry, a success which, as it happened, was surely his in his middle phase, could not possibly atone for failure to achieve the one goal he had chosen. He was one of those men to whom maturity does not bring the power cheerfully to abandon adolescent ambitions as being impossible of realization. Throughout his life, the reproachful memory of his early confident hopes burdened him like the Old Man of the Sea. There is much more than meets the eye in Edmund Gosse's report that Browning, in the last year of his life, said that he "marvelled, as he looked back, at the audacious obstinacy which had made him, when a youth, determine to be a poet and nothing but a poet."

Doubtless one reason for his marvelling at his early resolution was that curious verbal inadequacy which critics have remarked in him. His gift of language was insufficient for the messages he wished to deliver. Perhaps part of his trouble was that he did not understand clearly enough what he desired to communicate; but it is more certain that when he tried to communicate, his reach proved to exceed his grasp. " 'Language,' " he confessed to Miss Barrett, "is an organ that never studded this heavy head of mine."

Not only was his mastery of language inadequate for the task of "putting the infinite within the finite," which he told Ruskin was the proper business of the poet; but his lack of mental discipline, which prevented his reducing to coherence the teeming store of his brain, and perhaps above all his extraordinarily swift faculty of association, militated against the successful communication which he so much desired to achieve. In the period of his best work, it is true, he resolved the dilemma by abandoning the subjects which baffled him, by cultivating a colloquial style, and by adopting the congenial form of the dramatic monologue. But even in these poems the familiar knottiness appears, and the difficulty of his later verse amply proves that his old trouble revisited him and indeed was intensified.

It is by no means accidental that Andrea del Sarto, the frustrated artist, is the most profoundly and poignantly realized of all Browning's characters. No one who had not himself known the ashen flavor of failure could have written that moving poem, so filled with rationalizations which give but momentary solace. "All is as God over-rules"—that is well enough, but Andrea, like Browning, cannot take much comfort from it. The fault is within himself, and nothing can long alleviate the pain of eternally frustrated ambition, not even the satisfaction of possessing a flawless technique. Yet, hollow though Andrea's rationalizations may be in this poem, Browning repeatedly uses them elsewhere *in propria persona*. His fervent celebration of the glories of the incomplete, the imperfect, as being part of God's inscrutable but unquestionable plan for men, is far less the manifestation of an intellectual conviction than it is the result of Browning's growing need to salve his awareness of failure.

Conscious though he was of his own handicaps, he nevertheless was always nettled by the reluctance or the inability of his readers to meet him halfway. "You ought, I think," he wrote Ruskin in 1855, "to keep pace with the thought tripping from ledge to ledge of my 'glaciers,' as you call them; not stand poking your alpenstock into the holes, and demonstrating that no foot could have stood there; suppose it sprang over there?" Later in his life, when he beheld the labors of the Browning Society nurturing afresh the popular view that his poetry was unintelligible, he tartly remarked that he had never intended to write for the tired businessman. His annoyance was in part justified, of course; but it sprang also from an abiding sense of failure. He would have been happy enough to find tired businessmen liking his verse.

Beyond question, he was deeply hurt by the long critical

and popular indifference to his work. Usually he tried to joke about it; but one detects in his remarks a rankling grievance which went beyond mere ruefulness. He could never forget the bright ambitions which he had expressed in his letters to Miss Barrett. That they had been thwarted was the fault of a stupid and lazy audience. Had he been a conscious innovator, he would doubtless have found consolation in the belief that eventually the poetry-reading public would catch up with him; but, having little sense of the degree to which his own poetic method was at variance with the conventions of the age, he assumed that the public *was* fully capable of understanding and valuing him, but simply perverse. His attitude towards his audience after his early dreams of fame were dashed, an attitude marked by asperity and impatience, is a revealing measure of his sense of isolation. The underlying bitterness of his address to the "British Public, ye who like me not" marks the poet whose dream of ministering to the new age has been consistently frustrated—not so much, as he increasingly persuaded himself, through his own incapacity as through the wilful indifference of those whom he had considered himself destined to speak to.

Psychologically, then, Browning was doomed never to reach the particular heights to which he had aspired as a result of his early immersion in Shelley and the more visionary of the seventeenth-century poets. He may have had moments of ecstatic experience, and at all events it is certain that his inner life was so intense that he was driven by an almost demoniac compulsion to attempt to project it in language; but there were tragic barriers in the way. Perhaps even more formidable than those I have mentioned was that which led to his sudden assumption of the dramatic mask in his poetry. It is usually said that John Stuart Mill's comments on *Pauline* converted the young poet permanently to the "dramatic" rather than the deeply personal form of utterance, and unquestionably Browning's accidental encounter with those comments was a profound shock to him. But Mill's criticism would not have shaken the purpose of a Shelley. With Browning it was another matter; his whole upbringing in a highly conventional milieu had stressed decorum. One of his class did not pour out his innermost feelings with unrestrained candor, as he had done in *Pauline*. A youth might, indeed, go through a Shelleyan phase, as a youth of an earlier generation went through a Wertherian, and no harm done—unless he were to make public confession of his romantic passions. But Browning had made such a public confession, and he heeded Mill's voice, not alone as that of a respected critic but as that of a society whose standards of personal reticence and abhorrence of "morbidity" affected Browning more deeply than he knew.

And so, though deeply hurt, he made his decision. It is true that for the time being, despite his rejection of the first person singular, he clung to his great aspiration. In 1845 he was still sure that eventually he would write "R.B.—a poem," that sublime work of philosophical revelation which would place him with Shelley. But it never saw the light. Only in occasional poems, like "One Word More," "La Saisiaz," and the Epilogue to *Dramatis Personae,* does he emerge from behind his self-imposed mask and speak with unmistakable sincerity and passion in his own person.

The remarkable thing about that decision is that it was based, not upon a realization of the true quality of his genius and a determination to use it to the fullest, but upon the extraneous element of personal decorum. Browning, curiously, seems never to have analyzed correctly the peculiar character of his gifts. That he put them nevertheless to such magnificent use, in the two decades stretching from *Bells and Pomegranates* to *The Ring and the Book,* was the result of his being driven, not consciously attracted, to the dramatic form of utterance. What he hoped to do was to accomplish his Shelleyan mission in the mode of a Shakespeare: he wanted to be simultaneously a seer and a dramatist, to eat his cake and have it too. Under the circumstances, it is not surprising that his success as a writer of dramatic monologues left him unsatisfied. They were good of their kind, perhaps, but they were not what he had dedicated his life to doing. He was stifled by his mask, yet to write "R.B. —a poem" meant to speak out, and he could not allow himself to speak out, not even in the privacy of his letters to Miss Barrett (which are most revealing in their recurrent suggestion of all that went unrevealed), far less in the publicity of print. The compromise he chose, therefore, resulted inevitably in a deep-seated conflict, which he could have resolved only by doing one of two things—abandoning his first ambition and single-mindedly cultivating his talents for psychological analysis through the dramatic monologue, or casting aside the mask and speaking out, fearlessly and unashamedly, in the person of Robert Browning. And he could do neither.

That the second alternative was as impossible as the first is suggested by all that we know of his reticence. "You can know but little of me," he told the woman he loved. "For every poor speck of a Vesuvius or a Stromboli in my microcosm there are huge layers of ice and pits of black cold water. . . . I am utterly unused, of these late years particularly, to dream of communicating anything about *that* to another person." Even in the intimacy of their marriage, the reticence remained. He appears seldom to have discussed his poetic plans with his wife, and only infrequently showed the results to her before they were finished. Already he had sealed off the poet in a separate, almost impenetrable, compartment of his being, to which no one was to be given access except through the agency of cold type.

Yet, since the Shelley in him never died, there was still the fatal necessity of putting into words at least some portion of his inner experience, despite the inhibition which hardened through the years. No wonder, then, that the act of poetic creation, especially in retrospect, was shadowed by the torment of unfulfilled longings. No wonder that Browning not only was reluctant to talk about his own writing but had an active dislike for revision. If he had, as F. L. Lucas once remarked, the artistic conscience of a pavement artist, it was because once the act of creation was over, urgent though it had been, he would not relive it.

This picture of the private Browning as a disappointed idealist, a man whose fear of betraying his own heart drove him to the perpetually unsatisfactory device of speaking obscurely through the mouths of others, scarcely accords with his friends' untroubled assumption that he was the definition of self-assurance. But the truth seems to be—and it goes a long way towards explaining his abnormal reticence —that he was basically a most insecure man. In childhood he was protected to an unwholesome degree from the bruising contact with the world which brings emotional and social maturity. Except for three or four preadolescent years at a school from which he returned over weekends, and a disastrous interlude at the University of London, he stayed at home with his mother and his father's inexhaustible library. As an adolescent he seems to have delighted most in the company of two semi-intellectual young ladies, the adopted daughters of W. J. Fox. The woman he married was six years older than he, a fact which even those with the least possible tinge of Freudianism may find relevant. And when, after fifteen years, that marriage was ended by death, he found solace among women for the rest of his long life. Not that he actually shunned the company of men; he did have many male friends, and there is no evidence that they had any but the sincerest respect and affection for him. Yet his preference undoubtedly was for the softer companionship of women. And though, when he made his astonishingly gauche proposal to Lady Ashburton, he told her that he wished only to acquire a new mother for Pen and specifically disclaimed his need of a wife in the usual sense, one wonders whether he was not feeling, however unconsciously, another need. In any case, as we review the way in which his life was spent principally with women, the masculinity which all the books tell us is so conspicuous a quality of both the poet and the man seems in fact to have been a sort of overcompensation.

Yet most readers of Browning would object that if any proof is needed that the poet was emotionally secure, it can be found in his religious verse. Does not all received opinion exalt him as the great confident Voice of Faith? Yes—but received opinion is almost surely misleading. The burly assurance in his voice had no counterpart in his inner being. On the contrary, his famous positiveness in religious matters is a telling clue to his underlying insecurity.

Though we know little about the origin and development of his beliefs, it is plain that he had a thoroughly pious upbringing, in which emotion played a great part and intellectual conviction little or none. Such an upbringing could not possibly equip a man to face and conquer the stern challenges offered both by the backwash of eighteenth-century skepticism and by the rationalism of the new era.

Nor did Browning's native equipment atone for what his environment failed to give him. In his late teens, his reading of the unorthodox authors he found in his father's library and then his momentous discovery of Shelley converted him briefly to atheism. Superficially, this short-lived aberration had no lasting effect upon him. When it ended, he returned to the very same principles in which he had been reared, and which he was to assert in poetry throughout life: above all, to a reliance upon faith, faith alone, together with a deep, almost morbid distrust of whatever operations of the mind would cast doubt upon the truths which faith established. In returning to his first beliefs, however, Browning left behind a piece of unfinished business. He had failed to lay the ghost of Voltairian-Shelleyan anti-religion. He had learned that there were other answers to the great questions than those which comfortable nonconformity provided, answers from which, once his joy in adolescent rebellion had cooled, he flinched. In confusion he fled back to piety, because there alone his need for certainty, a need too insistent to await his working things out, could be gratified. But ironically, by his precipitance he made it impossible for himself ever to enjoy the luxury of certainty. Having lost the first battle by default, he was in no position to meet the new challenges to faith which were to roll in upon him, in wave after wave, as the Victorian age wore on.

For although a whole dismal shelf of treatises has been published on Browning as a thinker, actually he was not a thinker at all, either by native gift or by training. His reading in the classics of Western philosophy was unsystematic and spotty. Neo-Platonism he was well acquainted with— witness "Abt Vogler," one of the most Neo-Platonic poems of recent centuries—but he blandly admitted to Mrs. Orr that "he knew neither the German philosophers nor their reflection in Coleridge." What he read, he did not always understand; he ludicrously misinterpreted Mandeville's "Fable of the Bees." Compared with Tennyson or Arnold or Newman, he was philosophically illiterate, and he probably knew it. In social conversation he always shied away from serious subjects. The historian Oscar Browning, contrasting the poet's talk with that of George Eliot, commented, "She was always serious, always gave you of her best. Browning rarely discussed serious topics, philosophical, literary or artistic; his talk was that of a man of the world." Henry James had the same thing in mind when he wrote of Clare Vawdrey that "I never heard him utter a paradox or express a shade or play with an idea." We need not marvel, as some have done, that Browning, who as a poet exhibited intellectual powers that dazzled the undiscerning, as a man shunned the Metaphysical Society and fled to the undemanding precincts of fashion. Removed from his study, where he might consider knotty problems at leisure, he shrank from exposing the inadequacies of his knowledge or the possible frailty of his conclusions.

If he lacked grounding in the history of philosophy and the ability to understand it fully, his acquaintance with contemporary tendencies was equally sketchy. Yet, like thousands of mid-Victorians who were in no sense formal thinkers but simply educated readers, he knew enough about the trend of thought in his own time to be horrified by it. He read Strauss and Renan and immediately lashed out against the higher criticism of the Bible and the historical study of Jesus. The poems he wrote show that he by no means fully comprehended what Strauss and Renan were all about; was his reaction an honest failure of his intellect, or a stubborn refusal to recognize all the implications of what he read? In either case, it took no deep study but merely a normal sensitivity to the currents of popular thought eddying about him to make him realize that all liberalism, all rationalism, all science was leading mankind in a direction in which Robert Browning, the child of sincere and devoted dissenters, could not possibly go.

But unlike some of those who held high the banners of the traditional Christian faith, Browning did not, except in a few poems like "A Death in the Desert," specifically attack the movers and shakers. (And when he did, he failed, through either ignorance or choice, to meet the enemy on its own ground.) Instead, he retreated to his own citadel and, loftily disdaining to combat the powerful arguments of his adversaries, insisted upon his one cherished principle of faith—the faith that men hold, intuitively, even mystically, the knowledge of God and His love which is impossible to anyone who relies upon the deceptive charms of reason. The more he became aware, as the years passed, of the swelling tide of rationalism and agnosticism, the more passionately he insisted that divinely granted intuition was the only means to truth. He could not live without that supreme assurance, and therefore much of his life was occupied in reiterating it, as if in an attempt at self-hypnosis: "I believe . . . I believe . . . I believe . . . of course I believe."

But he dared not relax his vigilance. Notwithstanding the formidable opposition of his will, a small ugly hint of doubt, bred by his adolescent experience of skepticism and now persistently fed by the intellectual tendencies of the age, kept cropping up. The frequency with which the subject of doubt recurs in his poetry suggests that it was not a merely abstract problem: Browning wrote so much about doubt simply because he was himself never free from its temptations. Characteristically, he rationalized it. Doubt, too, was part of the divine plan, for it required one to shadowbox and thus to strengthen the fibres of belief; it was the "snake 'neath Michael's foot / Who stands calm just because he feels it writhe." Having put doubt into its place, he triumphantly dismissed it; it was no more serious a threat to faith than a pebble tossed at an elephant's flank. Yet, time after time, Browning felt obliged to put it *back* into its place.

The usual vehemence of Browning's assertion of his faith, then, is not, as most commentators have easily assumed it to be, a sign of his own inner confidence. Far from it; his unrelenting, sometimes hysterical insistence upon faith, his return to the theme over many years, suggests that he was obliged to keep talking down the intrusive devils of doubt. His poems on religion seem often like exorcization rituals.

As Paul de Reul has observed, "If he persuades us, it is through his attempt to persuade himself, by contagious emotion rather than logical demonstration."

How much easier it would have been for Browning had he been devoid of intellectual gifts and endowed simply with a fervent emotional life! But his predicament was complicated by an ironic twist of his makeup which endowed him with a natural faculty for a certain kind of mental operation. Although he was temperamentally unfitted to be a systematic philosopher, he had an almost abnormal mental agility, which found delight in taking an idea and following it, indeed pushing it, through all the convolutions and perversions that logic affords. His famous and seldom read casuistical poems, "Mr. Sludge, 'the Medium,'" *Prince Hohenstiel-Schwangau,* "Bishop Blougram's Apology," *Fifine at the Fair,* doubtless were intended to expose the hollowness and futility of mere mental gymnastics; but it is impossible to read them without feeling that Browning experienced an unholy joy in writing them. His acrobatic mind revelled in such exercises. And when he came to the end of such a poem, he realized that he had done his job too thoroughly, for, as Professor Hoxie N. Fairchild has pointed out, he hastened to tack on a "giveaway" to warn the reader that all that had gone before, despite its often attractive appearance, was sophistry pure and simple, and that the truth lay elsewhere: not in the head but in the unsophisticated heart that responded only to the promptings of God. He was a born dialectician, yet he was bidden by his deeper self to deny the efficacy of all reason. He admired the workings of the rationalizing mind, but since the results of reasoning seemed bound to work against the convictions his soul required, the only purpose to which he could devote his superb argumentative gift was to expose the futility of argumentation. He was obliged to load the dice against every speaker in his poems who chose to vindicate himself by reason rather than by intuition.

Browning's intellect, within its limits, was keen, but, as the structure of his poems proves, disorderly. And incapacity was the father of distrust. His intellectual myopia, which made him so aware of the details of an edifice of thought but prevented him from viewing it in its totality, led him to reject formal thought and to concentrate upon its antithesis —pure intuition, impulse—as the only possible way to truth, because it was the only way available to Robert Browning. It is somewhat surprising that a believer in the all-embracing benevolence of God should have placed so low a valuation upon reason, which is as much God's gift as the ability to receive irrational impulses from above; but he naturally valued highest what he himself could best depend on.

Browning was the victim of a tragic ambivalence. He wanted to be a philosopher-poet, but his genius dictated that he fulfill himself in quite another way. He wanted to address a wide audience, but he was cursed with verbal impotence when he tried to say the things he most needed to say. He wanted to speak out, loud and clear, in his own person, but a sense of inadequacy, a lack of self-confidence, bred an unconquerable reticence. He wanted to be firm in his Christian faith, but as an extraordinarily accomplished logician, he could not wholly protect himself from the blandishments of reason. Nature had lavished gifts and aspirations upon him, but they were so mixed and contradictory that only by a fortunate miracle did some of them conjoin to produce the rich poetry by which he is remembered.

That Browning was conscious of much inner malaise, especially in later life, is doubtful; the process of his spiritual recovery after Mrs. Browning's death may well have included the achievement of a *modus vivendi,* so that we cannot envision the other self of James's fancy brooding over his many sorrows. He probably never doubted that his mind was in the best of health. But he was not the best judge of his own condition. In Venice, a month or two before his death, he met at dinner a Dr. Bird, to whom, in the words of Edward Dowden, he "expressed confident satisfaction as to his state of health, and held out his wrist that his words might be confirmed by the regularity and vigor of his pulse. The physician became at once aware that Browning's confidence was far from receiving the warrant in which he believed." The man's gesture is admirably symbolic of his poetry: in it, he was always exposing his wrist, almost as an act of bravado, to demonstrate the perfect health of his mental as well as his physical organism. But some readers at least, like Dr. Bird, find that the pulse beat tells another story.

[1956]

KENNETH L. KNICKERBOCKER

A TENTATIVE APOLOGY FOR

ROBERT BROWNING

IN ONE OF the early issues of the *Victorian Newsletter* it was suggested that scholars should revaluate the major literary figures of the nineteenth century. Browning was singled out as particularly ripe for reappraisal. One would assume that such reconsideration would seek to correct the uncritical adulation of the Browningites who met for worship in the various Browning Societies. This sort of correction was not exactly overdue, for adverse attitudes toward Browning have been a regular part of Browning criticism from the beginning. Nevertheless, with more biographical material now available, one could welcome judgments which took this material into account.

It is curious to see how the old, traditional attitude toward Browning persists in the face of the new, somewhat iconoclastic attitude. In New York in 1950, for example, appeared Frances Winwar's routine, adulative book, *The Immortal*

Lovers. In 1952, a slender volume called *Ever a Fighter* by Dallas Kenmare (pseudonym) was published in London. *Ever a Fighter* has the somewhat misleading subtitle: *A Modern Approach to the Works of Robert Browning.* In a library copy of this book a graduate student has placed the correct marginal comment beside this subtitle: "The same, *old* approach of the Browning Society."

In opposition to this old approach one may cite as examples of the new approach Betty Miller's *Robert Browning: A Portrait* (London, 1952) and Richard Altick's "The Private Life of Robert Browning."[1] It must be admitted at the outset that Frances Winwar is no match for the brilliantly intuitive Betty Miller and that Kenmare's smoky candle has little chance against Altick's incandescence. In other words, the case against Browning has been better imagined, better stated, better documented than has the case for him. So far —with certain exceptions—only Crusaders and Saracens have been in the field. My own tendency is to defend Browning— to find excuses and rationalizations for him just as he looked for and found defenses for so many of his characters.

The Saracens—or young Turks—have interpreted the word "revaluate" to mean "value differently" or, in some instances, "to devaluate." Some have adopted the easy slogan: whatever has been, isn't. The purpose of these critics is not to polish up but to polish off. Whatever reasons we may think we have for admiring Browning are based upon misconceptions. Perhaps indicative of this icon-breaking is a statement such as this: "It seems to me that Browning gains in stature as a man if we assume that his marriage to Elizabeth Barrett was basically unhappy, but that he made it successful because he refused to admit its failure."[2] It is not clear in what way Browning would gain stature through our agreeing to this assumption—unless, of course, happy marriages are somehow unbecoming in poets. It would be carrying things a

bit far to assume that because *we* could not love Elizabeth
Barrett, Browning should be required to be as discriminating
as we are. The point is that there is little evidence of
Browning's not loving his wife and plenty of evidence to the
contrary. I cannot believe that any valid revaluation of
Browning can proceed from virtually baseless assumptions.
I do believe that revaluation must respect obvious, but
frequently neglected, principles. George Bernard Shaw announced the first principle when he advised members of the
London Browning Society to go home and read their poet
before talking any more about him. A great many people
talk about Browning, even write commentaries on Browning,
without taking the trouble to read what they are commenting on. A check will show, for example, that more than
half the critics who have had something to say about *Prince
Hohenstiel-Schwangau* do not know how that poem ends.

If the first principle in revaluation is to read the poet, the
second one is to make it obvious that one has done this. Any
genuine reappraisal of Browning should be filled with quotations from and references to the poems themselves. If one's
purpose is to differ with the critics of Browning, this purpose
can only be realized by the use of supporting arguments
from the poetry itself. It may be admitted that the Browning
Society was a missionary society with evangelical enthusiasm, but this quality in itself is not a valid reason for
denying that the mission was (and is) valid or for saying
that because a member of the Society believed this or that of
Browning, this or that must be wrong.

I should like to illustrate what seems to me to be the
danger of such a procedure by examining Professor Altick's
article, "The Private Life of Robert Browning." Space available to Mr. Altick was doubtless limited and the *Yale Review*, a serious but not a scholarly magazine, would have
rejected thorough documentation. These factors may partly

explain Mr. Altick's method. Nevertheless, the article takes such sharp issue with traditional views of Browning that it deserves to be looked at with some care.

First, then, though I am sure that he has, Mr. Altick does not make it obvious that he has read Browning. His general method is to take many of the well-known—and in some instances, firmly established—estimates of Browning, turn them upside down, and invite the reader to approve the new look. Somehow, this process reminds me of the familiar picture of an obstetrician holding an infant by his feet; the baby is all there, the view is interesting, but may leave one unconvinced that this is really the way to look at a baby.

Professor Altick tells us, for example, that Browning was healthy all right but so healthy that he was actually unhealthy: "A feverish flush on the cheeks, a fantastic cheerfulness of view, may betray a serious malady within." He adds: "We can grant to any poet a normal degree of satisfaction with the smooth flow of his endocrines, but in Browning's *poetry* there persists a palpable excess of health."[3] When we read Mr. Altick's remarks about the poet's endocrines, we are about to recall that an excessively breezy Browning nearly blew Thackeray out of his sickbed, but our memory is shunted into another direction when we find that it was not only Browning who was too healthy but also his poetry. There must be *many* poems of this sort, else the broad generalization ("in Browning's *poetry* there persists a palpable excess of health") would have been qualified. What poems does the author have in mind? He does not tell us but relies upon the reader to supply his own examples. The reader may be at a disadvantage since he is not told what a too-healthy poem is.

One other observation may be appropriate here. If Browning who professed to be healthy was in reality ill, was Carlyle, let us say, who professed to be chronically dyspeptic, in reality well? Did Keats die of too much health and was

Milton really blind? If Freudian interpretations work in one direction only, then the healthy are sick and the sick are sick too. A parlous state.

It must be admitted that one commits himself when he cites passages and poems to prove his contentions. Matthew Arnold's touchstone theory, for example, holds up excellently until Arnold, brave and honest, offers the touchstones themselves. Mr. Altick provides an example of this kind of honest but dangerous citation. One of his findings as revealed in "The Private Life" is that Browning was painfully conscious of his own failure. Such a contention would not, on the face of it, be difficult to believe. As part of the proof for this assertion, however, Mr. Altick virtually identifies Browning with Andrea del Sarto. "No one," says Mr. Altick, "who had not himself known the ashen flavor of failure could have written that moving poem, so filled with rationalizations which give but momentary solace."[4]

On every count, this assumption seems dubious critical doctrine. Browning, like Shakespeare and many other literary figures, would have had to be a monstrous and agile chameleon to *be* all the powerfully realized characters in his gallery. (Why not identify Browning with Guido Franceschini, a spectacular failure to whom Browning gave the special attention of two lengthy books in *The Ring and the Book?* And no character of Browning's rationalized his conduct any better than did Guido. Or, why not identify the poet with Cleon who found no comfort in a powerful intellect? Or with Sludge whose life was based on deception? Or with Blougram who exalted expediency?) Furthermore, Andrea, by Professor Altick's own reckoning, cannot stand for Browning. Andrea's tragedy was that his reach did not exceed his grasp. Browning's tragedy, if it may be so called, was, as Mr. Altick says, that "his reach proved to exceed his grasp." Finally, had Browning no knowledge that the things he had written—including "Andrea del Sarto"—are imperfect only in the sense that Giotto's campanile was imperfect and as all things human are imperfect? There is no convincing evidence from the poetry or the letters or the testimony of contemporaries that Browning regarded himself as a failure. Let us return for a moment to Mr. Altick's contention that Browning "came in time to regard his role of poet as a burden." I think this is true, but hardly surprising. The explanation could be a simple one: the process of composition is difficult, brain-stretching work; no matter how rewarding, it can become a burden. Browning was conscientious and because his one work in life was to be a poet, he continued grinding out volumes long after much of the zest for his job was gone. If Browning had died in 1869 at age fifty-seven, there would have been little evidence that the role of poet burdened him unduly. If he did not find being a poet irksome up to that time, one might suppose that fame, age, an exhaustion of fresh subjects took their toll—as always they take their toll of creators.

Mr. Altick's explanation is different. Browning's ambition, he says, was to be a "seer-poet," but the author of *Men and Women* was aware of a "curious verbal inadequacy" which frustrated his ambition. "His reach proved to exceed his grasp."[5] It would have been odd indeed if it had not. Thoughts which stand luminous and perfect in a poet's mind —in anybody's mind—rarely reach paper in an undimmed and still perfect condition. Shelley sorrowed over his own "verbal inadequacy." Browning doubtless knew but was not unduly distressed that his reach should exceed his grasp.

Besides the language fetter, Browning, says Mr. Altick, suffered from "a lack of mental discipline." It is true that Browning refused the traditional discipline of schools, as did Shelley and many other poets. Browning's reading was erratic, but would a more systematic course of reading have served him better? Who knows? During his best period, Mr. Altick observes, Browning partly solved his problem by "abandoning the subjects which baffled him."⁶ What subjects were these? Mr. Altick does not say. *Sordello* had baffled him for years, but he did not abandon it, though for the peace of everybody's mind, he might have. (Parenthetically, I should qualify this last statement, for there are those who greatly admire *Sordello*, including Ezra Pound who has this to say about it: "Victorian half-wits claimed that this poem [*Sordello*] was obscure and . . . used to pride themselves on grinning through the horsecollar: 'Only two lines of Sordello were intelligible'. . . . Browning had attained this limpidity of narration and published *Sordello* at the age of 28. . . . There is here a certain lucidity of sound that I think you will find with difficulty elsewhere in English, and you very well may have to retire as far as the *Divina Commedia* for continued narrative having such clarity of outline without clog or verbal impediment.")⁷ So far as I know, Browning in searching for a solution to his problem, did not abandon subjects which baffled him. Is Mr. Altick serious in thinking that Browning meant, literally, to write "R. B.—a poem"?⁸ In any but the most straitjacketed sense, the total of Browning's poetry is imaginable as "R. B.—a poem."

But Browning, we are informed, was harried by "an abiding sense of failure." Perhaps so; most artists are. He was hurt by indifference and neglect; most artists are. He blamed "a stupid and lazy audience"; most serious artists do, but Browning chiefly blamed his critics. "He was not a conscious innovator." We must pause here. Soon after *Men and Women* appeared, Browning wrote to his publisher: "As to my own Poems—they must be left to Providence and that fine sense of discrimination which I never cease to meditate upon and admire in the public: they cry out for new things and when you furnish them with what they cried for, 'it's *so* new,' they grunt."⁹ It is clear, I think, that Browning was thoroughly conscious of being an innovator, but it is fanciful to suppose that he, or any other innovator, would "take consolation," as Mr. Altick says, "in the belief that eventually the poetry-reading public would catch up with him."[10] Browning had consciously been providing new things for more than twenty years; yet there was little to hearten him in 1855—little evidence that the poetry-reading public would ever catch up with him.

Mr. Altick finds "underlying bitterness" in the address to the "British Public, ye who like me not." There may be a mild sort of jocular bitterness here, but what of the other line at the end of *The Ring and the Book:*

> So, British Public, who may like me yet
> (Mary and amen!)?

Is there bitterness here, too? Hardly. Browning had been cheered by a genuine second edition of *Dramatis Personae* and by the popularity of *Selections* from his poems. Now, he thought, his hugest effort would make solid his triumph, and he was right.

Browning donned the dramatic mask, Mr. Altick says, not because he wanted to, not because he realized "the true quality of his genius," but because he wished to be a model of decorum. Nevertheless, he retained the ambition to write a "sublime work of philosophical revelation which would place him with Shelley." This sort of speculation is, I think, neither reasonable nor unreasonable. All we know is that Browning did turn, *apparently whole-heartedly,* to the writing of dramatic monologues and that the results are so excellent we may easily be thankful—and with good conscience—that we do not have some "sublime work of philosophical revelation" in their place.

Mr. Altick continues in this fashion: Browning was "basically an insecure man . . . his famous positiveness in religious matters is a telling clue to his underlying insecurity." He had an "almost morbid distrust of whatever operations of the mind would cast doubt upon the truths which faith established." In summary, Browning "was not a thinker at all, either by native gift or by training."[11] Here is nadir, a flat statement which other critics have slowly approached and which, I suppose, was inevitably to be made some day by someone. Disregarding the dissenters, one may trace very roughly the course of criticism of Browning as a thinker: for a long time he was a great thinker; then he was simply a thinker; then a somewhat unsystematic thinker; now, he is no thinker at all.[12] Having arrived at rock-bottom, we must either stop or climb back to some former position. I suspect that we should climb back a pace or two.

The difficulty may lie in determining what one means by "think," or rather in what one supposes should be the end product of thinking. That Browning was not a systematic thinker—a ratiocinator, a philosopher—is evident enough. He was a poet. But the objection probably does not center here. It centers in the results of Browning's thinking, particularly his thinking about man and God. Browning did go through a short period of atheism. Did he think his way into that state? Once in, did he think his way out? Further, would he now be considered a thinker if, upon leaving atheism, he had moved no further than agnosticism and had remained there the rest of his life? Actually, as Mr. Altick recognizes, Browning was seldom sure, even though during intuitive moments he proclaimed his certainty.

If one supposes that he has thought all the thoughts and has concluded that *they* provide no satisfactory answers to any basic questions, he may stick doggedly to an earthbound intellect, in which event he will come quickly to the conclusion (in our time if not in Browning's) that we, along with clods and all else, are simply matter in motion. We note that it is the intellect which decides that its own answers to basic questions are unsatisfactory. It is the intellect, too, which decides whether or not to stew in its own juices. Browning, with an intelligence as keen as anybody's (including his ablest critics), was hungry for answers —and not dusty ones. His intellect could not pierce mysteries which no other intellect had pierced. Therefore, by *permission of his intellect,* he gingerly sought help from what he could feel. In taking this step, he no doubt lost caste with the redoubtables who would prefer to sink with all their intellectual gear intact (and sink they do) than to swim in speculative seas.

Browning preferred to swim. One wonders why it is that those who call him no thinker seldom demonstrate their own proficiency at speculation. Let us be specific. Basic to all Browning ever said about the relation of man to God is this line from *Christmas Eve:* "A scientific faith's absurd." If a scientific faith is absurd, then, clearly, so is a scientific doubt. Browning speculated concerning *faith, doubt,* and *imperfection.*

The evidence is clear, I think, that Browning *thought* his way into a distrust of thinking—as many a man has done before and since. He experienced within himself a *desire* for faith, a *fascination* in doubt, and *human* limitations which led to imperfection. He could have asked this question: is "matter in motion" responsible for what I find within myself? If matter in motion had had the power to do so, it would have forced an affirmative answer to this question. He could go a step further: if we wish to ignore intuition, we may—but if we really believe in the omnipotence of matter in motion, we must agree that it applies to all matter and to every motion matter makes; it must actually be responsible for intuition which, in turn, invents such things as faith, doubt, doctrines of imperfection and compensation, among other things. Matter in motion becomes a cause, as responsible for the feelings as for the intellect. Surely Browning could see this result, and just as surely he had an intellectual right to reject it. It is legitimate to ask, what should he have done? There are speculations different from those Browning arrived at, but in what way are they better? It is difficult to know because, Mr. Altick, among others, does not say what kind of guesses Browning should have espoused. As a postscript to this short and incomplete apology, I should like to close with three comments. First, Browning's power as a poet, as a seer in the sense of one who deeply understands human nature, is not in the slightest affected by the sniping at his thinking. Secondly, what appears to be a disorderliness (a lack of logical thinking) in the development of the monologues is almost always deliberate, a disorderliness not of the poet's mind but of the realistically groping minds of his characters. This lack of order in the personal poems is sometimes a result of carelessness but more often of intent, for the poet did not try to cover up the backing and filling in his thought processes. He had no reason, perhaps not even the ability, to develop a *system* of thought. There are plenty of systems and none of them satisfactory. Finally, Browning responded to his moods, just as all poets do. He made little effort to be obviously consistent, on the grounds, possibly, that life in any general sense is inescapably inconsistent anyway; only trivialities, rituals, formulas change not.

[1956]

ROBERT LANGBAUM

THE RING AND THE BOOK:

A RELATIVIST POEM

IN THE SAME sense that Dante's great poem can be said to derive its meaning from a Catholic, and Milton's from a Protestant, ethos—so Browning's *The Ring and the Book* derives its meaning from the relativist ethos predominant in Western culture since the Enlightenment. The first sign of the poem's relativism is in Browning's use of dramatic monologues to tell his story. For though he does not entirely succeed, his aim at least in telling the same story eleven times over through ten dramatic monologues and his own account in Book I, was to replace the objective view of events of traditional drama and narrative with points of view. Such a method can be justified only on the relativist assumption that truth cannot be apprehended in itself but must be "induced" from particular points of view, and that there can be sufficient difference among the points of view to make each repetition interesting and important as a psychological fact. Another sign of relativism is that Browning counted ·it such a virtue for his poem to be based on "pure crude fact." Facts figure as pure gold in the analogy of the ring, which Browning uses to justify stamping an interpretation upon the facts. The poet's imagination, the "something of mine," is likened to the alloy which the goldsmith uses to shape the gold into a ring. But the ring once made, the goldsmith bathes it in acid to free the gold from the alloy; so that in the end, we are assured, "the shape remains."

> Gold as it was, is, shall be evermore:
> Prime nature with an added artistry.   (I.28-29)[1]

It is significant that Browning should have felt it necessary to justify a liberty of interpretation which has always been granted poets.

But it was just the imputation of poetic license, relegating his work to the realm of fancy, entertaining but unimportant, that he did not want. His truth had to be taken seriously, which meant in a positivist age that it had to have the facts behind it, had to emerge from the facts. In answer to the difficult question, "Why take the artistic way to prove so much?"—Browning, speaking again in his own voice in the concluding passage of the poem, says the artistic way is best for criticizing a whole false view of things. Since falsehood is formulation that has got too far from the facts, to attack it with another formulation is to awaken resistance and have your true formulation judged false by the logical criteria that established the false formulation. "But Art," he says,

> may tell a truth
> Obliquely, do the thing shall breed the thought,

Nor wrong the thought, missing the mediate word.
So may you paint your picture, twice show truth,
Beyond mere imagery on the wall,—
So, note by note, bring music from your mind,
Deeper than ever e'en Beethoven dived,—
So write a book shall mean beyond the facts,
Suffice the eye and save the soul beside.   (XII.859-67)

Art, then, is truer than philosophical discourse because it is closer to the facts, taking into account more complexities, breeding the thought precisely. It shows the truth twice in that it shows the physical facts and the metaphysical meaning behind them—opening out an extra dimension "beyond . . . the wall" because it brings into operation the mind's deepest resource, imagination, what Wordsworth called "Reason in her most exalted mood." Above all, art is more convincing than philosophical discourse because, confronting false formulations with facts, it causes us to start again with the facts and construct the truth for ourselves.

Yet the judgments of *The Ring and the Book* are by no means "relative"—if we mean by the word that no one is either good or bad but a bit of both. Pompilia, Count Guido's young wife whom he murders, is presented in the final judgment as nothing short of a saint; while Guido is an incarnation of evil. His being evil remains as the real motive and the only one that can explain all the facts of his behavior—when, after two monologues totaling more than 4,500 lines, the complex layers of rationalized motivations have been finally stripped away. What he comes to understand, and we along with him, is that he has hated Pompilia for no other reason than that she is good. Let no one, he says,

                              think to bear that look
Of steady wrong, endured as steadily
—Through what sustainment of deluding hope? . . .
This self-possession to the uttermost,

[278]

> How does it differ in aught, save degree,
> From the terrible patience of God? (XI.1373-80)

And he cries out in an unguarded moment:

> Again, how she is at me with those eyes!
> Away with the empty stare! Be holy still,
> And stupid ever! (XI.2076-78)

He hates her, he reveals, because she did not hate him in return, did not wish him harm. But not until the end, when the black-hooded Brotherhood of Death has come to take him to execution, when the railing and the spite are no longer of use, nor the steadily shifting arguments ever retreating toward confession of his wolf nature—not until the extreme moment does he strip himself bare in a desperate call for help. He calls, in psychologically ascending order, upon the Abate and Cardinal who have attended him in the death cell, upon Christ, Maria, God, and in the final line:

> Pompilia, will you let them murder me? (XI.2427)

That cry is his salvation, acknowledging for the first time, without qualification or self-defense, Pompilia's goodness and his own evil. The implication is that he dies repentant.

Between the moral poles of Pompilia and Guido, the other characters are assigned no less definite places. Caponsacchi, the young priest who helps Pompilia escape from Guido, possesses the heroic as distinguished from the saintly virtues; he possesses, too, the weaknesses of the heroic character when its potentiality is unemployed—the weaknesses of dandyism and gallantry with women. But being good in the purely human way, Caponsacchi has a capacity for development not required by Pompilia's unchanging perfection. She is for him the *donna angelicata,* providing him with the crucial opportunity of his life—the chance for heroic exploit and the chance to recognize, in her, embodied goodness, and thus to be recalled to his priestly vows and the true meaning of Christianity.

Corresponding in moral position to Caponsacchi is the Pope, who represents the highest moral attainment of human wisdom, as Caponsacchi represents the highest in manliness and courage. Although not vessels of Divine Grace, like Pompilia, it is their distinction to be the only ones (except for Guido in his final line) who recognize her preeminence and learn from her. It is the Pope, in his capacity of final court of appeal for Guido, who pronounces all the authoritative judgments of the poem—"the ultimate / Judgment save yours" (I.1220-21) Browning calls it, addressing the reader. But if the reader has read correctly, his judgments should coincide with the Pope's; and to allow no mistake, Browning tells the main events of the story in his own voice in Book I, in such a way as to shape our judgments of the speakers before we have met them. The judgments of the poem are obviously not intended to be "relative"—if we mean by the word, 'indefinite' or 'a matter of opinion.'

To be sure, there are the characters of indefinite moral position. They people the world in which the significant action of the poem takes place; they are the poem's common clay, its chorus. Browning dubs in the "world" by means of the three speakers who represent the three lines of Roman opinion, the pro-Guido, the pro-Pompilia, and the impartial; by means of the two lawyers, prosecution and defense; and, although they never speak, by means of Pompilia's parents, the Comparini, who, through their mixture of motives and consistent pettiness, make the mistakes that involve their daughter in tragedy. But if these characters are in themselves indefinite, the judgment of them is quite definite. The Pope condemns the Comparini in terms general enough to apply to all the small-souled, morally indefinite inhabitants of the "world." "Sadly mixed natures," he calls the Comparini, who troop

> somewhere 'twixt the best and worst,
> Where crowd the indifferent product, all too poor
> Makeshift, starved samples of humanity! (X.1213-15)

Nor are they less culpable because indefinite:

> White shall not neutralize the black, nor good
> Compensate bad in man, absolve him so:
> Life's business being just the terrible choice. (X.1236-38)

What the Pope understands about the whole tragic Pompilia story, and what Guido also acknowledges in his final moments, is that it is sheer miracle that just this once the good has been vindicated and Pompilia's true worth recognized. All the established institutions for distinguishing right from wrong—the law, the Church, the authority of parents and husband—all have been either entirely wrong, or if partly right have still missed the main point, Pompilia's absolute goodness and Guido's badness. The courts, the lawyers, the representative of the impartial line of Roman opinion, all have committed the "relativist" fallacy of supposing that there must be both right and wrong on each side. Caponsacchi complains to the court of their "relativist" obtuseness. If I insist, he says, that my motives in helping Pompilia to escape were entirely pure and Christian, you cry "absurd!" But if I

> own flaws i' the flesh, agree
> To go with the herd, be hog no more nor less
> Why, hogs in common herd have common rights:
> (VI.1722-24)

why then you are indulgent of what you consider my peccadillo with a pretty woman. For the Pope, it is precisely the moral of the story that the good was vindicated by just the dandy priest doing what his vows and the laws of Church and State expressly forbid: running away with a married woman. "Be glad," says the Pope, apostrophizing Caponsacchi,

> Be glad thou hast let light into the world
> Through that irregular breach o' the boundary,
>
> (X.1205-206)

And this brings us to the proper sense in which *The Ring and the Book* can be called a relativist poem. It is relativist in that the social and religious absolutes are not the means for understanding the right and wrong of the poem; they are for the most part barriers to understanding. Pompilia is misled by all the constituted authorities, by "foolish parents" and "bad husband" as the Pope puts it, as well as by Church and State in the persons of the Archbishop and Governor of Arezzo, who send her back to Guido when she appeals to them for help. She even turns out to have been the offspring of vice, since Violante Comparini alleges in the course of the poem that she bought Pompilia from her real mother, a Roman prostitute. Nevertheless, in spite of all the wrong external influences, Pompilia finds the right way because her instinct is right. The Pope marvels at the flowering, just where the odds against it were greatest, of this one shining example of goodness vouchsafed his reign, while the plants so carefully nurtured by Church and respectability came to nought:

> While—see how this mere chance-sown cleft-nursed seed
> That sprang up by the wayside 'neath the foot
> Of the enemy, this breaks all into blaze,
> Spreads itself, one wide glory of desire
> To incorporate the whole great sun it loves
> From the inch-height whence it looks and longs! (X.1041-46)

In the same way, the Pope sees that Caponsacchi was in the position for "catching quick the sense of the real cry" just because he had strayed, had his "sword-hand" on the "lute" and his "sentry-station" at some "wanton's gate"; he had therefore a fresh ear for the contrasting moral cry, while pious Christians had grown "too obtuse / Of ear, through iteration of command" (X.1198-99). Caponsacchi did right not to reason out the merits of Pompilia's case, but to follow with passionate spontaneity his immediate perception of the good. "Blind?" asks the Pope,

> Ay, as a man would be inside the sun,
> Delirious with the plenitude of light
> Should interfuse him to the finger-ends—
> Let him rush straight, and how shall he go wrong?
> (X.1562-65)

Caponsacchi himself tells the court that in deciding to rescue Pompilia, he came to see that what official morality called sin was in this case virtue, that death was in this case life, salvation:

> Death was the heart of life, and all the harm
> My folly had crouched to avoid, now proved a veil
> Hiding all gain my wisdom strove to grasp. (VI.954-56)

Not only are the judgments of *The Ring and the Book* independent of official morality, they are for the most part in conflict with it—and in this sense *relative* to the particular conditions of the poem and to the motives and quality of the characters. Browning is not saying that all discontented wives are to be rescued from their husbands, but just this particular wife from her particular husband. Why? Because of what we understand Pompilia and Guido to *be*. Hence the use of repetition and the dramatic monologue—not because the judgments are a matter of opinion but because we must judge what is being said by who is saying it. The point is that all the speakers are eloquent to a fault and make the best possible case consistent with their own prepossessions and the facts accessible to them. Our judgments depend, therefore, on what we understand of them as people—of their motives, sincerity, and innate moral quality. Judgment goes on, in other words, below the level of the argument and hence the dramatic monologue, which makes it possible for us to apprehend the speaker totally, to subordinate what he says to what we know of him through sympathy.

Browning makes it clear, speaking in his own voice in Book I, that the judgments of the "world" are inadequate because of the personal inadequacies of the "worldly" speakers. The speaker who represents the Half-Rome that favors Guido is honest enough in his "feel after the vanished truth," but harbors all the same in that feel "A hidden germ of failure"—"Some prepossession" that causes "The instinctive theorizing whence a fact / Looks to the eye as the eye likes the look" (I.863-64). In recognizing the inevitability of personal distortion, Browning does not mean, as I understand it, that there is no truth, but that truth depends upon the nature of the theorizing and ultimately upon the nature of the soul of which the theorizing is a projection. After all, Browning justifies by the analogy of the ring his own instinctive theorizing of the facts of the Roman murder case; and there is disparity between the accounts of even such admirable characters as Pompilia and Caponsacchi. But the pro-Guido speaker of the monologue called "Half-Rome" reveals a prepossession hardly adequate to understanding the Pompilia story. He reveals toward the end that he is a married man worried about his wife's fidelity—and that his whole account, with its emphasis on Guido's just revenge, is by way of a warning that he wants delivered to his rival.

The pro-Pompilia speaker of the monologue called "The

Other Half-Rome" is, instead, a sentimental bachelor—yet no
more adequate as a judge. He represents

> the opposite feel
> For truth with a like swerve, like unsuccess,—
> Or if success, by no skill but more luck
> This time, through siding rather with the wife,
> Because a fancy-fit inclined that way,
> Than with the husband. (I.883-88)

Critics have objected to this unfavorable introduction of a
speaker who in his monologue strikes us as intelligent,
sensitive and sincere; and it must be admitted that we
would probably not discern the limitations of the pro-
Pompilia speaker, were we not specifically alerted to look
for them. But it is to alert us that Browning speaks in his
own voice in Book I; he wants us to see that the speaker's
interest in Pompilia is sentimental and literary rather than
moral, and hence a "fancy-fit." The speaker conceives
Pompilia as the beautiful wronged heroine of what he
himself calls the "romance-books." He characterizes her as

> the helpless, simple-sweet
> Or silly-sooth, unskilled to break one blow
> At her good fame, by putting finger forth.
> (III.805-807)

This is to miss the hard moral core of the saint, diluting her
into mere negative and vapid weakness; the conception, in
fact, matches Guido's when he pictures an Ovidian meta-
morphosis in which Pompilia will turn into water after her
death (XI.2050-55).

The speaker is preoccupied with Pompilia's beauty and the
theatrical effect of her death-bed scene. He is as inadequate
as the rest of the "world" in judging her relation with
Caponsacchi:

[285]

Men are men: why then need I say one word
More than that our mere man the Canon here
Saw, pitied, loved Pompilia?   (III.880-82)

though he is too well-versed in the conventions of the romance-books to suppose, like the others, that their love has
not been technically innocent:

oh, called innocent love, I know!
Only, such scarlet fiery innocence
As most folk would try to muffle up in shade.
(III.894-96)

Just as he casts Pompilia and Caponsacchi in the roles of
romance hero and heroine, so he casts Guido as romance
villain at some points, and at others as comic cuckold—in
both roles Guido is to be hated by sheer literary convention.
Guido is himself aware of literature's antipathy to the
betrayed husband and complains that literary and stage
precedents have turned opinion against him. The speaker of
"The Other Half-Rome" is so much concerned with the
melodramatic surface of the story, and so little with its moral
meaning, that he makes no moral distinction between Pompilia and the Comparini, characterizing the parents along
with the daughter as innocent lambs ravaged by the Franceschini wolves, Guido and his family.

Whether or not we grant that Browning has successfully
dramatized the limitations of the pro-Pompilia speaker, we
must agree that in its intention at least, "The Other Half-
Rome" is perhaps the poem's boldest stroke. For at the risk
of confusing us utterly, the poet forestalls just the facile
judgment the casual reader is likely to make; he takes a
stand not only against wrong judgments but against the
right judgment on the wrong grounds. "So, listen," he says
in concluding his introduction of the pro-Pompilia speaker,
"how, to the other half of Rome, / Pompilia seemed a saint

and martyr both!" (I.908-909); and there is, in the context
of what has preceded, a note of sarcasm in the last line. Yet
the last line does not differ from the Pope's "ultimate judgment" of Pompilia. The point for us, the point that explains
the use of the dramatic monologue in this poem, is that the
judgments are different because the men who pronounce
them are different.

If the first two Roman speakers go wrong through their
prepossessions—Tertium Quid, the representative of cultivated Roman opinion, goes wrong through his attempt to
evade moral judgment altogether. Browning introduces him
with evident sarcasm:

> Here, after ignorance, instruction speaks;
> Here, clarity of candour, history's soul,
> The critical mind, in short. (I.924-26)

The speaker's assumption that there is neither right nor
wrong in the case, but self-interested motives on both sides,
is itself a prepossession that leaves him in the end as "wide
o' the mark" as the other two.

As the institutional mechanism by which the "world"
passes judgment, law and the lawyers cannot be ignored,
though they are included mainly to be satirized. "Ignore
law," asks Browning with mock surprise,

> the recognized machine,
> Elaborate display of pipe and wheel
> Framed to unchoke, pump up and pour apace
> Truth till a flowery foam shall wash the world?
> The patent truth-extracting process,—ha? (I.1110-14)

Law is too mechanical to deal adequately with moral issues,
while the lawyers are immediately disqualified as judges
of the moral issue by the professional nature of their motives.
They speak for hire and subordinate the truth-extracting

process to winning the case and advancing their careers.
Arcangeli, the Procurator of the Poor who defends Guido,
has not only to win the case, but also

> All kind of interests to keep intact,
> More than one efficacious personage
> To tranquillize, conciliate and secure,
> And above all, public anxiety
> To quiet,   (I.1138-42)

and to render absurd his mixture of motives, he has in
addition domestic burdens, a birthday banquet to prepare
for his only son, "Paternity at smiling strife with law"
(I.1146).

His opponent, Bottini, the Fisc, because he is prosecuting
Guido finds himself

> Pompilia's patron by the chance of the hour,
> To-morrow her persecutor,   (I.1173-74)

her persecutor, we learn in a postscript to the poem in the
last Book, when after Pompilia's death he prosecutes a suit
for her property, which requires that he prove her to have
been a fallen woman. In prosecuting Guido, however, his
job is to vindicate Pompilia; but even in doing this, he grants
so much against her that his "best defence"—as is pointed
out by the Augustinian monk who heard Pompilia's last
confession—is itself a calumny. A bachelor, he has not the
domestic preoccupations of Arcangeli, but is preoccupied
instead with his own eloquence and ingenuity, and with the
frustrating awareness that his masterly argument is only to
be read by the court and will never enjoy the advantage of
his oral delivery. Bottini's extra preoccupations, like Arcangeli's, obscure the moral issue:

> ah, the gift of eloquence!
> Language that goes, goes, easy as a glove,
> O'er good and evil, smoothens both to one.   (I.1179-81)

Arcangeli and Bottini disqualify not only as lawyers but as men; and it was probably to reveal their personal inadequacies that Browning gave their pleas private and dramatic settings. (Arcangeli is doing a first draft of his plea at home; Bottini is rehearsing his aloud at home.) Arcangeli is much too normal, fat, domestic, and contented to appreciate the emotional and moral intensities of the case; while Bottini is the young-old man, disproportioned between emotional and intellectual development, a child with an old and corrupt mind:

> Just so compounded is the outside man,
> Blue juvenile pure eye and pippin cheek,
> And brow all prematurely soiled and seamed
> With sudden age, bright devastated hair. (I.1196-99)

With his intellectual virtuosity he manipulates passions and moral meanings he cannot begin to understand.

No less than the lawyers, the representatives of Roman opinion speak to show off their virtuosity. They all reveal at the end of their monologues self-interested motives which disqualify them as judges of the moral issue. The pro-Guido speaker has a vested interest in the authority of the marriage bond; the pro-Pompilia speaker is a bachelor with a sentimental, if not an active, interest in melodramatic violations of the marriage bond; and Tertium Quid reveals in his last two lines that he has been the whole time speaking to impress certain Princes and Cardinals:

> (You'll see, I have not so advanced myself,
> After my teaching the two idiots here!) (IV.1639-40)

he mutters after an Excellency and a Highness have departed.

By their motives shall ye know them! This is Browning's injunction throughout. In contrast to the inadequate motives of the "world," we have the Pope's high seriousness as he sits out

> the dim
> Droop of a sombre February day   (I.1235-36)
> With winter in my soul beyond the world's.   (X.213)

The Pope is aware of his responsibility as Christ's Vicar in making the ultimate judgment, and knows also that his judgment is fallible. He is confident, however, for even if it should turn out that he has made a mistake in judging Guido, he knows that he has judged according to the light given him, that his motives have been pure:

> For I am ware it is the seed of act,
> God holds appraising in His hollow palm,
> Not act grown great thence on the world below,
> Leafage and branchage, vulgar eyes admire.
> Therefore I stand on my integrity,
> Nor fear at all.   (X.272-77)

To add to the solemnity of the Pope's motives, he is eighty-six and aware that Guido's death may just precede his own, that his judgment of Guido may be his last official act, closely bound up with his own salvation.

The Pope's confidence in his judgment does not rest on the supposition that the truth is directly or easily apprehensible; but neither does he suppose that the truth cannot be found in the "pleadings and counter-pleadings" he has before him:

> Truth, nowhere, lies yet everywhere in these—
> Not absolutely in a portion, yet
> Evolvable from the whole: evolved at last
> Painfully, held tenaciously by me.   (X.229-32)

Truth is not in any one argument but can be "induced" from the particular viewpoints, the way Browning expects us to "induce" it from the ten dramatic monologues. And the judgments the Pope pronounces as evolved truth are the kind the dramatic monologue offers—judgments of character. The Pope does not weigh argument against argument, fact against fact, but cuts right through the facts to a sympathetic apprehension of the motives and essential moral qualities behind the deeds. He relies not upon logic to make his judgments, but upon talent, intuition, insight, the advantages of his own character gained through a long experience of life and people:

> dark, difficult enough
> The human sphere, yet eyes grow sharp by use,
> I find the truth, dispart the shine from shade,
> As a mere man may,

with "well-nigh decayed intelligence," if what the populace says of his senility is true, but "What of that?"

> Through hard labor and good will,
> And habitude that gives a blind man sight
> At the practised finger-ends of him, I do
> Discern, and dare decree in consequence,
> Whatever prove the peril of mistake.   (X.1241-52)

Thus, he decrees:

> First of the first,
> Such I pronounce Pompilia, then as now
> Perfect in whiteness: (X.1004-1006)

Caponsacchi sprang forth "the hero," and in spite of the compromising look of the facts,

> In thought, word and deed,
> How throughout all thy warfare thou wast pure,
> I find it easy to believe: (X.1169-71)

while in spite of all the arguments and legal rights that

[291]

Guido can adduce, "Not one permissible impulse moves the man" (X.537).

All the morally significant characters of the poem cut through facts in the same way. As soon as Pompilia and Caponsacchi lay eyes on each other, each recognizes the other's distinction. And their subsequent relation is carried on by means of such intuitive perceptions. Guido forges letters of crude solicitation which he has carried between them in order to compromise Pompilia. But each knows the other incapable of such letters. "As I," says Caponsacchi,

> Recognized her, at potency of truth,
> So she, by the crystalline soul, knew me,
> Never mistook the signs. (VI.931-34)

Their relation develops by means of the letters, in a direction contrary to the purport of the letters. In the course of receiving them and sending back refusals, Pompilia comes to realize that Caponsacchi is the honorable man she can trust to rescue her, while he comes to realize that she is the virtuous woman whom it would not be a sin to rescue. Guido himself cuts through his own false defenses to see in the end the moral truth. He stands, for this reason, a better chance of salvation than the inhabitants of the "world" who, by flattening out the moral issue, miss the final truth.

Thus, truth is psychologized in the sense that the facts do not reveal it, nor is it arrived at by any external yardstick, whether legal, Christian, or conventional. The moral judgments are definite and extreme, but they depend upon our total apprehension of the characters themselves. What we arrive at in the end is not *the* truth, but truth as the worthiest characters of the poem see it.

Truth is historicized as well, the historical meaning running parallel to the psychological. Just as the facts and arguments do not adequately reveal the moral issue between

Pompilia and Guido, so the legal and ecclesiastical machinery of the time proves inadequate to reveal and judge the moral issue. The Pope is distressed by the failure of the instituted machinery because he sees its significance in terms of historical dialectics. "We have got too familiar with the light" (X.1794), he says, comparing his own time, when Christianity is respectable and necessary for getting on in the world, with apostolic times when, as a minority sect, it could attract no one not sincerely committed to its essential meaning.

The time is 1698, almost the end of the seventeenth century and of the pontificate of Innocent XII (died 1700); almost the end, as the Pope points out, of Christianity's period of triumph, of the age when, for all the heresies and theological disputes, the authority of Christianity itself remained uncontested. The Pope foresees a new age to be ushered into life by his death, and asks whether it will be the mission of that age "to shake"

> This torpor of assurance from our creed,
> Re-introduce the doubt discarded, bring
> That formidable danger back, we drove
> Long ago to the distance and the dark? (X.1853-57)

He draws from Pompilia's case both despair and hope. On the one hand, her case presented a challenge which the instituted machinery showed itself unable to meet. The machinery of Christianity showed itself to be by now almost completely at odds with the meaning of Christianity. For was it not by daring to break the Christian rules that Caponsacchi came to virtue's aid; while where, asks the Pope, were "the Christians in their panoply?" "Slunk into corners!". (X.1566-71).

On the other hand, there is hope in the fact that Pompilia and Caponsacchi did find the right way in spite of all the wrong external guidance. Even in the anarchic age ahead, when men shall reject dogma and declare themselves a law unto themselves, some one Pompilia will keep essential Christianity alive through sheer right instinct:

> At least some one Pompilia left the world
> Will say "I know the right place by foot's feel,
> I took it and tread firm there; wherefore change?"
>
> (X.1885-87)

just as in the past Euripides anticipated Christian morality without benefit of Christian revelation. Thus, the Pope comes to see that the truth is something other than the machinery by which men try to understand it. He sees what is pointed out by St. John in Browning's "A Death in the Desert," that "the proofs shift," that myth, dogma, the machinery changes, but truth remains—never in equilibrium with the machinery and sometimes in direct conflict with it. He draws dialectical comfort from the necessary disequilibrium, for injustice shows up the old machinery as inadequate and helps

> to evolve,
> By new machinery in counterpart,
> The moral qualities of man.   (X.1378-80)

In other words, in trying to adapt the machinery of understanding to the truth, which remains always in advance of the machinery, man advances his moral understanding.

Just as, psychologically, the truth about a man is larger than and always in advance of our formulated understanding of him; so, historically, truth is larger than and in advance of the formulations and institutions of any age. Fra Celestino, the Augustinian monk who was Pompilia's last confessor, carries this idea beyond the possibility of dialectical comfort in a sermon, some paragraphs of which are quoted as execrable in a letter of Bottini in Book XII. Let no one suppose, says the Augustinian in his sermon, that

ROBERT LANGBAUM

Pompilia's vindication proves man capable of discerning truth or his judgments trustworthy. Let us rather draw from the case the contrary lesson that "God is true and every man a liar." For the fact that such a case has come to our attention should warn us of all the Pompilias who have died wronged and unknown. Nor is her vindication to the credit of human institutions, public opinion or

> The inadequacy and inaptitude
> Of that self-same machine, that very law
> Man vaunts,   (XII.576-78)

but the work of the Pope's miraculous insight, as much a gift of God as Pompilia's goodness itself:

> What I call God's hand,—you, perhaps,—mere chance
> Of the true instinct of an old good man
> Who happens to hate darkness and love light,—
> In whom too was the eye that saw, not dim,
> The natural force to do the thing he saw,
> Nowise abated,—both by miracle.   (XII.592-97)

The conclusion to be drawn both from the Pope's dialectical perception of the developing disequilibrium between truth and machinery, and Fra Celestino's somewhat antinomian perception of their eternal opposition, is that fixed principles and the institutions which embody them can never be adequate to judge the truth. Judgment must remain what it is in the Pope: a matter of talent, insight, and the essential moral quality of the judge. It must remain what it is in the dramatic monologue: a matter of total apprehension to which formulation is secondary and in some degree of disequilibrium. Truth in other words is relative —psychologically, to the nature of the judge and person being judged; historically, to the amount of disequilibrium, in any given age, between truth and the institutions by which truth is understood.

Not only does Browning give much attention to the inadequacy of most people to judge Pompilia, but he sets the action against a detailed historical background, the purpose of which is to show how far the disequilibrium between truth and machinery has gone by 1698. From every side, it is made clear that the Church has become a center of wealth and power, attracting to its service men whose motives are anything but religious. Guido's two younger brothers are priests as the only means of livelihood for younger sons of an impoverished noble family; and it is only the need to produce an heir for the family that has kept Guido himself from turning priest. He has, however, taken minor orders and served for thirty years as toady to a Cardinal in the hope of making his fortune. It is when the hope fails that he marries Pompilia for her money. The Pope finds it indicative of the condition of the Church that Guido has the effrontery to claim clerical privilege in appealing to the Pope the decision of the secular court of Rome. The Pope sees that the clerical privilege is now being used to protect crime.

Guido also expected the nobleman's privilege. "Who, using the old licence, dreamed of harm" (XI.780), he complains; and he cites as the kind of precedent he has in mind the brutal story of a stableman, Felice, who in the reign of the last Pope was beheaded for daring to strike a Duke who had abducted his sister. "Ah, but times change," Guido complains, "there's quite another Pope, / I do the Duke's deed, take Felice's place" (XI.276-77).

Both Guido and the Pope are aware that the general corruption of the time ought to have guaranteed Guido protection, and that justice in this case is unaccountable miracle, "luck" as Guido calls it: "What was there wanting to a masterpiece / Except the luck that lies beyond a man?" (XI.1566-67). The Pope knows that a routine bribe would unquestionably have obtained for Guido the scrap of paper necessary to leave Rome with horses and so escape to his native Tuscany, where the Grand Duke's court had already declared in his favor and the Papal court could not have touched him. That Guido, a thirty-years' resident of Rome and wise to its inside track, should have neglected to provide for such an obvious contingency, the Pope can only attribute to an act of God. And Guido completes the story by telling how in his frantic efforts to use bribery for obtaining horses without the necessary scrap of paper, it was his bad luck to have encountered just "the one scrupulous fellow in all Rome" (XI.1639).

It is a nice stroke, however, that the same general corruption which ought to have protected Guido would in any case have undone him in the end. For it is revealed in the Pope's monologue and again in Guido's second monologue that the four peasants from Guido's estate, who helped in the murder, were planning to murder him on the road from Rome to Arezzo because he had not paid them the money promised. Although Guido, in his first monologue, speaks of their feudal loyalty and keen sense of their lord's honor which caused them to volunteer vengeance for his wife's infidelity, the Pope reveals that they cared no more for feudal loyalty and honor than did their lord. "All is done purely for the pay," says the Pope,

> which, earned,
> And not forthcoming at the instant, makes
> Religion heresy, and the lord o' the land
> Fit subject for a murder in his turn.   (X.952-55)

And Guido, complaining in his second monologue of his bad luck, says that even if all else had gone well, there were still these "rustic four o' the family, sweet swains," planning to cut his throat.

In this second monologue, Guido again goes over the story of the murder, this time to show that he committed not a "crime" but a "blunder"; for the practice, as distinguished from the professed ideals of his time, gave him every reason to pursue the course he did. He complains of his trial in terms that make clear his disrespect for the legal machinery of the time. Were not his lawyers sufficiently "fools" to satisfy "the foolishness set to decide the case"? Did the lawyers lack skill in law, Latin or logic? Did they neglect to feign and flatter, and were not the judges clearly moved by the flattery? How then did the decision go against him? And in appealing finally to the Pope, had he not reason to expect indulgence from an old man about to die, who professed to be "pity's source and seat"? What is more to the point, he had every reason to expect

> A little indulgence to rank, privilege,
> From one who is the thing personified,
> Rank, privilege, indulgence, grown beyond
> Earth's bearing, even, ask Jansenius else! (XI.1778-81)

Actually, Guido and the Pope make the same historical observations, though for opposite reasons and with opposite judgments. Both see the age, to the Pope's distress and Guido's encouragement, as corrupt from top to bottom, and the murder case as symptomatic of the corruption. But they also see in the murder case, to the Pope's comfort and Guido's chagrin, signs that the corruption of the old order is giving birth to a regenerated new order. The ultimate origin of the crime in the poverty and vice out of which Pompilia was born, and in the property system which caused the Comparini to acquire Pompilia in order to preserve their claim to an inheritance; the cynical marriage barter of Pompilia's money for Guido's title; the precedents of injustice and abuse of privilege that Guido relied on and that were amply fulfilled by the decision of the Tuscan court in his favor; the failure of Church and State authorities to help Pompilia, forcing her to turn to Caponsacchi; the shameful conduct of the Roman convent that sheltered Pompilia, then sought after her death to defame her in order to inherit her property; the presence in the Church of men like Guido and his brothers; the brutality of Guido's peasants, which Guido first used to his advantage then found turned against him—these are signs that the ecclesiastical and feudal sanctions have ceased to apply, that the old order has died from within though the dead machinery still grinds. On the other hand, the unexpected accidents of which Guido complains, the approximately right judgment of the Roman court and the precisely right judgments of Fra Celestino and the Pope, even the exceptional scruples of the official who refused Guido the horses—these are signs that within the old institutions themselves lie the seeds of regeneration.

Psychologically, the right instinct of Pompilia and Caponsacchi is a guarantee that truth maintains itself in the human heart *in spite of* history, of external change. But historically, the murder case shows that truth maintains itself *by means of* history. The general corruption that made Guido's crime possible would also have destroyed him in the end, as it is destroying the old order he relied on. In addition, his crime aroused the almost forgotten conscience of the age to condemn him and the old order. That Pompilia and Caponsacchi found the right way in spite of the age, as Euripides found it in a pre-Christian era and some other Pompilia will find it in the coming post-Christian era, means that truth is different from and anterior to any cultural expression of it, and that the cultural expression must be renewed by being tested against truth's source in the human heart. But the dying order makes its own contribution to truth, by dying, and by summoning up its own conscience to condemn itself to death. By isolating the truth within itself against itself, the old order hands on essential truth to find embodiment in a new order.

The Pope is aware of the social and revolutionary implications of the murder case. He is aware that the privileged class expects him to uphold authority by declaring Guido to have acted within his rights as lord and husband. That is why the Pope has Guido executed not in the usual place, but in the Square frequented by the nobility: "So shall the quality see, fear and learn" (X.2114), learn that the age of special privilege is over. The Pope sacrifices the social order, and even the Christian era, to Christian truth. The act by which he condemns Guido and vindicates Pompilia is the great final act of his life, his gift as dying leader of the old order to the new order.

The historical meaning of the poem is symbolized by the references to Molinism, which recur like a leitmotif throughout.[2] Molinism was a fashionable sect in Italy during the 1670's and 1680's; "the sect for a quarter of an hour," Browning calls it. Since it was declared heretical and its leader, Molinos, condemned and imprisoned in 1687, it was undoubtedly, by the time of the murder case in 1698, a lost cause from which every one would be naturally eager to dissociate himself, if indeed people still spoke of it as ubiquitously as Browning makes out. But the very question of Browning's historical accuracy in giving so much emphasis in 1698 to Molinism is a sign that the short-lived heresy had advantages for his historical meaning. First, the restricted life of the heresy and its obscurity in the modern recollection help localize the poem historically, supplying the detail appropriate to no other time and place, and the authentic detail, since there it was though now almost forgotten. Second, the nature of the heresy suggests the stirrings within the Church that foreshadow the new order. Since Molinos was a Quietist who taught direct apprehension of God apart from ritual, Church, and even, in certain instances, the intermediary contemplation of the humanity of Christ, the heresy has affinities not only with Evangelical Protestantism, but—more to the point—with the kind of essential Christianity that the Pope finds in Pompilia, Euripides, and the future Pompilia of the post-Christian era.

Actually, the poem tells us nothing directly about Molinos' doctrine; we gather its purport indirectly from the characters who condemn as Molinism actions which strike us as adhering to the spirit, in opposition to the dogma and machinery, of Christianity. It is this pejorative use of Molinism as a recognition that the times are evil, and as a scapegoat on which to hang the evils of the time, that is its third and most important advantage in the poem. Molinism and the murder case are linked together as signs that "Antichrist surely comes and domesday's near," Guido's crime cropping forth

> I' the course of nature when Molinos' tares
> Are sown for wheat. (II.175-76)

We can almost rank the characters morally by the degree of their preoccupation with Molinism and the extent to which they use it as a scapegoat. On the one hand, Guido, the lawyers, and the pro-Guido speaker of "Half-Rome" find Molinists in every bush. Guido links the case against him with Molinism; Arcangeli, in defending Guido, calls it Molinist doctrine that would "bar revenge," the "natural privilege of man"; the Fisc, Bottini, calls Fra Celestino's sermon "Molinism simple and pure!" Caponsacchi's cynical old bishop, aware of the use to which charges of Molinism are put, half-jestingly accuses him of turning Molinist because he plays "truant in church all day long" from the more worldly duties laid upon him by the Church—duties of society priest and apostle to rich ladies. (To which Caponsacchi replies, "Sir, what if I turned Christian?") Pompilia, too, is jestingly accused of dipping into Molinist books because she is reluctant to give herself up to Guido's loveless embraces.

On the other hand, Pompilia, Caponsacchi, Fra Celestino,

and the pro-Pompilia speaker of "The Other Half-Rome" talk little about Molinism and say nothing against it; and the Pope even defends it:

> Leave them alone . . . those Molinists!
> Who may have other light than we perceive. (I.315-16)

The Pope sees the Molinists as heralds of the new era, who break up "faith in the report" to return to "faith in the thing." Remembering how Christianity broke up the "old faith of the world," the Pope wonders if it will be necessary in the new era for everyone to deny "recognized truths," as the Molinists do now, in favor of

> some truth
> Unrecognized yet, but perceptible?—
> Correct the portrait by the living face,
> Man's God, by God's God in the mind of man?
>
> (X.1871-74)

Just as Guido and the Pope display the same historical understanding of the age, so both the characters who condemn and those who do not condemn Molinism understand it in the same way—as an attempt to purify religion and as a herald of revolutionary changes to come. Whatever Molinos' actual doctrine, Molinism in Browning stands for an antidogmatic, an empirical and relativist, a psychological and historical approach to religion. Faith in the report must be replaced by faith in the thing; and the thing, the unformulated but perceptible truth, "God's God in the mind of man," is a step ahead of formulated truth, "man's God." Truth's ultimate source is in the individual mind; so that judgment of truth rests on judgment of character. Thus, the Pope is impressed by Molinism because its adherents make their denials "at peril of their body and soul," while the motives of orthodox Christians are questionable since orthodoxy is prudent for body and soul.

Nor is Browning's Molinism an antihistorical heresy that condemns the past as a mistake. It makes its protest within the limited historical context of 1698, a time when the disequilibrium between the thing and the report had grown too great. The Pope sees Molinism and the post-Christian era it foreshadows as history's way of producing again

> the Christian act so possible
> When in the way stood Nero's cross and stake,—
> So hard now when the world smiles "Right and wise!"
> (X.1831-34)

The Church's heresy hunting impedes the historical process by obscuring the truth, but it also advances history by advancing the decay of the old order. For the Pope sees that while the Church concentrates its attention on the frontier between orthodoxy and heresy, the Christian mainland inside, "quite undisputed-for," decays (X.1605-13). The historical point is that heresy was not required in Nero's time when no one was likely to profess Christian dogma who had not the faith, and will not be required in the new era when there will again be no disparity between dogma and faith. For we hear of no new Molinist dogma to replace the old Church dogma. Browning's Molinism would seem to leave truth at its source in the individual mind, to develop where and as the man of right instinct finds it.

Thus, by precept and example, by its ideas and structure, *The Ring and the Book* achieves its meaning through meeting the conditions of modern psychological and historical relativism. If Browning's poem does not offer the same order of satisfaction as Dante's or Milton's, or for that matter Homer's or Virgil's, it must be remembered that he starts with an almost opposite set of conditions, conditions unprecedented in major poetry before *Faust*.

First of all, Browning starts with Goethe's condition that

the poem is not to derive meaning from any external standard of judgment, but is to be the empiric ground giving rise to its own standard of judgment. (Faust spends the whole poem evolving the law by which his actions are to be judged, so that we have really to suspend judgment until the end.) Then Browning imposes upon Goethe's condition another still harder one, in that he does not take off from traditional categories, does not like Goethe give new meaning to an old myth, but draws his meaning out of "pure crude fact." He starts with history, and not even official history with its incrustation of myth, but with just the unmoralized and unhistoricized remains of the life that goes on below the level of history, with an old and forgotten scandal.

It is impossible to overemphasize the importance Browning attached to the crudely and even sordidly realistic quality of his story—since he himself recurs to its rock-bottom factuality over and over again in Book I, as though he could not exult enough about it. In his exultation he tosses the Old Yellow Book into the air, catches it again and twists it about by the crumpled vellum covers, all because it is "pure crude fact," likened to the "pure gold" of the ring. It has the shape of a book, he says returning to the subject, but is

> really, pure crude fact
> Secreted from man's life when hearts beat hard,
> And brains, high-blooded, ticked two centuries since.
> Give it me back! The thing's restorative
> I' the touch and sight. (I.86-90)

And again, with naive wonder, as though he could hardly believe in his good fortune:

> So, in this book lay absolutely truth,
> Fanciless fact, the documents indeed,
> Primary lawyer-pleadings . . .
> . . . real summed-up circumstance. (I.143-46)

The reverence and delight remind us of the ordinary Philistine's devotion to his facts and figures. For behind the devotion of both stands the positivist's faith that ultimate truth lies locked up in the facts.

Browning's purpose is to unlock the truth—not, however, by interpreting the facts according to some theory, but by restoring to the facts their life, the beating hearts and high-blooded, ticking brains of two centuries since. To do that he used the alloy of imagination, not as an interpretive but as a projective function: "I fused my live soul and that inert stuff."

> The life in me abolished the death of things,
> Deep calling unto deep: as then and there
> Acted itself over again once more
> The tragic piece.   (I.520-23)

For the repristination, the separation of the alloy from the gold once the ring has been shaped, Browning says he retained the sense and manner of the documentation:

> I disappeared; the book grew all in all,
> The lawyers' pleadings swelled back to their size,—
> Doubled in two, the crease upon them yet;   (I.687-89)

for once dramatized, imbued with life, the facts can be depended on to yield their meaning.

The only reason for dramatizing the story at all is not to impose truth upon it, but to make the truth accessible, as the smith makes the gold accessible by shaping it into a ring. For though the truth is all set down in the bookful of facts, what has hitherto come of it? Who remembers Guido and Pompilia?

> Was this truth of force?
> Able to take its own part as truth should,
> Sufficient, self-sustaining? Why, if so—

Yonder's a fire, into it goes my book,
As who shall say me nay, and what the loss? (I.372-76)

No loss because the poet adds nothing to the truth. In imitating in due proportion God's creativeness, man "Creates, no, but resuscitates, perhaps."

Man, bounded, yearning to be free,
May so project his surplusage of soul
In search of body, so add self to self
By owning what lay ownerless before,—
So find, so fill full, so appropriate forms—
That, although nothing which had never life
Shall get life from him, be, not having been,
Yet, something dead may get to live again,
Something with too much life or not enough,
Which, either way imperfect, ended once:
An end whereat man's impulse intervenes,
Makes new beginning, starts the dead alive,
Completes the incomplete and saves the thing.
(I.718-30)

Here is the new nineteenth-century theory of the nature and function of poetry. The poet is neither the "creator" of one traditional poetic theory, nor yet the "mirror" or "imitator" of another. For while he works only with extant facts, his meaning is not quite there for imitation; he must find his meaning by restoring to the facts a concreteness they have lost in the process of becoming facts, of being abstracted from their original human and historical situations. Thus, the poet as "resuscitator" is the superlatively effective psychologist and historian, the arch-empiricist who works toward greater concreteness and not, as in traditional poetic theory, toward general truths. His talent lies in the "surplusage of soul" which enables him to project himself into the facts, apprehend them sympathetically in other words, and thus apprehend their life. His poem establishes a pole for sympathy, so that the reader, too, can project himself into the facts and apprehend their life. For both poet and reader, to "see into the life of things" is to see their meaning. Meaning comes not from theoretical interpretation but from the intensest concreteness.

Thus, meaning is not separable from the facts, and is in that sense psychological and historical, coextensive with the facts of character and setting. Any formulation of the meaning in terms applicable beyond the conditions of the poem remains partial and problematical as an account of the poem. Even the Pope's interpretation of the events is presumably partial and problematical, though we favor it above other interpretations because of what we apprehend about him as a person. Hence Browning's use of dramatic monologues, to make it clear that no one point of view is identifiable with the truth. "The same transaction," Browning said of the poem, "seen from a number of differing points of view, or glimpses in a mirror."³ Just as we perceive the third dimension because each eye gives a different report, so the disparity in points of view gives the life-like effect. Our apprehension of the total three-dimensional picture is the meaning. But when we try to rationalize our apprehension, break it up into moral or legal judgments, or even judgments of fact, we are reduced to partial views, the variegated refractions of truth in the mirror.

These then are the unprecedented conditions of *The Ring and the Book*—not only that the poem was to be no mere illustration of an external principle from which the facts would derive meaning, but that the facts themselves, all of them, unselected and as they came to hand (their sordidness was all the better as a guarantee that they were unselected), were to yield the meaning. It can be argued that Browning does not entirely let the facts speak for themselves; for he not only speaks in his own voice in Books I and XII, but he makes the Pope too authoritative.⁴ It is certainly a valid criticism of *The Ring and the Book* that good and evil are not sufficiently interfused. Our judgment is forced from the beginning, whereas it would seem to be peculiarly the genius of a poem treating different points of view toward the same story to treat each point of view impartially, allowing judgment to arise out of the utmost ambiguity.

But such a criticism raises the question whether facts really can speak for themselves; whether a poet can, with the mere accumulation of prosaic details and a workable middle style seldom rising to passages which can in themselves be called poetry, achieve the high transcendental meaning Browning wanted. For he wanted nothing less than to portray in Pompilia the most exalted saintliness (Dante's Beatrice was not, I should imagine, beyond his mark), revealing itself amid and by means of the ordinarily vicious human motives and judgments. The poetry, the total illumination, lies in the dynamism of the whole scheme, really in the backward glance, the reader's sense of having come a long way.

However we measure Browning's achievement, his aim—to make poetry rise out of prose and spirituality out of the world's common clay, to meet in other words the conditions for modern intellectual and moral conviction as Tennyson in the *Idylls*, Arnold in *Sohrab* and Morris in *Sigurd* do not— would have to be the aim, I should think, of any genuinely modern literature. If his method seems to pertain more closely to the novel than to poetry, so much the better for my point. For to judge Browning's poem adequately, we would want to know whether other poets have managed to pitch their meaning higher, given the same weight of clay; or whether the long poem is, for that matter, the vehicle for sublimating a weight of clay.

The relativist conditions for modern conviction might explain, for example, the decline of the long poem and the rise of the novel in the nineteenth century, as well as the almost universal retreat by twentieth-century poets into

ROBERT LANGBAUM

short poetry—the poetry of momentary illumination in which
the illumination is made possible through a personal and
temporary rejection of the facts, or rather of the prevailing
system of ideas through which we perceive the facts. Certainly, the relativist conditions make the virtues of classical
narrative and dramatic poetry difficult to achieve. The
weight of clay makes difficult what Arnold, protesting against
the effect on poetry of modern culture, called the "grand
style"; while the differing points of view, the variegated
refractions in the mirror are, according to the new *ars
poetica*, a virtue—though a virtue quite opposite from that
singleness of view Arnold admired and envied so much in
Sophocles, "who saw life steadily and saw it whole."

[1957]

ROMA A. KING

EVE AND THE VIRGIN

Browning characteristically begins "Andea del Sarto" in the middle of an action, and concentrates the painter's situation into a single climactic experience. Yet before the drama is finished this pinpointed moment has been related to the whole of Andrea's drab life. We have both the intense moment of revelation and the slow movement in time of past events which make the painter's final insight possible.

The poem is a psychological study in which the time element is an important part of structure. Andrea's initial surrender to his wife's demand that he paint for money is totally damning to the artist; its completeness and finality divert interest from what may happen to why it has happened, from suspense in action to character analysis. The action moves from present to past, from past to present, and finally, to an imaginary future in the New Jerusalem.

Andrea's restless dissatisfaction with any time signals his personal disturbances, his unwillingness to accept himself in any role, real or imaginary, and provides a significant clue to the poem's meaning. There can be no question about the sordidness of the present, for Browning presents its most repelling aspects. Andrea, uncomfortable over his capitulation to his wife, seeks renewed self-esteem in the past which he tries to make palatable by recalling what he once was, or what he imagines he was. A less honest nature might have found comfort in such an escape, but Andrea, much too sensitive to be easily deluded, is driven first to face and then to rationalize his obvious failure. Ironically, he achieves not peace, but an increasing self-awareness that makes the past as uncomfortable as the present. In his primitive Garden he finds both the Tree of Knowledge and an Eve. He comes to see that his failure is at least twofold—both as artist and as lover —and that somehow these two are inseparably related. His initial surrender of his art to Lucrezia is paralleled by a final surrender of Lucrezia to her lover. From the reality of both past and present, he is driven finally to seek refuge in an imaginary heaven where, with Leonardo, Rafael, and Agnolo, he achieves illusory fulfillment.

This account of action inadequately describes the drama of the poem, however, for it is given complexity and intensity both by Andrea's conscious attempts to reject what he unconsciously knows to be true, and by a series of dialectical movements within the poem. Part of the intensity comes from the opposition of pairs, all symbolic: summer and autumn, twilight and darkness, youth and age, past and present, heaven and earth, hope and failure.

The first suggestion of meaning comes in the ambivalent subtitle, "The Faultless Painter." The phrase, recognized as ironic, is too often understood to mean that Browning said a thing ridiculous in order to enforce a contradictory meaning. Accordingly, he did not mean that Andrea was faultless, but that he was totally depraved. A thoughtful reading discredits this one-dimensional interpretation. Empson makes a statement about irony which applies here: "An irony has no point unless it is true, in some degree, in both senses; for it is imagined as a part of an argument; what is said is made absurd, but it is what the opponent might say." Precisely so in "Andrea del Sarto." In a sense, Andrea is a faultless painter; at the same time he is a mere craftsman. On another level, he is both husband and pander; Lucrezia is at once his Virgin and his Eve.

Andrea's roles are many and often contradictory. He becomes participant with the lover in a twofold drama, one in which lover and mistress provide contrasting comment upon husband and wife, and the other in which the two vie for Lucrezia's favor. Still again, Andrea is unwittingly cast in opposition to Agnolo and obliged to defend his faultless paintings against his rival's superior accomplishments. Torn between opposite but equally demanding claims and made constantly aware of failure, Andrea achieves not wholeness, but destructive self-realization.

His impulses run in counter directions. A remark of self-justification is followed by one of self-accusation; a spirit of bravado and assertiveness, by one of passive acceptance. His attitude toward Lucrezia fluctuates from contempt to deference; toward the lover, from resentment to grudging admiration; toward his public, from disdain to obsequiousness.

Andrea oscillates between assertiveness and passiveness, between projection and receptivity. His vision of what he should do as artist is remarkably clear and his desire for a normal relationship with Lucrezia is intense, but a spiritual and physical enervation prohibits him from being satisfactorily either the husband or artist. The conflict of the poem is between asserted artistic and masculine virility and a steadily increasing awareness of debility.

Andrea attempts to establish himself by recalling with justified pride the praise of his contemporaries; he is, indeed, a facile craftsman, and his attempt to improve Rafael is not mere bravado. He likes also to fancy himself as being masculine and irresistible. In the lines

> Your soft hand is a woman of itself,
> And mine the man's bared breast she curls inside

the words "bared breast" suggest masculine strength, and the "soft hand" feminine dependency and affection. The hand appropriately curls in his, a symbol of the personal union which he desires.

At the same time, he is aware of the superiority of Rafael's paintings, and he realizes too that his own sense of form and line can never compensate for an insight which he does not have. Simultaneously, he knows that the lover possesses Lucrezia in a way that he can never hope to rival. Suspecting that he is incapable of passion and devoid of masculine attractiveness, Andrea resembles a character out of the early Auden, Eliot's Prufrock, or James's Marcher, save that he, perhaps, is more aware of his deficiency. His despair is produced partly by the realization that Lucrezia can be, indeed has been, won. Even as he presses his ineffectual suit, outside waits a lover to whom she is willingly drawn. His failure and the lover's success tantalize him into speculation:

> Ah, but what does he,
> The Cousin! what does he to please you more?

If Andrea could answer this question he would at the same time answer a great many more. For his failure with

Lucrezia is only a part of his total failure as son, friend, and artist. His strange, almost abnormal devotion to a woman who has so degraded him cannot have been other than devastating to his art. Yet, he realizes clearly that she is not wholly the cause of his failure:

> Beside, incentives come from the soul's self;
> The rest avail not. Why do I need you?
> What wife had Rafael, or has Agnolo?

What he calls lack of incentive from the soul's self is really passiveness, debility, receptivity. These qualities make necessary his attempts to escape from time and self and produce his ultimate weariness and despair.

Stopford Brooke and William Lyon Phelps have called attention to Andrea's uxoriousness, his "unconquerable passion," but have failed to note that what they speak of is largely illusory. Indeed, Andrea does seem to give up everything for Lucrezia—his family, his friends, his integrity, and finally his creative vision; yet with equal submissiveness he hands her over to the lover at the end of the poem: "Again the Cousin's whistle! Go, my Love." His attitude toward her wavers. His subservience is counterpointed by a bitterness, an antagonism that makes itself felt much too often to be ignored: "You don't understand / Nor care . . . ," "Had I been two, . . ." "Had you enjoined them on me, given me soul," "Had you, with these same, but brought a mind!" "And had you not grown restless. . . ."

Clearly, uxoriousness is only one manifestation of a more basic weakness. Attracted as he is by Lucrezia's body, he lacks, nevertheless, the virility of Fra Lippo Lippi and the passion of Sebald. What seems physical desire is partly enthusiasm for artistic form, and in the following it is the craftsman who speaks: "perfect ears . . . oh, so sweet," "perfect brow, / And perfect eyes, and more than perfect mouth, / And the low voice. . . ." Enamoured of his wife's beauty, Andrea runs his hands through her hair and remarks that it serves to frame her picture-perfect face:

> Let my hands frame your face in your hair's gold,
> You beautiful Lucrezia that are mine!

Actually, he is surprisingly passive and physically undemanding:

> . . . and it seems
> As if—forgive now—should you let me sit
> Here by the window with your hand in mine
> And look a half-hour forth on Fiesole,
> Both of one mind, as married people use,
> Quietly, quietly the evening through,
> I might get up to-morrow to my work
> Cheerful and fresh as ever.

The half-hour over, he states complacently:

> You loved me quite enough, it seems to-night.

That "enough" reflects a characteristic of Andrea's which is given additional emphasis by the poem's structure. Diction, sound repetition, rhythm, and sentence structure all unite to create an impression, emotionally and sensuously, of placidity and greyness, qualities by which Andrea describes his life and work.

The diction, lacking the colorfulness of Fra Lippo Lippi's, is abstract and conceptual rather than perceptive and sensory. There are an unusually large number of substantives and relatively few modifiers, an almost equal number of concrete and abstract nouns. Clear and sharp but not particularly sensuous, the concrete nouns are used primarily to establish character and setting. Many are descriptive or technical: *sun, tree, star, moon, bird, picture, chalk.* Others show a painter's interest in man's anatomy: *hand, head, face, breast, ears, arms, neck, shoulders.* Andrea habitually speaks professionally, detachedly of the human body. It is as model that he refers most often to Lucrezia. The small number of modifiers suggests subordination of sensuous appeal. Only a few are sensory, and of these, two alone, *grey* and *golden,* appear more than once; even they lose most of their sensuousness since they are used as symbols, as I shall show later. On the whole, the diction in "Andrea del Sarto" contrasts sharply with that of the Ottima-Sebald scene in *Pippa Passes,* where Browning attempts to communicate physicality.

The greater number of modifiers is qualitative and quantitative: *glad, perfect, past, little, same, poor, great, good,* and *better.* Only a sprinkling of adjectives, *sober, pleasant, strange, festal, melancholy,* and *bright,* are romantically atmospheric. Browning begins "Andrea del Sarto" with a simple, straightforward, unemotional statement:

> But do not let us quarrel any more,
> No, my Lucrezia; bear with me for once:
> Sit down and all shall happen as you wish.

Andrea himself suffers from emotional sterility, reflected both by his "faultless" paintings (contrasted with the "soulful" works of his contemporaries) and by his relations with Lucrezia. His pleading, his promises, his bribes, elicit less response from her than the whistle of the lover. Andrea offers everything, the cousin nothing. Yet his "less" is "more," just as Rafael's is.

In "The Bishop Orders His Tomb" Browning partly characterizes the Bishop by frequent repetition of vowel sounds used for purely sensuous effects, but no such attempts is made in "Andrea del Sarto." Governed by the central meaning of the poem, he does avoid cacophony, the general placidity helping to present both in concept and in emotional texture Andrea's "grey world" and his "autumnal" and "twilight" life and work.

There is considerable alliteration, but it does not function primarily to convey sensuousness or to provide poetic decoration. Frequently, it emphasizes idea by calling attention to important thoughts, as in "mine the man's bared breast she curls inside." This line, containing a basic image, commands special attention because of the alliteration. Browning uses repetition (the *l*'s and the *f*'s in the following, for example) to link sentences and to gain conceptual unity and compactness:

> Love, we are in God's hand.
> How strange now, looks the life he makes us lead;
> So free we seem, so fettered fast we are!
> I feel he laid the fetter: let it lie!

My point is that Browning does not use alliteration in "Andrea del Sarto," as, for example, Swinburne does in "Dolores," to produce emotional and sensuous effects apart from meaning. Even when repetition calls attention to lines that appear sensuous the effect is actually ironic. For example, "Let my hands frame your face in your hair's gold" counterpoints sensuous with artistic attraction, passion with a painter's professional appraisal of a good subject.

Alliteration is used further as part of rhythm. Stressing lightly conceptually unimportant syllables, and calling attention to others by heavy stress and alliteration, Browning achieves simultaneously in some lines both the artistic effect of alliterative verse and an emphasis on idea. Thus, the rhythmic pattern of the poem becomes a part of the meaning much more profoundly than by merely echoing the sense. Though irregular, the poem is "unmusical" only if judged by Spenserian and Tennysonian standards. Closer to the Wyatt-Donne tradition, Browning uses a line basically conventional in that it has a predetermined number of syllables and stresses, but breaks with the musical tradition in the placement of syllables within the line, proposing to relate closely what is felt and said with the manner of saying it, to use rhythm both to create and to support meaning. The absence of a strong sensuous movement, such as that, for example, which creates so vividly the physicality of Shakespeare's "Venus and Adonis" and Marlowe's "Hero and Leander," emphasizes Andrea's passivity; its brokenness reflects at the same time his psychological chaos. Andrea's weariness—physical, intellectual, emotional—is expressed both overtly and structurally.

> I often am much wearier than you think,
> This evening more than usual,

he says. And again:

> Too live the life grew, golden and not grey,
> And I'm the weak-eyed bat no sun should tempt
> Out of the grange whose four walls make his world.

Andrea's debility contrasts significantly with Lucrezia's assertiveness.

Such frequently used words as *silver, dream, quietly, evening, grey, greyness, twilight, autumn* create atmosphere and texture more because of their conceptual meaning than their emotional connotations. Their effect, therefore, is clear and sharp rather than vague and diffuse. Browning's diction, here and elsewhere, has a specificity not found in that of any other nineteenth-century poet before Meredith, Hardy, and Hopkins. It was this quality more than any other that recommended him to Ezra Pound in the twentieth century.

The small number of verbs slows down the action and heightens the sense of weariness. Browning uses a minimum of action words:

I surely then could sometimes leave the ground,
Put on the glory, Rafael's daily wear,
In that humane great monarch's golden look,—
One finger in his beard or twisted curl
Over his mouth's good mark that made the smile,
One arm about my shoulder, round my neck,
The jingle of his gold chain in my ear,
I painting proudly with his breath on me,
All his court round him, seeing with his eyes,
Such frank French eyes, and such a fire of souls
Profuse, my hand kept plying by those hearts,—
And, best of all, this, this, this face beyond,
This in the background, waiting on my work,
To crown the issue with a last reward!

In fourteen lines there are only three finite verbs. Others are implied, and participles function suggestively as verbs. By implication and substitution, however, Browning avoids disturbing the quiet autumnal atmosphere with active verbs. Some lines lack even participles:

But all the play, the insight and the stretch—
Out of me, out of me! And wherefore out?

The effect here should be contrasted with that of "Fra Lippo Lippi," where relatively a great many more verbs are used. Obviously, a difference in subject matter requires a difference in technique: Lippo, in contrast to Andrea, is virile and sensuous.

The structure of Andrea's sentences is on one level a projection of his inner emptiness, and on another a suggestion of his struggle against self-realization. They express an unwillingness to grapple realistically with his problem, a passive receptiveness of "fate" that contradicts his half-hearted attempts at assertiveness.

His imperatives, never strong, are characteristically more often entreaties than commands. He timidly requests that

Lucrezia grant him partly what by rights he should command wholly. And though numerous, the interrogatory sentences are not at all like Lippo's startling demand:

> Come, what am I a beast for?

Andrea's is not a searching mind attempting to discover truth, but a timid one afraid of discovering too much. Lippo, more confident of himself, could with greater comfort face his problems. Andrea's exclamations lack force, the shock of immediate experience and spontaneous utterance having been absorbed by retrospection. The opening sentence reveals an emotional staleness produced by a situation so often repeated that it has lost all immediacy.

Andrea's speech, though not "literary," lacks the colloquial directness, the force, of Lippo's or Bishop Blougram's. Lucrezia is protagonist but not in the sense that Gigadibs and the Watchman are. Symbolic of the whole pattern of Andrea's life, she is in a sense a much richer auditor than either of the others. Her presence in the room, the turn of her head that brings face but not heart, the careless sweep of her skirt against wet paint, her indifference to Andrea's reputation among his contemporaries, her impatience to join her lover all combine to elicit from Andrea a complex response. In a sense, he speaks more to himself than directly to Lucrezia, and although we never forget that she is with him, we feel that she too is overhearing. Actually, the poem belongs somewhere between dramatic conversation and internal monologue. Andrea does not develop his thoughts logically, for he is not reasoning and coming to conclusions; rather he is reminiscing, justifying, excusing, and accepting. Consequently, units of expression often consist of conceptual or emotional rather than grammatical groups. Their unity is imaginative, hence not always immediately apparent.

These groups are frequently only fragments, many times containing a series of substantives and few or no verbs:

ROMA A. KING

That Francis, that first time,
And that long festal year at Fontainebleau!

Their fragmentariness, the omission of coordinates and verbs,
is significant. The absence of verbs I have already discussed
as one indication of his passiveness. The omission of co-
ordinate conjunctions between independent clauses serves to
break the poem into a series of ungrammatically related reflections, and at the same time signals his incapacity for
integrating counterimpulses and for forming relationships.
Lack of structural formality creates the impression of
emotional and intellectual instability. In general, Andrea's
sentences are of two types: either segmented, brief, independent clauses frequently not syntactically related to a
larger unit; or complex sentences consisting of introductory
independent clauses followed by one or more subordinate
clauses. These complex sentences are frequently split into
two or more segments by interpolations which may or may
not be syntactically related:

Well, I can fancy how he did it all,
Pouring his soul, with kings and popes to see,
Reaching, that heaven might so replenish him,
Above and through his art—for it gives way;
That arm is wrongly put—and there again—
A fault to pardon in the drawing's lines,
Its body, so to speak: its soul is right,
He means right—that, a child may understand.

The complex sentences, the numerous subordinations, the
interpolations, the exclamations, the lack of syntactical connections give the effect of thought in conflict, of intellectual
uncertainty and emotional instability. Andrea's aim is self-
justification, but since he has not ordered his thinking, he
cannot proceed straightforwardly as Lippo does; rather he
muses disjointedly and inconclusively on first one aspect and

then another of his unpleasant experience. Andrea is afraid to pursue his speculations to a logical conclusion for he partly knows and rejects what he would find if he did. His sentences reflect the tortured flow of thought that can neither stop nor come to a logical conclusion, a surplus of diffused intensity that decreases the finality of what he says. The *pasticcio* quality of his thinking is demonstrated by the fact that a reader is hardly aware of either the beginning or the end of many of his constructions.

Thus, the dialectical opposition between Andrea's physical and spiritual debility and his effort to avoid self-realization is communicated materially and structurally. These opposing forces are given both more precise definition and artistic unity particularly through symbol. Lucrezia herself is the dominant symbol. Briefly, Andrea's devotion to her "soulless" beauty signifies a personal and artistic deficiency; and her perfidy, fate's compensation to him for his weakness. She is the materialization of his desires for human relationships and artistic achievement, reflecting his erroneous judgment, his false standard of values.

She is the symbol of the emptiness which Andrea comes to understand. He speaks of himself rightly as a "half-man." The famous "Ah, but a man's reach should exceed his grasp" is ironical, for Andrea is vaguely conscious of the discrepancy between his higher vision (personal and artistic) and his spiritual and emotional faculties to achieve; he is tormented by a stimulus greater than his power to respond.

His eventual capitulation and destruction are suggested by a group of frequently repeated words associated with values: *worthy, pay, gold, silver, gain, reward.* Each has a literal meaning, but as a group and in context they are also symbolically significant. The two basic adjectives are *golden* and *silver* (grey): in his "kingly days" Andrea enjoyed the monarch's "golden look"; he worked with Francis' arm about

him, the jingle of his gold chain in his ears; a "fire of souls"
kept his hand plying until "too live the life grew, golden and
not grey. . . ." He left the "golden look" of the monarch for
the gold of Lucrezia's hair, and his whole world changed:

> . . . the whole seems to fall into a shape
> As if I saw alike my work and self
> And all that I was born to be and do,
> A twilight-piece.

His attitude toward his work changed; seeing it degenerate
into a commodity, he came to speak of it in marketplace
terms:

> I'll work then for your friend's friend, never fear,
> Treat his own subject after his own way,
> Fix his own time, accept too his own price,
> And shut the money into this small hand
> When next it takes mine.

He uses the same terminology when he attempts to describe
the relation between himself and his painting:

> I know both what I want and what might *gain*,
> And yet how *profitless* to know. . . .

The words *gain* and *profitless* suggest the hold which buying
and selling have upon him. His painting itself takes on the
color of commercialism:

> All is silver-grey
> Placid and perfect with my art.

Lucrezia is blamed because she failed to urge that he "never
care for *gain*" (a pun that is ironic). Because of his perverted values, Andrea becomes paradoxical when he recog-

nizes that Rafael, though lacking his technical skill, is the greater painter:

> Yet do much less, so much less, Someone says,
> (I know his name, no matter)—so much less!
> Well, less is more, Lucrezia.

Toward the conclusion of the poem, these market terms appear more frequently and in positions of greater emphasis. Heightening emotion and sharpening the irony, they become effective mediums for expressing meaning. The brick walls appear cemented with fierce bright gold; Andrea took money from Francis; he neglected to give money to his mother and father; he failed to make money for himself and Lucrezia. Most significantly they depict the degeneration of Andrea's standards of values, his genuine confusion, and ultimately his compromise with the tawdry and commonplace. They are all echoed in the lines:

> That Cousin here again? he waits outside?
> Must see you—you, and not with me? Those *loans?*
> More gaming *debts* to *pay?* you smiled for that?
> Well, let smiles *buy* me! have you more to *spend?*
> While hand and eye and something of a heart
> Are left me, work's my *ware*, and what's it *worth?*
> I'll *pay* my fancy.

Here everything is reduced to a mart where the lover makes debts which Andrea must pay, where Lucrezia barters her love, and where Andrea pays for her smiles with second-rate paintings. The climaxing line, "I'll pay my fancy," suggests the ironic state of Andrea's existence: the delight which he finds in his relationship with Lucrezia is capricious, not real, and even for that he pays dearly.

The words *golden* and *grey* have still another meaning. *Grey* best suggests Andrea's passive, colorless personality, and used in contrast to *golden* points up the difference between the life that he now lives and that he once lived; they also suggest, on another level, the breach between his actual existence and his imagined one.. There was a time when life itself was golden, but that time is gone: "A common greyness silvers everything. . . ." Dusk falls outside as Andrea talks; dusk has long since settled over his life. Summer has given way to autumn in the natural world; within Andrea's inner world "autumn grows, autumn in everything." The merging of the outer world with the inner illustrates the success with which Browning handles symbol. Andrea's work, as well as his life, has been affected. "All that I was born to be and do" is "a twilight-piece." "My youth, my hope, my art, being all toned down. . . ." This is the figure which he uses to contrast his work with that of his more successful contemporaries. His is the hand of a patient, skilful, but uninspired craftsman, while in the works of his contemporaries "There burns a truer light of God. . . ."

Andrea regrets his lack of light, but at the same time, paradoxically, fears to venture into full day. In one powerful figure he expresses his inner paralysis and brings together the golden-grey with the wall figure. He says, referring to his earlier life with Francis:

> Too live the life grew, golden and not grey,
> And I'm the weak-eyed bat no sun should tempt
> Out of the grange whose four walls make his world.

The emphasis is on the "weak-eyed bat"—the natural lover of darkness. Andrea prefers the calm security and the comforting shades of four walls to the penetrating light of the world. Lucrezia is a symbol of darkness which he welcomes rather than fears, and he follows his own self-destroying impulses when he chooses her in preference to

the world of Rafael and Agnolo. Now he lives within his
four walls and takes comfort in the dusk of the late afternoon, his only light a false reflection created by a guilty
conscience:

> . . . oft at nights
> When I look up from painting, eyes tired out,
> The walls become illumined, brick from brick
> Distinct, instead of mortar, fierce bright gold,
> That gold of his I did cement them with!

His personal limitations are imposed upon his paintings.
He realizes that an artist should break through the bounda-
ries of here and now to participate in the limitlessness of
eternity. Spiritually and artistically imprisoned, however, he
is unable to transcend the market place. His failure sets him
apart from his more illustrious contemporaries:

> Their works drop groundward, but themselves, I know,
> Reach many a time a heaven that's shut to me,
> Enter and take their place there sure enough,
> Though they come back and cannot tell the world.
> My works are nearer heaven, but I sit here.

Indeed, it is understandable that in a moment of despair
he should say, "I feel he laid the fetter: let it lie!"
Paradoxically, also, he realizes that Lucrezia is a part of
his failure and sometimes blames her for the whole of it;
yet he holds tenaciously to the small security which she
brings. The fact that he legally possesses her beautiful body
is comforting compensation for his personal ineffectualness.
She is there as a bulwark against complete self-realization.
The epithet "serpentining beauty" is rich in connotations.
It calls to mind the Garden of Eden story with its suggestions
of feminine deception, loss of innocence, the curse of God,
and spiritual death. In a sense, Lucrezia is his Eve; at the
same time she is also his Virgin, the prototype of his tech-

nically faultless painting. Another expression of his ambivalent attitude toward her appears in the following:

> And the low voice my soul hears, as a bird
> The fowler's pipe, and follows to the snare.

The fowler is a destructive figure; the snare, a kind of trap
serving to restrict and imprison. Browning uses the word
snare and not *trap* because the snare quietly entangles; while
a trap, more violent, suggests action inappropriate to the
tone of the poem. Here, as in the serpent figure, the emphasis is on deception, and yet it must be noted again that
Andrea's is a willing deception. He is the weak-eyed bat
who "came home" to Lucrezia. If she were a deceiver, if he
were snared, she was also his deliverer; he found a home, a
resting place in the snare.

Browning uses these figures to achieve tragic irony.
Andrea both desires and fears light, both resents and welcomes the snare; he prefers the grey autumnal shades, yet
nostalgically recalls his golden days. His desire to break
his prison walls and reach the heaven of others is expressed
in the ironic figure coming at the conclusion of the poem:

> What would one have?
> In heaven, perhaps, new chances, one more chance—
> Four great walls in the New Jerusalem,
> Meted on each side by the angel's reed.

Andrea is tragically incapable of either conceiving or enjoy-
ing complete freedom.

Actually, in the "bared breast" figure, quoted earlier as an
expression of Andrea's desire for a normal marital relationship, the word *bared* is a pun. Literally, it suggests qualities
of masculine strength which Andrea desires, at the same
time points up the bareness of his soul. There is nothing
there for Lucrezia. In fact, ultimately it is Andrea who seeks

Lucrezia's breast, not she his. This reversal of roles should be noted. It is Lucrezia who calls, not Andrea; she who is the assertive, Andrea the receptive member of the pair. Andrea's behavior contrasts with that of the lover; his passive submission to Lucrezia's call, with the command of the lover's whistle. Equally ironic and effective as the subtitle is the line: "You beautiful Lucrezia that are mine." For she was never his. It was Andrea's misfortune to know this.

B. R. JERMAN

BROWNING'S WITLESS DUKE

A NUMBER of critics who have written on Browning believe that the Duke's little chat with the emissary of the Count in "My Last Duchess"[1] constitutes a clever man's instructions as to the sort of behavior he expects of his next wife. Mrs. Sutherland Orr, for example, says that the Duke's "comments on the countenance of his last Duchess plainly state what he will expect of her successor."[2] Others, like Edward Berdoe, S. S. Curry, Ethel C. Mayne, William Lyon Phelps, and Ina B. Sessions,[3] not to mention numerous editors and anthologists,[4] find a similar purpose in the Duke's monologue. Although Berdoe's reading of the poem (p. 282) is perhaps not typical, it summarizes what the other critics have in mind: "When the Duke said 'Fra Pandolf' by design, he desired to impress on the envoy, and his master the Count, the sort of behavior he expected from the woman he was about to marry. He intimated that he would tolerate no rivals for his next wife's smiles. When he begs his guest to 'Notice Neptune—taming a sea horse,' he further intimated how he had tamed and killed his last duchess. All this was to convey to the envoy, and through him to the lady, that he demanded in his new wife the concentration of her whole being on himself, and the utmost devotion to his will." Browning himself is often quoted in support of at least the first part of this argument. Asked what the Duke meant by the words "by design," the poet answered briefly but equivocally, "To have some occasion for telling the story, and illustrating part of it."[5]

There is good reason to doubt, however, that the Duke is intentionally warning his intended bride, as these critics believe. In the first place, we know that Browning was uncomfortable with factual-minded people who persisted in asking him what he had meant by this or that line or poem.[6] We also know that he, like most good poets, felt that it was necessary to make ambiguous statements about his poetry.[7] Again like most good poets, Browning wanted his readers to do their own interpreting, once even going so far as to tell an acquaintance that poetry was not "a substitute for a cigar, or a game of dominoes, to an idle man."[8] In the second place, if we must use Browning's statement about his poem (which he made, incidentally, nearly fifty years after the poem was first published), we need not necessarily conclude from it that the Duke is moralizing—as I hope to show. In the third place, although we, the audience (and certainly the emissary), might very well be aware of what His Grace expects of his wives, I see little in the poem to support the notion that the Duke is consciously warning, demanding, taking precautions to inform, insinuating, hinting, implying, or intimating—or whatever other terms these critics employ —that he expects or wants the envoy to tell the Count's daughter how she must behave once she is his wife. Finally, if he is not issuing a warning to his intended bride, it follows that the Duke, in pointing out the statue of Neptune taming the sea horse, is not suggesting "That's the way I break them in!" (Phelps, p. 175) or "just so do I tame my wives" (Rogers, p. 519). A closer analysis of "My Last Duchess" should show that the Duke does not have this purpose in mind. The Duke of Ferrara is an art collector, not a moralist.[9] He is, further, a splendid dilettante who prides himself on his possessions.[10] As the poem opens, he is in his sublime role of collector, pointing out his various acquisitions to his visitor. I hardly think that he went to all the trouble to lead the emissary upstairs so he could, by telling the tale of the Duchess' demise, warn the Count's daughter, even by indirection. More probably the Duke has been taking the emissary on the rounds of his art gallery, a common courtesy in great houses, after chatting briefly about his bride-to-be ("as I avowed / At starting"). When they come to one particular picture, the Duke flings back the curtain which covers it, and, after determining his guest's reaction to the portrait, goes into his act. He is pleased, even inspired, to talk about this work of art.

> That's my last Duchess painted on the wall,
> Looking as if she were alive. I call
> That piece a wonder, now: Frà Pandolf's hands
> Worked busily a day, and there she stands.

His first mention of the artist is, as it were, bait. The envoy may have exclaimed, "What a beautiful portrait! Who on earth did it?" "Picasso, of course!" the Duke replies. The bait is out, and the Duke knows, from having stalked other prey, what questions such a man as the envoy would ask. He is suave and confident in this matter:

> I said
> "Frà Pandolf" by design, for never read
> Strangers like you that pictured countenance,

The depth and passion of its earnest glance,
But to myself they turned (since none puts by
The curtain I have drawn for you, but I)
And seemed as they would ask me, if they durst,
How such a glance came there; . . .

Although the Duke might ask him to "sit and look at her," we can be certain that the envoy's eyes are soon turned to the speaker, for the Duke quickly draws attention to himself. The focus is, as Browning intended it to be, on the Duke, who is less concerned with this man's knowing how the artist managed to paint the Duchess than he is in pointing up his own stature as an art collector. The name of the famous artist, then, is designed to give the Duke a gambit, or as Browning called it, an "occasion for telling the story" of what he had to go through to get this so-called "wonder."

The Duchess was no doubt a very attractive but not necessarily beautiful woman, whose great asset, and paradoxically, liability, was her warm personality. Although the Duke disparages her personality (and well he might),[11] he praises her portrait as being a "wonder," and his explanation of how this artist managed to paint her "earnest glance" is all in a day's work to him as an elegant connoisseur. He describes the portrait's virtues, which were his Duchess' faults, in such phrases as the "depth and passion of its earnest glance," "such a glance," "spot of joy," "blush," and "smile," suggesting, to be sure, that the portrait is a revelation of the woman's "soul," possibly a masterpiece. However, in deflating the real-life Duchess, surely to inflate himself before this nameless messenger, the Duke reveals that all the artist had to do was to paint what was on the surface, for she was shallow, undiscriminating, common. She smiled at everyone and everything ("Sir, 't was all one!"). Even the artist could call up that "spot of joy" by using commonplace flattery, he says. Moreover, Frà Pandolf painted the portrait in "a day," surely a supreme achievement even for a master doing a perfunctory job, let alone painting a "wonder." What appears at first glance to be a masterpiece, then, is (on the basis of the Duke's own description of its history, it must be remembered) a mechanically reproduced, realistic picture of a photogenic woman, a dilettante's trophy. Frà Pandolf would be quick to agree that his patron's knowledge of art is more apparent than real.

The Duke, of course, plays down the annoyance the real-life Duchess caused him, saying:

> Sir, 't was not
> Her husband's presence only, called that spot
> Of joy into the Duchess' cheek:

and, later:

> Oh sir, she smiled, no doubt,
> Whene'er I passed her; but who passed without
> Much the same smile?

In other words, the Duke explains "how such a glance came there" not, I think, because he feels compelled to make an accounting of his motives for getting rid of his last Duchess, thereby drawing a moral, but to state the "price" he had to pay for the portrait. A man as proud as His Grace would not condescend to explain why he had her put away.

The most obvious point against the notion that the Duke is warning his bride-to-be is in this very matter of pride, which can best be seen in his attitude towards instructing her. "I choose / Never to stoop," he declares coldly. Petty wrangling, even polite suggestion that she might not spread her personality so thin, would have been beneath his dignity, he insists—and we believe him. After all, she was a duchess —His Duchess—and she should have known better than to have degraded him and his "nine-hundred-years-old name" by being "too easily impressed." It seems unlikely, therefore, that he would consciously unbend to tell "strangers" like the emissary, directly or even subtly, what he expects of this new woman.

As I see it the Duke's "design" is to exhibit his possessions, to pose as a patron of the arts, and to explain how he suffered to get the Duchess on canvas—all for the single purpose of directing attention to himself. In person she was a nuisance because he could not possess her. Framed, the object of inquiries which appeal to his vanity and, therefore, the subject of what he believes is a great portrait, she was kept in his art gallery along with other presumed "rarities" like the statue of Neptune taming a sea horse, which another apparently well-known artist cast in bronze for "me!" Now, he has no more feeling for the one than for the other. He could as easily be talking about the statue. He moves, not callously but unwittingly, from one to the other, never guessing that because of the proximity of the two *objets d'art* to each other, his audience might see him as Neptune. He keeps the portrait of his last Duchess covered because he, like a jealous and insecure child, wants to show complete possession of her "smile." He can now turn that smile on or off at will, simply by pulling a rope.

The Duke would, in all likelihood, adopt similar measures against a new, smiling Duchess who refused to be possessed, but he does not draw a parallel between the two women, possibly because he sees no parallel. He says he wants to marry the Count's daughter because she is "fair" (that is, beautiful), certainly a tactful statement, not because she has a personality equal to or better than that of his last Duchess. In spite of his insistence that he is interested in the daughter's "self" and not her dowry, money is probably important to him, but he is too proud to bargain for it. If it is money that he wants, it would seem that he and the Count are indulging in out-and-out horse trading: he is offering a position of dignity and an old name in exchange for the

Count's money. The Duke remembers to mention the Count's "known munificence." Only a man who has money can afford to have the reputation for being generous.

"My Last Duchess," then, is a clever character study of a Renaissance nobleman who does not appear to be as clever after all as some critics would have him. This monologue is done with the same extraordinary irony exhibited in "Soliloquy of the Spanish Cloister," its usual companion piece, where the petty and lecherous monk, too, unmasks himself unwittingly. Where jealousy blinds the monk, vanity and pride blind the Duke. His Grace is so pleased with himself that he does not realize that he has given himself away. Nor would it ever occur to so vain and possessive a dilettante that this conducted tour of his art gallery had revealed his "soul," as Browning would term it, just as it would never occur to him to utilize the tale of his sinister treatment of his last Duchess and the statue of Neptune taming the seahorse as warnings to the Count's daughter about her behavior. The excellence of the poem lies in the dramatic irony of the Duke's witlessness, for we can be certain that the envoy, unless he sees and feels less than we do, will advise the Count against a marriage which might have put money in the Duke's pocket. As one discerning critic observes, some of Browning's "best effects are produced by a kind of dramatic irony, by which the speaker reveals himself as infinitely better or (more often) worse than he supposes himself to be."[12]

[1959]

LAURENCE PERRINE

BROWNING'S SHREWD DUKE

B. R. JERMAN's challenge to the traditional view of Browning's Duke of Ferrara ("Browning's Witless Duke," *PMLA*, LXXII, June 1957, 488-93)[1] should not pass without a rebuttal. According to Jerman, the Duke is not at all the clever man he has usually been thought, who utilizes a casual conversation on his last Duchess to insinuate what he expects of his next one; rather, he is a "witless" man who, blinded by vanity and pride, "does not realize that he has given himself away" to the Count's emissary, with whom he is speaking. "The excellence of the poem lies in the dramatic irony of the Duke's witlessness, for we can be certain that the envoy, unless he sees and feels less than we do, will advise the Count against a marriage which might have put money in the Duke's pocket."

I shall contend, quite otherwise, that the Duke, vain and

proud as he assuredly is, is also a shrewd bargainer and master diplomat who, while exposing himself fully to the reader, not improbably obtains high commendation from the emissary in his report to the Count. Inordinate egotism and intellect frequently cohabit, as may be seen in characters from history (e.g., Benvenuto Cellini) or from Browning's other poems (e.g., Cleon); and vanity, though it puffs a man up, by no means necessarily blinds him in matters of self-interest.

If it seems paradoxical that the Duke should expose himself to the reader without giving himself away to the Count's envoy, we must remember that the envoy (1) does not have the privilege of viewing him through the lens of literature, as we have, and (2) has not been subjected, as we have been for over two hundred years, to such sentiments as "a man's a man for a' that" and "Kind hearts are more than coronets, / And simple faith than Norman blood." The reader is fully prepared to dismiss the Duke's position and family name as hollow trumperies, and to be scornful of their possessor; but the envoy, living in a day when the prerogatives of birth were still unquestioned, standing in the very presence of the Duke, and surrounded by all the appurtenances of his power, may well have been impressed and even dazzled.

We cannot know, however, how the envoy responded; we can only know how the Duke handled him.[2] And first, why has the Duke summoned him to an upper room? I agree with Mr. Jerman that he hardly "went to all the trouble to lead the emissary upstairs so he could, by telling the tale of the Duchess' demise, warn the Count's daughter," without joining him in the speculation that he "has been taking the emissary on the rounds of his art gallery." The purpose of their interview seems clearly indicated in the poem:

> I repeat,
> The Count your master's known munificence
> Is ample warrant that no just pretense
> Of mine for dowry will be disallowed;

The Duke and the Count's envoy have been closeted for a business conference: they have been discussing terms for the Duke's alliance with the Count's daughter. The Duke is indeed "indulging in out-and-out horse-trading": it is his position and nine-hundred-years-old name for her money. Such arrangements were probably common enough in those days of marriages of convenience; nevertheless, the Duke is too polished and subtle to avow openly that the dowry is his principal interest, so he adds,

> Though his fair daughter's self, as I avowed
> At starting, is my object.

The words "I repeat" and "as I avowed / At starting" are important. The Duke has mentioned both of these matters before, in reverse order; he is now driving them home in order of their real importance, making sure he is clearly understood. Notice also that the Duke's claiming of the Count's "fair daughter's self" as his object in marriage, is not at all equivalent, as Jerman says it is, to saying that he wants to marry the Count's daughter "because she is 'fair'."

The prime argument for the Duke's shrewdness is his skill in speech. His disclaimer of such skill is part of the evidence for it, and should remind the reader of a similar disclaimer by Shakespeare's Mark Antony in his oration on Caesar, for it serves a similar purpose. It is a rhetorical trick, to throw the listener off his guard. The Duke's momentary groping for words a few lines above ("She had / A heart— how shall I say?—too soon made glad") by no means supports his disclaimer, for actually the words he finds when he finds them are just the right words and, moreover, the break in the sentence serves very subtly to throw emphasis on the words which follow the break, which otherwise might have followed too smoothly, as if rehearsed. But the real proof of the Duke's skill in speech is the beautifully modulated passage, above quoted, in which he couches his demand for dowry. These lines are a masterpiece of diplomatic circumlocution. The nature of the demand is made amply clear, yet it is gloved in a sentence softened by a double negative and by a skillfully tactful and euphemistic choice of diction: not "riches" but "munificence"; not "proves" but "is ample warrant"; not "my demand" but "no just pretense of mine"; not "refused" but "disallowed." The hard bargaining is thus enveloped in an atmosphere of perfect courtesy and good breeding.

The Duke's skill in diplomacy is to be seen not only in his speech, however, but also in his whole deportment toward the emissary, which is subtly designed to flatter. Having risen from their business conference, they pass in the hall the portrait of the Duke's last Duchess. We need not assume that the Duke has planned it this way: he is simply quick to take advantage of the opportunity. To show the emissary a specimen of his art collection is indeed, as Jerman says, a courtesy, but it hardly has the manner of a "common" courtesy when the Duke tells him, "none puts by / The curtain I have drawn for you, but I"; it is rather a special courtesy. The envoy may well feel honored that the Duke should thus draw aside the curtain for him and chat in a friendly manner about personal affairs. This friendly courtesy, from the man who is accustomed to give commands and who objected to too much courtesy in his Duchess, is apparent throughout the interview: "Will't please you sit and look at her? . . . Will't please you rise?" And when the envoy, having risen, waits respectfully for the Duke to precede him downstairs, as befits his eminence, the Duke, perhaps taking him by the elbow, tells him, "Nay, we'll go / Together down, sir." And so the envoy walks side by side down the stairway with the possessor of a nine-hundred-years-old name who has just said, "I choose / Never to stoop." Why shouldn't the envoy be flattered?

Mr. Jerman's interpretation would seem to assume that *because* the Duke is glorying in showing off his possessions, he is *not* using the occasion also to intimate his prescriptions for his next wife. But the poem does not present us with any such *either-or* proposition. The Duke is a complex, not a simple individual, and Browning's is a complex characterization. The Duke is compounded of egotism and astuteness, cruelty and politeness, pride of possession and love of art, all at once. In his interview with the emissary his motives are at least three. He wishes (1) to stipulate politely but clearly exactly what he expects for his share in this bargain, both as to dowry and as to daughter, (2) to impress the envoy with his position, his power, and his importance, and (3) to flatter the envoy so as to ensure a favorable report on the envoy's return to his master. He accomplishes all three purposes. When he has been so subtle in presenting his demands for dowry, we need not balk at imputing to him subtlety also in presenting stipulations for his next bride. Mr. Jerman may find the irony he requires in the fact that when the Duke says,

> Even had you skill
> In speech—which I have not—to make your will
> Quite clear to such an one,

he is at that very moment by indirection making his will most clear to the envoy as to what he expects of his next wife. The Duke is vain, but he is no fool.

To support his interpretation Mr. Jerman advances the "obvious" point that the Duke who chooses "never to stoop" to correct his first wife, would find it beneath his dignity to stipulate, even indirectly, what he expects of his next wife.

But surely there is a difference between making clear what is wanted in a purchase and wrangling over the goods after they are provided. The man who is very particular in ordering a custom-built piece of furniture may simply cancel the order, rather than haggle over details, if it doesn't meet specifications on delivery. Moreover, if the Duke can "stoop" to state plainly what he expects in dowry, why should he not state subtly what he expects of a wife?

Another point that Mr. Jerman advances for the Duke's "witlessness" is his regarding as a "wonder" a portrait that had been painted in a day. There are various ways of meeting this objection. One is to question whether a masterpiece may not be painted in a day. Whistler, when cross-examined about one of his paintings, said he asked two hundred guineas for it, not for the labor of two days but "for the knowledge of a lifetime." Another is to question how literally the phrase "a day" is to be interpreted: perhaps only the sitting lasted a day. But suppose we grant that the painting may not have been the masterpiece the Duke thought it? We may grant a shallowness in his art appreciation without impairing our claim for cleverness in matters that touch him more personally. The Duke is proud of being a collector and art patron at a time when such patronage was fashionable. Millionaire collectors today often have very faulty artistic taste without being any less shrewd in their personal transactions with people.

One other suggestion made by Mr. Jerman requires contention. He apparently regards the Duchess as superficial and insipid, and quotes approvingly the opinion of Margaret H. Bates that it was "the deadly monotony" of the Duchess' smile that got on the Duke's nerves. The poem does not support this view of the Duchess. Our reactions to the Duchess are controlled by the warmth of her response to compliments, by her graciousness to inferiors, and especially by the things she takes delight in: the beauty of a sunset, the gift of a bough of cherries, a ride round the terrace on a white mule. Her response to these things indicates a genuine and sensitive nature, which takes joy in simple, natural things rather than in gauds and baubles or the pomp of position and power which attract the Duke. To the Duke, who seldom smiles, the Duchess may seem to smile excessively. The Duke thinks his Duchess should be proud and unbending, like himself; she should give commands to her inferiors, not stoop to thank them for small favors. The Duke's response to her, therefore, is to do away with her. But the response of others in the poem is to bring her a bough of cherries or to remark on "the faint / Half-flush that dies along her throat."

Mr. Jerman ends his article by quoting H. V. Routh's comment that some of Browning's "best effects are produced by a kind of dramatic irony, by which the speaker reveals himself as infinitely better or (more often) worse than he supposes himself to be." The excellence of "My Last Duchess" does indeed lie in this kind of dramatic irony, in fact, in a double use of it, for the Duke while revealing himself as infinitely worse than he supposes himself to be (in human worth, not wit), is at the same time revealing his last Duchess as infinitely better than he supposed her to be. The Duke is trying to build himself up and run his Duchess down. He is given all the words, and he uses them skillfully. But for the reader (not necessarily for the envoy), he accomplishes just the reverse.

[1959]

ROBERT PREYER

A READING OF THE

EARLY NARRATIVES

THE EARLY poetry of Robert Browning is certainly interesting enough in its kind, and varied enough within
its kind, to warrant a special approach. I want here to
consider not only the nature of that kind but also Browning's
approach to the making of it; and to explore a little the
relations between this early work and the later dramatic
monologue which came eventually to replace it. Commentators and biographers have noted that there was indeed
a major shift of emphasis around 1840; some have called
attention to the poet's efforts to discount the earlier productions. Yet the nature of that early work and the reason for
abandoning it continue to perplex. A purely psychological
explanation such as we find in Mrs. Miller's biography of the
poet sounds convincing until we recall that a similar shift
occurs in the writing of Tennyson. And if we consider the
blighted careers of poets who continued writing according

to the idea of poetry with which Tennyson and Browning began—I refer to Beddoes, Darley, Clare, and the "Spasmodic" group—then the shift begins to appear as a major cultural fact and no mere private idiosyncrasy. Something of importance was occurring to the mind of England in the interregnum period of the 1830's, and as one might expect, it was taking a toll among those artists most exposed to the resulting conflicts.

The testimony of writers who live through such troubled periods is instructive. They insist that alterations introduced into style directly reflect alterations in the psyche. Or they claim that had they continued writing according to the traditions available to them in youth the result might have been both artistic and psychological disaster. (I am thinking especially of Wordsworth and Coleridge, Keats, Tennyson, and Yeats.) Browning certainly felt much the same; and he would doubtless subscribe to Yeats' well-known quatrain which reads,

> They that hold that I do wrong
> Whenever I remake a song
> Should recollect what is at stake:
> It is myself that I remake.

I dwell on this subject because it seemed of major importance to all the artists in the 19th century. To remake the style meant to remake the self; and woe to the artist who attempted to continue, in his life or work, as he began. Wordsworth warns:

> We poets in our youth begin in gladness,
> But thereof comes in the end despondency and
> Madness.

Arnold's sage, the doomed Empedocles, knows what fate is awaiting the youthful Callicles: When young, he reflects,

> we receive the shock of mighty thoughts
> On simple minds with a pure natural joy!

but once past this youthful stage

> Joy and the outward world must die to him
> As they are dead to me
> . . . .
> But Callicles will learn.

Yeats, with an even larger perspective of ruined poets behind him, declares that it is youth with its dreams which destroys the mature artist by preventing any further development of his powers:

> The best-endowed, the elect,
> All by their youth undone,
> All, all, by that inhuman
> Bitter glory wrecked.

His proud yet bitter cry of triumph is this: the child in him is no longer father of the man.

> But I have straightened out
> Ruin, wreck, and wrack;
> I toiled long years and at length
> Came to so deep a thought
> I can summon back
> All their unwholesome strength.

Neither Arnold nor Browning was able to make such a dazzling, if unclear claim—nor Wordsworth, with his

> We will grieve not, rather find
> Strength in what remains behind
> . . . .
> In years that bring the philosophic mind.

[345]

All these writers are plunged into dejection and despair or guilt and frustration when they summon back the "unwholesome strength" of their youth. That is an experience from which few poets recover; they all try to fight clear of its potent spell and the debilitating sense of loss and nostalgia which recollection evokes.

This is especially the case with Browning, who suffered intermittently all his life from the conviction that he had somehow sold his poetic birthright. "You speak out" he wrote his wife, "I never do"![1] And in the introduction to his masterpiece *The Ring and the Book,* he is at pains to explain that he deliberately does *not* speak out. The implication seems to be that he writes under a self-imposed restriction. It is of course the figure of Shelley that looms large in his youthful dedication to art; and it was the Shelleyan mode of speaking out which he repressed. The "inhuman bitter glory" of the Sun Treader both enthralled him and seemed to threaten his ruin. Browning was eventually to make a great symbolist poem out of the complex lure of his youthful ideal: "Childe Roland." Consciously he determined not to be "undone," as Childe Roland was, by the dream of his fervent youth. Yet the attraction remained; out of this tension was born the great symbolist poem.[2]

Browning seems to have arrived at this decision very early in his career. In *Paracelsus* (1835) and *Sordello* (1840) he is offering apologies for the "misguided" hero who had set out on the quest for the ideal. Even in *Pauline* (1833) the strain is evident. It is to these works we must return if we want to understand the choice which Browning saw before him. I shall be arguing that one path led directly into symbolism and its obsessive subject-matter, a direction Browning tried to avoid. The other path led on to the remarkable discoveries in the handling of a wide range of subjects which we find in the dramatic monologues. The decision Browning made was crucial, for the man as well as the artist; and the fact that others made similar decisions in these decades proved decisive for the development of English poetry.

II

Around 1800 European literature had become preoccupied with the discrepancy between the relatively inexhaustible reservoir of potentiality within the individual psyche and the drastically reduced field of action in which it could be deployed. The aspiration toward individual self-realization had collided head on with the demands imposed by a reactionary and repressive social order.

It was the age of Werther, of the Byronic hero, and of Rousseau's *Confessions;* an age which recognized that the stress was falling most heavily on its youth. It was also an age which developed a remarkable genre, the spiritual confession or monodrama, to convey the acuteness of this stress. We may go to the Preface of Shelley's *Alastor or the Spirit of Solitude* (1815) to get some idea of the area of experience governed by the form. This poem, Shelley tells us, is "allegorical of one of the most interesting situations of the human mind. It represents a youth of uncorrupted feelings and adventurous genius led forth by an imagination influenced and purified through familiarity with all that is excellent and majestic, to the contemplation of the universe. . . . So long as it is possible for his desires to point towards objects thus infinite and unmeasured he is joyous, and tranquil, and self-possessed. But the period arrives when these objects cease to suffice. His mind is at length suddenly awakened and thirsts for intercourse with an intelligence similar to itself." That "intelligence" appears (in a dream) as a young lady and the poet pursues her through a magical landscape until he is exhausted and dies. Death takes place, appropriately, in a curious setting half way between a blank heaven and an impersonal earth; a scene of total alienation. The argument in both poem and Preface is not well articulated but its direction is evident when we consider the curse Shelley calls down upon those who *deliberately* "keep aloof from sympathies with their kind." It is the presence of this stolid mass of people which makes it so difficult for the young idealist to feel at home in the world. As a consequence he is the predestined victim of "illustrious superstition," develops "too exquisite a perception" of the actuality of Platonic ideas, and ends his days pursuing a phantom of the imagination. The implication seems to be that in a better society "the pure and tender-hearted" need not "perish through the intensity of their search after . . . communities." Or in terms of the narrative, a sympathetic young lady might have prevented the young man from pursuing a female phantasm, might conceivably have subdued what Shelley interestingly calls the "sacred thirst for dubious knowledge." (We shall have occasion, shortly, to pursue some of the implications of that "sacred" yet "dubious" thirst for knowledge.)

The Byronic version of dramatic confession does not, at first glance, resemble what we have found in *Alastor*. His hero is first seen, as a rule, in the guise of the pampered child of fortune, bored, disdainful, inactive. It is only the uncontrollable glint in his eye that marks him as melancholy's own, a guilty wanderer in the abyss of self. The protagonist may have had a stormy past—occasionally he is depicted as some giaour operating adventurously on the fringes of Europe—or he may have been stopped on the brink of action, having contracted a mysterious guilt in some unimagined, perhaps unimaginable past. Whatever the reason, he is excluded from normal occupations, normal activity. He exists in a social void. These heroes invariably possess superior talents, insight, or intensity—and the implication is there that these gifts are responsible for his being cut off from his fellows and from normal modes of experience. Frequently the "conflict" in such a narrative commences when the hero begins to feel an attraction for a conventional pure young maid. She is the point of intersection between the subjective, daemonic world inhabited by the hero's feelings and the world of marriage, society and children.

Such a young lady cannot understand the nature of the threat she poses, even if it were possible for her to interrupt the prolonged declamations her presence seems to occasion. Will he cling to his gifts and to the more intense world of feeling he inhabits? If he accepts the obligations of normal love will he sink into the common herd? These and other questions are bruited about in a strenuous and often tiresome fashion. Meanwhile the young lady awaits the outcome of all this ranting in placid uncomprehending silence.[3]

It should be clear by now that Byron deals in the "matter" of *Alastor* but in such a way that elements of probability tend to obscure the romantic and allegorical nature of the myth. The same thing seems to have happened in the narratives of the Spasmodic School. This had unfortunate consequences; it led readers to presume that all the characters were of the same degree of "roundness." Actually there is but one round character, the protagonist; all the others are something less than flat. As Robert Langbaum observed,[4] it would seriously distort the intention of *Faust* if the reader treated Gretchen as though she existed on the same level of actuality as the protagonist—and the same thing applies in Byron's work. Essentially, these authors were engaged in the production of *monodramas*. The focus is upon the developing soul of the protagonist; the other characters are there to show forth or articulate that development in all its particularity.

According to Langbaum, minor characters in monodrama are sharply differentiated: black villains (often the devil himself), pure young maids and so on. What looks like melodrama is a convention of characterization designed to provide a rapid means of entry into the real subject of the narrative. The reader who accepts the convention will notice that subsidiary characters open up some possibility of action or aspect of mind which pertains to the protagonist. The plot then is not quite the silly business of a young man trying to decide whether to marry the pure maiden. It defines the mind's attempt to reconcile warring attitudes through a process of self-development. On this showing a pure maid may represent good instincts whereas the critical friend (Oswald in Wordsworth's *The Borderers* for instance) may be an incarnation of the devilish spirit of abstract thought. (The problem then might be how to keep one's friend and the girl as well.) The possibilities of the form are many, the opportunities for parody obviously rich. We may notice at this point a curious fact. The poet and the alchemist became almost interchangeable figures in the literature of spiritual confession. We have as protagonists in this form Faust, Paracelsus, the English necromancer Michael Scott (around whom Coleridge *planned* a stirring work) and a host of others. The presence of such figures should have removed some of the temptations to parody, if only by emphasizing anew the allegorizing tendency in the genre and its obsessive attention to a particular subject matter. Such figures, as Northrop Frye reminds us, have usually been treated as comic, their pretensions ridiculed as mere fraud. It was only with the honorific emphasis on "becoming" and "process" in the late 18th Century that they recover their dignity, becoming, in fact, emblematic of the aspiring soul of the poet.[5] In recent times Cassirer, Warburg, and Saxl have documented the analogy, arguing that pseudo-sciences like astrology provide a link between a mythical and a rational view of the world. If we translate this into the language of psychology, myth is seen as the product of emotion, reason as the product of the intellect. Poetry, as the romantics conceived it, had as one of its most urgent concerns the reforging of the links between these two areas of experience. The analogy between poet and alchemist is thus an exact one. Marcel Raymond has written that poetry in modern times tended to become "some sort of irregular instrument of metaphysical knowledge" with the (largely unconscious) aim of "reconquering man's irrational powers and transcending the dualism of the self and the universe."[6] If we keep in mind that, for an Englishman, society makes up a large component of the "universe," then this remark neatly defines the intention of the dramatic confessional.

It is easy enough to read works in this genre as incredibly crude examples of bourgeois tragedy or, for that matter, comedy of manners. But to do so is to miss the point. We will be equally wide of the mark if we read with the eyes of a pseudo-psychologist and dismiss these works because they enact attitudes and actions associated with adolescent daydreams. A clumsy parody like Prof. Wilson's *Firmilian: A Spasmodic Tragedy* is preferable to the modern cant which damns this form as "adolescent" or immature. (Let us hope that *Catcher in the Rye* marks the beginning of a renewed interest in the problematic quality of adolescent experience.) I am not arguing now, about the worth of individual works within the genre. I am simply saying that one must be clear about the intentions of the form, and its conventions. The form offers many intractable difficulties and we will speak of them in a moment. But it offers some unique opportunities as well, enabling a writer to penetrate quickly and effectively into the recesses of consciousness and define there the area of feeling which is being mutilated by the pressure of conventional social norms. When we replace these works in the explosive and frustrating milieu to which they are a response—the age of Metternich and Tory repression—their relevance is apparent. It is the lament of these "unemployable" idealists that their potentialities can find no vent in creative social action. As Browning put it in *Pauline*, "I have nursed up energies, they will prey on me." Precisely: for that energy of spirit is internalized, goes rotten, and poisons not only the individual victim of the *malaise* but all those with whom he comes into contact. *Corruptio optimi pessima.* The old Latin tag takes us to the heart of the romantic dilemma.

I have said that the risk of failure in this genre seems inordinately great—just as the possibilities, if one succeeds, are remarkable. The trouble comes with the attempt to harmonize plot, character, and setting. If the projected feelings or aspects of mind are developed into believable or interesting characters, then the drama of reconciliation through self-development is lost sight of and the imaginary landscape seems a needless imposition. If, on the other hand, the personified feelings are not given enough substance or identity it is impossible to see the point of the episodes they act out—or at least it is impossible to interest oneself in them. *Sordello* is tiresome precisely because Browning's attempt to introduce historical characters, local color, and politics, makes a shambles of the "drama of internal development" and a nuisance of the evocative landscapes. One feels that in the seven years of its composition (1833-40) Browning began to overlay the original mode with conventions borrowed from current theatrical productions—historical settings, the intrigue plot, full characterization of a half dozen protagonists and so on.[7] Enough of both intentions remained to baffle future readers and cause at least one contemporary to think he had lost his mind. There are no keys to this muddle—or rather there are too many keys that almost fit. In *Paracelsus* (1835) we have a more successful drama which suffers from the fact that the hero's identity is clearly meant to include that aspect of mind personified by the character Aprile but evidently does not include that of the two other leading characters, Festus and Michal. Mrs.

Miller surmises that these intrusive friends really represent the poet's mother and father. This seems likely enough. Whatever their source, they do not fit into a scheme which allows us to envisage characters as interacting aspects of a single consciousness. According to its Preface, *Strafford* (1837) was a play of "Action in Character, rather than Character in Action." Once more we wander between two sets of conventions not knowing which to apply at any given point. Browning's friend Milsand put his finger on the difficulty when he remarked that Browning was attempting, perhaps unconsciously, "the fusion of two kinds of poetry into one," the dramatic and the lyrical.[8] The result, as might have been anticipated, was that his works became increasingly obscure—until the fusion was complete and a proper form discovered. *Pauline* (1833), the earliest of these works is also the least troubled by the effort to reconcile and combine two sorts of poem. *Sordello* (1840) and *Strafford* (1837) are almost total failures, *Paracelsus* (1835) is somewhere in between. It is to *Pauline* therefore that we must turn if we want to see in its "purest" state the sort of poem and poetic with which Browning began—and from which he struggled to free himself in the transitional works that followed. It is one of the best poems of its kind in English; and if we wish to explore the relations between the early work and the later dramatic monologues here is the obvious point of departure.

III

Pauline appears to be a variant on the genre we have been describing. (The subtitle reads, "A Fragment of a Confession.") As in *Paracelsus* the author set out to "reverse the method usually adopted by writers whose aim is to set forth any phenomena of the mind or passions, by the operation of persons and events" and to "display somewhat minutely

the mood itself in its rise and progress. . . ." By presenting
the feelings he hopes to compose in the reader's mind an
image of the personality which is their ground of being.
Prof. DeVane's words on *Paracelsus* apply here as well: "the
moods and thoughts are the characters and the stage is the
soul."[9] What is behind this effort to construct a drama out
of subjective feelings? Why does Browning want to exclude
the subject matter dramatized by what he calls, in the Shelley essay, "objective artists," namely actions that are "sub-
stantive, projected from himself, distinct"? The reason seems
to be that he is consciously modelling *Pauline* on the method
of Shelley, whom he terms the greatest modern writer in the
subjective tradition. A subjective poet, *because* he is excluded from action, is enabled to achieve a special form of
cognition which amounts to a direct insight into the structure
of reality. This is Browning's conviction, affirmed often in
his youth, and formulated in these words in 1850:

Not what man sees, but what God sees—the *Ideas* of Plato, seeds
of creation lying burningly on the Divine Hand—it is toward these
that he [the subjective poet] struggles.

Browning glories in this exalted and comprehensive role
assigned to the poet; he believes, further, that the subjective
poet has a means, at once simple and profound, of attaining
to such knowledge. It is the means employed in *Pauline* and
described in the Shelley essay with these words:

Not with the combination of humanity in action, but with the
primal elements of humanity he has to do; and he digs where he
stands,—preferring to seek them in his own soul as the nearest
reflex of that Absolute Mind, according to the intentions of
which he desires to perceive and speak.

The road to the absolute is through the subjective. A
century later we find St. J. Perse recommending the same

procedure: "French literature . . . is rediscovering its infinite in the very depths of the well of the human heart."[10] The romantic (and symbolist) assumption behind both these statements seems to be this. Certain minds are so constituted they can respond to the "summons from the deep," body forth as images a reality that cannot be transposed to the plane of discursive intelligence. Now this verges on magic; and I think that Browning was uneasily aware of the fact. We should take quite seriously the Latin quotation from Cornelius Agrippa which served as an admonitory preface to the first edition of *Pauline*. Agrippa is quoted as saying some will cry out "that we are teaching forbidden things, are scattering the seeds of heresies. . . . To these I now give counsel not to read our book, neither to understand it nor remember it; for it is harmful, poisonous; the gate of Hell is in this book . . . FOR I DO NOT RECOMMEND THESE THINGS TO YOU: I MERELY TELL YOU OF THEM." I submit that Browning, in appending that quotation, had grounds other than a delight in mystification; that he had caught sight of a conflict between reason, the Revelation of Scripture, and the revelation offered by the vatic poet. "I consider Shelley's poetry as a sublime fragmentary essay towards a presentment of the correspondency of the universe to Deity, of the natural to the spiritual, and of the actual to the ideal" he was to declare. In other words, he attributed to Shelley a revelation of what Arthur Symons grandly called "that central secret of the mystics, from Pythagoras onwards, the secret which the Smaragdine Tablet of Hermes betrays in its 'As things are below, so they are above'; which Boehme had classed in his teaching of 'signatures' and Swedenborg has systematized in his doctrine of 'correspondence'. . . ."[11] This revelation down through the centuries had been granted alike to Christian and non-Christian—that was one difficulty for Browning. But another difficulty was the irrational quality of this revelation. These were the dangers which led him to append the long warning from Cornelius Agrippa's *Concerning Occult Philosophy:* for some readers the gate of Hell might well be in this book. As the despairing Paracelsus cries out,

> Ha, have I, after all
> Mistaken the wild nursling of my breast?
> Knowledge it seemed, and power, and recompense!
> . . . .
> God! Thou art mind! Unto the master-mind
> Mind should be precious. Spare my mind alone!
> (II. 221-23, 229-30)

If we look closely at *Pauline* I think we will begin to see how deeply Browning had become immersed in such vatic revelations. As the above quotation makes clear, Browning felt that Shelley elucidated a system of "vertical" correspondences, i.e. that he read appearances as signs or symbols reflecting a supra-sensible world behind them. This means that there exists an intermediate common language which makes it possible for the actual and the ideal, both spiritual in their essence, to reveal themselves and recognize each other. This is the "language" of analogies and symbols, a musical, alogical discourse relying on synaesthesia very heavily and syntax and the logical rendering of sequential events as lightly as possible.

The effect of the discovery of such a language, and a good account of its structure, is provided by a long passage in *Pauline* beginning on line 411. Browning tells us he had begun to hear the *melodies* of passion in which Shelley "clothed" his aspirations. The passage continues:

> such first
> Caught me and set me, slave of a sweet task,
> To disentangle, gather sense from song:
> Since, song-inwoven, lurked there words which seemed
> A key to a new world, the muttering

Of angels, something yet unguessed by man.
How my heart leapt as still I sought and found
Much there, I felt my own soul had conceived,
But there living and burning! Soon the orb
Of his conceptions dawned on me . . .

I am not here concerned with the "doctrine" but with Browning's way of discovering it. These words, sounding here and there from their lurking places in the "song-in-woven" verses, seem to form among themselves an esoteric order of meaning. We have, apparently, the symbolist tendency to use words as if they were recurring *leitmotifs* in a musical structure—a structure that is superimposed upon the narrative sequence and the normal sentence syntax which orders it. The two kinds of meaning exist simultaneously and we must resort to the spatial metaphor of two levels of meaning to describe them. On one level a bait is provided to occupy the watchdog of the intellect. On the other level, and as a consequence, the imagination is freed to wander about in a sort of conceptual space, where all things bear witness to a common kinship, words with emotions, thoughts with sounds, images with feelings. The verse rhythms and the narrative satisfy the intellect and simultaneously awaken a sense of the correspondency between words, thoughts, and feelings. Eventually they point beyond this world to "something yet unguessed by man."

As befits one who believed significant actions can occur outside the narrative dimension of time,

> I . . . who lived
> With Plato and who had the key to life

—Browning listens intently for the chimes of magical correspondence, for the "song," "passion's melodies," which provide a second level of awareness for the initiate.

"Music," he had written, "is earnest of a heaven, / Seeing

we know emotions strange by it, / Not else to be revealed." Yet Shelley had shown him that words and images could be used to recreate the same effects—just as the "song" in "Kubla Khan" enabled the poet to "see" a vision. Nor was that all. Browning was capable himself of creating a verse which rendered these effects. Having said that music was the sole means at our disposal for revealing a certain order of emotional experience he goes on to manage an analogous feat in words:

> For music . . . is like a voice
> A low voice calling fancy, as a friend
> To the green woods in the gay summer time:
> And she fills all the way with dancing shapes
> Which have made painters pale, and they go on
> Till stars look at them and winds call to them
> As they leave life's path for the twilight world
> Where the dead gather.

This could easily be mistaken for the very best of the early Yeats—the ending of "When You Are Old" for example, where we are told

> how love fled
> And paced upon the mountains overhead
> And hid his face amid a crowd of stars.

It is the evocative "magic" of the romantic image, a poetry which aspires to the condition of music.[12]

No wonder we find him writing as one "Created by some power whose reign is done, / Having no part in God and his bright world." He is deeply immersed in the underworld of feeling, a daemonic region well below the surface of normal everyday affairs. Nor is that all. Browning feels that he is trembling on the verge of some occult meaning which is "revealed" in music (and the "music" of verse) but is otherwise inexpressible. These arts revealed "correspondences" between levels of existence rather than propositions that could be validated by analysis. Perhaps this was the form which thinking took in the golden age of the poets. At any event Browning thought of himself as living in some earlier age ("Created by some power whose reign is done") and spoke of the total identification he felt when reading the mythical literature of early Greece:

> And I myself went with the tale—a god
> Wandering after beauty, or a giant
> Standing vast in the sunset—an old hunter
> Talking with gods, or a high-crested chief
> Sailing with troops of friends to Tenedos.
> I tell you nought has ever been so clear
> As the place, the time, the fashion of those lives:
> . . . .
>   never morn broke clear as those
> On the dim clustered isles in the blue sea,
> The deep groves and white temples and wet caves:
> And nothing ever will surprise me now—
> Who stood beside the naked Swift-footed,
> Who bound my forehead with Proserpine's hair.

The result of this

> Was a vague sense of power though folded up—
> A sense that, though those shades and times were past,
> Their spirit dwelt in me, with them should rule.

Is it too far-fetched to suggest that he saw a connection between this second, alogical or musical mode of meaning in the arts and the mythical world he had delighted in as a boy? If so, it is but a step to the esoteric doctrines which Cornelius Agrippa retailed; and Browning lets us know that he was already deep in Neo-Platonism. Here indeed was consolation (I had almost said fatal consolation) for the isolated artist—so much so that he can hardly find it in him to take Pauline and the problem she posed quite seriously.

> Thou art not more dear
> Than song was once to me.

The excitements of the esoteric were beginning to carry him
away from the serious social import of his narrative, namely
the effects of isolation and self-centeredness on a young man
whose potential has been ignored by society. Browning
seems to be caught up in that lonely pride which led the
youthful Yeats to confide exultantly, "in the second part of
Oisin under disguise of symbolism I have said several things
to which only I have the key. The romance is for the readers.
They must not even know there is a symbol anywhere." His
credentials as poet seem somehow bound up with his ability
to sense the presence of some symbolic or occluded meaning:

> And, though this weak soul sink and darkness whelm
> Some little word shall light it, raise aloft,
> To where I clearlier see and better love,
> And I again go o'er the tracts of thought
> Like one who has a right, and I shall live
> With poets, calmer, purer still each time,
> And beautous shapes will come for me to seize,
> And unknown secrets will be trusted me
> Which were denied the waverer once . . .

As the passage above indicates, Browning had moments
when the whole elaborate structure seemed nonsense.

> 'T was my plan to look on real life,
> The life all new to me; my theories
> Were firm, so them I left, to look and learn
> Mankind, its cares hopes, fears, its woes and joys;
>
> . . . .
> And suddenly without heart-wreck I awoke
> As from a dream: I said " 'T was beautiful,
> Yet but a dream, and so adieu to it!"

Nevertheless, when Browning wanted to indicate a revival
of his poetic powers he commenced with an account of a

magical landscape with obvious symbolic ramifications—as in lines 729 through 810. When these powers flag he is overwhelmed with symbolic nightmares,

> dreams in which
> I seemed the fate from which I fled; I felt
> A strange delight in causing my decay.

Two marvelous dreams display guilt fixations centered upon the arrogance and self-preoccupation that seemed necessary to a poet intent upon reaching the absolute through the subjective (ll. 95-123). In this state he is prepared to "give up all gained, as willingly / As one gives up a charm that shuts him out / From hope or part or care in human kind." He is appalled at the fate he has deliberately courted

> Sure I must own
> That I am fallen, having chosen gifts
> Distinct from theirs—that I am sad and fain
> Would give up all to be but where I was,
> Not high as I had been if faithful found,
> But low and weak yet full of hope . . .
> I would lose
> All this gay mastery of mind, to sit
> Once more with them, trusting in truth and love
> And with an aim—not being what I am.

The poem wavers back and forth: one moment on fire with vatic ambitions, the next moment longing for release from these alienating dreams. As the quotations indicate, Browning can't decide what tenses to use in describing his state of mind. The muddled time sequences mime his state of mind:

> Sad confession first
> Remorse and pardon and old claims renewed,
> Ere I can be—as I shall be no more.
> I had been spared this shame if I had sat
> By thee forever from the first, in place

[361]

Of my wild dreams of beauty and of good,
Or with them, as an earnest of their truth:

Eventually he was led to abandon the struggle, unable to sustain that "reckless courage in entering into the abyss of himself"[13] which Yeats demanded of the symbolist poet. The poem concludes with a touching appeal: he hopes Shelley will understand why he must abandon these esoteric poetic excitements in favor of the life of morality and social commitment. The magic was dead or dying, the spell broken. It had been recognized by the young poet as a compensatory device for one who could not actively enter into the life about him. But was it only that?

To sum up: in the 1830's Browning felt all the attraction of the hero gifted above others in his power of experiencing and comprehending excellence. He could see that such a man, for the very reason that he was fated to experience an intenser range of emotional experiences, was subject to loneliness and misunderstanding. But he could not as yet see how to get beyond this static Gloomy Egotist stereotype without calling in some form of magic. The obsessive subject matter of his youth had become the self and its prehensions seen as other than or opposed to society and reason. But it was no easy problem (as Goethe had discovered before him) to drive beyond this "subjectivity" and replace, at the center of his art, the relations and interconnections between the self and society. That he did so is evident in the masterpieces of his maturity; but the effort cost him almost ten years of sustained effort and defeat.

One of the traditional functions of the artist has been to remind us of the enduring human needs and desires which must somehow be satisfied by any organization of society which seeks to be just and humane. At times he will envisage a paradisiacal society where the constructive powers of the psyche are placed under the least possible restraint and energy finds a release in "toil that does not bruise the soul."

At other times he will count the cost, in broken or twisted lives, that a repressive society exacts—for sometimes society loses all sense of its humane goal. Now we have observed that there is a great hole in the middle of this romantic literature around 1800, a blank in that portion of the canvas usually given over to the celebration of "works and days." It is as though the authors have been stunned by the inhumanity of both Tory repression and middle class industrialism. They can conceive of no joy or dignity or meaning in the toil such a society offered its victims. Hence they stand aloof, become revolutionary, or fill the void with some magical dream of poetry. A situation had arisen which, in the words of Marcel Raymond, "aggravated to an almost intolerable degree the natural discordance between the total exigencies of the mind and the limited existence which is the lot of man." The human demands that custom and religion had managed to exorcize or channel into acceptable forms of work were ignored in the new society. Hence there arose that longing for a happiness which the world of common experience made no pretense of satisfying, a disillusionment that sprang from the clash between the inner dream and the empty, hostile environment.

Browning was among the first to realize the extent of the cost of the romantic vision, the price that it exacted of its adherents. And he was also aware of the nobility of that dream. He knew that Romantic disillusionment, romantic contempt for normal living, could easily turn into something contemptible: an evasion of moral choices and a striking of attitudes. But he also knew that romantic disillusionment could spring from the conflict between impulses and emotions that were often sound and the prevailing middle-class *bêtise* that corroded them. It was this double knowledge which came to expression, eventually, in the great gallery of criminals, quacks, poseurs, and artists who constitute the *dramatis personae* of the dramatic monologues.

[1964]

PHILIP DREW

HENRY JONES ON

BROWNING'S OPTIMISM

Browning's fame as a poet in the 1890's, as Professor Boyd Litzinger has shown,[1] was closely connected with his reputation as an optimistic philosopher. When the philosophy was discredited the poetry suffered also; critics today seldom offer to explore, much less to defend, any areas of Browning's work that border on the religious or metaphysical. In this article I shall consider in what senses Browning may be correctly termed an optimist and suggest that his optimism is not of a kind which necessarily involves an admission of poetic inadequacy.

I

There are two prevalent misconceptions of the nature of Browning's optimism, one simple, the other sophisticated. No time need be wasted on the crude misjudgment which ascribes to Browning himself opinions which he has put into the mouth of his characters for dramatic purposes. A common example is the acceptance as representative of Browning's own thought of the celebrated lyric from *Pippa Passes* which finishes:

> God's in his heaven—
> All's right with the world.[2]

What is true of the lyrics in the dramas is true of the dramatic monologues. Even "Rabbi Ben Ezra," for example, which at first sight completely lacks the characteristic refraction of vision which normally distances the speaker, can be used only with the greatest caution as evidence of Browning's personal view of the world.

It can be readily shown that many accounts of Browning as a Victorian Soame Jenyns can be set aside on the grounds that they fail to take account of the dramatic element in his poems. It is less easy to counter the suggestion that Browning's optimism lies in his persistent undervaluing of the intellect in order to justify his wilful refusal to see the world as it is. This is the direction of attack encouraged by Sir Henry Jones, although he offers also some elegant variations on the main line. *Browning as a Philosophical and Religious Teacher* appeared in 1891, just over a year after the poet's death. Its influence on the assessment of Browning as a poet has been incalculable.[3] It is a long book, and apparently very thorough and detailed, but, as A. C. Bradley noticed, it is diffuse and repetitive. The main argument which Jones is concerned to establish runs on these lines. "Browning tries to demonstrate that there is an utter severance between the intellect and the emotions, between the heart and the head: that the heart is an infallible guide to conduct and the intellect worthless. Logically his contempt for the intellect should lead him to complete agnosticism and pessimism: in fact he arbitrarily asserts an optimistic view of the world, holding that ignorance of God's purposes is essential to our moral growth." Having set this up as Browning's position, Jones attempts to demolish it, and claims to have done so. His final chapter begins:

I have tried to show that Browning's theory of life, in so far as it is expressed in his philosophical poems, rests on agnosticism; and that such a theory is inconsistent with the moral and religious interests of man. The idea that truth is unattainable was represented by Browning as a bulwark of the faith, but it proved on examination to be treacherous. His optimism was found to have no better foundation than personal conviction, which any one was free to deny, and which the poet could in no wise prove. The evidence of the heart, to which he appealed, was the evidence of an emotion severed from intelligence, and, therefore, without any content whatsoever. 'The faith,' which he professed, was not the faith that anticipates and invites proof, but a faith which is incapable of proof.[4]

This severe indictment has been generally accepted as satisfactorily proved. In addition many critics have accepted the further implication that, since his optimism is valueless and his poetry is optimistic, his poetry is marred by this central deficiency.

The first step in a defense of Browning against such a charge must be to indicate briefly the unsoundness of any argument which treats poems as if they were prose essays, for such an argument will provide no standard for judging the poems as *poetry*, since its criterion is logical or metaphysical consistency instead of imaginative coherence, and may well miss even the philosophic value of the poem through a failure to see that the poet is making his points not by logical argument but by an appeal to imaginative conviction. Jones is apparently aware of the danger of what he calls "the interpretation of a poet from first principles" (p. 10; see also pp. 89-90), but he continues, "Nevertheless, among English poets there is no one who lends himself so easily, or so justly, to this way of treatment as Browning." He does not show why it is just to treat Browning in this way, utterly ignoring the admirable sentiments of his Introduction.

But even if we allow Professor Jones the right to treat the poems as essays in metaphysics, there are many unsatisfactory features in his book. I should like to mention two points especially, first the evidence which he offers in support of his case and secondly his treatment of that evidence.

II

Perhaps his most serious deficiency is that he makes no attempt to consider the whole of Browning's "teachings" on religion and philosophy. He does not, for example, comment on Browning's distinctive views on such subjects as the historical evidences for Christianity, the relationship between the Church and the Christian, love between human beings, the relationship of ends and means, the importance of choice in the life of the individual and the allied problem of free will. Nor does he have much to say about such a characteristic tenet of Browning's as personal immortality. Indeed the innocent reader of Jones's book would reasonably but erroneously conclude that the only philosophical and religious topics that the poet treated with any seriousness were questions of perception and knowledge and the problem of evil.

The reason for this eccentric view of Browning's thought is that Jones limits his attention to a very small number of poems, a sample far too small to establish any general point whatever. The crucial steps of his argument are in effect drawn from the following poems: *Christmas-Eve and Easter-Day, La Saisiaz,* the "Parleying with Francis Furini," "A

Pillar at Sebzevar" and "A Bean-Stripe" (both from *Ferishtah's Fancies*), and "Reverie" (from *Asolando*). He ignores or hardly considers such important poems as "Caliban upon Setebos," the Epilogue to *Dramatis Personae*, "Bishop Blougram's Apology," most of the *Parleyings*, and "Mr. Sludge, 'The Medium,'" to name only a few. It will be noticed that the poems which he does choose are in an obvious sense not typical of Browning, since they are not dramatic in form.[5]

Jones's avoidance of these important poems not only leads him to ignore large tracts of Browning's more metaphysical poetry, but sends him astray in his treatment of the poems he does choose to deal with. While it is true that each of Browning's poems is self-sufficient, it is also true that in the later poems, such as those in *Ferishtah's Fancies*, Browning is using a vocabulary which he has forged in his major poems. To take only the most obvious examples, "love" in Browning is not simply a mindless instinct, ignorant of its object: it comes almost to stand for everything that is valuable in human life. Similarly we have learned from Browning's great gallery of sophists and casuists that by "knowledge" he means particularly the kind of unreal ratiocination which tries to replace the experience of the individual by an abstract generalization. If we have read and comprehended the whole body of Browning's work and appreciated his constant efforts to *animate* his terms, we shall not misunderstand Browning's exaltation of love at the expense of knowledge. Although the whole of his last chapter implicitly admits the need of a broader approach, Jones attempts hardly any interpretation of this kind. The only poems he uses with any consistency for the purpose of explaining Browning's life-long attempts to supply a full definition of these crucial elements in his vocabulary are "A Death in the Desert" and the Pope's monologue from

The Ring and the Book, the latter quoted as respectfully as if it were Holy Writ.

Jones, then, limits himself to a small fraction of Browning's work, but even in the poems which he considers with some care he leaves out of account passages which do not accord with the main lines of his argument. For instance, he uses passages from the "Parleying With Francis Furini" to support his contention that Browning utterly condemns all the activities of the human intellect, yet in that very poem Furini speaks of himself as follows:

> Made to know on, know ever, I must know
> All to be known at any halting-stage
> Of my soul's progress.[6]

Similarly when Jones refers us from Chapter X back to Chapter VIII for proof of the statement that "demonstrative, or certain, or absolute knowledge of the actual nature of things would, Browning asserts, destroy the very possibility of a moral life," we find that he relies on "Francis Furini" once more and on "A Bean-Stripe," of which he offers what appears to be a paraphrase, finishing:

The argument ends by bringing us back

> To the starting-point,—
> Man's impotency, God's omnipotence,
> These stop my answer. (p. 262)

But these lines are not, as Jones implies, the conclusion of the poem (in fact they occur in the first half), nor does Ferishtah simply apply the closure with a plea of ignorance. Instead he argues, in a passage which Jones ignores,

> Even so
> I needs must blend the quality of man
> With quality of God, and so assist

Mere human sight to understand my Life,
What is, what should be, —understand thereby
Wherefore I hate the first and love the last,—
Understand why things so present themselves
To me, placed here to prove I understand. (ll. 351-58)

Finally, from *La Saisiaz*, a most important poem, whose theme bears very closely on the topics which Jones particularly discusses, he quotes the following couplet,

Take the joys and bear the sorrows—neither with
extreme concern!
Living here means nescience simply: 't is next life
that helps to learn. (ll. 467-68)

Jones comments, "It is hardly necessary to enter upon any detailed criticism of such a theory of knowledge as this which is professed by the poet" (p. 241). But the couplet which Jones derides is taken from an intermediate stage in the debate between Fancy and Reason which establishes the condition of Man's moral existence. The two speakers in the debate proceed, as it were, by trial and error, postulating a condition of existence and then examining the consequences if it is fulfilled. This is a postulate, which in fact they decide *cannot* be fulfilled:[7] it is absurd to attribute it to Browning as a positive opinion and to use it as a necessary link in an elaborate argument about his theories of knowledge.

In short, Jones gives an unsatisfactory account of the philosophical implications of Browning's poetry and pays little attention to the essential points of Browning's religious faith. He is not concerned to interpret Browning's speculations, much less to illuminate the poems. His continual labor is to sift through a few pieces and to extract from them those passages which suit his purposes. Upon this material he imposes a rigid pattern, forcing a definite opposition where Browning is content to indicate a disharmony. As I have indicated his basic fallacy is to treat the poet as a rival philosopher. Jones says (p. 275), "He offers a definite theory to which he claims attention . . . on the ground that it is a true exposition of the moral nature of man. . . . Browning definitely states, and endeavours to demonstrate a theory of knowledge, a theory of the relation of knowledge to morality, and a theory of the nature of evil." But this is not so. Browning has written a number of poems for which part of his raw material was arguments about these subjects. They were written at various times and in varying tones, some in his own person, some not, and in each poem Browning made use of the ideas which suited the poem best. What the poems have to say about life they say not by making a series of flat theoretical statements about ethical problems but by presenting an enactment of a complex and fluid situation. They were not intended to be literally consistent with each other, much less to form an ordered philosophic system. The fact that Jones can produce a logical dilemma by setting a snippet from one poem against a snippet from another shows not the confusion of Browning's thought but the unsoundness of Jones's method. His book, *The Philosophy of Lotze* (Glasgow, 1895), a thorough and penetrating critique, covers very much the same ground as his *Browning*, and repeats some of his earlier arguments. In each work he is in effect defending Hegel by attacking those who found Idealism simply a collection of "pale and vacant general ideas": his error is to suppose that the poet and the philosopher can be answered by the same arguments.

III

So much for Professor Jones's presentation of Browning's "philosophy": I turn now to his attempts to refute it. It is notable that even when he has simplified the poet's ideas and erected them into a suitable argument he is often unable to show their error. For example, in a central passage of the book (pp. 237-41) Jones deals with Browning's theories of the imperfection of human knowledge. Browning emphasizes the difficulty of being certain of more than one's own existence, and of maintaining that one's own judgment is more accurate than another's or that the laws that govern one's own life govern anybody else's. These are valid questions, and Browning raises them to show how difficult it is for the intellect to arrive at general truths. In short he points out a celebrated metaphysical dilemma. Jones's comment on this is that if Browning carries this line of reasoning to a logical conclusion he will find himself in a celebrated metaphysical dilemma. Similarly (on pp. 310-11) Jones reverts to a consideration of Browning's difficulty in reconciling perfect knowledge with moral responsibility. He says, "It is impossible to conceive how the conduct of a being who is moral, would be affected by absolute knowledge; or, indeed, to conceive the existence of such a being. . . . A being so constituted would be an agglomerate of utterly disparate elements, the interaction of which, in a single character, it would be impossible to make intelligible." But this is precisely the point Browning is making—that we cannot conceive moral responsibility coexisting with complete knowledge and must therefore suppose that lack of certain knowledge is a necessary condition of moral development and thus not irreconcilable with the idea of a just God. On this line of speculation Jones comments in a favorite phrase (Cf. pp. 9, 241, 248, 262), "I do not stay here to inquire whether sure knowledge would really have this disastrous effect of destroying morality, or whether its failure does not rather imply the possibility of a moral life." Nowhere in the book does he show directly that Browning is in error in supposing that, if retribution followed Sin as cer-

tainly as pain followed fire and it were as certainly known
that this was so, then avoiding Sin would be of as little moral
worth as avoiding fire is now.

Again, after his inaccurate summary of "A Bean-Stripe"
Jones says, "I shall not pause at present to examine the value
of this new form of the old argument, 'Ex contingentia
mundi.'" In fact, he never resolves the paradox which
Browning deals with in the poem. His reply is always that
rightly viewed the paradox vanishes, but his own explanations of the correct point of view cause more confusion than
they remove. For instance, one of Browning's great problems is how to argue from his own experience to a truth
which will hold good for other people, that is, how to
develop a generally valid argument on the basis of subjective
knowledge. In Chapter IX Jones attempts a criticism of
Browning's view of knowledge, apparently including the
poet among the "relativists, phenomenalists, agnostics, scep-
tics, Kantians[8] or neo-Kantians—all the crowd of thinkers
who cry down the human intellect." Here Jones seems to be
considering Browning as a subjective idealist, whose work
will result in reducing all Idealism to the absurdity of
solipsism.

He sees the difficulty which confronted Browning and
which eventually led him to doubt the infallibility of intellectual processes, but, declaring that "the method of fixed
alternatives" is "inapplicable," refuses to offer any direct
refutation of Browning's main point that human knowledge
is conditioned and relative. Instead he first asserts that
"our thought is essentially connected with reality" (p. 297)
and then embarks on a long parallel between thought and
the moral consciousness:

In morality (as also is the case in knowledge) the moral ideal,
or the objective law of goodness, grows in richness and fulness
of content with the individual who apprehends it. *His* moral

world is the counterpart of *his* moral growth as a character. Goodness for *him* directly depends upon his recognition of it. . . . In morals, as in knowledge, the mind of man constructs its own world. And yet . . . *the moral law does not vanish and reappear with its recognition by mankind* [italics mine]. . . . With the extinction of self-consciousness all moral goodness is extinguished. The same holds true of reality. (p. 299)

This seems to me indistinguishable from the subjectivism which Jones criticized in Browning, although it will be observed that the sentence I have italicized runs counter to the rest of the argument. Jones proceeds to enlarge at considerable length on his basic premise that "the negative has no meaning, except as the expression of a deeper affirmative." He makes the application to Browning by saying,

If he acknowledges that the highest revealed itself to man, on the practical side, as love, he does not see that it has also manifested itself to man on the theoretical side, as reason. The self-communication of the Infinite is incomplete; love is a quality of God, intelligence a quality of man; hence, on one side, there is no limit to achievement, but on the other there is impotence. Human nature is absolutely divided against itself; and the division, as we have already seen, is not between flesh and spirit, but between a love which is God's own and perfect, and an intelligence which is merely man's and altogether weak and deceptive. (p. 307)

These last two sentences, which are presumably Jones's version of what Browning thinks, are not refuted by the first sentence which Jones offers as a solution of the dilemma, for it evades the precise difficulties which Browning continually confronts. If both love and the intelligence are manifestations of the Infinite, how is it that they so often prompt a man in different directions? And while they can theoretically be reconciled as aspects of the same harmonious whole, if in practice a man is forced to choose between them, as in fact often happens, which is he to choose? In short Jones's concern is with the soundness of a metaphysical theory: Browning's concern is with life, which he sees as a succession of extraordinarily difficult ethical choices. "Duty and love, one broad way, were the best— / Who doubts? But one or other was to choose" ("Bifurcation," ll. 17-18).

Jones in the course of a brief but entertaining summary of European thought, early in Chapter III, says that with the new light of the philosopher-poets of Germany "the antagonism of hard alternatives was at an end." To Jones this meant the reconciliation of opposites in statements such as, "The negative implies the affirmative and is its effect" (p. 141), and, "The process towards truth by man is the process of truth *in* man: the movement of knowledge towards reality is the movement of reality into knowledge" (p. 304). Browning, although usually classified as an Idealist, is not content with vapid formulas of this kind for reconciling individual responsibility with Divine omnipresence. In short to Jones's affirmation, "The individual does not institute the moral law; he finds it to be written both within and without him" (p. 142), Browning opposes simply a series of instances of conflict between the "law within" and the "law without."

Browning then, as indeed is a commonplace of criticism, is concerned with men as individuals and with their relationships to their fellow men. Jones, on the contrary, is always concerned to avoid recognition of men as individuals. In Chapter III he offers a typically disingenuous evasion of the notorious weakness of Hegelianism, that it diminishes the status of the individual. He writes:

Thus, when spirit is spiritually discerned, it is seen that man is bound to man in a union closer than any physical organism can show; while 'the individual,' in the old sense of a being *opposed* to society and *opposed* to the world, is found to be a fiction of abstract thought, not discoverable anywhere, because not real.

A few pages later he says, "Individualism is now detected as scepticism and moral chaos in disguise."⁹

From such a point of view Browning is clearly in error since he insists on the reality of the individual as the very foundation stone of all knowledge. His skill in philosophical argument may be called in question, but in the poems of his maturity his grasp of life as it is never falters. His poetry is grounded in his own experience; if therefore he encounters a paradox in his own nature or in his picture of the world or in his apprehension of God he does not attempt to resolve it in the interests of the tidiness of a metaphysical theory, but gives it full expression.

For example, he constantly makes the distinction between certain knowledge and religious faith, which he finds in his own experience to be a unique order of belief. Jones as persistently affects to misunderstand this vital distinction. I have already quoted the passage in which he says of Browning, " 'The faith,' which he professed, was not the faith that anticipates and invites proof, but a faith which is incapable of proof." But Browning, like most people, would deny that any faith was required to believe that which could be demonstrated.¹⁰ For him an act of trust was an essential element in faith: this meant believing even when the reason withheld its assent. When his poetry has a design upon the reader that design is very often to convince him of the contingent nature of the reason and thus to make it easier for him to perform the decisive act of trust.

In the same way Jones complains about Browning's optimism that it "was found to have no better foundation than personal conviction, which any one was free to deny, and which the poet could in no wise prove." Jones does not, of course, show that there *is* any proof of an optimistic view of the world. In default of this, what better foundation could a man have than personal conviction, or, indeed, without personal conviction, what foundation at all?

IV

I should not, however, like to suggest that nothing is to be learned from the book. Jones establishes the following useful points. First that "A Bean-Stripe," "A Pillar at Sebzevar," and the "Parleying with Francis Furini" are not the best of Browning. Jones has, as I say, treated the poems unfairly, but even so most readers will agree that his unfavourable verdict on them has some critical justification. Secondly, he stresses the irrationality of Browning's optimism, indeed of all his ethical and metaphysical speculations. As I have said, Browning would not have denied this, arguing that faith transcends logic: this is a position which he has reached with open eyes and by diligent self-searching, and with continual insistence on the need for each individual to discover its truth for himself. Nevertheless Jones properly draws attention to the *voulu* element in Browning's cheerfulness, which brings it at times close to heartiness. It is true to say that a quality in which Browning is deficient is the determination to follow his reason steadfastly even when it is in conflict with all he most values. But to say this, of course, is simply to describe the converse of one of his most striking gifts.

Thirdly, Jones's book is valuable if it encourages or provokes readers to look on Browning's works not as metrical tracts from which stray sentences are to be selected as ethical mottoes but as poems which happen to take a metaphysical dilemma as their starting point.

Finally Jones rightly emphasizes, as every critic has done, the importance of love in Browning's poetry, and the remarkable way in which Browning continually suggests the correspondence between human love and divine love, which is the *raison d'être* of the Universe, a correspondence which at once ennobles human love and makes divine love more intelligible. Indeed in Chapter VI and in most of Chapter XI

Jones offers a substantially accurate summary of the ideas in many of Browning's important poems: it is hard to understand how he reconciles his generous tributes to the poet's insight in these chapters with his general condemnations elsewhere in the book.

V

With every allowance made for its good points Jones's book still stands condemned as fundamentally defective in method and infinitely mischievous in effect. Its claim to enlighten the reader on Browning as a philosophical and religious teacher is weakest precisely where expert assistance would be most helpful, on the extremely difficult point of the relation of Browning's metaphysical and epistemological views to his religious beliefs. Not only does Jones fail to see the distinction which, in some poems, Browning makes between logical conviction and an act of faith, but he apparently does not realize the bearing of the attacks which, in other poems, Browning makes upon the reason in the interests of faith. Browning makes one point repeatedly, that all our intellectual processes are incapable of proof—we cannot *prove* that the external world exists; we cannot *prove* the law of cause and effect; we cannot *prove* that other people even see the world as we do, much less that they ought to agree with our moral and religious conclusions; we cannot *prove* that our wills are free; we cannot even *prove* that we are awake. But we know that it is unthinkable to live as if all these points were open questions, and so we bridge the gap by an act of faith.

Browning is prepared to concede that to live at all one must accept certain basic assumptions unproved, but he does not allow the reader to forget the existence of these initial acts of faith. If then religion is attacked in the name of reason, he points out that reason itself is based on an act of trust, and argues that if everyone accepts unprovable intellectual postulates because life would be meaningless unless one did, then he is himself justified in accepting unprovable postulates about religion and the nature of man because his life would be meaningless unless he did.

Thus at the core of Browning's philosophical and speculative poems we find not an impulsive and emotional denial of man's intellectual responsibilities but a constant awareness of his intellectual limitations.[11] This, together with a mind incapable of drawing comfort from dogma, forces Browning always into a position of questioning and doubting. He characteristically finds himself in a situation where he must choose between hope and utter despair.

The argument, then, of Browning's metaphysical poetry is not, as Jones represents it, a simple Panglossian optimism, accompanied by a deliberate smothering of the reason lest it should inconveniently draw attention to certain deficiencies of the Creation. On the contrary its origin is very often in a mood of grief or anxiety, doubt or distress, caused perhaps by the death of someone near to him, or by a sceptical attack on religion, or by a sudden realization of the problems of pain or evil.[12] A rational consideration of such events seems to constrain man to a pessimistic view of the world. By temperament Browning reacted to them not by listless acquiescence but by an energetic attempt to establish from his total experience of life a picture of the world which should not be entirely hopeless. To do this he used all the resources of his intellect, exploring possible solutions, and never expecting short answers to difficult problems. A favorite pattern is for this intellectual analysis to continue until, as it were, mentally exhausted, the poet falls back on Montaigne's question, "Que scais-je?" It is only when he has proved, or even enacted, the inefficacy of the intellectual processes that Browning decides to perform the crucial act of trust. Even then he is fully aware of what he is doing, as the last stanza of the Epilogue to *Ferishtah's Fancies* clearly shows.

This general pattern is of course varied enormously in the individual poems. In many of them there is a genuine sense that Browning is not ignoring but transcending the knowledge of the head: in others it is, I think, fair to complain that the resolution which Browning accepts is too easy. But in all of them the reader senses that Browning's starting point is not a conviction but a question, that he has brought to it a mind unshackled by prejudice, and that his final position is held sincerely but undogmatically. It is characteristic of Browning that what he wants to maintain is not that everything is for the best in the best of all possible worlds, but that for himself personally there is still room, if not for certainty, at least for hope.

Jones, as I have shown, takes issue with this modest claim, accusing Browning simultaneously of pernicious scepticism and pernicious optimism. Once we have realized the incompleteness and inaccuracy of his argument, the way is open for a reconsideration of those poems in which Browning offers such resolutions as a poet may of the great paradoxes of human thought.

[NOTES]

INTRODUCTION

[1] Apparently the first dissertation on Browning appeared in Copenhagen in 1891. The first American dissertation was C. W. Hodell's work on *The Ring and the Book,* Cornell, 1894. Of the 77 dissertations on Browning produced from 1891 to 1958, 15 were written during the period from 1891 to 1920, 32 from 1921 to 1940, and 37 from 1941 to 1958. Significantly, if one is interested in the fluctuations of Browning's status at universities, only 5 dissertations appeared from 1941 to 1950 (the war and postwar years) and 25 from 1951 to 1958. See Richard D. Altick and William R. Matthews' very useful *Guide to Doctoral Dissertations in Victorian Literature 1886-1958,* Urbana, 1960, pp. 35-37.

[2] See Philip Drew's "Henry Jones on Browning's Optimism," pp. 364-80 in this volume.

[3] London, 1952, p. 21 and p. 187.

WILLIAM C. DeVANE: *The Harlot and the Thoughtful Young Man*

[1] The most ambitious and suggestive account of the relationship is to be found in R. L. Mégroz, *Dante Gabriel Rossetti, Painter Poet of Heaven in Earth* (London, 1928), pp. 308-12. See also pp. 290 ff.

[2] *The Browning Collections,* Sotheby, Wilkinson and Hodge Catalogue (London, 1913), p. 57.

[3] *Memoir of Dante Gabriel Rossetti* (London, 1895), pp. 101-102.

[4] *Autobiographical Notes of the Life of William Bell Scott,* ed. W. Minto (London, 1892), II, 138.

[5] *Letters from Robert Browning to Isa Blagden* (Waco, Texas, 1923), pp. 50-51.

[6] *The Browning Collections,* p. 59.

[7] *Memoir of D. G. R.,* p. 305.

[8] *Autobiographical Notes,* II, 171. Scott indicates that this incident occurred in June 1872. Rossetti learned of Buchanan's authorship of the *Review* article almost immediately after its publication. Scott refers, in that part of his account which I have omitted, to the article in the *Contemporary Review,* as if that were the cause of Rossetti's

NOTES

distraction; the date that he gives is shortly after the publication of the pamphlet.

⁹ *Memoir of D. G. R.*, p. 307.
¹⁰ *Memoir of D. G. R.*, p. 308.
¹¹ *Autobiographical Notes*, II, 171.
¹² *Some Reminiscences* (London, 1919), I, 245.
¹³ A. C. Benson, *Rossetti* (London, 1904), p. 120.
¹⁴ *Autobiographical Notes*, I, 289; II, 127, 115-16. The publication of "Jenny" in 1870 may well be a contributing factor to Scott's aversion to Rossetti, ill-concealed in his *Autobiographical Notes*.
¹⁵ *PreRaphaelite Diaries and Letters*, ed. W. M. Rossetti (London, 1900), pp. 144, 148.
¹⁶ *Memoir of D. G. R.*, p. 166.
¹⁷ *Ruskin: Rossetti: PreRaphaelitism. Papers, 1854 to 1862*, ed. W. M. Rossetti (London, 1899), pp. 233-34. The italics are mine.
¹⁸ *Idem*, p. 233.
¹⁹ *Letters of Dante Gabriel Rossetti to William Allingham, 1854-1870*, ed. G. B. Hill (London, 1897), p. 247.
²⁰ Hall Caine, *Recollections of Rossetti* (London, 1928), pp. 197-203.
²¹ *Memoir of D. G. R.*, p. 274.
²² *Rossetti Papers, 1862-70.* A Compilation by William Michael Rossetti (New York, 1903), p. 473. The letter is to Madox Brown.
²³ *Memoir of D. G. R.*, p. 166. See also *D. G. R. as Designer and Writer*, p. 151, and *Rossetti Papers*, p. 413. Swinburne recognized new passages in "Jenny" a little later. That Swinburne was of great assistance in the final writing of "Jenny" may be seen in Mr. T. J. Wise's *A Swinburne Library* (London, 1925), pp. 47-56.
²⁴ *Letters of D. G. R. to his Publisher, F. S. Ellis*, ed. Oswald Doughty (London, 1928), p. 10.
²⁵ *Rossetti Papers*, p. 529.
²⁶ *Family Letters*, ed. W. M. Rossetti (London, 1895), p. 227.
²⁷ The quarrel was an old one, dating back to the publication of Swinburne's *Poems and Ballads* of 1866. For the fullest account of the quarrel see Harriet Jay's *Robert Buchanan. . . .* (London, 1903), pp. 159-68.
²⁸ *Contemporary Review*, XVIII (October 1871), 343-45.
²⁹ *Athenaeum*, December 16, 1871, pp. 792-94.
³⁰ Mégroz, *Dante Gabriel Rossetti*, p. 192.
³¹ *The Fleshly School of Poetry. . . .*, p. 4.
³² *Idem*, p. 64. See also p. 39.
³³ *Idem*, p. 64.
³⁴ *Idem*, p. 86. See also p. 92.
³⁵ W. Hall Griffin and Harry Christopher Minchin, *Life of Browning* (London, 1910), pp. 248-49.

NOTES

³⁶ See A. W. Crawford, "Browning's Cleon," in *Journal of English and Germanic Philology*, XXVI (October 1927), 485-90.

³⁷ See W. O. Raymond, "Browning and the Higher Criticism," in *Publications of the Modern Language Association*, XLIV (June, 1929), 590-621; and W. Kirkconnell, "The Epilogue to *Dramatis Personae*," in *Modern Language Notes*, XLI (April 1926), 213-19. There is a full and excellent master's essay upon the contemporaneity of *Dramatis Personae*, as yet unpublished, in the Yale University Library, by Nellie Elizabeth Pottle, now Mrs. John Hankins.

³⁸ This suggestion was made by my friend, Mr. Gordon Haight.

³⁹ Quoted from Domett's diary by Griffin and Minchin, *Life of Browning*, p. 257.

⁴⁰ *Critical Comments on Algernon Charles Swinburne and Dante Gabriel Rossetti, by Robert Browning.* A series of letters privately printed by Mr. T. J. Wise, 1919, p. 11.

⁴¹ Harriet Jay, *Robert Buchanan*, p. 162.

⁴² Caine, *Recollections of Rossetti*, pp. 94-95.

F. E. L. Priestley: *Blougram's Apologetics*

¹ W. C. DeVane, *A Browning Handbook* (New York, 1935), p. 215. Cf. E. Dowden, *Robert Browning* (London, 1904), pp. 197 ff.: "a nineteenth century sceptic's exposition of his Christian faith." Cf. also J. Fotheringham, *Studies of the Mind and Art of Robert Browning* (London, 1898), pp. 363 ff. Recognition in various degrees of what I take to be Browning's real intention is to be found in E. M. Naish, *Browning and Dogma* (London, 1908), pp. 63-91; J. A. Hutton, *Guidance from Robert Browning in Matters of Faith* (Edinburgh, 1903), pp. 24-42; and C. R. Tracy, "Bishop Blougram," *Modern Language Review*, XXXIV (1939), 422-25: "Browning's real purpose was to comment on the problem of faith in a sceptical world."

² G. K. Chesterton, *Robert Browning* (New York, 1903), p. 201.

³ *Ibid.*, p. 188.

Donald Smalley: *Special Pleading in the Laboratory*

¹ *Letters of Robert Browning to Miss Isa Blagden*, arranged by A. J. Armstrong (Waco, Texas, 1923), pp. 196, 197.

² *The Diaries of William Charles Macready, 1833-1851*, ed. William Toynbee (London, 1912), II, 72.

³ Richard H. Wilde, *Conjectures and Researches concerning the Love, Madness, and Imprisonment of Torquato Tasso* (New York, 1842).

[4] [Professor Smalley in reprinting Browning's *Essay on Chatterton* numbered the lines. His numbers locate the passages as they appear in his book but naturally do not conform to our printing of the quotations.]

[5] "How much that establishes old convictions," Browning exclaims at one point (80-81), "and how little that is even supplementary to them, have we here!"

[6] Wilde also gained some recognition as a poet. His lyric "My life is like the summer rose," published in the *Analectic Magazine* for April 1819, was set to music by Sidney Lanier. *Hesperia: A Poem* was published posthumously in 1867, edited by his son William Cumming Wilde. See *Dictionary of American Biography*, XX, 206-207, for further details of his life.

[7] LIV, 502.

[8] *Conjectures and Researches*, I, 7.

[9] *Ibid.*, II, 268.

[10] See lines 145-67 of the Essay. In context, Browning's quotation from Wilde is seen to be merely an argument for the genuineness of Tasso's sentiments in certain lines of his poetry. The sentence immediately following the last one quoted by Browning makes this clear: "At the period when these lines were composed, it is hard to imagine what motive could exist for such a deception; and if the fiction usually attributed to poetry is relied on as a sufficient cause for doubting whatever appears in rhyme, we must reject, as feigned, much that the world has long received as true." Wilde was not attempting to clear Tasso's character, but to authenticate a portion of his own evidence.

[11] *Conjectures and Researches*, I, 77-78.

[12] For this purpose "Bishop Blougram's Apology" (1855), "Mr. Sludge, 'The Medium'" (1864), *Prince Hohenstiel-Schwangau* (1871), and *Red Cotton Night-Cap Country* (1873) will be used.

[13] Pompilia, Caponsacchi, and Guido, it is true, speak more publicly, with necessity rather than favorable conditions urging them to self-revealment.

[14] "Robert Browning," in *Formative Types in English Poetry* (Boston, 1917), p. 307.

[15] See "Bishop Blougram's Apology," lines 78-85.

WILLIAM O. RAYMOND: *The Infinite Moment*

[1] William Clyde DeVane, *A Browning Handbook* (New York, 1935), p. 79.

[2] *The Letters of Robert Browning and Elizabeth Barrett Barrett, 1845-1846* (London, 1899), I, 17.

NOTES

[3] A. M. Terhune, *The Life of Edward FitzGerald* (New Haven, 1947), p. 254.

[4] From George Santayana, *Interpretations of Poetry and Religion* (New York, 1900), p. 189. [In this volume, p. 57. Succeeding references are to page numbers in this volume.]

[5] *Ibid.*, p. 69.

[6] F. L. Lucas, *Ten Victorian Poets* (Cambridge, 1948), pp. 36, 23.

[7] Cf. Browning's letter to Isabella Blagden, cited in *Letters of Robert Browning*, collected by Thomas J. Wise and ed. by Thurman L. Hood (New Haven, 1933), p. 82. See also F. R. G. Duckworth, *Browning: Background and Conflict* (London, 1931), p. 121.

[8] *The Works of John Ruskin*, ed. by E. T. Cook and Alexander Wedderburn, XXXVI (London, 1909), xxxiv.

[9] *An Introduction to the Study of Browning* (London, 1916), p. 27.

[10] "Lady Geraldine's Courtship," stanza 41.

[11] G. K. Chesterton, *Robert Browning* (New York, 1903), p. 149. [In this volume, p. 92.]

[12] "By the Fire-side," ll. 244-45.

[13] *The Brownings* (London, 1928), p. 338.

[14] "Old Pictures in Florence," ll. 149-52.

KENNETH L. KNICKERBOCKER: *A Tentative Apology for Robert Browning*

[1] *Yale Review*, XLI (Winter 1952), 247-62. [In this volume, pp. 247-64. Succeeding references are to page numbers in this volume.]

[2] *Victorian Newsletter* (Autumn 1955), p. 1.

[3] Altick, p. 249.

[4] *Ibid.*, p. 253.

[5] *Ibid.*, pp. 251-52.

[6] *Ibid.*, p. 252.

[7] *ABC of Reading* (Norfolk, Connecticut, 1951), p. 191.

[8] Altick, p. 255.

[9] *New Letters of Robert Browning*, ed. William C. DeVane and K. L. Knickerbocker (New Haven, 1950), p. 92.

[10] Altick, p. 254.

[11] *Ibid.*, p. 259.

[12] Mr. Boyd Litzinger in his recently published book, *Time's Revenges: Browning's Reputation as a Thinker, 1889-1962* (Knoxville, Tenn., 1964), shows a rising tide of critical dissatisfaction with Browning as a thinker. The depression thirties, naturally disdainful of anything that smacked of optimism, delivered blow after blow at Browning's reputation. F. L. Lucas called the poet "a rather childish philosopher" (*Ten Victorian Poets*, Cambridge, 1940, p. 25).

Lascelles Abercrombie found Browning's personal thinking "of scarcely any importance at all" ("Robert Browning, 1812-1889," *The Great Victorians*, ed. H. J. and Hugh Massingham, New York, 1932, p. 82). F. R. G. Duckworth discovered "a root contradiction" in Browning's thinking which goes beyond such things in even "the least philosophical of poets" (*Browning: Background and Conflict*, New York, 1932, p. 182). So many others join this chorus of derogation, right up to the present, one must conclude that Browning appears to be an easy mark, a dead horse which it is safe to beat.

ROBERT LANGBAUM: *The Ring and the Book: A Relativist Poem*

[1] I shall quote by Book and line number from Volumes V and VI of the Centenary edition of Browning's *Works* (London, 1912).

[2] See "Molinos and the Molinists," Appendix VIII of A. K. Cook's *A Commentary Upon Browning's "The Ring and the Book"* (London, 1920).

[3] Quoted in Betty Miller, *Robert Browning: A Portrait* (London, 1952), p. 231.

[4] Henry James, who saw a point-of-view novel in *The Ring and the Book*, considers dropping the Pope from his hypothetical novelized version—"as too high above the whole connection functionally and historically for us to place him within it dramatically" ("The Novel in *The Ring and the Book*," in *Notes on Novelists*, London, 1914, p. 316).

B. R. JERMAN: *Browning's Witless Duke*

[1] See William C. DeVane, *A Browning Handbook* (2nd ed.; New York, 1955), pp. 102-103, 107-109, for details of publication. First entitled "Italy," the poem is said to catch the temper of the Italian Renaissance. Edward Dowden, *The Life of Robert Browning* (London, 1915), p. 79, observes that "the Duke is Italian of Renaissance days; insensible in his egoistic pride to the beautiful humanity before him." Pearl Hogrefe, *Browning and Italian Art and Artists* (Lawrence, Kans., 1914), p. 19, says that the poem sums up "the entire decadent Renaissance attitude toward art so fully that no historical names could improve it."

[2] *A Handbook to the Works of Robert Browning* (London, 1939), p. 251.

[3] *The Browning Cyclopaedia* (London, 1892), p. 282; *Browning and the Dramatic Monologue* (Boston, 1908), p. 98; *Browning's Heroines* (London, 1913), pp. 173-74; *Robert Browning* (Indianapolis, 1932), p. 175; "The Dramatic Monologue," *PMLA*, LXII

(1947), 510. It should be clear that I have not made a collection here of the variant interpretations of "My Last Duchess." I cite only a handful to illustrate what seems to be the prevailing interpretation of the poem, however.

⁴ A representative few are Charlotte Porter and Helen A. Clarke, ed., *The Complete Works of Robert Browning* (New York, 1901), IV, 384; William H. Rogers, ed., *The Best of Browning* (New York, 1942), pp. 518-19; James Stephens, Edwin L. Beck, and Royall H. Snow, ed., *Victorian and Later English Poets* (New York, 1937), p. 1198; R. R. Kirk and R. P. McCutcheon, ed., *An Introduction to the Study of Poetry* (New York, 1934), p. 20; Cleanth Brooks, John P. Purser, and Robert Penn Warren, ed., *An Approach to Literature* (New York, 1952), p. 293.

⁵ See A. Allen Brockington, "Robert Browning's Answers to Questions Concerning Some of his Poems," *Cornhill Magazine,* XXXVI (1914), 316-18. On 22 Feb. 1889 Browning answered in writing the queries put to him by a member of The Day's End Club of Exeter, a literary group studying contemporary writers. The queries dealt with not only "My Last Duchess," but also "In a Gondola," "Earth's Immortalities," and "Parting at Morning." Brockington reprints this information in his *Browning and the Twentieth Century* (Oxford, 1932), pp. 117-18.

⁶ On his reticence, see Richard D. Altick, "The Private Life of Robert Browning," *Yale Review,* XLI (1951), 247-62. [In this volume, pp. 247-64.]

⁷ Such statements abound in Browning scholarship, perhaps reinforcing the often repeated idea that what a poet has to say about his work is frequently not the most revealing word on the subject. One of Browning's comments on "My Last Duchess" should illustrate the poet's point, however. An American professor once asked him if the Duke's commands were that the Duchess be killed. Browning "made no reply, for a moment, and then said, meditatively, 'Yes, I meant that the commands were that she should be put to death.' And then, after a pause, he added, with a characteristic dash of expression, and as if the thought had just started in his mind, 'Or he might have had her shut up in a convent.'" This interviewer wisely points out that when Browning wrote the poem he most likely had not thought out exactly what the commands were. His art purpose was satisfied, nevertheless, in having the smiles stopped, whatever the method. See Hiram Corson, *An Introduction to the Study of Robert Browning's Poetry* (Boston, 1886), pp. vii-viii.

⁸ Letter to W. G. Kingsland, dated 27 Nov. 1868 in *Letters of Robert Browning,* ed. Thurman L. Hood (New Haven, 1933), pp. 128-29.

⁹ Louis S. Friedland, "Ferrara and 'My Last Duchess,'" *SP,* XXXIII (1936), 656-84, convincingly establishes the Duke as Alfonso II, 5th

NOTES

Duke of Ferrara (1553-98); the Duchess as the daughter of Cosimo I de Medici, the Duke of Florence; the Count as the Count of Tyrol; the envoy as possibly one Nikolaus Madruz of Innsbruck, etc. It is useless to suppose that Browning had all of these people in mind as the actual personages in the poem. Nevertheless, since he located the poem in Ferrara, there is every reason to believe that he meant the speaker to be the Duke of Ferrara and not some other Italian grandee, as John D. Rea suggests in " 'My Last Duchess,' " *SP*, XXIX (1932), 120-22. If the envoy is not patterned after Madruz, Browning surely intended him to be an intelligent and respected commoner, say, a scholarly diplomatist, and not an ordinary servant, as some readers might believe him to be.

[10] Elizabeth Nitchie, "Browning's 'Duchess,' " *Essays in Criticism*, III (1953), 475-76, once again calls attention to "my" in the title and the first line of the poem as being significantly in keeping with the Duke's pride of possession. We may add that a reading of the poem aloud with increased emphasis on the personal pronouns should reveal this important aspect of the Duke's character.

[11] One can hardly resist the temptation to agree that "It was the deadly monotony [of her smile] that got on the man's nerves." See Margaret H. Bates, *Browning Critiques* (Chicago, 1921), p. 84, for this spirited note. Browning told The Day's End Club (q. v.) that the Duke used her shallowness "As an excuse—mainly to himself—for taking revenge on one who had unwittingly wounded his absurdly pretentious vanity, by failing to recognize his superiority in even the most trifling matters."

[12] H. V. Routh, *Towards the Twentieth Century* (Cambridge, 1937), p. 107.

LAURENCE PERRINE: *Browning's Shrewd Duke*

[1] Reprinted in this volume, pp. 329-35.

[2] However, if historical evidence counts for anything, the marriage did take place. In 1565 Alfonso II, Duke of Ferrara, took for his second duchess the daughter of Ferdinand I, Count of Tyrol. That these historical figures were the prototypes of Browning's characters is convincingly established by Louis S. Friedland in "Ferrara and *My Last Duchess*," *SP*, XXXIII (1936), 656-84.

ROBERT PREYER: *A Reading of the Early Narratives*

[1] Quoted in Betty Miller, *Robert Browning: A Portrait* (New York, 1953), p. 14. The passage continues, "I only make men and women

speak—give . . . the truth broken into prismatic hues, *and fear the pure white light.*" (my italics)

² "Childe Roland" was composed in Paris, Jan. 2, 1852, at the height of the excitement over Napoleon III's *coup d'état.* It was at this time also that the Shelley essay was written. The poem came to him "in a sort of dream" he reported, a final image of guilt, despair, and hopeless heroism. It seems to me that these emotions were appropriate to the occasion—an occasion which underscored the impossible grandeur of the Shelleyean quest for an ideal liberty.

³ The notes J. S. Mill jotted down in a review copy of *Pauline* suggest that he was on the right track until sidetracked by moral considerations. "If she *existed* and loved him, he treats her most ungenerously and unfeelingly," he wrote. Precisely: but as Mill knew, she did not exist as a character and therefore it was not a fault that "all his aspirings and longings and regrets point to other things, never to her."

⁴ *The Poetry of Experience* (London, 1957).

⁵ Northrop Frye, *Anatomy of Criticism* (Princeton, 1957), p. 172.

⁶ *From Baudelaire to Symbolism* (London, 1957), pp. 5-6.

⁷ William C. DeVane, *A Browning Handbook* (New York, 1935). Prof. DeVane distinguishes at least four poetic directions in *Sordello.*

⁸ Quoted in Langbaum, *The Poetry of Experience,* p. 81.

⁹ DeVane, *A Browning Handbook,* p. 52.

¹⁰ "André Gide: 1909," trans. Mina Curtiss, *Sewanee Review,* LX (1952), 601.

¹¹ Quoted in Frank Kermode, *Romantic Image* (London, 1957), p. 111.

¹² Browning often attempted musical effects in verse and (more significantly) the effect of music on its listeners or on musicians: cf. "Abt Vogler," "A Toccata of Galuppi's," etc. Perhaps the most "romantic" of all such passages occurs in *Pauline:*

> At first I sang as I in dreams have seen
> Music wait in a lyrist for some thought
> Yet singing to herself until it came.

¹³ Quoted in Richard Ellman, *Yeats: The Man and the Masks* (New York, 1948).

PHILIP DREW: *Henry Jones on Browning's Optimism*

¹ "Browning's Reputation as a Thinker, 1889-1900," *TSL,* IV (1959), 43-50.

² H. B. Charlton brings out well the full dramatic effect of this lyric. "Browning as Dramatist," *BJRL,* XXIII (1939), 57-67.

³ The world's leading Browning scholars speak of the book with

unstinted praise. "The most detailed, sympathetic, and yet judicious treatment of Browning's ideas upon philosophy and theology." "The most profound and excellent of books of this kind on Browning." (William C. DeVane, *A Browning Handbook*, 2nd ed., New York, 1955, pp. 478, 587); "Brilliant and profound." "A masterpiece of exposition." (H. B. Charlton, "Browning's Ethical Poetry," *BJRL*, XXVII [1942-43], 43, 272); "A classic of literary criticism." (W. O. Raymond, *The Infinite Moment*, Toronto, 1950, p. 38). See also C. R. Tracy, "Browning's Heresies," *SP*, XXXIII (1936), 611.

⁴ Henry Jones, *Browning as a Philosophical and Religious Teacher*, (2nd ed.; Glasgow, 1892), p. 342. All page references, as indicated hereafter in the text, are to this edition.

⁵ This at least saves Jones from the elementary error of ascribing the speaker's sentiments directly to the poet, although he twice quotes "God's in his heaven" as if it were a simple statement of a cheering truth.

⁶ *Parleyings*, (1st ed.; London, 1887), p. 150.

⁷ As the next step in the theodicy Fancy says, "I also will that man become aware / Life has worth incalculable" (ll. 476-77).

⁸ Note that Jones has earlier relied on Kant to refute Berkeley.

⁹ It is only fair to say that Jones's attack on individualism at this point apparently has its origin in his conviction that individualism is necessarily incompatible with social responsibility.

¹⁰ In this connection it is interesting to compare Coleridge, *Biographia Literaria*, Chapter X: e.g., "It [the existence of God] could not be intellectually more evident without becoming morally less effective; without counteracting its own end by sacrificing the life of faith to the cold mechanism of a worthless because compulsory assent." See also *Christmas-Eve*, Section v:

[God's plan was] To create man and then leave him
Able, His own word saith, to grieve Him,
But able to glorify Him too,
As a mere machine could never do,
That prayed or praised, all unaware
Of its fitness for aught but praise and prayer,
Made perfect as a thing of course.

Jones quotes this passage with approval in his concluding chapter.

¹¹ Cf. Coleridge again: "Wherever the forms of reasoning appropriate only to the *natural* world are applied to *spiritual* realities, it may be truly said, that the more strictly logical the reasoning is in all its *parts*, the more irrational it is as a *whole*." *Aids to Reflection* ("Aphorisms on Spiritual Religion," Reflections Introductory to Aphorism x).

¹² See, for example, the first stanza of the Epilogue to *Ferishtah's Fancies*.

[BIBLIOGRAPHY]

THIS BIBLIOGRAPHY has been compiled to provide the serious student of Robert Browning with a useful supplement to the excellent bibliography compiled and edited by Professors Broughton, Northup, and Pearsall, published in 1953 by the Cornell University Press. We have attempted to list everything which has been published on Browning since 1950, both the important and the incidental, feeling that those who will use such a compilation will prefer a surplusage to a shortage of material. Having been forced, nonetheless, to place some limitations upon ourselves, we have not provided (as the Cornell bibliographers have) bibliographical descriptions of books which have been published; nor have we listed reprints or later editions, except where these contain substantial new material. We have given a sampling of the reviews of the more important books treating Robert Browning. This bibliography indicates something of the breadth of present scholarly and critical interest in the poet; and if—as bibliographies often do—it stimulates still further interest in Browning, it will have served a useful purpose.

1951

Altick, Richard D. "The Private Life of Robert Browning," *Yale Review*, XLI (1951), 247-62.

Armytage, W. H. G. "Some New Letters of Robert Browning, 1871-1889," *Modern Language Quarterly*, XII (1951), 155-58.

Brown, E. K. "The First Person in 'Caliban upon Setebos,'" *Modern Language Notes*, LXVI (1951), 392-95.

Buckley, Jerome H. *The Victorian Temper: A Study in Literary Culture*. Cambridge, Massachusetts, 1951.

Dickson, Arthur. "Browning's 'Serenade at the Villa,'" *Explicator*, IX (1951), Item 57.

BIBLIOGRAPHY

Fairchild, Hoxie N. "Browning's Pomegranate Heart," *Modern Language Notes,* LXVI (1951), 265-66.

―――――. "Browning's 'Whatever Is, Is Right,'" *College English,* XII (1951), 377-82.

Foster, J. T. "Browning's 'The Inn Album,'" *Explicator,* X (1951), Item 18.

Himelick, Raymond. "Bayard Taylor and Browning's 'Holy Vitus,'" *South Atlantic Quarterly,* L (1951), 542-51.

Howling, Robert Tunis. "Browning's Theory of the Purpose of Art," *Susquehanna University Studies,* IV (1951), 215-28.

Knickerbocker, Kenneth L., ed. *Selected Poetry of Robert Browning.* New York, 1951.

Lewis, Naomi. "Browning's Poetry," *The New Statesman and Nation,* XLI (1951), 161.

Lind, Sidney E. "James's 'The Private Life' and Browning," *American Literature,* XXIII (1951), 315-22.

McAleer, Edward C., ed. *Dearest Isa: Robert Browning's Letters to Isabella Blagden.* Edited and with an Introduction. Austin, Texas, 1951.

―――――. "Isa Blagden to Kate Field," *Boston Public Library Quarterly,* III (1951), 210-20.

Nowell-Smith, S., ed. *Browning: Poetry and Prose.* Cambridge, Massachusetts, 1951.

"Poetry and Crime," *Times Literary Supplement,* February 23, 1951, p. 117.

Rundle, James Urvin. "Burns' 'Holy Willie's Prayer' and Browning's 'Soliloquy of the Spanish Cloister,'" *Notes and Queries,* CXCVI (1951), 252.

Super, R. H. "Review of *New Letters of Robert Browning,*" *Modern Philology,* XLIX (1951), 136-42. "Rejoinder," *Modern Philology,* XLIX (1952), 275-77.

Thaler, Alwin. "Whittier and the English Poets," *New England Quarterly,* XXIV (1951), 53-68.

Tillotson, Geoffrey. *Criticism and the Nineteenth Century.* London, 1951.

Wallace, Sarah A. "Robert Browning in London Society," *Modern Language Notes,* LXVI (1951), 322-24.

BIBLIOGRAPHY

Weber, Carl J. "Much Ado about Browning," *Colby Library Quarterly*, III (1951), 44-45.

1952

Armytage, W. H. G. "Robert Browning and Mrs. Pattison: Some Unpublished Browning Letters," *University of Toronto Quarterly*, XXI (1952), 179-92.

Bowman, W. P. "Browning Anecdote," *Modern Language Notes*, LXVII (1952), 473-74.

Burrows, Leonard. *Browning: An Introductory Essay.* Perth, Australia, 1952.

Burtis, Mary Elizabeth. *Moncure Conway, 1832-1907.* New Brunswick, New Jersey, 1952.

Cohen, J. M. *Robert Browning.* London, 1952.

_____. "Seeing Browning Plain," *Spectator*, CLXXXIX (1952), 637-38.

Corrigan, Beatrice. "New Documents on Browning's Roman Murder Case," *Studies in Philology*, XLIX (1952), 520-33.

Coyle, William. "Molinos: 'The Subject of the Day' in *The Ring and the Book*," *PMLA*, LXVII (1952), 308-14.

Greer, Louise. *Browning and America.* Chapel Hill, North Carolina, 1952.

Harding, Joan O. H. "Charles Morgan and Browning," *Hibbert Journal*, LI (1952), 55-62.

Jamieson, Paul F. "Browning's 'Pictor Ignotus, Florence, 15___,' " *Explicator*, XI (1952), Item 8.

Johnson, Edward Dudley Hume. *The Alien Vision of Victorian Poetry: Sources of the Poetic Imagination in Tennyson, Browning, and Arnold.* (Princeton Studies in English Series, No. 34.) Princeton, 1952.

Kenmare, Dallas. *Ever A Fighter: A Modern Approach to the Work of Robert Browning.* London, 1952.

Lowe, Robert L. "Scott, Browning, and Kipling," *Notes and Queries*, CXCVII (1952), 103-104.

McLachlan, H. John. "A Browning Letter," *Times Literary Supplement*, February 8, 1952, p. 109.

BIBLIOGRAPHY

Miller, Betty. "Elizabeth Barrett and her Brother," *Cornhill Magazine*, VIII (1952), 221-28.

_____. *Robert Browning: A Portrait*. New York, 1952. Rev. by R. D. Altick, in New York *Herald Tribune Book Review*, Mar. 22, 1953, p. 3; by W. C. DeVane, *Saturday Review*, XXXVI (Mar. 7, 1953), 22; by J. M. Cohen, *Spectator*, CLXXXIX (Nov. 14, 1952), 637; by Eugene Davidson, *Yale Review*, XLII (1953), 613; by Francis Steegmuller, New York *Times*, Mar. 8, 1953, p. 6; in *Times Literary Supplement*, Nov. 14, 1952, p. 742.

Morgan, Charles, *Rapporto tra arte e genio Considerazioni sull' Andrea del Sarto di Browning*. Rome, 1952.

Osgood, Charles Grosvenor. *The Voice of England: A History of English Literature*. New York, 1952.

Pearsall, Robert B. "Browning's Texts in Galatians and Deuteronomy," *Modern Language Quarterly*, XIII (1952), 256-58.

Purves, John. "New Letters of Robert Browning," *Times Literary Supplement*, June 6, 1952, p. 377.

Stevenson, Lionel. "The Pertinacious Victorian Poets," *University of Toronto Quarterly*, XXI (1952), 232-45.

Super, R. H. "A Grain of Truth about Wordsworth and Browning, Landor and Swinburne," *Modern Language Notes*, LXXVII (1952), 419-21.

Weaver, Bennett. "A Primer Study in Browning's Satire," *College English*, XIV (1952), 76-81.

Willey, Dale H. "Moral Meanings in *The Ring and the Book*: Three Symbols and an Allegory," *Research Studies of the State College of Washington*, XX (1952), 93-111.

1953

Boulton, J. A. "Browning: A Potential Revolutionary," *Essays in Criticism*, III (1953), 165-76. See also comment by Elizabeth Nitchie, III, 475-76.

Bowra, C. M. "Dante and *Sordello*," *Comparative Literature*, V (1953), 1-15.

Broughton, Leslie Nathan; Clark Sutherland Northup; and Robert Pearsall, comps. *Robert Browning: A Bibliography, 1830-*

BIBLIOGRAPHY

1950 (Cornell Studies in English Series, Vol. XXXIX). Ithaca, New York, 1953.

Charlton, H. B. "The Making of the Dramatic Lyric," *Bulletin of the John Rylands Library,* XXXV (1953), 349-84.

Chesterton, Gilbert Keith. "Browning and his Ideal," *A Handful of Authors.* Ed. Dorothy Collins. New York, 1953.

Coombes, Henry. *Literature and Criticism.* London, 1953.

Duncan, Joseph E. "The Intellectual Kinship of John Donne and Robert Browning," *Studies in Philology,* L (1953), 81-100.

Furnivall, F. J., ed. "Acquisitions," *Huntington Library Quarterly,* XVI (1953), 437.

Gwynn, Frederic L. "Browning's 'Home Thoughts from the Sea,' " *Explicator,* XII (1953), Item 12.

Hogarth, Henry. "The Mystery of Molinos," *London Quarterly and Holborn Review,* 6th ser., XXII (1953), 6-10.

Horsman, E. A., ed. *The Diary of Alfred Domett, 1872-1885.* New York, 1953.

Joseph, D. C. "A Browning Book," *Times Literary Supplement,* April 3, 1953, p. 221.

Kaiser, Leo M. " 'Urbs Roma' and Some English Poets," *Classical Journal,* XLVIII (1953), 179-83.

————. " 'Urbs Roma' and Some English Poets," *Classical Journal,* XLIX (1953), 181-85.

Kenmare, Dallas. "Robert Browning," *Contemporary Review,* CLXXXIV (1953), 355-59.

King, Roma A., Jr. "Some Studies in the Shorter Poems of Robert Browning: Stylistic Interpretations," *Dissertation Abstracts,* XIII (1953), 810.

Kirby, Thomas A. "Browning on Chaucer," *Modern Language Notes,* (1953), 552-53.

Klomp, Henry. "The Idea of Aspiration in Early and Mid-Victorian Literature," *Dissertation Abstracts,* XIII (1953), 389.

Longaker, Mark, and Edwin C. Bolles. *Contemporary English Literature.* New York, 1953.

Lovelace, Robert Eugene. "A Note on Arnold's 'Growing Old,' " *Modern Language Notes,* LXVIII (1953), 20-23.

————. "Wordsworth and the Early Victorians: A Study of his

BIBLIOGRAPHY

Influence and Reputation, 1830-1860," *Summary of Doctoral Dissertations, University of Wisconsin,* XIII (1953), 382-83.

Lowe, Robert Liddell. "Browning and Donne," *Notes and Queries,* CXCVIII (1953), 491-92.

Mauer, Joseph A. "The Clitumnus," *Classical Weekly,* XLVI (1953), 113-18.

Maurois, André. "Les Browning," *Revue de Paris,* LX (1953), 7-27.

McCormick, James Patton. "Robert Browning and the Experimental Drama," *PMLA,* LXVIII (1953), 982-91.

Metzdorf, Robert F. "The Full Text of Rossetti's Sonnet on *Sordello,*" *Harvard Library Bulletin,* VII (1953), 239-43.

Miller, Betty. "'This Happy Evening,'" *Twentieth Century,* CLIV (1953), 53-61.

Nitchie, Elizabeth. "Browning's 'Duchess,'" *Essays in Criticism,* III (1953), 475-76.

Parr, Johnstone. "The Date of Composition of Browning's 'Love among the Ruins,'" *Philological Quarterly,* XXXII (1953), 443-46.

––––––––. "The Site and Ancient City of Browning's 'Love among the Ruins,'" *PMLA,* LXVIII (1953), 128-37.

Pearsall, Robert B. "The Forthcoming Bibliography of Browning," *Victorian Newsletter,* No. 3 (1953), 5-6.

Perrine, Laurence. "Browning's 'Respectability,'" *College English,* XIV (1953), 347-48.

Reilly, Sister M. Paraclita, C.S.J. *Aubrey de Vere: Victorian Observer.* Lincoln, Nebraska, 1953.

Short, Clarice. "John Keats and 'Childe Roland,'" *Notes and Queries,* II (1953), 218-19.

Smith, Charles D. "Browning's 'How They Brought the Good News from Ghent to Aix,'" *Explicator,* XI (1953), Item 42.

Stone, Wilfred H. "Browning and 'Mark Rutherford,'" *Review of English Studies,* new ser. IV (1953), 249-59.

Treves, Guiliana Artom. *Anglo-Fiorentine de cento anni fa.* Florence, 1953.

Worthington, Mabel Parker. "Don Juan: Theme and Development in the Nineteenth Century," *Dissertation Abstracts,* XIII (1953), 399.

BIBLIOGRAPHY

Wright, Maureen. " 'Karshish,' " *Times Literary Supplement,* May 1, 1953, p. 285.

1954

Akamine, Yoyoi. " 'Robert Browning, you writer of plays,' " *Athenaeum,* I (1954), 33-39.

Archibald, R. C. "Musical Settings of Robert Browning's Poetry and Drama," *Notes and Queries,* I (1954), 270.

Brundidge, Harry T. "Browning in Texas," *American Mercury,* LXXXIX (1954), 45-47.

Condee, Ralph W. "On Browning's 'Meeting at Night' and 'Parting at Morning,' " *Explicator,* XII (1954), Item 23.

Dahl, Curtis. "A Note on Browning's 'Ben Karshook's Wisdom,' " *Modern Language Notes,* LXIX (1954), 569-72.

Daniel, Robert N. "Robert Browning, Poet of Affirmation," *Furman Studies,* new ser. I (1954), 1-14.

Du Bos, Charles. "Pauline de Browning. Extraits d'un cours inedit," *Etudes anglaises,* VII (1954), 161-64.

Federle, Walter. *Robert Brownings dramatisches Experiment.* Zurich, 1954.

Greer, Louise. "Browning in America: A Study of Browning Criticism and of Browning Reputation in the United States, 1839-1890," *Dissertation Abstracts,* XIV (1954), 1073-74.

Hartung, Charles Vincent. "Browning and Impressionism," *Dissertation Abstracts,* XIV (1954), 358.

Hilton, Earl. "Browning's *Sordello* as a Study of the Will," *PMLA,* LXIX (1954), 1127-34.

Hood, Thurman L. "Browning's Hellenism," *Trinity College Library Gazette,* I (1954), 13-15.

Lloyd, Francis V., Jr. "On 'How They Brought the Good News from Ghent to Aix,' " *Explicator,* XII (1954), Item 31.

Stange, G. Robert. "Browning and Modern Poetry," *Pacific Spectator,* VIII (1954), 218-28.

"The Stature of Browning," *Times Literary Supplement,* June 4, 1954, p. 361.

Trevelyan, G. M. *A Layman's Love of Letters.* London, 1954.

Williams, W. E., ed. *Browning: A Selection.* Harmodsworth, 1954.

Badger, Kingsbury. "'See the Christ Stand!': Browning's Religion," *Boston University Studies in English,* I (1955), 53-73.

Baetzhold, Howard George. "Mark Twain's Attitudes toward England," *Summary of Doctoral Dissertations, University of Wisconsin,* XV (1955), 595-97.

Dahl, Curtis. "The Victorian Wasteland," *College English,* XVI (1955), 341-47.

DeVane, William Clyde. *A Browning Handbook.* 2nd ed. New York, 1955.

Duffin, H. C. "Mysticism in Browning," *Hibbert Journal,* LIII (1955), 372-75.

Glen, Margaret Eleanor. "The Meaning and Structure of *Pippa Passes,*" *University of Toronto Quarterly,* XXIV (1955), 410-26.

Groom, Bernard. *The Diction of Poetry from Spenser to Bridges.* Toronto, 1955.

Katope, Christopher G. "Patterns of Imagery in Robert Browning's *The Ring and the Book,*" *Dissertation Abstracts,* XV (1955), 403-404.

Kaufman, Marjorie Ruth. "Henry James's Comic Discipline: The Use of the Comic in the Structure of his Early Fiction," *Dissertation Abstracts,* XV (1955), 2534.

Maurois, André. *Robert et Elizabeth Browning.* Paris, 1955.

Parrott, Thomas M., and Robert B. Martin. *A Companion to Victorian Literature.* New York, 1955.

Priestley, F. E. L. "A Reading of *La Saisiaz,*" *University of Toronto Quarterly,* XXV (1955), 47-59.

Pucelle, Jean. *L'Idealisme en Angleterre, de Coleridge à Bradley: Être et Penser.* Neuchâtel, 1955.

Raymond, William O. "'The Jewelled Bow': A Study in Browning's Imagery and Humanism," *PMLA,* LXX (1955), 115 31.

Ruffin, D. "Browning's 'Childe Roland' and Chaucer's *House of Fame,*" *Essays in Honor of Walter Clyde Curry.* Nashville, Tennessee, 1955, pp. 51-60.

Sanders, Charles Richard. "Carlyle's Letters," *Bulletin of the John Rylands Library,* XXXVIII (1955), 199-224.

Thale, Jerome. "Browning's 'Popularity' and the Spasmodic

Poets," *Journal of English and Germanic Philology*, LIV (1955), 348-54.

1956

Adams, Norman O. W., Jr. "Byron and the Early Victorians: A Study of his Poetic Influence, 1824-1855," *Dissertation Abstracts*, XVI (1956), 336-37.

Beall, Chandler B. "A Dantean Simile in Browning," *Modern Language Notes*, LXXI (1956), 492-93.

Corrigan, Beatrice, trans. and ed. *Curious Annals: New Documents Relating to Browning's Roman Murder Story*. Toronto, 1956.

Davison, Edward. "The Line of Caponsacchi," *Great Moral Dilemmas in Literature, Past and Present*. New York, 1956, pp. 61-72.

De Selincourt, Aubrey. *Six Great Poets*. London, 1956.

Dietrichson, Jan W. "Obscurity in the Poetry of Robert Browning," *Edda*, LV (1956), 173-91.

Duffin, Henry Charles. *Amphibian: A Reconsideration of Browning*. Cambridge, England, 1956. Rev. by W. C. DeVane, *Modern Language Review*, LII (1957), 265-66; by H. J. McLachlan, *Hibbert Journal*, LV (1957), 193-94; by Donald Smalley, *Modern Language Notes*, LXXII (1957), 137-38.

Faverty, Frederic E., ed. *The Victorian Poets: A Guide to Research*. Cambridge, Massachusetts, 1956.

Going, William T. "The Ring and the Brownings," *Modern Language Notes*, LXXI (1956), 493-95.

Hardy, Barbara. "Mr. Browning and George Eliot," *Essays in Criticism*, VI (1956), 121-23.

Harrison, Thomas P. "Birds in the Poetry of Browning," *Review of English Studies*, new ser. VII (1956), 393-405.

Hill, Archibald A. "Pippa's Song: Two Attempts at Structural Criticism," *University of Texas Studies in English*, XXXV (1956), 51-56.

Jeffrey, Lloyd N. "Browning as Psychologist: Three Notes," *College English*, XVII (1956), 345-48.

BIBLIOGRAPHY

Keller, J. C. *Literature and Religion*. Rindge, New Hampshire, 1956.

Knickerbocker, Kenneth L. "A Tentative Apology for Browning," *Tennessee Studies in Literature*, I (1956), 75-82.

Langbaum, Robert. "*The Ring and the Book:* A Relativist Poem," *PMLA*, LXXI (1956), 131-54. Included in *The Poetry of Experience*, pp. 109-36.

Lloyd-Jones, Richard. "Common Speech—A Poetic Effect for Hopkins, Browning, and Arnold," *Dissertation Abstracts*, XVI (1956), 957.

Lowe, Robert Liddell. "Robert Browning to Percy William Bunting: An Unpublished Letter," *Notes and Queries*, III (1956), 539-41.

McAleer, Edward C. "Browning's 'Cleon' and Auguste Comte," *Comparative Literature*, VIII (1956), 142-45.

McNeir, Waldo F. "Lucrezia's 'Cousin' in Browning's 'Andrea del Sarto,'" *Notes and Queries*, III (1956), 500-502.

Raymond, William O. "Truth in *The Ring and the Book*," *Victorian Newsletter*, No. 10 (1956), 12-13.

Roppen, George. *Evolution and Poetic Belief: A Study in Some Victorian and Modern Writers*. (Oslo Studies in English Series, No. 5). Oslo, 1956.

Schneck, Jerome M. "Robert Browning and Mesmerism," *Bulletin of the Medical Library Association*, XLIV (1956), 443-51.

Schweik, Robert C. "Bishop Blougram's Miracles," *Modern Language Notes*, LXXI (1956), 416-18.

Singer, Armand E. "Supplement to a Bibliography of the Don Juan Theme: Versions and Criticism," *West Virginia University Philological Papers*, X (1956), 1-36.

Smalley, Donald, ed. *Poems of Robert Browning*. New York, 1956.

Tillotson, Geoffrey. "Victorian Novelists and Near-Novelists," *Sewanee Review*, LXIV (1956), 663-75.

Williams, Luster J. "Figurative Imagery in *The Ring and the Book:* A Study in Browning's Poetic Technique," *Dissertation Abstracts*, XVI (1956), 2153-54.

Windolph, Francis Lyman. *Reflections of the Law in Literature*. Philadelphia, 1956.

BIBLIOGRAPHY

1957

Altick, Richard D. "Browning's 'Karshish' and Saint Paul," *Modern Language Notes,* LXXII (1957), 494-96.

Baker, Joseph E. "Religious Implications in Browning's Poetry," *Philological Quarterly,* XXXVI (1957), 436-52.

Dahl, Curtis. "*Neblaretai* and *Rattei* in Browning's 'Aristophanes' Apology,'" *Modern Language Notes,* LXXII (1957), 271-73.

De Courten, M. L. Giartosio. "Pen, il figlio dei Browning," *English Miscellany,* VIII (1957), 125-42.

Dudley, Fred A. "'Hy, Zy, Hine,'" *Research Studies of the State College of Washington,* XXV (1957), 63-68.

Erdman, David V. "Browning's Industrial Nightmare," *Philological Quarterly,* XXXVI (1957), 417-35.

Fairchild, Hoxie N. *Religious Trends in English Poetry. Vol. IV: 1830-1880, Christianity and Romanticism in the Victorian Era.* New York, 1957.

Gordan, John D. "New in the Berg Collection: 1952-1956," *Bulletin of the New York Public Library,* LXI (1957), 303-11, 353-63.

Gray, Donald Joseph. "Victorian Verse Humor: 1830-1870," *Dissertation Abstracts,* XVII (1957), 1083.

Halliburton, M. "Browning's Other Romance," *American Mercury,* LXXXV (1957), 46-57.

Henry, Marjorie Ruth. "The Pope in *The Ring and the Book,*" *Dissertation Abstracts,* XVII (1957), 2010.

Houghton, Walter E. *The Victorian Frame of Mind, 1830-1870.* New Haven, Connecticut, 1957.

Jerman, B. R. "Browning's Witless Duke," *PMLA,* LXXII (1957), 488-93.

Kenmare, Dallas. *The Browning Love Story.* London, 1957.

King, Roma A., Jr. *The Bow and the Lyre: The Art of Robert Browning.* Ann Arbor, Michigan, 1957. Rev. by Thomas P. Harrison, *College English,* XX (1958), 59; by Robert Langbaum, *Victorian Newsletter,* No. 13 (1958), 12-13; by Patrick J. McCarthy, *Arizona Quarterly,* XIV (1958), 72-73; by Robert Stange, *Victorian Studies,* I (1958), 289-90.

Langbaum, Robert. *The Poetry of Experience: The Dramatic*

Monologue in Modern Literary Tradition. London, 1957. Rev. by John Bayley, *Spectator,* July 26, 1957, p. 143; by John Jones, *New Statesman,* LIV (Aug. 3, 1957), 153; by A. W. Phinney, *Christian Science Monitor,* July 25, 1957, p. 5; by Chad Walsh, New York *Herald Tribune Book Review,* Aug. 4, 1957, p. 6; in *Times Literary Supplement,* Aug. 2, 1957, p. 4721.

Lewis, Naomi. *A Visit to Mrs. Wilcox.* London, 1957.

Litzinger, Boyd. "A Note on 'Master Hughes of Saxe-Gotha,'" *Notes and Queries,* IV (1957), 266.

_____. "Robert Browning's Reputation as a Thinker, 1889-1955," *Dissertation Abstracts,* XVII (1957), 123.

McAleer, Edward C. "Pasquale Villari and the Brownings," *Boston Public Library Quarterly,* IX (1957), 40-47.

Miller, Betty. "The Seance at Ealing: A Study in Memory and Imagination," *Cornhill Magazine,* CLXIX (1957), 312-24.

Pepperdene, Margaret W. "Browning's 'Fra Lippo Lippi,' 70-75," *Explicator,* XV (1957), Item 34.

Perrine, Laurence, and Edwin M. Everett. "Browning's 'Fra Lippo Lippi,' 70-75," *Explicator,* XVI (1957), Item 18.

Praz, Mario. "Browning's 'A Grammarian's Funeral,'" *Times Literary Supplement,* December 6, 1957, p. 739.

Reeves, James, ed. *Selected Poems.* London, 1957.

Slatin, Myles. "'Mesmerism': A Study of Ezra Pound's Use of the Poetry of Robert Browning," *Dissertation Abstracts,* XVII (1957), 125.

Szladits, Lola L. "Browning's French Night-Cap," *Bulletin of the New York Public Library,* LXI (1957), 458-67.

Wain, John. *Preliminary Essays.* London, 1957.

Wishmeyer, William Hood. "The Myth in *The Ring and the Book,*" *Dissertation Abstracts,* XVII (1957), 3026.

1958

Adrian, Arthur A. "The Browning-Rossetti Friendship: Some Unpublished Letters," *PMLA,* LXXIII (1958), 538-44.

Arnold, Marian. *The Two Brownings.* London, 1958.

Cutts, John P. "Browning's 'Soliloquy of the Spanish Cloister,'" *Notes and Queries,* V (1958), 17-18.

DeVane, William C. "Robert Browning," *Victorian Newsletter,* No. 13 (1958), 22.

Fiorini, Natale. *Robert Browning.* Torino, 1958.

Foakes, Reginald A. *The Romantic Assertion: A Study in the Language of Nineteenth Century Poetry.* New Haven, Connecticut, 1958.

Ford, Boris, ed. *Pelican Guide to English Literature. Vol. VI: From Dickens to Hardy.* Baltimore, 1958.

Herring, Jack W. "Critical Attitudes toward Browning since his Death," *Dissertation Abstracts,* XIX (1958), 798.

Hill, A. G. "Three Modes in Poetry," *Times Literary Supplement,* September 12, 1958, p. 512.

Johnson, Agnes Boswell. "The Faust Motif in Browning's *Paracelsus,*" *Dissertation Abstracts,* XIX (1958), 319.

Kano, Hideo. *Crisis and Imagination.* Tokyo, 1958.

Landis, Paul, and Ronald E. Freeman, eds. *Letters of the Brownings to George Barrett.* Urbana, Illinois, 1958. Rev. by Samuel C. Chew, New York *Herald Tribune Book Review,* July 6, 1958, p. 5; by William Irvine, *Victorian Studies,* II (1958), 85-87; by Fraser Nieman, *American Scholar,* XXVIII (1958), 116; by Frances Winwar, New York *Times Book Review,* July 6, 1958, p. 4; in *Times Literary Supplement,* May 16, 1958, p. 270.

Litzinger, Boyd. "Browning on Immortality," *Notes and Queries,* V (1958), 446-47.

Marks, Emerson R. "Browning's 'Abt Vogler,' 43-56," *Explicator* XVI (1958), Item 29.

McCrory, Thomas E. "Browning and Dante," *Dissertation Abstracts,* XIX (1958), 813.

Morse, J. Mitchell. "Browning's Grammarian, Warts and All," *CEA Critic,* XX (1958), 1, 5.

Page, David. "Split in Wain," *Essays in Criticism,* VIII (1958), 447-50.

Porter, Katherine A. *Through a Glass Darkly: Spiritualism in the Browning Circle.* Lawrence, Kansas, 1958.

Rivers, Charles Leo. "Browning's Theory of the Poet, 1833-1841,"

Abstracts of Dissertations, The University of Southern California, 1958, 52-53.

Salingar, L. G. "Robert Browning," *Pelican Guide* [1454], VI (1958), 245-55.

Shackford, Martha Hale. "Browning Selected Four Poems," *Talks on Ten Poets: Wordsworth to Moody.* New York, 1958.

Tanzy, C. E. "Browning, Emerson, and Bishop Blougram," *Victorian Studies,* I (1958), 255-66.

Watkins, C. C. "Browning's 'Fame Within These Four Years,'" *Modern Language Review,* LIII (1958), 492-500.

_____. "Browning's *Men and Women* and the Spasmodic School," *Journal of English and Germanic Philology,* LVII (1958), 57-59.

Zamwalt, Eugene B. "Christian Symbolism in 'My Last Duchess,'" *Notes and Queries,* V (1958), 446.

1959

Albrecht, Sister Mary Catherine de Ricci. "Robert Browning's Classification of his Monologues in 1868," *Dissertation Abstracts,* XIX (1959), 104.

Alberich, Jose. "El obispo Blougram y San Manuel Bueno," *Revista de litteratura,* XV (1959), 90-94.

Altick, Richard D. "Browning's 'Transcendentalism,'" *Journal of English and Germanic Philology,* LVIII (1959), 24-28.

Bell, Martha S. "Special Women's Collections in United States Libraries," *College and Research Library,* XX (1959), 235-42.

Bevan, Bryan. "Poet's Novel," *Poetry Review,* L (1959), 29-31.

Britton, John. "Browning's 'Bishop Blougram's Apology,' 702-709," *Explicator,* XVII (1959), Item 50.

"A Browning Exhibit in the Treasure Room," *The Boston Public Library Quarterly,* XI (1959), 50-52.

Bryson, John. *Browning.* (Writers and Their Work Series, No. 106.) London, 1959.

Cundiff, Paul A. "Robert Browning: 'Our Human Speech,'" *Victorian Newsletter,* No. 15 (1959), 1-9.

Goldsmith, Richard Weinberg. "The Relation of Browning's

Poetry to Religious Controversy 1833-1868," *Dissertation Abstracts*, XIX (1959), 2612.

Honan, Park. "Browning's Poetic Laboratory: The Use of *Sordello*," *Modern Philology*, LVI (1959), 162-66.

Hughes, R. E. "Browning's 'Childe Roland' and the Broken Taboo," *Literature and Psychology*, IX (1959), 18-19.

Johnson, Charles E., Jr. "The Dramatic Career of Robert Browning: A Survey and Analysis," *Dissertation Abstracts*, XIX (1959), 2601.

Knickerbocker, Kenneth L. "Robert Browning: A Modern Appraisal," *Tennessee Studies in Literature*, IV (1959), 1-11.

Lindberg, John. "Grail-themes in Browning's 'Childe Roland,'" *Victorian Newsletter*, No. 16 (1959), 27-30.

Lindsay, Norman. "The Mask of Robert Browning," *Southerly*, XX (1959), 182-200.

Litzinger, Boyd. "Browning's Reputation as a Thinker, 1889-1900," *Tennessee Studies in Literature*, IV (1959), 43-50.

Maxwell, J. C. "Browning and Christopher Smart," *Notes and Queries*, VI (1959), 449.

Perrine, Laurence. "Browning's Shrewd Duke," *PMLA*, LXXIV (1959), 157-59.

Preyer, Robert. "Robert Browning: A Reading of the Early Narratives," *Journal of English Literary History*, XXVI (1959), 531-48.

Ransom, H. H. "The Hanley Library," *Library Chronicle of the University of Texas*, VI (1959), 33-35.

Raymond, W. O. "Browning's 'The Statue and the Bust,'" *University of Toronto Quarterly*, XXVIII (1959), 233-49.

Singer, Armand E. "Third Supplement to a Bibliography of the Don Juan Theme: Versions and Criticism," *West Virginia University Philological Papers*, XIII (1959), 44-68.

Smalley, Donald. "Browning's View of Fact in *The Ring and the Book*," *Victorian Newsletter*, No. 16 (1959), 1-9.

Smidt, Kristian. "The Intellectual Quest of the Victorian Poets," *English Studies*, XL (1959), 90-102.

Stange, G. Robert. "Browning's 'James Lee's Wife,'" *Explicator*, XVII (February, 1959), Item 32.

BIBLIOGRAPHY

Stevenson, Lionel. "'My Last Duchess' and Parisina," *Modern Language Notes,* LXXIV (1959), 489-92.

Trawick, Buckner B. "The Moon Metaphor in Browning's 'One Word More,'" *Notes and Queries,* VI (1959), 448.

Vanson, Frederic. "Robert Browning—Christian Optimist," *London Quarterly and Holborn Review,* CLXXXIV (1959), 331-35.

Watkins, Charlotte Crawford. "The 'Abstruser Themes' of Browning's *Fifine at the Fair,*" *PMLA,* LXXIV (1959), 426-37.

1960

Assad, Thomas J. "Browning's 'My Last Duchess,'" *Tulane Studies in English,* X (1960), 117-28.

Barbery, Y. "La critique moderne face à Elizabeth et Robert Browning," *Études anglaises,* XIII (1960), 444-51.

Barnett, Howard A. "Robert Browning and the Drama: Browning's Plays Viewed in the Context of the Victorian Theatre: 1830-1850," *Dissertation Abstracts,* XX (1960), 4097.

Bevington, Merle M. "Three Letters of Robert Browning to the Editor of the *Pall Mall Gazette,*" *Modern Language Notes,* LXXV (1960), 304-309.

Bodkin, Maud. "A Note on Browning's 'Childe Roland,'" *Literature and Psychology,* X (1960), 37.

Brown, T. J. "English Literary Autographs XXXV: Elizabeth Barrett Browning, 1806-1861, and Robert Browning, 1812-1889," *Book Collector,* IX (1960), 317.

Corrigan, Beatrice. "Browning's Roman Murder Story," *English Miscellany,* XI (1960), 333-400.

————. "Vernon Lee and the Old Yellow Book," *Colby Library Quarterly,* V (1960), 116-22.

Cowan, James. "Literary Criticism and Projection," *Kansas Magazine* (1960), 84-87.

Cundiff, Paul A. "Robert Browning: 'Indisputable Fact,'" *Victorian Newsletter,* No. 17 (1960), 7-11.

Dougherty, Charles T. "Browning's Letters in the Vatican Library," *Manuscripta,* IV (1960), 164-69.

Garriott, Harold M. "Characterization through Metaphor in

BIBLIOGRAPHY

The Ring and the Book, with Special Reference to the Guido Monologues," *Dissertation Abstracts,* XXI (1960), 892-93.

Honan, Park. "Browning's *Pauline*: The Artistic Safety Device," *Victorian Newsletter,* No. 18 (1960), 23-24.

Jones, T. H. "The Disposition of Images in Browning's *The Ring and the Book," Journal of the Australasian Universities Language and Literature Association,* XIII (1960), 55-69.

Kendall, J. L. "Lippo's Vision," *Victorian Newsletter,* No. 18 (1960), 18-21.

Langbaum, Robert. "The Importance of Fact in *The Ring and the Book," Victorian Newsletter,* No. 17 (1960), 11-17.

Litzinger, Boyd. "Did Cardinal Wiseman Review *Men and Women?" Victorian Newsletter,* No. 18 (1960), 22-23.

Millet, Stanton. "Art and Reality in 'My Last Duchess,'" *Victorian Newsletter,* No. 17 (1960), 25-27.

Palmer, Rupert E., Jr. "The Uses of Character in 'Bishop Blougram's Apology,'" *Modern Philology,* LVIII (1960), 108-18.

Pipes, B. N. "The Portrait of 'My Last Duchess,'" *Victorian Studies,* III (1960), 381-86.

Porter, Jenny Lind. "Physical Locale in *The Ring and the Book," Personalist,* XL (1960), 48-59.

Poston, Lawrence, III. "Ritual in 'The Bishop Orders His Tomb,'" *Victorian Newsletter,* No. 17 (1960), 27-28.

Reed, Joseph W., Jr. "Browning and Macready: The Final Quarrel," *PMLA,* LXXV (1960), 597-603.

Sanders, Charles Richard. "Carlyle, Browning, and the Nature of a Poet," *Emory University Quarterly,* XVI (1960), 197-209.

Smalley, Donald. "Browning's View of Fact in *The Ring and the Book," Victorian Newsletter,* No. 16 (1960), 1-9.

Starkman, Miriam K. "The Manichee in the Cloister: A Reading of Browning's 'Soliloquy of the Spanish Cloister,'" *Modern Language Notes,* LXXV (1960), 399-405.

Waters, D. Douglas, Jr. "Does Browning's 'Great Text in Galatians' Entail 'Twenty-Nine Distinct Damnations'?" *Modern Language Review,* LV (1960), 243-44.

Wilkinson, D. C. "The Need for Disbelief: A Comment on *Pippa Passes," University of Toronto Quarterly,* XXIX (1960), 139-51.

Willoughby, John W. "Browning's Familiarity with the Bible," *Notes and Queries*, VII (1960), 459.

1961

Austin, James C. "The Hawthorne and Browning Acquaintance: Including an Unpublished Browning Letter," *Victorian Newsletter*, No. 20 (1961), 13-18.

Bevington, Merle M. "Browning and Wordsworth: The Argument for Immortality in 'Saul,'" *Victorian Newsletter*, No. 20 (1961), 19-21.

Blair, Carolyn L. "Robert Browning as a Literary Critic," *Dissertation Abstracts*, XXII (1961), 1974.

Buhl, Paulina E. "A Historical and Critical Study of Browning's *Asolando* Volume," *Dissertation Abstracts*, XXII (1961), 562.

Chiarenza, Frank J. "Browning's 'The Bishop Orders His Tomb at St. Praxed's Church,' 73-79; 99-100," *Explicator*, XIX (1961), Item 22.

Cox, Mary Elizabeth. "With Bernard de Mandeville," *West Virginia University Philological Papers*, XIII (1961), 31-36.

Docherty, H. A. "Browning's Use of History: Its Effect on Meaning and Structure in his Poetry," *Dissertation Abstracts*, XXII (1961), 3659.

Gray, Donald J. "Arthur, Roland, Empedocles, Sigurd, and the Despair of Heroes in Victorian Poetry," *Boston University Studies*, V (1961), 1-17.

Hagopian, John V. "The Mask of Browning's Countess Gismond," *Philological Quarterly*, XL (1961), 153-55.

Harper, James W. "Browning and the Evangelical Tradition," *Dissertation Abstracts*, XXI (1961), 3089-90.

Harrison, Thomas P. "Browning's 'Childe Roland' and Wordsworth," *Tennessee Studies in Literature*, VI (1961), 119-23.

Hess, M. Whitcomb. "Graham Greene's Travesty on *The Ring and the Book*," *Catholic World*, CXCIV (1961), 37-42.

Honan, Park. *Browning's Characters: A Study in Poetic Technique.* New Haven, Connecticut, 1961. Rev. by Robert Langbaum, *Victorian Studies*, V (1962), 269-71.

BIBLIOGRAPHY

Johnson, E. D. H. "Robert Browning's Pluralistic Universe: A Reading of *The Ring and the Book*," *University of Toronto Quarterly*, XXXI (1961), 20-41.

Kelley, Lachlan Phil. "Robert Browning and George Smith," *Quarterly Review*, CCXCIX (1961), 323-35.

Kilburn, Patrick E. "Browning's 'My Last Duchess,'" *Explicator*, XIX (1961), Item 31.

King, Roma A. "Browning: 'Mage' and 'Maker'—A Study in Poetic Purpose and Method," *Victorian Newsletter*, No. 20 (1961), 22-25.

Litzinger, Boyd. "Incident as Microsm: The Prior's Niece in 'Fra Lippo Lippi,'" *College English*, XXII (1961), 409-10.

———. "A Note on Browning's Defense of Chatterton," *Victorian Newsletter*, No. 19 (1961), 17-19.

———. "The Prior's Niece in 'Fra Lippo Lippi,'" *Notes and Queries*, VIII (1961), 344-45.

———. "Browning's 'The Statue and the Bust' Once More," *Studies in Honor of John C. Hodges and Alwin Thaler.* Knoxville, Tennessee, 1961. Pp. 87-92.

McAleer, Edward C. "Browning's 'Nationality in Drinks,'" *Explicator*, XX (1961), Item 34.

McNally, James J., Jr. "The Political Thought of Robert Browning," *Dissertation Abstracts*, XXII (1961), 1629.

Mendl, R. W. S. "Robert Browning, the Poet-Musician," *Music and Letters*, XLII (1961), 142-50.

Nathanson, Leonard. "Browning's 'My Last Duchess,'" *Explicator*, XIX (1961), Item 68.

Orenstein, Irving. *A Fresh Interpretation of 'The Last Ride Together'* (Baylor Browning Interests Series, No. 18). Waco, Texas, 1961. Pp. 3-10.

Peattie, D., and L. Peattie. "Immortal Romance," *Readers Digest*, LXXIX (1961), 304-309.

Poisson, Jean. "Georges Connes: le livre et l'anneau de Browning," *Études anglaises*, XIV (1961), 354-55.

Puckett, W. M. "The Nineteenth Century Foundations of the Robert Browning-Ezra Pound Bridge to Modernity in Poetry," *Dissertation Abstracts*, XXII (1961), 3205.

BIBLIOGRAPHY

Rivers, Charles. *Three Essays on Robert Browning's Theory of the Poet.* Northwest Missouri State College Studies, XXV, No. 3 (1961).

Rosenbaum, Robert A. *Earnest Victorians.* New York, 1961.

Sanders, Mrs. Steven. *A Supplementary Calendar of Letters* (Baylor Browning Interests Series, No. 18). Waco, Texas, 1961. Pp. 11-20.

Schweik, Robert C. "The Structure of 'A Grammarian's Funeral,'" *College English,* XXII (1961), 411-12.

Shanks, Edward, ed. *Poems of Robert Browning.* London, 1961.

Sypher, Wylie, ed. *The Ring and the Book.* With an Introduction. New York, 1961.

Thane, Adele. "'Pied Piper of Hamelin': Dramatization of the Poem by Robert Browning," *Plays,* XXI (1961), 37-47.

Wasserman, George R. "The Meaning of Browning's Ring-Figure," *Modern Language Notes,* LXXVI (1961), 420-26.

Woodard, Charles R. "The Road to the Dark Tower: An Interpretation of Browning's 'Childe Roland,'" *Studies in Honor of John C. Hodges and Alwin Thaler.* Knoxville, Tennessee, 1961. Pp. 93-99.

1962

Benziger, James. *Images of Eternity: Studies in The Poetry of Religious Vision, from Wordsworth to T. S. Eliot.* Carbondale, 1962.

Clarke, C. C. "Humor and Wit in 'Childe Roland,'" *Modern Language Quarterly,* XXIII (1962), 323-26.

Curran, E. M. "Browning: Tallow and Brown Sugar?" *Colby Library Quarterly,* Ser. VI (1962), 169-75.

Davies, Hugh Sykes. *Browning and the Modern Novel.* The St. John's College Lecture, 1961-62.

De Laura, David J. "The Religious Imagery in Browning's 'The Patriot,'" *Victorian Newsletter,* No. 21 (1962), 16-18.

Dougherty, Charles T. "Three Browning Letters to His Son," *Manuscripta,* VI (1962), 98-103.

Fletcher, Richard M. "English Romantic Drama: 1795-1843. A Critical and Historical Study." *Dissertation Abstracts,* XXIII (1962), 1364.

BIBLIOGRAPHY

Hess, M. Whitcomb. "Browning: An English Kierkegaard," *Christian Century*, LXXIX (1962), 569-71.

————. "Browning Sesquicentennial," *Contemporary Review*, CCI (1962), 268-70.

Kemper, Frances Claudette. "Irony and Browning's *Fifine at the Fair*," *Dissertation Abstracts*, XXIII (1962), 1351-52.

Kendall, J. L. "Browning's *Fifine at the Fair*: Meaning and Method," *Victorian Newsletter*, No. 22 (1962), 16-18.

Kendall, Lyle H., Jr., "A New Browning Letter," *Notes and Queries*, IX (1962), 298-99.

Kenmare, Dallas. *An End to Darkness: A New Approach to Robert Browning and His Work*. London, 1962. Rev. by Gilbert Thomas, *English*, XIV (1962), 155-56; in *Times Literary Supplement*, July 27, 1962, p. 536.

"Letters from the Brownings," *Listener* (1962), p. 842.

Litzinger, Boyd. "Browning's Reputation as a Thinker, 1900-1910," *Cithara*, I (1962), 8-23.

————. *Robert Browning and the Babylonian Woman* (Baylor Browning Interests Series, No. 19). Waco, Texas, 1962.

Orel, Harold. "Browning's Use of Historical Sources in *Strafford*," *Six Studies in Nineteenth-Century English Literature and Thought*, ed. Harold Orel and George J. Worth. (University of Kansas Publications. Humanistic Studies, No. 35.) Lawrence, Kansas, 1962. Pp. 23-27.

Pietch, Frances. "The Relationship between Music and Literature in the Victorian Period: Studies in Browning, Hardy, and Shaw," *Dissertation Abstracts*, XXII (1962), 2386.

Ryals, Clyde De L. "The Poet as Critic: Appraisals of Tennyson by His Contemporaries," *Tennessee Studies in Literature*, VII (1962), 113-25.

Seturaman, V. S. "Browning's 'By the Fireside': 'The Path Grey Heads Abhor,'" *Notes and Queries*, IX (1962), 297-98.

Stevenson, Lionel. "The Hawthorne and Browning Acquaintance: An Addendum," *Victorian Newsletter*, No. 21 (1962), p. 16.

Tilton, J. W., and R. D. Tuttle, "A New Reading of 'Count Gismond,'" *Studies in Philology*, LIX (1962), 83-95.

Willoughby, John W. "Browning's 'Johannes Agricola in Meditation,'" *Explicator*, XXI (1962), Item 5.

BIBLIOGRAPHY

1963

Adair, Virginia H. "Browning's 'Soliloquy of the Spanish Cloister,' 65-72," *Explicator,* XXII (1963), Item 24.

Altick, Richard D. "'A Grammarian's Funeral': Browning's Praise of Folly?" *Studies in English Literature,* III (1963), 449-60.

_____. "Memo to the Next Annotator of Browning," *Victorian Poetry,* I (1963), 61-68.

Balliet, Conrad A. "'Growing Old' Along with 'Rabbi Ben Ezra,'" *Victorian Poetry,* I (1963), 300-301.

Barnes, Warner. "The Browning Collection," *Library Chronicle of the University of Texas,* VII (1963), 12-13.

Cary, Richard. "Robinson on Browning," *Victorian Newsletter,* No. 23 (1963), 19-21.

Columbus, Robert Rudolph. "A Critical Explication of Robert Browning's *Parleyings with Certain People of Importance in Their Day,*" *Dissertation Abstracts,* XXIII (1963), 3370.

Crowell, Norton B. *The Triple Soul: Browning's Theory of Knowledge.* Albuquerque, New Mexico, 1963. Rev. by Boyd Litzinger, *Cithara,* IV (1964), 77-78.

Drew, Philip. "Browning's *Essay on Shelley,*" *Victorian Poetry,* I (1963), 1-6.

Fleisher, David, "'Rabbi Ben Ezra', 49-72: A New Key to an Old Crux," *Victorian Poetry,* I (1963), 46-52.

Fryxell, Lucy Dickinson. "Browning's 'Soliloquy of the Spanish Cloister,' 65-72," *Explicator,* XXII (1963), Item 24.

Gainer, Patrick W. "'Hy, Zy, Hine,'" *Victorian Poetry,* I (1963), 158-60.

Graves, Robert. "Pretense on Parnassus," *Horizon,* V (1963), 81-85.

Guerin, Wilfred L. "Irony and Tension in Browning's 'Karshish,'" *Victorian Poetry,* I (1963), 132-39.

Holloway, Sister Marcella M. "A Further Reading of 'Count Gismond,'" *Studies in Philology,* LX (1963), 549-53.

Howard, John. "Caliban's Mind," *Victorian Poetry,* I (1963), 249-57.

Johnson, Wendell Stacy. "Browning's Music," *Journal of Aesthetics and Art Criticism,* XXII (1963), 203-207.

BIBLIOGRAPHY

Kelley, Philip, and Ronald Hudson. "The Letters of the Brownings," *Victorian Poetry*, I (1963), 238-39.

Kishler, Thomas C. "A Note on Browning's 'Soliloquy of the Spanish Cloister,'" *Victorian Poetry*, I (1963), 70-71.

Leary, Lewis. "An American in Florence Meets the Brownings," *Columbia Library Columns*, XII (1963), 7-16.

Martin, Hugh. *The Faith of Robert Browning*. London, 1963.

Maxwell, J. C. "Browning's Concept of the Poet: A Revision in *Pauline*," *Victorian Poetry*, I (1963), 237-38.

McCall, John. "Browning's Uncloseted Dramas," *Iowa English Yearbook*, No. 8 (1963), 51-55.

Miles, Josephine. "Toward a Theory of Style and Change," *Journal of Aesthetics and Art Criticism*, XXII (1963), 63-68.

Miller, J. Hillis. *The Disappearance of God: Five Nineteenth-Century Writers*. Cambridge, Massachusetts, 1963. Rev. by A. Dwight Culler in *Yale Review*, LIII (1964), 440; by R. L. Perkins in *Library Journal*, LXXXVIII (1963), 4222; by Boyd Litzinger in *Journal of English and Germanic Philology*, LXIII (1964), 818-20; by Basil Willey, in *Modern Language Review*, LIX (1964), 467-68; in *Times Literary Supplement*, Feb. 27, 1964, p. 168; in *Virginia Quarterly Review*, XL (1964), xvii.

————. "The Theme of the Disappearance of God in Victorian Poetry," *Victorian Studies*, VI (1963), 207-27.

Monteiro, George. "Browning's 'My Last Duchess,'" *Victorian Poetry*, I (1963), 234-37.

Paganelli, Eloisa. "Il teatro di Robert Browning," *Convivium*, XXXI (1963), 191-210.

Page, David. "And So Is Browning," *Essays in Criticism*, XIII (1963), 146-54.

Raymond, William O. "Browning and the Harriet Westbrook Shelley Letters," *University of Toronto Quarterly*, XXXII (1963), 184-92.

Ridenour, George M. "Browning's Music Poems: Fancy and Fact," *PMLA*, LXXVIII (1963), 369-77.

Ryan, William M. "The Classifications of Browning's 'Difficult' Vocabulary," *Studies in Philology*, LX (1963), 542-48.

Sanders, Charles Richard. "Some Lost and Unpublished Carlyle-

BIBLIOGRAPHY

Browning Correspondence," *Journal of English and Germanic Philology,* LXII (1963), 322-35.

Slakey, Roger L. "Browning's 'Soliloquy of the Spanish Cloister,' " *Explicator,* XXI (1963), Item 42.

Stevens, Lewis Robert. "Robert Browning as a Myth-Maker in *The Ring and the Book," Dissertation Abstracts,* XXIV (1963), 1164.

Tobias, R. C. "The Year's Work in Victorian Poetry: 1962," *Victorian Poetry,* I (1963), 223-30.

Truss, Tom J., Jr. "Browning's 'Childe Roland' in Light of Ruskin's *Modern Painters," University of Mississippi Studies in English,* II (1963), 13-21.

Whitla, William. *The Central Truth: The Incarnation in Browning's Poetry.* Toronto, 1963. Rev. by Park Honan in *Victorian Poetry,* II (1964), 214-15; by Boyd Litzinger in *Cithara,* IV, (1964), 77-78; in *Times Literary Supplement,* Aug. 20, 1964, p. 748.

Willoughby, John. "Browning's 'Childe Roland to the Dark Tower Came,' " *Victorian Poetry,* I (1963), 291-99.

1964

Armstrong, Isobel. "Browning's *Mr. Sludge, 'The Medium,' " Victorian Poetry,* II (1964), 1-9.

Bachem, Rose M. "Musset's and Browning's 'Andrea del Sarto,' " *Revue de Littérature Comparée,* XXXVIII (1964), 248-54.

Bonner, Francis W. "Browning's 'The Bishop Orders His Tomb at Saint Praxed's Church,' " *Explicator,* XXII (1964), Item 57.

Cadbury, William. "Lyric and Anti-lyric Forms: A Method for Judging Browning," *University of Toronto Quarterly,* XXXIV (1964), 49-67.

Collins, Thomas J. "Browning's *Essay on Shelley:* In Context," *Victorian Poetry,* II (1964), 119-24.

Columbus, Robert R., and Claudette Kemper. "Sordello and the Speaker: A Problem in Identity," *Victorian Poetry,* II (1964), 251-67.

Combecher, Hans. "Drei victorianische Gedichte," *Neueren Sprachen,* XIII (1964), 257-67.

Drew, Philip. "Henry Jones on Browning's Optimism," *Victorian Poetry*, II (1964), 29-41.

Fleming, John Vincent. "Browning's Yankee Medium," *American Speech*, XXXIX (1964), 26-32.

Friend, Joseph H. "Euripides Browningized: The Meaning of *Balaustion's Adventure*," *Victorian Poetry*, II (1964), 179-86.

Honan, Park. "Belial upon Setebos," *Tennessee Studies in Literature*, IX (1964), 87-98.

_____. "Browning's Testimony on His Essay on Shelley in 'Shepherd v. Francis,'" *English Language Notes*, II (1964), 27-31.

Hooreman, Paul. "Promenades romaines. La recontre inopinée de Stendhal et de Robert Browning," *Stendhal Club*, VI (1964), 185-200.

Irvine, William. "Four Monologues in Browning's *Men and Women*," *Victorian Poetry*, II (1964), 155-64.

Jennings, C. Wade. "Diderot: A Suggested Source of the Jules-Phene Episode in *Pippa Passes*," *English Language Notes*, II (1964), 32-36.

Kramer, Dale. "Character and Theme in *Pippa Passes*," *Victorian Poetry*, II (1964), 241-49.

Litzinger, Boyd. *Time's Revenges: Browning's Reputation as a Thinker, 1889-1962*. Knoxville, Tennessee, 1964.

Melchiori, Barbara. "Where the Bishop Ordered His Tomb," *Review of English Literature*, V (1964), 7-26.

Mendel, Sydney. "Browning's 'Andrea del Sarto,'" *Explicator*, XXII (1964), Item 77.

Nelson, Charles Edwin. "Creative Consciousness in *The Ring and the Book*," *Dissertation Abstracts*, XXIV (1964), 4179.

Perrine, Laurence. "Browning's 'Caliban Upon Setebos': A Reply," *Victorian Poetry*, II (1964), 124-27.

Poston, Lawrence Sanford, III. "Five Victorians on Italian Renaissance Culture: A Problem in Historical Perspective," *Dissertation Abstracts*, XXV (1964), 484.

Priestley, F. E. L. "The Ironic Pattern of Browning's *Paracelsus*," *University of Toronto Quarterly*, XXXIV (1964), 68-81.

Rivers, Charles. "The Twin Revealment: Subjective-Objective

Polarity in the Poetry of Robert Browning," *Northwest Missouri State College Studies*, XXVIII (1964), 3-31.

Shaw, W. David. "The Analogical Argument of Browning's 'Saul,'" *Victorian Poetry* II (1964), 277-82.

————. "Character and Philosophy in 'Fra Lippo Lippi,'" *Victorian Poetry*, II (1964), 127-32.

Tamagnan, Jean. "Fenêtre ouverte sur Browning," *Études anglaises*, XVII (1964), 163-70.

Tillotson, Geoffrey. "A Word for Browning," *Sewanee Review*, LXXII (1964), 389-97.

Triesch, Gisela. "Der dramatische Monolog in Robert Brownings *The Ring and the Book*," *Neueren Sprachen*, XIII (1964), 153-64.

Truss, Tom J., Jr. "Browning's Ambiguities and *The Ring and the Book*," *University of Mississippi Studies in English*, V (1964), 1-7.

Watkins, Charlotte Crawford. "Browning's *Red Cotton Night-Cap Country* and Carlyle," *Victorian Studies*, VII (1964), 359-74.

1965 (through May)

Altick, Richard D. "The Symbolism of Browning's 'Master Hughes of Saxe-Gotha,'" *Victorian Poetry*, III (1965), 1-7.

Dahl, Curtis. "Who Was Browning's Cleon?" *Cithara*, IV (1965), 69-74.

Hudson, Gertrude Reese, ed. *Browning to His American Friends: Letters Between the Brownings, the Storys, and James Russell Lowell, 1841-1890*. London, 1965.

Huebenthal, John. "'Growing Old', 'Rabbi Ben Ezra', and 'Tears, Idle Tears,'" *Victorian Poetry*, III (1965), 61-63.

Merivale, Patricia. "The Pan Figure in Victorian Poetry: Landor to Meredith," *Philological Quarterly*, XLIX (1965), 258-77.

Preyer, Robert. "Two Styles in the Verse of Robert Browning," *ELH*, XXXII (1965), 62-84.

Raymond, William O. *The Infinite Moment, and Other Essays in Robert Browning*. 2nd ed. Toronto, 1965.

BIBLIOGRAPHY

Smalley, Donald. "Joseph Arnould and Robert Browning: New Letters (1842-50) and a Verse Epistle," *PMLA*, LXXX (1965), 90-101.

Stevens, L. Robert. "Aestheticism in Browning's Early Renaissance Monologues," *Victorian Poetry*, III (1965), 19-24.

Timko, Michael. "Browning upon Butler; or, Natural Theology in the English Isle," *Criticism*, VII (1965), 141-50.

[INDEX OF BROWNING'S WORKS]

TITLES published separately are set in large and small CAPITAL LETTERS. Italicized *numbers* following a title indicate that a quotation from the work appears on those pages.

[GENERAL INDEX]